Forgotten Aerodromes of World War I

Forgotten Aerodromes of World War I

British military aerodromes, seaplane stations,
flying-boat and airship stations to 1920

Martyn Chorlton

www.crecy.co.uk

Crécy Publishing Ltd

www.crecy.co.uk

First published in 2014 by Crécy Publishing

Copyright 2014 Martyn Chorlton

A CIP record for this book is available from the British Library

ISBN 9780859 791816

Printed and bound in Malta by Melita Press

Crécy Publishing Limited
1a Ringway Trading Estate, Shadowmoss Road,
Manchester M22 5LH

www.crecy.co.uk

Front Cover: Airmen of the RFC and the USAAC pose around a Bristol Scout 'C' at Waddington with a General Service hangar in the background.

Back cover main picture: Braemar Mk II C4297 is pictured at Filton in late 1918 prior to its maiden flight in February 1919.

Back cover inset top: Hornsea Mere 1918.

Back cover inset bottom: The Moxton Road is clear heading towards Andover in this aerial view taken from 1,200 feet during an air display. *Via Stuart Leslie*

Back cover colour profile: One of a batch of 100 DH.9A constructed by Mann Egerton & Co. Ltd, Norwich, 'E9665' was supplied to the Wireless Experimental Establishment at Biggin Hill in September 1918 and used for trials. © *Inkworm.com*

Front flap top: Handley Page staff at Cricklewood pause momentarily for the camera from their work of producing the rear nacelle/cowling for the /400's Eagle VIII engines. *Via Stuart Leslie*

Front flap bottom: A part-built Gnosspelius single-float monoplane stands outside the flight sheds at Bowness-on-Windermere.

Table of Contents

An atmospheric image of a pair of early machines arriving at Hendon in September 1913, with the flying school flight sheds of W. H. Ewen and Deperdussin beyond. The furthest machine is the Grahame-White Five-Seater; the two large dots on the lower mainplanes are two engineers enjoying the ride!

DEDICATED to my youngest daughter, Eleanor Grace, for her efforts in keeping her Dad happy by showing an interest in aeroplanes!

A typical early flying machine that would have been seen at Brooklands during the pre-First World War period was this Sopwith-Wright Hybrid. Also known as the Sopwith No 1 'Three-Seat Tractor', the aircraft is pictured in 1912 being flown by the man himself, Tommy Sopwith. Note the racing circuit behind and the curve of the banking on the left-hand side.

Introduction

WHEN I began this project I planned to include every aviation-related site in the whole of Great Britain, but soon realised that I had bitten off more than I could chew. Luckily, unlike some of my previous works, I recognised this from a very early stage and managed to discipline myself into keeping the subjects of this book confined to aerodromes, airship stations, seaplane stations, kite balloon stations and manufacturers' aerodromes. Locations of Wing and Group HQs and a few other non-flying establishments have inevitably slipped into the mix, but generally the majority would have been used by a flying-machine of some sort or another.

While the title narrows the subject matter to the First World War, the time frame covered is from the turn of the 20th century through to 1920, give or take a few years, as a large number of sites remained in military hands until the latter date. Those few that were retained will only have a very thin round-up of their later history and any details of the First World War-related infrastructure that may still be in place to this day. Many of the locations, especially the Landing Grounds (LG), which were hastily brought into service as part of the nation's huge Home Defence (HD) network, were little more than fields that had been requisitioned from the 'compliant' landowners, who were always well compensated for their trouble and often inherited any structures that were left behind. A large number of these sites look exactly the same as they did when the RFC or RNAS arrived and, with no permanent buildings constructed on the vast majority of them, no evidence that they were there in the first place will remain. If you ever visit one of these locations, all you have to do is imagine a few tents and a handful of biplanes and you will be just about there. Don't expect to find a 'billiard table' flat area of land either, as many of these locations, which averaged around just 50 acres, were undulating to say the least. It is the larger, more complex aerodromes that are more likely to have been erased today as their prime land has been consumed by industry or housing, especially those sites that continued to be used until the end of the Second World War and beyond. However, there are exceptions to every rule and it is surprising how many of the sites listed in this book are easily traceable, despite being established around 100 years ago, a number of them being out of use for at least 90 of them.

Of those aerodromes that did feature more permanent structures, only in recent years have the likes of English Heritage and the general restoration movement begun to take notice, not only from a historical point of view but also an architectural one. An increasing number of memorials have also been erected in recent years, very few of them influenced by national centenaries but rather by local enthusiasts and individuals who care about their local history. Some county councils have realised the importance of their aviation history, a good example being Lincolnshire, which is famous for its Second World War activities but is also recognising the First World War sites.

With the foreground occupied by a diminutive R.A.F. FE.2D and the background filled by giant airship sheds, Farnborough was the centre for military aviation prior to the beginning of the war.

As with virtually all military sites over the years, the majority were opened before completion and, even when closure was on the horizon, construction continued so that contracts could be upheld. This is Felixstowe during the launch of a Felixstowe F.3 flying-boat, with one of the site's unique flying-boat sheds under construction on the right.

I have laid out this book county by county, rather than chronologically, as I'm not expecting the reader to consume this tome from start to finish; instead, it is designed to be dipped into. Some counties, especially those in the East and South East, are understandably bulging with sites, while others contain just a handful or even none at all. Each entry gives the name of the site, and an alternative local name in brackets, above a set of Google Earth coordinates, a traditional eight-figure Ordnance Survey reference and a description of where the site is with regard to the current lie of the land and non-period features. The body text, which ranges from 40 to several hundred words, will inform the reader, where known, what type of aerodrome/site it is, for example an NLG1, which translates as a Night Landing Ground Category 1 (this will be explained in detail in the first chapter), the size of the site in acres, and its dimensions in yards. Details of the main

structures on the site will include the type of hangars, their size in brackets and a general overview of other significant buildings. Finally, the larger aerodromes' entries will include their own 'main units' panel; each unit will have its date of formation or arrival, the location from which it came, the departure location or date of disbandment (DB), and in brackets the main types of aircraft operated. These panels are designed to give the reader an overview of the site at a glance with regard to how busy it was; only the most significant units are listed, which are still numerous.

This tome is little more than a 'toe-dipping' exercise, as the majority of sites covered demand a much larger entry than is possible, while others do well to reach the 40 words provided. The complex organisations that controlled all of these sites have also been omitted; the Brigades, Groups and Wings involved were planned for an appendix that would have

While buildings made their mark, it was people who brought an aerodrome alive, typified by this image of a cheery group of 3 Wing, RNAS, Gunlayers at Eastchurch on 5 June 1917 outside 'Hut 5'.

By 1917 the training structure to create a skilled fighting unit such as 85 Squadron, pictured here with its new SE.5As, had become more disciplined. Created from 'C' Flight of the CFS at Upavon in August 1917, the squadron was not ready for action until May 1918.

One of three slipways is under construction at Lee-on-Solent, with Short Type 184 seaplanes on a calm Solent beyond. Before the slipways were built at this busy seaplane station, the aircraft were lifted into the water by a crane from the shallow cliff through which the cutting has been made for this slipway. *Via Stuart Leslie*

One of 'The Howden Pigs' was this Coastal Class non-rigid airship, serialled *C21*. More than 195 feet long, 52 feet high and with a diameter of 37 feet, the Coastal Class was a very capable airship, and carried out long anti-submarine patrols around Britain's coast from 1916 through to the end of the war.

added another 30,000 words! The main aim is to show the vast number of military aviation sites that were spread across the country during the First World War; many more locations that were used for the aforementioned organisations have also been omitted. As many buildings as possible, their type, size and use, are also included, but this is a vast subject with virtually every site having at least one unique feature.

Just as in the Second World War this island nation of ours became the world's largest aircraft carrier, and by the end of it Britain could boast the largest air force in the world, only for it to be whittled away to a fraction of its former self during the inter-war peace.

Above: Submarine Scout airship *SSZ17* comes in to land at the Pembroke Airship Station (Class C) in 1917. Both of the station's 300-foot-long Airship Sheds can be seen in the background.

Left and below: These two images, taken at Marske during 2 Fighting School's tenure in 1918, present us with an internal view of the Repair Shop and a well-stocked Mechanics Shop. *Via Stuart Leslie*

Acknowledgements

VERY special thanks to Mick Davies (Cross & Cockade) for allowing me to use a large number of his excellent plans and technical information along the way; Colin Durrant (Suffolk Aviation Society); Rose Gibson (Area Development Librarian, Information and Digital Services, www.leodis.net); Alastair Goodrum (photos); Stuart Leslie (photos); Alan Smith (Martlesham Heath Museum); and Tarkey Barker (Martlesham Heath Museum). I would also like to acknowledge the Airfield Research Group, whose on-line forum provides an incredible wealth of information on virtually every aviation-related site in Britain and large chunks of the 'rest of the world'. Finally, Cross & Cockade International has been producing an excellent quarterly magazine since 1970, packed with original material about everything relating to aviation and the First World War – long may it continue.

Abbreviations

Landing grounds

ALG	Advanced Landing Ground
DLG	Daylight Landing Ground
DLG1	1st Class Daylight Landing Ground
DLG2	2nd Class Daylight Landing Ground
DLG3	3rd Class Daylight Landing Ground
ELG	Emergency Landing Ground
LG	Landing Ground
NLG	Night Landing Ground
NLG1	1st Class Night Landing Ground
NLG2	2nd Class Night Landing Ground
NLG3	3rd Class Night Landing Ground
RLG	Relief Landing Ground

General

A&AEE	Aeroplane & Armament Experimental Establishment
AAP	Aircraft Acceptance Park
ADS	Aircraft Dispatch Section
AES	Armament Experimental Station
AFC	Australian Flying Corps
amsl	above mean sea level
ARD	Aircraft Repair Depot
ARS	Aeroplane Repair Section
ASRMCU	Air Sea Rescue Marine Craft Unit
ATC	Air Training Corps
Aux	Auxiliary
BB	Balloon Base
BEF	British Expeditionary Force
(BS)	Baby Seaplane
CAF	Canadian Air Force
CFS	Central Flying School
C-in-C	Commander in Chief
CO	Commanding Officer
CRO	Civilian Repair Organisation
DB	Disbanded
DFTDC	Defence Fire Training & Development Centre
DGIFC	Defence Geospatial Intelligence Fusion Centre
DS	Depot Squadron
ERD	Engine Repair Depot
ETPS	Empire Test Pilots School
(F)	Fighter
(FB)	Flying-boat
FG	Fighter Group
FIS	Flying Instructors School
FOIS	Flying Officers Instructors School
FS	Fighting School
GS	General Service
HD	Home Defence
IWM	Imperial War Museum
JFIG	Joint Forces Intelligence Group
JNCO	Junior Non-Commissioned Officer
JSSO	Joint Service Signals Organisation

JSSU	Joint Service Signal Unit
(LB)	Light Bomber
MAD	Marine Acceptance Depot
MAED	Marine Aircraft Experimental Depot
MAEE	Marine Aeroplane Experimental Establishment
MGS	Machine Gun School
MT	Mechanical or Motor Transport
MU	Maintenance Unit
NCO	Non-Commissioned Officer
(N)TS	(Night) Training Squadron
OS	Observers School
RAF	Royal Air Force
R.A.F.	Royal Aircraft Factory
RAFA	Royal Air Force Association
RAS	Reserve Aeroplane Squadron
RCAF	Royal Canadian Air Force
REP	Renault Esnault-Pelterie
RFC	Royal Flying Corps
RMLI	Royal Marine Light Infantry
RNAS	Royal Naval Air Service
RS	Reserve Squadron
(S)	Seaplane
SAG	School of Aerial Gunnery
(SD)	Special Duty
SDP	Stores Distribution Park
SNCO	Senior Non-Commissioned Officer
SP&AES	Seaplane & Armament Experimental Station
SoAC	School of Army Co-Operation
SoAF	School of Aerial Fighting
SoAF&BD	School of Aerial Fighting & Bomb Dropping
SoAF&G	School of Aerial Fighting & Gunnery
SoAG	School of Aerial Gunnery
SoN&BD	School of (Aerial) Navigation & Bomb Dropping
SoAP	School of Air Pilotage
SoSF	School of Special Flying
SoWT	School of Wireless Telephony
SSQ	Station Sick Quarters
TB	Training Brigade
T(C)S	Training (Control) Squadron
TDS	Training Depot Station
TF	Training Flight
TS	Training Squadron or School
TSS	Training Squadron Station
TTS	Torpedo Training Squadron
TU	Training Unit
USAAS	United States Army Air Service
USN	United States Navy
USNAS	United States Naval Air Station
VGS	Volunteer Gliding Squadron
WC	Water Closet
W/T	Wireless/Transmitter
YMCA	Young Men's Christian Association

It started with a field

An Army and Navy with wings

IT WAS from 1909 that the first purpose-built aerodromes began to appear in Britain, starting with Larkhill in Wiltshire, although Farnborough, originally intended as a balloon station, is the spiritual birthplace of military aviation in this country. That year also saw the birth of Barking, Castle Bromwich, Eastchurch, Gosport, Hendon, Hounslow Heath and Leysdown, although several of these were used for little more than early flying experiments, some more successful than others.

While the Imperial Defence Committee debated whether the airship or the aeroplane should serve the military, the Air Battalion of the Royal Engineers was formed at Farnborough on 1 April 1911. Split into two companies, No 1 operated airships under the command of Capt E. Maitland from Farnborough while No 2, commanded by Capt J. Fulton, was equipped with aeroplanes, including the Bristol Boxkite, at Larkhill. By November 1911 the Secretary of State for War wisely proposed the formation of a British Aeronautical Service made up of a Military and Naval Wing and a Central Flying School (CFS). On 13 April 1912 the Royal Flying Corps (RFC) was formed with just five squadrons to its name, and only seven by the beginning of the First World War. Despite this low number, a complex training programme, both technical and flying, was created, the latter being catered for by the CFS at Upavon and the former with schools at Coley Park, Netheravon and Reading.

In late 1913 the First Sea Lord, Winston Churchill, announced that the Naval Wing would be retitled the Royal Naval Air Service (RNAS). Prior to the outbreak of the war the aerial defence of the nation was in the hands of the RFC, but virtually all of the service's aircraft had been allocated to the British Expeditionary Force (BEF) in France, and the responsibility fell on the RNAS (officially formed/recognised on 1 July 1914). Under the command of Capt Murray Sueter, the RNAS expanded its bases rapidly prior to and during the early stages of the war, including a number of seaplane stations along the East Coast. These included the Isle of Grain, which was surveyed in 1912, and the airship station at Kingsnorth, which was opened in March 1914.

In June 1914, as the clouds of war gathered over Europe, a large exercise was staged at Netheravon involving 2, 3, 4, 5 and 6 Squadrons and a Kite Section. A vast 'concentration camp' was created at Netheravon to accommodate the influx of units, and several large tents, or marquees, were erected to shelter the aircraft. The main thrust of the exercise that followed was reconnaissance and observation with tasks that included spotting and reporting the positions of 'enemy' troops and vehicles. One exercise was to spot a pair of MT lorries moving along a road, then record the distance between the two vehicles. At least one balloon involved in the exercise was used to imitate a powerless airship, and squadrons were asked to record its exact position.

By 1915, with the war gaining momentum, it soon became apparent that a single centralised training establishment could not cope with the huge numbers of volunteers. As a result, specialised training aerodromes began to spring up all over the country, from Beaulieu in the south to Catterick in the north. These aerodromes, called training squadron stations, supported several new reserve squadrons, later renamed training squadrons, which were formed to help replace the large number of pilots that were being lost in Northern France. A handful of these training stations were original landing grounds, while the majority were brand-new sites, all of which were built to the same standard pattern. When the new RAF organised itself from April 1918, these training aerodromes became known as training depot stations and, just like the training stations, were all built or expanded to the same format.

While thousands of men volunteered for flying duties, the number of aircraft they would fly into action also began to increase. To cope with the numbers of aircraft being built, several Aircraft Acceptance Parks (AAP) were positioned around the country to receive brand new machines direct from the manufacturer. The aircraft would arrive by road, rail or air and, once received, each was carefully examined and prepared with military equipment, then dispatched direct to the unit. AAPs, which were manned by both military and civilian personnel, received aircraft from local manufacturers. For example, Lincoln was a vibrant centre for aircraft manufacturing; two AAPs, one at Lincoln (West Common Racecourse) and one at Bracebridge Heath accepted aircraft from Clayton & Shuttleworth, Ruston Proctor & Co, Robey & Co and Marshall & Sons from 1915 until the Armistice.

Repair of aircraft was also carried out on an industrial scale and began with the Aeroplane Repair Section (ARS), which tended to be housed in a single GS (General Service) Shed located on a number of aerodromes where basic repairs and maintenance took place. For more serious damage, which would have entailed a complete rebuild, the machine was sent to one of nine Aircraft Repair Depots (ARD), which covered large areas of the country; for example, No 5 (Eastern) ARD at Henlow looked after most of East Anglia. Each ARD was located close to a major section of the rail network and each only accepted aircraft from within its designated area and would only dispatch the repaired machine back into that area.

The network of sites across Britain was huge, all interconnected and controlled by Wings, Groups and Brigades. By 1918 the pace of construction of aerodromes increased and a large number were still being built by the time of the Armistice. If the war had lasted any longer, Sir Hugh Trenchard's Independent Air Force would have made the network even larger, as it supported more Handley Page O/400s and the larger V/1500 bombers. The presence of a growing number of American servicemen in the country also saw an increasing number of aerodromes either expanded or occupying new sites, but their late entry into the conflict saw very few actually completed.

By the end of the war the RAF had 22,647 aircraft on strength and 188 operational squadrons, not to mention the innumerable training and support units. It was the largest air force in the world, but many of the squadrons saw their existence cut short when they returned from the continent, were reduced to a cadre, then disbanded. Aerodromes and seaplane stations were closed down wholesale, the vast majority of LGs by early 1919 while the sites of training depot station size clung on until 1920. Only a comparative handful survived the swingeing cuts of the post-war period, and it was only through the tenacity of the 'Father of the RAF' that the service survived at all.

The Landing Grounds

The vast majority of sites within this book were NLGs (Night Landing Grounds), which were first opened in late 1914 for the use of the RNAS and HD duties. It was not long before many of these early NLGs were either abandoned or placed on the back burner as the expected swarms of enemy airships and aircraft never came. However, by April 1916 large numbers of sites were opened across Britain when the RFC became responsible for the nation's defence as the threat of the Zeppelin became all too real. A colossal HD network across the country was brought into play, which kept at least 10,000 personnel and large numbers of operational squadrons away from the rest of the war. Several of these sites had an RFC and later RAF presence, but were very rarely used other than for emergency use. Although early aircraft in difficulties would more likely make for any unobstructed field in daylight, it was a different matter at night. This was when the NLG could be a life-saver, as the vast majority could be lit by the ubiquitous 'Money' and 'Gooseneck' flares. The 'Money' flare was little more than a metal cage containing an asbestos wick soaked in paraffin, which would burn at a rate of 1¼ gallons per hour. The 'Gooseneck' was a metal can with a spout, filled with paraffin with a wick sticking out. It proved to be a very effective method of lighting up a remote NLG, the glow being visible from more than a mile away. The down side was that it could also draw in the enemy like a moth to a flame, and there are instances of Zeppelins dropping a bomb or two on an unsuspecting NLG.

The majority of Landing Grounds (LGs) were surveyed by one or two officers armed with a local survey map, who would mark out the proposed site on paper, which was followed by the landowner being approached and a requisition order issued. There was no real science to finding the correct site, and there are several examples where LGs were found to be unsuitable. It was not uncommon for LGs to be literally moved to the next field, which had the added bonus of not having to change the location's name. With regard to naming the LG, very often the farm from which the land was requisitioned was used, or the nearest village. It was not unusual for an official name to be allocated by the military and a different name to be used by the locals or the units operating from the site. Throughout this book you will see the official name first and the local name in brackets.

There were two main types of LG that received a category from Class 1 through to Class 3, depending upon landing restrictions. Each site could be categorised as an NLG or DLG or both, complete with a Class number. For example, a 1st Class or Category 1 LG meant that there were no, or very few, restrictions with regard to landing from any direction. A 2nd Class site could also be approached from any direction but at least one of the approaches would have a building and/or trees that would be categorised as a hazard. A 3rd Class site not only had just one strip or axis to land on, but would also have the same obstacles as a 2nd Class LG. This system, when applied, would show the site to be an NLG1, 2 or 3, and or a DLG1, 2 or 3, and, depending on night or day operations, the class of approach could be different. Just to throw the system slightly, some sites were not given a class number, but at least the method of classifying LGs was standardised from January 1917 and by the middle of that year many sites were recategorised. For example, Gooderstone (aka Warren Farm) was opened as an HD NLG3 in August 1916, but by March 1917 was upgraded to an NLG2. Generally prefixed with HD, the task of Home Defence was the sole purpose of these sites.

The aerodromes

The next step up from the humble LG was the HD station, of which there were two types, the HD Flight Station and the HD Squadron, both of them controlled by 6th (Home Defence) Brigade from October 1917. Typical examples of an HD Flight Station, which were little bigger than an NLG but with better facilities, were Buckminster, Holt, Manston and Scampton. Facilities would have included HD-pattern Flight Sheds which averaged 80 by 65 feet in size, as well as the ubiquitous Bessonneau hangar. The very first standard transportable hangar for the RFC and RAF, the Bessonneau remained in production until the 1930s, when the Bellman took over. With a structure of wood and a covering of canvas, the Bessonneau could be erected by a team of twenty men in the space of 48 hours. Built in varying sizes, a few examples survived until late in the 20th century, although one stalwart was still extant at RAF Odiham until 2010. Examples of the larger HD Squadron Stations were Biggin Hill, Detling, Elmswell and Throwley. These aerodromes also featured HD-type Flight Sheds, including the rarer all-timber twin shed, not to mention an array of support buildings.

A fair representation of a typically complex First World War aerodrome would be the training squadron stations, which by 1918 were all redesignated as training depot stations. In describing each site I have tried to simplify the layout by describing the buildings as being 'technical' and 'domestic'. The former were involved in the day-to-day operation of the aircraft, fronted by, on average, seven GS (General Service) Sheds, which changed pattern several times between 1915 and 1918. The GS Sheds transformed the capability of military aerodromes, enabling large numbers of aircraft to be sheltered from the elements. On average, these large sheds measured 170 by 80 feet and at first were constructed throughout from timber, but later versions had brick side walls. The key feature of the GS Shed was the roof trusses, commonly known as the 'Belfast' truss. There were several variations of the truss, but all comprised criss-cross bracing within the truss, which gave it great strength and the ability to span a large area. The general layout for the seven main hangars was six coupled (pairs joined together) and the seventh serving as an ARS. GS Sheds also often had a 60-foot-wide plane store attached to the side.

Behind the line of hangars the plethora of subsidiary technical buildings were constructed. Not every aerodrome was the same, but examples of an armoury, blacksmith's shop, carpenter's shop, coal and wood store, depot offices, dope shop, instruction huts, MT (Motor Transport) yard, metal workshop, powerhouse, salvage shed, squadron offices, technical store and a water tower could be found on most early aerodromes. The vast majority of these buildings were built from timber, although as the war progressed brick (described as 'temporary' brick) became more available.

Domestic buildings were segregated, where possible, away from the technical site, very often by a public road, which was not ideal from a security point of view. Accommodation was usually divided into three groups: the officers' mess and their quarters; the regimental institute; and men's barracks and women's accommodation. It was standard practice to place the officers' quarters between the men's and women's quarters.

The officers' facilities were made up of a bath house, ablutions and WC, the mess and cabin-type accommodation. The 'regimental' buildings, a description harking back to army days, were much larger mainly because the 'rank and file' were the main personnel on all aerodromes. The biggest domestic complex of all was made up of barrack huts, a drying room, bath house, ablutions (which were sub-divided into NCO pilots' ablutions and WCs), NCO pilots' mess and NCO pilots' quarters. Each regimental area also had an institute, cookhouse, stores and a YMCA. Again continuing the Army tradition, all of the buildings were constructed in rows, with all of the aforementioned facilities contained with their own group. It was not uncommon for buildings to be connected by covered corridors, especially in areas where the weather was less forgiving, and each domestic area was fenced off. Officers' accommodation tended to be grouped closely around the mess. Quarters for the women, of which there were on average 100 on strength at a training depot station, were facilitated with ablutions, a bath house, sleeping accommodation, a kitchen and WCs.

Like the technical ones, domestic buildings were initially constructed from timber, but 'temporary' brick was used as the war progressed. To speed up construction of these areas, a variety of prefabricated buildings were brought into use, giving an air of standardisation. Common prefabricated buildings were the Adrian (98 by 27 feet), the Armstrong, Detchet (60 by 16 feet), Nissen Hospital hut (60 by 20 feet), Tarrant Mk I (60 by 20 feet) and the Tarrant Mk II (60 by 16 feet). Just like the many buildings constructed on airfields during the Second World War, they were only designed to last for a short period of time and it is amazing that so many 'temporary' brick buildings survive from both World Wars.

All at sea

Seaplane and flying-boat stations, by the very nature of the type of aircraft operating from them, required considerably less acreage of land. Early seaplanes, such as the Short 184, required very little space to operate, although the type operated for the entire war. Hangarage tended to be within cambered-roof flight sheds, which averaged 70 by 70 feet in size, sufficient to accommodate a pair of Short 184s with their wings folded. As the war progressed and aircraft became larger, the RNAS introduced a standardised shed (aka the Type G) measuring 180 by 60 feet with an unequal-pitch roof. Examples of the latter could be found at Calshot, Cattewater and Newlyn to name but a few, and several survive today. Slipways varied in length depending on how far out the deep water was at low tide; the three at Killingholme were exceptionally long at 700 by 60 feet and 850 by 35 feet, while the average was considerably shorter. Several larger-capacity slipways for the bigger Felixstowe and Curtiss-type flying-boats were furnished with rails to make handling much easier. Cattewater utilised the breakwater already in situ and laid a railway line along it; this supported a steam-powered crane that lifted the seaplanes into the water. In fact, many short-lived seaplane bases were little more than a crane on a harbour wall or moorings in the harbour.

Just like the aerodromes, many seaplane stations became Marine Operations (Seaplane) Stations from mid-1918 onwards. Their effectiveness was proven by the rapid reduction in U-boat successes around the coast of Britain during the final months of the war.

Airships and balloons

Airship stations were obviously very large sites, which could measure 2,000 yards square and occupy several hundred acres. Dominated by skyline-changing sheds, which could be anything up to 700 feet long and 100 feet high to accommodate the large rigid airships, the first stations were already in place before the outbreak of the war, the most obvious example being Farnborough. During the war airship stations came under seven main classes depending on the type and number of airships being operated, including the Mooring Out Station (Class E) and civilian-run Airship Construction Stations. Class A was only one step up from a mooring-out station, but would have at least one portable hangar as part of its limited facilities. Class B airship stations were larger sites with at least one main shed, several also serving as Marine Operation (Aeroplane) Stations, although this would have been a more opportunistic use rather than part of the site's original classification. Class B sites at Luce Bay and Anglesey also had sub-stations to expand their area of operations. The airship station class system continued from Class C to Class G, the latter being exemplified by Cranwell, Howden, Kingsnorth, Longside and Pulham.

A typical large airship station contained many buildings that were unique to airship operations, such as gasholders and a gas plant house, both taking up a large area of land. The main buildings on these sites included an acetylene-generator house, barracks, garage, magazine, officers' mess, powerhouse, stores and a variety of workshops.

Mooring-out stations, in comparison, were functional sites, usually consisting of an area of woodland that was cleared to accommodate an airship of SS-Type size. While they may have been basic, they proved a very welcome haven for tired crews who, after a long patrol over the sea, could not back to the parent station because of a shortage of fuel or deteriorating weather. Several major airship stations had their own mooring-out stations, including Bude (mooring-out station at Mullion), Lowthorpe (Howden), Chathill (East Fortune), Kirkleatham (Howden and Cramlington), and Auldbar (Longside).

Generally only occupying a few acres of land, balloon stations, whether operating free or kite-type balloons, provided a useful method of observation and protection for convoys operating around the coast of Britain. The balloons, which were accommodated in specialist sheds (100 by 36 feet) when not in use, were towed behind Royal Navy warships at an average height of 3,000 feet, providing the observer with an outstanding and efficient view over a great distance. A vital part of marine operations, this method of protecting convoys, combined with the use of aeroplanes and airships, significantly reduced convoy losses.

Lest we forget

As we enter the '100 years since' period, with regard to the beginning of the First World War, the senses of the general public are heightened towards remembering that most appalling conflict. It usually takes such a major anniversary to make people think of the sacrifice that so many young men made and the important role played by various aerodromes across Britain between 1914 and 1918. With regard to the gallant men of the fledgling RFC and RNAS, many were recognised at the time of their loss, and even those pioneering airmen who were killed before the conflict were memorialised at the time. A number of memorials appeared across the country from the South East of England to Scotland, recognising the efforts of these young airmen, the majority of whom lost their lives before getting close to a German machine over the Western Front.

While it is impossible to protect and preserve every remnant of the First World War in this country, it is always possible to remember and acknowledge this period of our history. There will always be the tell-tale white headstones in the local churchyard to make us think, or the memorial on the roadside, seemingly in the middle of nowhere, which will make the curious want to find out more.

Index of aerodromes

ENGLAND

Bedfordshire
Bedford (Cardington)
Biggleswade
Flitwick (Ampthill)
Goldington (Bedford)
Henlow
Leagrave
Little Staughton (Bedford)

Berkshire
Ascot Racecourse

Buckinghamshire
Cheddington
Halton (Wendover)
Hanslope (Newport Pagnell)
High Wycombe
Lavendon (Bedford)

Cambridgeshire
Bainton, Huntingdonshire
Coldham (Wisbech)
Cottenham
Duxford
Fowlmere
Hardwick
Horseheath
Little Downham (Ely)
Old Weston (Thrapston),
    Huntingdonshire
Orton
Portholme Meadow,
    Huntingdonshire
Upwood (Bury/Ramsey)
Walton (Peterborough)
Wyton, Huntingdonshire
Yelling (St Neots)

Cheshire
Heaton Chapel, Greater
    Manchester
Hooton Park, Merseyside

Cornwall
Bude
Merifield (Tor Point)
Mullion
Newlyn (Penzance)
Padstow (Trevose House)

Cumbria
Bowness-on-Windermere
    (Cockshot Point/Hill of Oaks)
Solway House

Derbyshire
Lullington (Burton-on-Trent)
Roston (Ashbourne)
Stanton-by-Dale

Devonshire
Berry Head
Cattewater (Batten Camp)
Laira (Plymouth)
Okehampton
Poole (Upton)
Prawle Point
Toller (Bridport, aka Powerstock)
Torquay Harbour (Beacon
    Quay/Haldon Pier)
Westward Ho!

Dorsetshire
Chickerell (Weymouth)
Kinson
Moreton (Dorchester)
Portland Harbour
Sandbanks (Poole Harbour)
Winton (Talbot Village)

Durham
Bishopton
Catley Hill (Trimdon)
Cleadon (Sunderland/South
    Shields)
Easington (Seaham Harbour)
Horsegate
Hylton (Usworth)
Sadberge
Seaton Carew I and Seaton
    Carew II (Tees Bay)
Spennymoor
West Town Moor

East Yorkshire
Atwick (Hornsea)
Barmby Moor (Pocklington)
Bellasize (Gilberdyke)
Beverley (Racecourse)
Brough
Eastburn (Driffield)
Flamborough
Hedon (Hull)
Hornsea Mere
Howden
Lowthorpe
Owthorne (Withernsea)
South Cave

Essex
Barking (Creekmouth), London
    Borough of Barking
Barking (Longbridge Farm)
Beaumont, Essex
Blackheath Common
    (Colchester)
Bournes Green (Shoeburyness)
Braintree
Broomfield Court (Chelmsford)
Broxted
Burnham-on-Crouch
Chelmsford
Chelmsford (Writtle)
Chingford, London Borough of
    Waltham Forest
Clacton-on-Sea
East Hanningfield
Easthorpe
Fairlop
Fyfield (Ongar)
Goldhangar (Gardener's Farm,
    aka possibly Maldon)
Hainault Farm (Romford)
Horndon-on-the-Hill (Woodcock
    Field)
Loughton (Kings Oak Hotel, High
    Beech)
Mountnessing
North Benfleet (Sadlers Farm)
North Ockendon
North Weald (Bassett)
Orsett I and II
Palmers Farm (Shenfield)
Plough Corner (Little Clacton)
Rochford (Eastwood)
Runwell
Sible Hedingham
Stow Maries
Sutton's Farm
Thaxted
Widford
Woodford Green, London
    Borough of Redbridge
Woodham Mortimer
Wormingford (Bures)

Flintshire
North Shotwick
South Shotwick
    (Chester/Queensferry)

Greater London
Battersea Park, London Borough
    of Wandsworth
Hurlingham (Polo Ground),
    London Borough of
    Kensington & Chelsea
Hackney Marshes, London
    Borough of Hackney
Hyde Park (Marble Arch &
    Rotten Row), London
    Borough of Westminster
Kennington (The Oval), London
    Borough of Lambeth
Kensington Gardens, London
    Borough of the City of
    Westminster
Putney Heath
Regent's Park, City of
    Westminster
Richmond Park (Beverley
    Brook), London Borough of
    Richmond-upon-Thames
Richmond Park (Kingston Hill),
    London Borough of
    Richmond-upon-Thames
Shooters Hill

Gloucestershire
Bristol (Filton/Patchway)
Brockworth
Cirencester
Leighterton (Bowldown Farm)
Minchinhampton
Rendcomb
Yate (Chipping Sodbury)

Hampshire
Aldershot (Balloon Square,
    Alison's Road, aka Stanhope
    Lines)
Andover (Weyhill)
Beaulieu (East Boldre)
Calshot
Chattis Hill (Training
    Gallops/Stockbridge)
Eastleigh (Southampton)
Eversley
Farnborough
Fleet Pond
Gosport (Fort Grange and Fort
    Rowner)
Gosport (Marine)
Hamble
Hilsea (aka Cosham)
Hythe (Southampton Water)
Lee-on-Solent (Gosport)

Lopcombe Corner
Northam
Tipner
Woolston
Worthy Down

Hertfordshire

Bishops Hatfield
Hertford (Ware)
London Colney
Sawbridgeworth I
Sawbridgeworth II
Stanstead Abbots (Stanstead St Margarets)
Therfield (Heath Farm/Baldock)
Willian (Hitchin)

Kent

All Hallows (Sheerness)
Bekesbourne
Biggin Hill (Westerham)
Broad Salts (Sandwich)
Broomfield (Herne Bay)
Capel (Capel-le-Ferne/Folkestone)
Detling
Dover (Dover Harbour/Marine Parade)
Dover (Guston Road)
Dover (Swingate Down/St Margaret's, aka Langdon)
Dymchurch (Hythe/Palmarsh)
Dymchurch (Redoubt)
Eastchurch (HMS Pembroke II)
Farningham
Frinsted (Harrietsham)
Godmersham Park
Grain and Port Victoria, Isle of Grain
Grove Park, London Borough of Bromley
Guilton (Ash)
Harty
Hawkinge (Folkestone)
Hunton (Maidstone)
Kings Hill (West Malling)
Joyce Green
Kingsnorth (Hoo/Chatham)
Leigh (Tonbridge)
Leigh Green (Tenterden)
Leysdown (Shellbeach)
Lidsing (Chatham)
Lydd
Lydd (Dering Farm)
Lydd Camp
Lympne
Lympne (Hythe)
Manston (Manstone)
Marden (Staplehurst)

New Romney (Littlestone)
Old Romney
Penshurst (Chiddingstone Causeway)
Pluckley
Plumstead Marshes, London Borough of Bexley
Queenborough
Ramsgate
Rochester (Chatham)
Sheerness I and II, Isle of Sheppey
Sole Street (Crundale)
South Ash (Wrotham)
Swingfield
Throwley (Faversham)
Walmer
Westgate (St Mildred's Bay and Mutrix Farm)
Wittersham
Wye

Lancashire

Aintree Racecourse, Merseyside
Barrow-in-Furness (Cavendish Dock)
Barrow-in-Furness (Walney Island)
Blackpool Sands
Didsbury (Manchester/Alexandra Park)
Flookburgh
Lytham
Manchester (Burnage)
Manchester (Miles Platting)
Manchester (Trafford Park)
Oldham (Chadderton/Hollinwood)
Scale Hall (Lancaster/Morecombe)

Leicestershire

Blaston (Uppingham)
Brentingby (Melton Mowbray)
Burton on the Wolds (Loughborough)
Castle Donington
Loughborough Meadows
Peckleton (Desford)
Queniborough
Scalford (Melton Mowbray)
Welham

Lincolnshire

Anwick/Ruskington Fen (Sleaford)
Blyborough
Bracebridge Heath (Robey's Aerodrome)

Braceby
Buckminster
Bucknall (Horncastle)
Cranwell (North and South)
Cockthorne (Market Rasen)
Cuxwold
Elsham
Freiston
Gosberton (Spalding)
Goxhill
Greenland Top (Stallingborough)
Harlaxton
Harpswell (Hemswell)
Immingham (Aerodrome)
Immingham (Kite Balloon Base)
Kelstern (Louth)
Killingholme
Kirton Lindsey (Manton)
Leadenham
Lincoln (Handley Page Field)
Lincoln (West Common Racecourse)
Market Deeping
Moorby (Horncastle)
New Holland
North Coates Fitties (North Coates)
Scampton (Brattleby)
Scopwick
Skegness (Burgh Road)
South Carlton
Spittlegate
Swinstead (Grimsthorpe)
Tydd St Mary (Wisbech)
Waddington
Wellingore
Willoughby Hills
Winterton (Roxby)

Merseyside

Southport (Hesketh Park Sands)
Waterloo Sands (Blundellsands/Bootle)

Middlesex

Acton (Ealing/Hangar Hill/Hanger Hill Garden Estate/London Aviation Ground)
Cricklewood, London Borough of Brent
Edgware (Stag Lane), London Borough of Brent
Feltham, London Borough of Hounslow
Hayes (Harlington), London Borough of Hillingdon
Hendon

Hounslow Heath, London Borough of Hounslow
Kingsbury (Church Lane), London Borough of Brent
Kingsbury (Grove Park), London Borough of Brent
Northolt
North Wembley, London Borough of Brent
Westpole Farm
Wormwood Scrubs (HMS President), London Borough of Hammersmith & Fulham

Norfolk

Bacton
Bexwell
Bircham Newton
Earsham
Feltwell
Freethorpe
Frettenham
Gooderstone (Warren Farm)
Harling Road (Roudham)
Hickling Broad
Hingham
Holt (Bayfield)
King's Lynn
Marham
Marsham
Mattishall
Methwold
Narborough (The Great Government Aerodrome)
North Elmham (Dereham)
Norwich (Aylsham Road)
Norwich (Mousehold Heath)
Pulham St Mary
Saxthorpe (Aylsham)
Scoulton
Sedgeford
Sporle
Taverham
Thetford (Snarehill)
Tibenham
Tottenhill
West Rudham
Yarmouth (South Denes I and II)

Northamptonshire

Clipston (Market Harborough),
Easton-on-the-Hill
Finedon
King's Cliffe (Peterborough)
Litchborough
Moulton (Northampton)
Stamford
Welton

CHANNEL ISLANDS
St Peter Port (Guernsey)

ISLE OF MAN
Ramsey

ISLE OF WIGHT
Bembridge Harbour
    (Bembridge Point)
Brading
Cliff End
Cowes East and West
Foreland (New Bembridge)
Golden Hill
Wight (Cowes/Somerton)

ISLES OF SCILLY
Porth Mellon, Isles of Scilly
Tresco (Abbey Wood),
    Isles of Scilly
Tresco (New Grimsby),
    Isles of Scilly

NORTHERN IRELAND

Antrim
Ballycastle
Bentra (Whitehead, aka Larne)
Broughshane

Down
Aldergrove
Ballywalter
Bangor
Bryansford (Newcastle)
Slidderyford Bridge

SCOTLAND

Borders
Cairncross (Reston)
Eccles Tofts
Horndean
Whiteburn (Grantshouse)

Central
Alloa (Forthbank/Caudron)
Stirling (Kincairn/Gargunnock)
Stirling (Raploch/Falleninch Farm)

Dumfries & Galloway
Castle Kennedy
Luce Bay
Tinwald Down Farm

Fife
Crail
Donibristle

Hawkcraig Point
Inverkeithing Bay
Kilconquhar
Leuchars (Leuchars Junction)
Leven
Methil
North Queensferry
Port Laing (Carlingnose)
Rosyth
St Andrews Sands
South Kilduff (Kinross)

Grampian
Auldbar (Albar/Montrose)
Longside (Lenabo/Peterhead)
Peterhead Bay
Strathbeg

Highland
Cromarty
Delny House
Fort George
Nigg
Thurso

Lothian
Belhaven Sands, East Lothian
Colinton (Edinburgh),
    Mid-Lothian (Edinburgh)
East Fortune, East Lothian
Gifford
    (Townhead/Haddington),
    East Lothian
Gilmerton (Edinburgh),
    Edinburgh
Granton, Edinburgh
Gullane (West Fenton),
    East Lothian
Hoprig Mains, East Lothian
Myreside (Edinburgh),
    Edinburgh
Penston I and II, East Lothian
Skateraw (Innerwick),
    East Lothian
South Belton (Dunbar),
    East Lothian
Turnhouse (Edinburgh),
    Mid-Lothian
Tynehead, Mid-Lothian

Orkney
Caldale
Houton Bay
Houton (Orphir)
Kirkwall Bay
Pierowall (Westray)
Scapa
Smoogroo
Stenness (Stenness Loch)

Shetland
Balta Sound (Unst)
Catfirth
Lerwick (Grimista/Gremista)

Strathclyde
Ayr (Racecourse)
Bogton (Dalmellington)
Carmunnock
    (Cathcart/Glasgow)
Dalmuir (Robertson Field)
Helensburgh
Inchinnan
Loch Doon I, II and III
Machrihanish (Strabane)
Renfrew (Moorpark)
Turnberry

Tayside
Balhall
Barry
Broughty Ferry
Dundee (Stannergate)
Edzell
Montrose (Broomfield)
Montrose (Upper Dysart)

WALES

Gwynedd
Anglesey (Llangfni or Llangefni),
    Anglesey
Bangor, Caernarvonshire

England

BEDFORDSHIRE

Bedford (Cardington)

52°06′31″N/00°25′19″W, TL081467. 0.75 miles SW of Cardington village, 2.7 miles SE of Bedford town centre

IN 1915 Short Brothers purchased 1,064 acres of land south-west of the small Bedfordshire village of Cardington with the intention of constructed airships there for the Admiralty. As with all airship stations of the day, the site was complex and included new housing for the employees, which was called Shortstown. A single Airship Shed (700 by 180 by 110 feet) was constructed for the *R31* and the *R32*, first flown in July 1918 and September 1919 respectively. The station had its own railway sidings connected to the Bedford-Hitchin branch line, and a construction area that was fronted by impressive general offices. Behind the offices were a gondola shop and sheet metal works, storage for girders, a balloon gas testing room, a duralumin metal rolling shop, hydrogen storage for cylinders and a gas-making plant.

Although this photo of Cardington was taken during the early 1930s, the view, with the exception of the second airship shed, which arrived from Pulham in 1928, is little changed from the First World War period.

Nationalised in April 1919, Cardington became the Royal Airship Works, its most notable product being the ill-fated *R101*. To build the *R101* the airship shed had its roof raised by 35 feet and it was lengthened to 812 feet. It was not until 1928 that the second shed was erected, having been dismantled at Pulham. With the loss of the *R101* in October 1930 construction of airships in Britain came to an abrupt halt. Today the two giant sheds remain an impressive sight, although the technical site is now making way for new houses.

Biggleswade

52°06′33″N/00°14′23″W, 1 mile W of Sutton, 2 miles NE of Biggleswade town centre

ALLOCATED only to 75(HD) Squadron as its most westerly LG, Biggleswade was only in use between July and September 1917.

Flitwick (Ampthill)

52°00′38″N/00°29′07″W, TL040357. On N edge of Maulden Road Industrial Estate, 0.7 miles NE of Flitwick railway station

AN NLG near Flitwick was only operational from October 1916 through to July 1917 for the use of 75(HD) Squadron.

Goldington (Bedford)

52°09'39"N/00°27'13"W, TL058525. Off Kimbolton Road (B660) in region of Avon Drive, 2 miles NNE of Bedford railway station

DESIGNATED as an HD NLG3, Goldington was the home of 75(HD) Squadron, which arrived from Tadcaster on 12 October 1916 with BE.2Cs and BE.12s. Detachments by the squadron to Yelling, Old Weston and Therfield were carried out from here until the unit moved to Elmswell on 8 September 1917. During the squadron's occupation Goldington was redesignated as an NLG2 on 31 March 1917, and from 30 June was classified as a DLG only during its last few weeks of military use. The site today has been swallowed up by the sprawl of Bedford.

Henlow

52°01'10"N/00°18'06"W, TL165359. N and S of Hitchin Road (B659), current RAF Henlow, 1.8 miles WSW of Arlesey railway station

CONSTRUCTED by Holland, Hannen & Cubitt Ltd in late 1917 and early 1918, Henlow was opened as an ARD and ERD on 15 February 1918. Six 1917-pattern GS Sheds (170 by 80 feet), built as three coupled units, a pair of 1918-pattern GS Sheds (170 by 100 feet) coupled, and two nine-bay 1918-style sheds as a coupled unit with a double pitched roof were all built for the main unit, which was officially designated as No 5 Eastern Area ARD & ERD. The site occupied 228 acres, 35 of them covered by buildings, and measured 1,600 by 1,200 yards; at its peak the ARS produced 100 aircraft per month and the ERD up to 300 Rolls-Royce and Liberty engines per month. A large number of buildings were constructed on both sides of the Hitchin Road, just as they are today. This type of unit needed a large number of personnel, and at its peak 75 officers, 230 SNCOs, 270 JNCOs, 2,349 other ranks and 1,072 women, 91 of whom were 'household', served here. All were accommodated on an extensive site to the south of the Hitchin Road, running parallel with Bedford Road; the WRAF block alone was the biggest in the country.

Today the site remains an active RAF station and all eight sheds are extant, with preservation orders in place.

Leagrave

51°53'59"N/00°27'44"W, TL058234. Electrolux site off Oakley Road, 2.5 miles NW of Luton city centre

IN May 1914 aircraft manufacturer Hewlett & Blondeau bought a piece of land at Leagrave to build Farmans. A new factory, which covered 120,000 sq ft by the end of the war, was named 'The Omnia Works', and at its peak the company employed 700 workers.

The military surveyed the site as a potential aerodrome for the RFC, and it was recommended on 10 February 1916, but no further action was taken. In the meantime Hewlett & Blondeau continued to build aircraft at a good rate, including 350 FK.3s and several Avro 504s.

By late 1920 the business was failing, and it was later sold to Electrolux, which has been at Leagrave ever since. Extensively redeveloped over the years, the small LG has been swallowed up by housing, although some original buildings still remain.

Little Staughton (Bedford)

52°15'43"N/00°23'27"W, TL099640. S of Great Staughton road, SW of New Farm, 0.75 miles NW of Little Staughton

LITTLE STAUGHTON was one of several LGs that served 75(HD) Squadron during its tenure at Goldington. Opened in October 1916 as an HD NLG1, the site was abandoned only weeks before the unit moved to Elmswell in September 1917.

BERKSHIRE

Ascot Racecourse

51°24'58"N/00°40'35"W, SU921694

AN Examination Ground & Aircraft Park was formed at Ascot in 1916, but was disbanded the following year, to be replaced by No 6 Stores Depot HQ. The depot for the latter unit was located at Hurst Park, while both HQ and depot were under the total control of the Central Aircraft Depot at Kennington from 1 January 1917. The CAD became the Central Aircraft Repair Depot on 11 January.

By 27 January Ascot became a separate park under the Inspector of Repair Depots. Ascot Racecourse, 6 SD, occupied The Farm, established an Aeroplane Section in the grandstand, and operated Engine & Packing Sections within the yard of the Royal Hotel. The unit also had detachments at King Street, Hammersmith, London; Brook Green Skating Rink, Hammersmith, London; Austin's Stores, Northfield, Birmingham; Dudley Skating Ring, Dudley; and The Zoo, Glasgow.

The depot at Hurst Park moved to Ascot in 1918 and remained into the post-war period when 6 SD was redesignated as the Packing Depot until it was finally disbanded on 23 May 1929.

BUCKINGHAMSHIRE

Cheddington

51°50'18"N/00°39'30"W, SP924162. 0.65 miles SSE of Cheddington village, 0.5 miles E of disused Long Marston airfield

OPENED in March 1917 for 39(HD) Squadron as an HD NLG1, Cheddington was reclassified as a DLG1 on 14 September 1917, but was closed by the following month.

Halton (Wendover)

51°46'13"N/00°43'41"W, SP878085. Either side of Tring Road (B4009), surrounding Roborough Copse on W and towards Boddington and Haddington Hill/Wendover Woods to E

AN area of land very close to Halton House was used by 3 Squadron for manoeuvres at the invitation of the owner, Alfred de Rothschild, in 1913. After making a gentlemen's agreement with Lord Kitchener, Rothschild allowed to Army to use his estate for training for the remainder of the war, and ever since the name Halton has been associated with the military.

The RFC showing an interest in the open land in 1916 and moved its School of Technical Training (Men) here from Coley Park, Reading, on 10 September 1917. The many huts and workshops needed to support such a unit were built by German POWs, including an aerodrome measuring 833 by 766 yards. The school taught all of the RFC's mechanical trades, with courses lasting from eight to sixteen weeks, together with advanced and refresher courses on new engines and equipment, which lasted from two to four weeks. The camp was huge, with a maximum capacity of more than 9,000 airmen and airwomen at its peak. Bessonneau and a variety of portable hangars protected many aircraft, which were used for general engine running and taxying, although many visitors did fly in and out during this early period.

No 5 Cadet Wing was reformed here in September 1917, when 7 and 8 Cadet Wings amalgamated after arriving from Farnborough; an AFC Training Centre was also formed here in 1918. The main training school was redesignated the Boys Training Depot in December 1919 and continued to be one of the main training centres of the RAF into the post-war period.

The current RAF Halton is as active as ever and accommodates a number of units, including the Recruit Training Squadron. The airfield today is not the First World War site; this area is now covered by Halton Camp.

Hanslope (Newport Pagnell)

52°08'01"N/00°49'19"W, SP807490. At Salcey Green off the M1, S of Salcey Forest, 1.3 miles NNE of Hanslope

This HD NLG1 and DLG was used solely by 75(HD) Squadron from December 1916 through to the summer of 1918.

High Wycombe

51°36'35"N/00°48'46"W, SU823908. Off Marlow Road (B482), SW end of Wycombe Park main runway, 3 miles SW of High Wycombe

ONLY open from January to July 1917 as an HD NLG2 for 39(HD) Squadron, the same site was surveyed at the beginning of the Second World War to become RAF Booker from 1941. Closed in 1963, the site reopened in civilian hands as Wycombe Air Park.

Lavendon (Bedford)

52°10'53"N/00°38'57"W, SP924546. Off Harrold Road, 0.8 miles NE of Lavendon, 3 miles NE of Olney

DESPITE the alternative 'Bedford' name, Lavendon NLG1 was located literally yards within the Buckinghamshire border. Opened in October 1916 for 75(HD) Squadron, it was reclassified as an NLG2 on 5 January 1917, but later changed back to an NLG1 and DLG. Measuring 600 by 500 yards, the site was abandoned by mid-1918.

CAMBRIDGESHIRE

Bainton, Huntingdonshire

TF091066A. Two miles E of Barnack railway station

AN NLG near the village of Bainton was only in use during 1916 for 75(HD) Squadron, flying the BE.2C and BE.12 from Tadcaster. The unit's most southerly LG by far, Bainton was 90 miles south of the main airfield.

Coldham (Wisbech)

52°35'38"N/00°06'46"W, TF432016. E of B1101, 0.4 miles NE of Rutlands Farm, 0.75 miles S of Coldham, 3.2 miles NNE of March

THIS 37-acre HD NLG3 was opened in the middle of the remote Fens in early 1917, initially for the use of 51(HD) Squadron. Measuring 400 by 300 yards, the site was also later used by 75(HD) Squadron before it was closed down in June 1919.

Cottenham

52°18'02", 00°05'50"W, TL431690. 0.6 miles NNE of Rampton off Cow Lane, 1.4 miles NW of Cottenham

COTTENHAM was opened in April 1916 as an HD NLG1 for the use of 75(HD) Squadron. The LG took up 85 acres and measured 660 by 300 yards. Reclassified as an NLG2 on 3 March 1917, Cottenham later hosted aircraft from 192 NTS from Newmarket flying FE.2s and BE.2s. Cottenham remained open until April 1919.

Duxford

52°05'38", 00°07'45"W, TL463457. IWM, 1.25 miles from Duxford, 7 miles S of Cambridge

ONE of the busiest historic aviation centres in Britain, Duxford has remained active since it first opened in March 1918 as a Training Squadron Station. The arrival of 119, 123 and 129 Squadrons quickly brought this airfield to life in a military career that was destined to continue into the 1960s and beyond in the hands of enthusiasts, who have helped to create one of the country's leading aviation museums.

It was initially furnished with nine Bessonneau hangars, along the side of the Cambridge-Royston road (A505),

Looking north-east along the Royston to Cambridge road, this view clearly shows how Duxford occupied both sides, with the main technical site and flying field to the right. Note the line of Bessonneau hangars to the south-west of the main GS sheds.

Handley Page O/400 bombers huddle close together, thanks to their foldings, inside one of Duxford's 1918-pattern GS Sheds, six of which survive today.

pending the construction of seven 1918-pattern GS Sheds (Esavian doors) of 170 by 100 feet, three of them coupled and one as a single ARS with a pair of plane stores attached. Technical and domestic buildings were constructed on both sides of the A505, while the flying site, which measured 1,000 by 1,000 yards, was located on the south-eastern side of the road, as it is today. The entire site occupied 223 acres, 30 of which were taken up by technical buildings by the time the site was fully completed as a TDS. 35 TDS was the main occupant, formed from 12 and 25 TS at Thetford on 15 July 1918; the unit moved to Duxford on 21 August with a variety of aircraft including the DH.4, DH.6, 504 and RE.8. The unit was disbanded into 31 TS at neighbouring Fowlmere on 31 May 1919, and it looked as if Duxford would be closed, but instead the training squadron returned in the shape of 2 FTS in April 1920 and the airfield's future was secured.

Today the most obvious remnant of Duxford's late First World War existence are its six GS Sheds and many brick-built technical buildings, which have survived many years of military use. In fact, right up to the airfield's closure by the RAF in 1968, the original infrastructure remained and it is only in recent years with the expansion of the IWM that the airfield has changed its appearance. The airfield was famously used for the making of the classic war film *Battle of Britain* in 1968, which included a very realistic Luftwaffe bombing raid that spectacularly brought about the demise of the missing seventh ARS Shed.

Duxford main units, 1918-19

119 Sqn from Andover, 1 Mar 1918; to Thetford,
19 Aug 1918 (various aircraft)

123 Sqn from Waddington, 1 Mar 1918; to Thetford,
21 Aug 1918 (DH.9)

129 Sqn formed 1 Mar 1918; DB 4 Jul 1918 (DH.9)

159th Aero Sqn, USAAS, from USA 15 Mar 1918;
departed 1918

137th Aero Sqn, USAAS, by 17 Jul 1918;
departed 1918

23rd Aero Sqn, USAAS, from Thetford Jul 1918;
to France, Nov 1918

151st Aero Sqn, USAAS, by 1918; to France, Nov 1918

35 TDS from Thetford, 21 Aug 1918;
DB into 31 TS Fowlmere, 31 May 1919
(DH.4, DH.6, 504 and RE.8)

256th Aero Sqn, USAAS, by 1918;
departed 1918

268th Aero Sqn, USAAS, by 1918;
departed 1918

23rd Aero Sqn, USAAS, from Thetford, 2 Sep 1918;
to Codford, 5 Nov 1918 (DH.4)

8 Sqn from Sart, 28 Jul 1919;
DB 20 Jan 1920 (FK.8 and F.2B)

Fowlmere

52°04'36"N/00°03'49"W, TL415440. Next to London Road, 1 mile SSW of Fowlmere village, 3 miles WSW of IWM Duxford

FOWLMERE was first surveyed and recommended as an aerodrome by 7th Wing (based in Norwich) in July 1916. A generous site, it occupied 247 acres and measured 1,100 by 1,100 yards. The following month the site was classified as an NLG1 and was allocated to 75(HD) Squadron, which remained until December 1917. By then Fowlmere was earmarked for expansion, and in March 1918 became a Training Squadron Station and TDS. A domestic site was constructed on the eastern side of London Road and a large technical site on the western side, with the flying field beyond. One feature of Fowlmere's seven GS Sheds (170 by 100 feet) was that they had sliding doors rather than the concertina type that can still be seen at nearby Duxford.

After a flurry of operational units passed through Fowlmere, the main training unit, 5 TS, moved in from Castle Bromwich on 10 August 1918 with a variety of aircraft ranging from BE types to the 504, DH.9 and Camel. Redesignated as 31 TDS from 1 September, and again to 31 TS on 14 March 1919, this large unit remained at Fowlmere until the end, when it was disbanded into 2 FTS at Duxford on 26 April 1920. Fowlmere was closed down by end of that year, although buildings lingered on until 1923.

A second airfield was established here between 1940 and 1946, and the current active airfield, which covers both original sites, retains a link with aviation.

Fowlmere units, 1918-19

124 Sqn from Old Sarum, 1 Mar 1918;
DB 10 Aug 1918 (DH.9)

125 Sqn from Old Sarum, 1 Mar 1918;
DB 17 Aug 1918 (DH.4 and DH.9)

126 Sqn from Old Sarum, 1 Mar 1918;
DB 17 Aug 1918 (DH.9)

165th Aero Sqn 'C' and 'D' Flts, (USAAC), from USA,
15 Mar 1918; fate unknown

5 TS from Castle Bromwich, 10 Aug 1918;
redesignated 31 TDS, 1 Sep 1918 (various aircraft)

31 TDS (ex-5 TS), 1 Sep 1918; redesignated 31 TS,
14 Mar 1919 (DH.4, DH.9, 504K and BE.2D/E)

16 Sqn (cadre) from Auchy, 12 Feb 1919;
DB 31 Dec 1919

15 Sqn from Vignacourt, 16 Feb 1919;
DB 31 Dec 1919 (RE.8)

21 Sqn from Coucou, 14 Feb 1919;
DB 1 Oct 1919 (RE.8)

31 TS (ex-31 TDS), 14 Mar 1919;
DB into 2 FTS, 26 Apr 1920 (504K)

De Havilland DH.9 C2228 of 31 TDS, named 'Nichette', at Fowlmere in September 1918.

Below: 155 Squadron DH.9A E8553 'N' visits Fowlmere from Chingford in 1918.

Hardwick

52°11'53", 00°00'16"W, TL371574. NE of Asplins Farm off Main Street, 0.75 miles S of Hardwick, 6.5 miles W of Cambridge railway station

HARDWICK was a private aerodrome and the home of the Cambridge School of Flying. The same 80-acre site hosted several RFC machines for army manoeuvres in 1911. The flying school remained into the post-war period, operating DH.6s, 504s and Caudrons. In 1919 a flying course on the DH.6 cost the princely sum of £100, and the 504 £180.

Horseheath

52°05'50", 00°22'05"W, TL623470. W of Horseheath Park Farm, S of Acre pond off Park Hill (A1307), WNW of Haverhill

A 55-ACRE site measuring 600 by 450 yards, Horseheath opened in April 1916 as an HD NLG3 for the use of 75(HD) Squadron. Later reclassified as an NLG2 on 5 January 1917, Horseheath also played host to aircraft of 192 Depot Squadron (192 NTS from December 1917) from Newmarket in October 1917. The LG was closed down by April 1919 and returned to the soil.

Little Downham (Ely)

52°26'02", 00°13'42"W, TL514844. Off Mill Hill Road (B1411) on W side of village, NW of Tower Farm, 2.75 miles NW of Ely

AT 30 feet amsl, the field chosen for this HD NLG2 was higher than most in Fenland. Opened in April 1916 for the use of 75(HD) Squadron, the LG was also used by 192 Depot Squadron (later 192 NTS) at Marham from October 1917, and possibly from Newmarket from November. Occupying 60 acres and measuring 700 by 580 yards, the site was closed down in April 1919.

Old Weston (Thrapston), Huntingdonshire

52°23'27"N/00°23'16"W, TL097782. 0.5 miles due N of Old Weston village, 1.3 miles E of RAF Molesworth (650 yards from end of wartime main runway)

USED exclusively by 75(HD) Squadron operating from Goldington, Old Weston served as an HD Flight Station from October 1916 to July 1917. 'C' Flight was the first occupant when it formed here on 12 October 1916 flying the BE.2C and BE.12. 'C' Flight moved to Therfield in December, and 'B' Flight moved from Yelling. 'B' Flight returned to Yelling on 1 July 1917 and Old Weston was closed down.

Orton

52°32'43"N/00°17'54"W, TL155955. 1.5 miles from Overton railway station

A 40-ACRE aerodrome measuring 450 by 420 yards, Orton was opened in December 1916 for the use of 75(HD) and 90(HD) Squadrons. 38(HD) Squadron may also have briefly used the aerodrome during 1918, the site remaining in military hands until June 1919.

Portholme Meadow, Huntingdonshire

52°19'15"N/00°11'08"W, TL235705. Hemmed in by River Ouse, A14 to N, East Coast Main Line to W, 0.7 miles S of Huntingdon

PORTHOLME MEADOW first witnessed aviation on 19 April 1910 when James Radley demonstrated a Blériot to more than 300 spectators. As a result, the Earl of Sandwich thought the 360-acre meadow, possibly the largest in the country, would make an ideal site for a combined aerodrome and racecourse, and on 18 November 1910 the decision was made to proceed. The following year, in March, the Portholme Aircraft Co Ltd was formed here by James Radley and William Barnard Rhodes-Moorhouse*. The company's first aircraft, the Radley Monoplane, was unsuccessfully tested here in July 1911, but success followed with several Blériot-type designs and the two-seater Radley-Moorhouse Monoplane in November 1911. By August 1915 the company won its first military contract to build twenty Short Wright 840 seaplanes; only three were built, but more successful production would follow with 250 Camels and 100 Snipes.

The military first arrived in 1917 when aircraft from 20 and 31 TS moved in from Wyton, by which time the aerodrome occupied 130 acres and measured 1,000 by 900 yards. Only temporary Bessonneau hangars were ever erected, despite the fact that the station was upgraded when 211 TDS was formed here on 1 April 1918 with the DH.6, Pup and BE.2E. The unit was redesignated as 59 TDS on 18 July, only to move to Scopwick on 15 October. The aerodrome was up for sale by 1920 and was closed down in 1922, but was used briefly again by Sir Alan Cobham's circus during the 1930s.

*Lt W. B. Rhodes-Moorhouse, while serving with 2 Squadron, won the Victoria Cross for his action over Kortrijk, Belgium, on 26 April 1915. He died of his injuries the following day.

Visiting Handley Page O/400 D9702 has its wings locked back into place at Portholme Meadow. The exact number of Bessonneau hangars on the aerodrome is unknown, but three examples can be seen in the background, with a fourth under construction.

Upwood (Bury/Ramsey)

52°26'27"N/00°08'02"W, TL269842. On N side of ex-RAF Upwood, 1.25 miles SW of Ramsey

THE first of two airfields built to the south-west of Ramsey was opened in 1917 with the name of Bury (Ramsey), classified as an NLG for the occasional use of 75(HD) Squadron operating from Elmswell. By 1918 the site was renamed Upwood and work began on expanding the site into an HD station. The aerodrome took up 160 acres and measured 1,075 by 750 yards. The infrastructure was big, occupying 25 acres of the site alone, including four Aeroplane Sheds of 180 by 100 feet. Personnel strength included 16 officers, 50 officer pupils, 15 SNCOs, 15 JNCOs, 117 other ranks and 71 women, 24 of whom were 'household'.

Upwood's first flying unit was 191 NTS from Marham, equipped with a large number of aircraft including the BE.2D/E, DH.6 and FE.2B. 190 NTS arrived from Newmarket on 5 October 1918 with its 504Ks. By the time both training squadrons had settled in the war was over, but both units clung on into mid-1919; 190 NTS disbanded first on 1 May, and 191 NTS followed on 26 June. The site was rapidly closed down and cleared, but this excellent location was not overlooked, as a much larger bomber airfield opened in 1937 and was destined not be fully vacated by the military until 2012.

Walton

52°36'03"N/00°16'18"W, TF171017. Between Enterprise Way and W of main railway line, 2 miles NNW of Peterborough railway station

THIS was a manufacturer's LG for Frederick Sage & Co Ltd, whose shopfitting factory on the eastern side of the main East Coast Main Line produced a large number of aircraft during the war. These included B.E.2Cs and Avro 504s, a large number of which would have been towed across the railway line for test flying and/or delivery. The original Sage factory was only demolished a few years ago but, following a local campaign, a unique water tower has been saved.

Wyton, Huntingdonshire

52°21'29"N/00°07'12"W, TL283751. Within W boundary of current RAF Wyton and E of A141 under old bomb dump, 2.9 miles NE of Huntingdon

ANOTHER active RAF station with a long history, Wyton still remains in use, but not for much longer from an aviation point of view, as the Cambridge UAS, University of London Air Squadron and 5 AEF should have relocated to Wittering by the time this book is published. However, Wyton will remain as an RAF station for the foreseeable future as JFIG and DGIFC make this historic site their home.

The original First World War aerodrome, which was destined to be swallowed up by the 1930s expansion airfield, was located on either side of the A141, the flying site on the east and domestic buildings on the west, south-east of Hungary Hall. The site was large at 151 acres, and measured 1,150 by 630 yards. Thirty acres of the aerodrome were occupied by buildings, including five Aeroplane Sheds (two of 210 by 65 feet, two 170 by 80 feet, and one 140 by 65 feet).

Opened in April 1916, a variety of units passed through Wyton, including operational squadrons, training squadrons and units from the USA and Canada. The aerodrome was classified as a three-squadron Mobilisation Station in 1918, but by mid-1919 was already being wound down. The majority of the buildings lingered on through the 1920s and 1930s, and Alan Cobham's circus briefly saw aviation return, before the site was earmarked as a bomber station in 1935.

DH.9 C6117, which originally served with 5 TDS at Easton-on-the-Hill, is seen in service with 31 TS at Wyton, where it received the nickname 'Umpikoff'.

Wyton main units, 1916-19

46 Sqn from Brooklands, 20 Apr 1916;
to St Omer, 20 Oct 1916 (BE.2C and Nieuport 12)

65 Sqn, formed 1 Aug 1916;
to La Lovie, 27 Oct 1917 (various aircraft)

31 (Reserve) Sqn, formed 1 Oct 1916;
redesignated 31 TS, 1 Jun 1917 (various aircraft)

54 (Reserve) Sqn, formed 15 Feb 1917;
redesignated 54 TS, 1 Jun 1917 (DH.5 and Mono Avro)

20 TS from Wye, 1 Jun 1917; to Spittlegate, 15 Sep 1917
(BE.2C/D, BE.12A, 504, RE.8, DH.2, FK.3, DH.6 and JN.4)

31 TS (ex-31 (Reserve) Sqn), 1 Jun 1917;
DB 2 Sep 1918 (various aircraft)

54 TS (ex-54 (Reserve) Sqn), 1 Jun 1917;
to Harlaxton, 17 Mar 1917 (DH.5 and Mono Avro)

104 Sqn, formed 4 Sep 1917; to Andover, 16 Sep 1917 (DH.9)

83 Sqn from Spittlegate, 15 Sep 1917;
to Narborough, 12 Dec 1917 (various aircraft)

5 TS from Castle Bromwich, 12 Dec 1917;
to Fowlmere, 10 Aug 1918
(Shorthorn, Longhorn, BE.2C/E, BE.12 and DH.9)

8th Aero Sqn, USAAS, detached from Joyce Green (DH.4)

72 TS, formed 10 Jan 1918;
to Beverley, Jan 1918 (SE.5, Camel and 504)

24th Aero Sqn, USAAS, detached from Wye, 31 Jan 1918;
to Narborough, 1 May 1918 (aircraft unknown)

130 Sqn, formed 1 Mar 1918;
to Hucknall, 7 Mar 1918 (DH.9)

151st Aero Sqn, 'A' & 'B' Flight, USAAS, detached, arrived by
17 Jul 1918

153rd Aero Sqn, 'A' Flight, USAAS, arrived by 17 Jul 1918

165th Aero Sqn, 'A' Flight, USAAS, arrived by 17 Jul 1918

124 Sqn from Fowlmere, 10 Aug 1918;
DB 17 Aug 1918 (DH.4 and DH.9)

119 Sqn from Thetford, 26 Sep 1918;
DB 19 Nov 1918 (various aircraft)

96 Sqn, reformed 28 Sep 1918;
DB 9 Dec 1918 (Salamander)

156 Sqn, formed 12 Oct 1918;
DB 9 Dec 1918 (no aircraft)

81 Sqn/1 Sqn CAF, reformed 13 Nov 1918;
to Upper Heyford, 20 Nov 1918

120 Sqn from Bracebridge Heath, 23 Nov 1918;
to Hawkinge, 20 Dec 1919 (DH.9)

117 Sqn from Norwich, 30 Nov 1918;
to Tallaght, 29 Mar 1919 (DH.4, DH.9 and RE.8)

211 Sqn from Thuilles, 15 Mar 1919;
DB 24 Jun 1919 (DH.9)

Yelling (St Neots)

52°14'42"N/00°10'08"W, TM173141. 0.6 miles W of
Yelling, 1.5 miles SE of Graveley WW2 airfield

THIS small LG was made ready in early October 1916 for
the use of 75(HD) Squadron and its BE.2Cs from
Goldhanger. Yelling remained active until 75(HD) Squadron
moved to Elmswell in September 1917, the site being
relinquished the following month.

CHESHIRE

Heaton Chapel, Greater Manchester

53°25'58"N/02°11'18"W, SJ871930 (aerodrome),
SJ875928 (factory). E of Errwood Road, S of Crossley
Road, 0.6 miles W of Mauldeth railway station

BEFORE the war Crossley Motors Ltd built a new engine
factory alongside the railway line at Heaton Chapel.
Following further expansion, this became the site of National
Aircraft Factory No 2 (de Havilland Shadow Factory) from
October 1917, specifically for the construction of the Airco
DH.9. A manufacturer's aerodrome was established on the
western side of the factory alongside Errwood Road, and from
here 326 DH.9s were flight-tested, the first of them delivered
to the RFC on 16 March 1918. Two hundred DH.10s followed,
but after the Armistice the site lay empty until it was purchased
by Fairey in 1934. Today the original offices and factory site
are extant and the aerodrome is still open ground.

Hooton Park, Merseyside

53°18'11"N/02°56'28"W, SJ373788. Vauxhall Motors
site, off M53, 2.3 miles NW of Ellesmere Port railway
station

ON the outbreak of war a large area of land on the western
bank of the River Mersey was requisitioned by the War
Office as a training area for the Army. The area was originally
a racecourse, set in the grounds of Hooton Hall, and by 1917
the site was surveyed as a potential aerodrome.

Hooton Park was destined to become a TDS, work
beginning on the 200-acre aerodrome, which measured 1,250
by 1,000 yards, in the summer of 1917. The work was allocated
to Sir Lindsay Parkinson Ltd, in a contract worth £800,000. The
site's buildings were all concentrated on the western boundary
and included seven 1917-pattern GS Sheds (170 by 80 feet),
three of them coupled and one built behind as an ARS.

4 TDS was formed here on 19 September 1917, although
the units that would form the nucleus, 'A' Flight from Ternhill,
'B' Flight from Wyton and 'C' Flight from Scampton, all
began arriving from 1 September. Equipped with a wide range
of aircraft, the TDS's main role was to train pilots to fly single-
seat fighters. Service fighters such as the Pup and Camel were
available to the TDS, but by mid-1918 the main types were
the 504 and the Dolphin; more than seventy of them were on
strength at any one time during 1918.

Hooton Park was earmarked to assemble American-built O/400s from mid-1918, and at least two prospective USAAS units were resident between February and October, but the big bombers never arrived before the Armistice and the idea was shelved. 4 TDS was redesignated as 4 TS on 14 March 1919 and remained training pilots in a reduced capacity until it was disbanded on 31 May. The site was placed under Care & Maintenance until May 1920, when it was closed down. After languishing unused until 1927, Hooton Park was reopened, going on to enjoy a rich aviation history beyond the remit of this book. Closed down in the late 1950s, the site was bought by Vauxhall Motors Ltd in 1962, and covers virtually all of the original site and the later expanded airfield.

A few gems still survive today, thanks to the efforts of local volunteers and the Hooton Park Trust. Six of the seven GS Sheds survive, although one pair now has no roof, but this is in hand for repair and restoration. Behind the shed line, a few hardy survivors from 4 TDS days also remain as part of this historic site.

Hooton Park main units, 1917-19

4 TDS formed 19 Sep 1917; redesignated 4 TS, 14 Mar 1919 (Dolphin, 504A/J/K, Pup, Camel, DH.10, F.2B, SPAD and FK.8)

185th Aero Sqn, 'B', 'C' and 'D' Flts, USAAS, from Romsey, 28 Feb 1918; to Flower Down, 7 Aug 1918

185th Aero Sqn, 'A' Flt, USAAS, from Ternhill, 5 Apr 1918; to Flower Down, 7 Aug 1918

43rd Aero Sqn, USAAS, detached from South Carlton, 24 Aug 1918; to Codford, 14 Oct 1918

37 Wing HQ from Little Sutton, 3 Nov 1918; DB 9 Apr 1919

4 TS (ex-4 TDS), 14 Mar 1919; DB 31 May 1919 (504K)

Storage Section formed Mar 1919; DB 1919

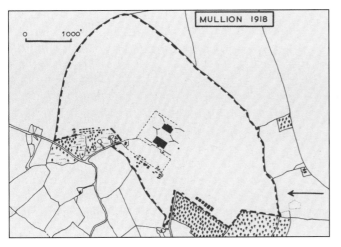

CORNWALL

Bude

50°47'06"N/04°30'01"W, SS238013. 0.3 miles WSW of Titson, 3.5 miles SE of Bude

A SUB-STATION for Mullion, Bude served as a mooring outstation specifically for non-rigid airships during 1918 and 1919. Under the charge of 77th Wing, there was also a small LG here, but units credited with using it are unknown.

Merifield (Tor Point)

50°23'19"N/04°12'27" (W site), 50°23'17"N/04°12'23"W (E site), SX431566 (W site), SX434565 (E site). NE of Wilcove, occupying N half of Cove Head and E of Cove Plantation, 1 mile NW of Torpoint

S PLIT by a minor road, Merifield was divided into two sites – the western site, north of Peter House, and the eastern site, surrounding Whitehall Farm. The entire site, which occupied just 13 acres, was opened in 1917 as Kite Balloon Station Merifield, equipped with six balloons. Merifield was credited with having six canvas Balloon Hangars (100 by 36 feet), but later plans showed nine in residence on the western site. Each balloon was walked across the road to the eastern site, where they were launched.

The station was redesignated as No 16 Balloon Base in April 1919, and was then redesignated again in July 1919 as No 1 Balloon Training Base. The base was disbanded on 16 October 1919 and Merifield was closed down in early 1920. Today the western site is covered in houses (Cove Meadow), while the eastern site remains unaltered.

Mullion

52°02'44", 05°12'17"W, SW705210. Bonython (Goonhilly Downs) Wind Farm, 1 mile W of Goonhilly Earth Station, 2 miles NE of Mullion

M ULLION played an important role in stemming the U-boat threat during the war, with both airships and aircraft operating from the same site. Mullion was opened as a Class F Airship Station in June 1916 for the operation of non-rigid airships. It was a large site occupying 320 acres and measuring 1,933 by 1,100 yards, and was allocated three sub-stations at Bude, Laira and St Mary's. A pair of sheds were constructed, one non-rigid Airship Shed (300 by 100 by 70 feet) and one portable Airship Shed (220 by 70 by 70 feet). An array of supporting technical buildings including a gas storage plant, several workshops and domestic buildings were erected along the western boundary.

The majority of airship operations carried out from here was by Coastal Class airships, although many SS and SSZ Class airships also passed through the station. Sightings of U-boats were rare, which was probably a sign of the airships' patrol success, but at least one was recorded as being attacked on 12 February 1917. The commander of a Coastal airship, Flt Sub Lt C. S. Coltson, spotted a U-boat surfacing below him off the Cornish coast. From a height of 1,000 feet two bombs were dropped; one just missed its target while the second struck the conning tower. Coltson reported that oil and a large amount of bubbles were seen on the surface, as the U-boat disappeared below the waves. However, no U-boat was reported missing that day, but Coltson and his three crew were all awarded the DSC. Three more DSCs and nine Mentions in Dispatches were awarded to airship crewmen at Mullion.

From April 1917 Mullion was also classified as a Marine Operations Station, the first 'fixed-wing' occupant being an RNAS (Royal Naval Air Station) Special Duties Flight. This unit would evolve into one of many specialist flights tasked with a variety of coastal duties, including anti-submarine patrols. In the meantime 515 and 516(SD) Flights were formed here on 16 May 1918, and a few days later the original SD Flight was redesignated as 493(LB) Flight; the former units operated the DH.6 and the latter the DH.9. Six Bessonneau hangars were erected in the south-west corner of the aerodrome for 515 and 516, which by May had become part of 254 Squadron, while 493 Flight came under 236 Squadron control from August. The latter unit was formed here and remained until disbandment on 31 May 1919.

The site was rapidly closed down, but today is still open land, albeit for the occupation of a wind farm, which helps to protect the two extant airship shed bases.

Mullion main units, 1917-19

SD Flt RNAS formed Apr 1917; DB 1917

SD Flt RNAS/RAF formed Dec 1917;
redesignated 493 Flt, 30 May 1918

515(SD) and 516 Flt formed within 254 Sqn,
16 May 1918; to 236 Sqn, 10 Aug 1918 (DH.6)

493(LB) Flt (ex-SD Flt), 30 May 1918;
into 236 Sqn, 20 Aug 1918 (DH.9 and 1½ Strutter)

236 Sqn (ex-493, 515 and 516 Flts) formed Aug 1918;
DB 31 May 1919 (DH.6 and DH.9)

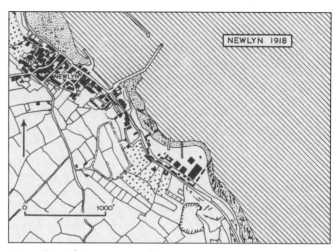

Newlyn (Penzance)

50°05'56N/05°32'32"W, SW467280. Off Fore Street, opposite quarry entrance, 0.2 miles S of South Pier, 0.6 miles SSE of Newlyn

POSITIONED on a shallow 5-acre promontory, which has since eroded away, Newlyn was opened as a Seaplane Station in 1917. With three Bessonneau hangars (66 by 66 feet), a single slipway and few technical buildings, the officers were accommodated in 'York House', while all other ranks made do in a pair of requisitioned houses in Newlyn. Personnel had the luxury of a tramway, which ran from the station into Newlyn.

A single War Flight with 184s carried out anti-submarine patrols until 20 May 1918, when 424 and 425(S) Flights were formed here with six aircraft apiece. On 20 August 235 Squadron was formed here to control the two flights, which continued to operate the 184. By this time a more permanent Type G Seaplane Shed (180 by 60 feet) had been erected, providing appreciated cover for the dozen seaplanes now operating from here. 235 Squadron was disbanded on 22 February 1919, the station following suit in the spring.

All three of RNAS Newlyn's Bessonneau hangars are evident in this view, and the base of the Type G Seaplane Shed can be seen to the left under construction. The small peninsula on which this seaplane station was established has since been taken by the sea.

Nine DH.6s of 500 and 501(SD) Flights can be seen in front of Padstow's three Bessonneau hangars in the summer of 1918.

Padstow (Trevose House)

50°32'59"N/04°58'00"W, SW897764. Due W of Crugmeer, NE of Porthmissen, 1.5 miles NW of Padstow

WITH its north-western boundary little more than 200 yards from Longcarrow Cove, the aerodrome at Padstow would have been both a dramatic and very exposed place from which to fly in the DH.6s and DH.9s that operated from here.

Originally under construction for the RNAS in early 1918, by the time Padstow was completed it was in RAF hands and classified as a Marine Operations (Aeroplane) Station. The technical site to this aerodrome was huddled close to the western side of Crugmeer, while the 50-acre aerodrome spread out towards Porthmissen. The site measured 500 by 550 yards, and four Bessonneau hangars (66 by 66 feet) were erected with a few technical buildings. The 30 officers and 119 other ranks that ran the station were all billeted locally.

The first unit here was the DH.9 or SD Flight, which became 494(LB) Flight from 30 May 1918, and part of 250 Squadron, which was formed here on 10 May with DH.6s and DH.9s. Joined by 500 and 501(SD) Flights on 31 May, the station provided aircraft for continuous anti-submarine patrols along the north Cornwall coast until the Armistice. 250 Squadron remained until it was disbanded on 31 May 1919, and the station was closed down by the end of the year. While no traces of buildings remain, the flying field is unaltered.

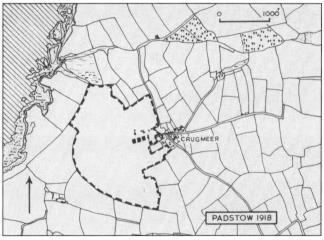

Padstow main units, 1918-19

DH.9 Flt (aka SD Flt) formed 2 May 1918; redesignated 494 Flt, 250 Sqn, 30 May 1918 (DH.9)

250 Sqn formed (494, 500, 501, 502 and 503 Flts) 10 May 1918; DB 31 May 1919 (DH.6 and DH.9)

494(LB) Flt, 30 May 1918; DB 15 May 1919 (DH.9)

500(SD) and 501(SD) Flt formed 31 May 1918; DB 15 May 1919 (DH.6)

CUMBRIA

Bowness-on-Windermere (Cockshot Point/Hill of Oaks)

54°21'35"N/02°55'52"W, SD395964. Cockshot Point, 0.6 miles SW of Bowness-on-Windermere

A PRIVATE experimental seaplane station was established here by the Lakes Flying Co Ltd and the Melley Flying School in 1911. The first aircraft flown from here was the Lakes Water Bird, but this was destroyed in March 1912 when its hangar was destroyed in a storm. Both Lakes Flying and the school were swallowed up by the Northern Aircraft Co Ltd in November 1914, which trained future RNAS seaplane pilots from January 1915. Northern Aircraft was wound up in August 1916 and no further flying took place from Cockshot Point.

Solway House

54°54'34"N/03°16'46"W, NY180579. Centre of Anthorn Radio Station, 0.65 miles SE of Cardurnock, 0.75 miles W of Anthorn

L OCATED on the northern shore of Moricambe Bay, and inlet of the Solway Firth, an LG was located near a property called Solway House, between the hamlets of Cardurnock and Anthorn, which was demolished to make way for the new airfield during the Second World War. Not much is known about the LG, but it is highly likely that it would have been used by a Scottish-based HD squadron on anti-Zeppelin patrols. Known as RNAS Anthorn (HMS *Nuthatch*) from 1943 to 1958, the site has been used as an important radio station since the early 1960s.

A view of Hill of Oaks across Lake Windermere, complete with an RNAS flying over the seaplane flying school.

Below: A part-built Gnosspelius single-float monoplane stands outside the flight sheds at Bowness-on-Windermere.

DERBYSHIRE

Lullington (Burton-on-Trent)

52°43'17"N/01°38'55"W, SK238139A. 1 mile SSW of Coton in the Elms, 6 miles due S of Burton-on-Trent

A SMALL HD NLG2, Lullington was only used by 38(HD) Squadron operating from Melton Mowbray. Opened on 1 October 1916, the site was closed down on 24 March 1917.

Roston (Ashbourne)

52°57'39"N/01°46'43"W, SK148403. SW of Birchwood Park, 1.3 miles ESE of Roston, 4.3 miles SSW of Ashbourne

A LARGE, open site, Roston was only classified as an HD NLG2 for the use of 38(HD) Squadron between October 1916 and September 1918. Occupying 69 acres and measuring 930 by 500 yards, the site was reclassified as a DLG2 from 14 September 1917.

Stanton-by-Dale

52°55'59"N/01°19'09"W, SK457375. Off No Man's Lane, SE of High Lodge Farm, 0.5 miles SW of Stanton-by-Dale

O PENED by early October 1916, this HD NLG3 was reclassified as an NLG2 in January 1917, then from September, only as a DLG. Used by 38(HD) Squadron until the unit moved to Buckminster, Stanton-by-Dale was closed down by August 1918.

DEVONSHIRE

Berry Head

50°23'57"N/03°29'04"W, SX945565. Berry Head, 1.1 miles ENE of Brixham

U NDER the control of 10 (Operations) Group, Berry Head was a Kite Balloon Base for a single balloon detached from Merifield (Tor Point) during 1918.

Cattewater (Batten Camp)

50°21'33"N/04°07'38"W, SX487531. Mount Batten Point, accessed by Lawrence Road, 1 mile NW of Hooe

T HE naturally sheltered Cattewater in Plymouth Sound was first used for seaplane trials in 1913, but it took until 1916 to recognise the fact that it would make a good home for an RNAS Seaplane Station. Making full use of Mount Batten breakwater, the station was located on Mount Batten Point, occupying 30 acres, and the site stretched southwards towards Clovelly Bay, where one of three slipways was constructed. A pair of F Type Sheds (200 by 100 feet) and two 1916-pattern Seaplane Sheds (180 by 60 feet) gave good shelter to the large number of Short 184s that served there carrying out anti-submarine patrol duties. The 184s operated from the breakwater and were lifted into the water by a steam crane that ran up and down a railway track.

The Short 184s of 237 Squadron are seen on Mount Batten breakwater complete with the steam crane and railway line visible in front of the seaplanes. *Via Stewart Leslie*

By 1918 the site was designated as a Marine Operations (Seaplane) Station with several seaplane flights in residence, which would later gel into 237 and 238 Squadrons. These flights introduced much larger flying-boats in the shape of the Curtiss H.16 and Felixstowe F.2s and F.3s. These big aircraft would be the first of many flying-boats to operate from Cattewater, but not before 237 was disbanded in May 1919 and 238 Squadron in March 1920. By 1928 the site was renamed RAF Mount Batten, with Southamptons becoming a familiar site until the mid-1930s, followed by the iconic Sunderland during the Second World War.

Mount Batten was an MU and the Marine Craft Training School by the late 1950s and a centre for the RAF Marine Branch, which did not close down until 1986. The RAF did not fully vacate the site until 1992, and its long time in military hands is one of the reasons why the two F Sheds still survive to this day, on the edge of Clovelly Bay.

Cattewater main units, 1917-22

RNAS Seaplane War Flight formed Jul 1917;
redesignated 420 and 421 Flts, 30 May 1918

RAF Flying Boat War Flight formed 1918;
redesignated 347 Flt, 15 Jun 1918

420(S) and 421 (S) Flt formed May 1918;
joined 237 Sqn, 20 Aug 1918 (Short 184)

347(FB) Flt formed 15 Jun 1918;
joined 238 Sqn, 20 Aug 1918 (H.16 and F.3)

348(FB) Flt formed 15 Jul 1918;
joined 238 Sqn, 20 Aug 1918 (H.16 and F.3)

349(FB) Flt formed 18 Oct 1918;
joined 238 Sqn, 18 Oct 1918 (H.16 and F.3)

237 Sqn (420 and 421 Flts), 20 Aug 1918;
DB 15 May 1919 (Short 184)

238 Sqn (347, 348 and 349 Flts), 20 Aug 1918;
detachments at Holy Island, Killingholme and Calshot,
reduced to cadre 15 May 1919 (H.16, Short 184, F.2A and F.3);
DB 22 Mar 1920

Laira (Plymouth)

50°22'35"N/04°05'49"W, SX510550. On Chelson Meadow, 0.75 miles NE of Laira Bridge, 2 miles E of Plymouth

FOLLOWING mooring experiments carried out here in March 1918, a permanent site was established from May 1918. Laira was used for airship moorings and as a sub-station for operations from Mullion. Several non-rigid airships passed through the site from May to November 1918, but it closed in early 1919. The RNAS carried out mooring experiments here in March 1918.

Okehampton

50°43'18"N/03°59'57"W, SX589932. NE of Okehampton Camp, close to Gunnery Lodge, 1.1 miles SSE of Okehampton

THIS was the location for a Kite Balloon Station, specifically for balloon and artillery co-operation with the RFC.

Poole (Upton)

50°44'14"N/02°00'54"W, SY989929. N of Upton Country Park, 0.6 miles W of Upton, 2 miles NW of Poole town centre

AIRSHIP moorings were constructed here during 1917 for the use of SS-Type non-rigid airships. One of two sub-stations for Polegate, Poole's airships carried out anti-submarine patrols until 1918, when the site was closed down.

Prawle Point

50°13'04"N/03°43'01"W, SX775367. 0.4 miles NW of East Prawle, 2.75 miles SE of Salcombe

LOCATED less than half a mile from the coast, Prawle Point was an ideal location for carrying out coastal operations. The site was opened as an RNAS Marine Operations Station in April 1917 with a single War Flight in residence. Only 50 acres in size, the site measured 700 by 400 yards and was only provided with four Bessonneau hangars.

The station was closed down in the winter of 1917 and 1918, reopening in the same role in February. A SD Flight operating the DH.9 was formed in April 1918 and redesignated as 492(LB) Flight in May. The same month Prawle Point became much busier when 254 Squadron was formed here, made up of three flights, 517, 518 and 525(SD), all operating the DH.6 for anti-submarine duties. This task was carried out until the Armistice by 517 and 518(SD) Flights, which remained until 22 February 1919, when the parent unit was disbanded.

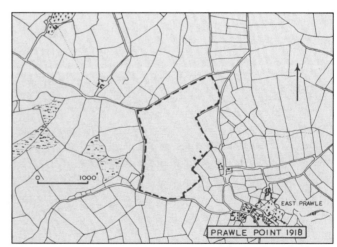

Prawle Point main units, 1917-19

RNAS War Flt formed Apr 1917; DB Aug 1917

Special Duty Flt formed 18 Apr 1918;
redesignated 492(LB) Flt, 30 May 1918 (DH.9)

492(LB) Flt formed 30 May 1918;
within 254 Sqn, 15 Aug 1918 (DH.9)

254 Sqn formed 18 May 1918;
DB 22 Feb 1919 (DH.6 and DH.9)

517(SD) and 518(SD) Flt formed 6 Jun 1918;
DB 22 Feb 1919 (DH.6)

525(SD) Flt formed 6 Jun 1918;
to Ashington, 28 Jun 1918 (DH.6)

Toller (Bridport, aka Powerstock)

50°46'47"N/02°39'11"W, SY540980. NW of Gray's
Farm in Regent's Coppice, 1.4 miles W of Toller
Porcorum

OPENED as a sub-station with airship moorings for Mullion, Toller was only active from April to November 1918.

Torquay Harbour
(Beacon Quay/Haldon Pier)

50°27'30"N/03°31'30"W, SX918631. On edge of Beacon
Quay, N of Haldon Pier, 0.25 miles S of Torquay town centre

ON 15 June 1918 Torquay played host to the formation of 418(S) Flight equipped with the Short 184 for anti-submarine patrol duties. Established at Beacon Quay, RNAS Torquay Harbour took over the area between the South Pier and Haldon Pier, an area of approximately 4 acres. The Seaplane Station had four Seaplane Sheds (48 by 60 feet) and four canvas hangars (66 by 66 feet), two of them coupled, and a few technical buildings erected in the limited space available. A third hangar (105 by 60 feet) was used by No 16 Balloon Base, based at Merifield, to house three dummy balloons for operations under the control of the C-in-C, Devonport, until the parent unit disbanded in September 1919.

The station was run by 29 officers, 11 SNCOs, 13 JNCOs

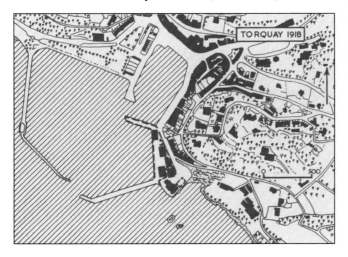

and 103 other ranks. Sea Lawn Hotel was used to accommodate some of Torquay's personnel, and the 17 women who were stationed here were billeted in No 11 Beacon Terrace, which became a temporary women's hostel. The Coastguards' Boat House was also used as the women's mess.

On 20 August 1918 418 Flight was redesignated as 239 Squadron, still equipped with the Short 184 and remaining at Torquay until it was disbanded on 31 May 1919. Torquay Harbour was then closed down, but during the Second World War slightly larger 'seaplanes' in the shape of Sunderlands returned to Torquay, operating from a pontoon south of Haldon Pier.

Westward Ho!

51°03'09"N/04°13'04"W, SS446305. Now Northam
Burrows Country Park, 1 mile N of Northam, 1.3 miles
NE of Westward Ho!

LOCATED on the exposed North Devon coast, Westward Ho! was ideally situated for anti-submarine operations over the Bristol Channel. Established in the spring of 1918 as a Marine Operations (Aeroplane) Station, this aerodrome occupied 90 acres and measured 700 by 700 yards. Aircraft were protected from the elements by several Bessonneau hangars, and personnel were accommodated in Armstrong huts. Personnel strength at its peak was 27 officers, 16 SNCOs and 89 other ranks.

On 6 June 1918 502(SD) and 503(SD) Flights were

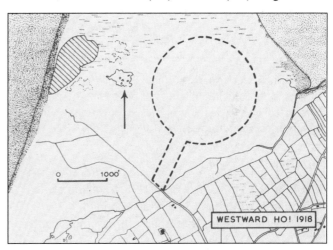

formed here with six DH.6s each as part of 260 Squadron, which established its HQ here. 260 Squadron also operated the DH.9 from here, but from 18 August 502 and 503 Flights were transferred to 250 Squadron, which had a permanent detachment from Padstow based here. In March 1919 both flights were disbanded and Westward Ho! quickly returned to its sandy origins, leaving no trace of its aviation past.

DORSETSHIRE

Chickerell (Weymouth)

50°37'13"N/02°29'18"W, SY655802. Wessex Golf Centre, 0.75 miles ESE of Chickerell, 1.5 miles NW of Weymouth

THIS 60-acre site, measuring 650 by 450 yards, was opened as a Marine Operations Station in June 1918. The first occupant was 513 Flight ('D' Flight), 253 Squadron, which was formed here on 7 June with DH.6s, although its HQ was established at Bembridge. On 20 August the unit was redesignated as 513 Flight, 241 Squadron, and, retaining its DH.6s, operated from Chickerell until its disbandment on 23 January 1919.

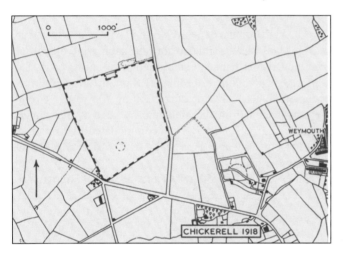

Facilities were sparse, although a pair of Bessonneau hangars gave Chickerell an aviation feel until they were dismantled and the site was closed down following 241 Squadron's disbandment.

Kinson

50°44'36"N/01°53'50"W, SZ080955. In region of Leybourne Avenue and Saxonhurst Road in Northbourne, 3 miles N of Bournemouth town centre

THIS was the home of the Bournemouth Aviation Co, which made the short move from Winton (Talbot Village) in 1917. The 88-acre site was in the region of Ensbury Park, which by the early 1920s became Ensbury Park racecourse. Air racing was popular from here until 1927, and the aviation company remained until 1932, after which redevelopment of the area for housing began.

Moreton (Dorchester)

50°42'09"N/02°20'18"W, SY764895. Due S of Woodsford, 4.5 miles E of Dorchester town centre

DESIGNED to fill the 250-mile gap between the airship stations at Polegate and Mullion, this 355-acre site was still under construction when the war ended. It measured 1,930 by 1,330 yards, and a large number technical buildings had

already been constructed when work was halted. At least two of these still survive today, on the south side of the site. Concrete roads and a large floor section of airship shed also remain.

Portland Harbour

50°34'04"N/02°26'06"W, SY693743. Centre of Portland Port, Castletown, 0.3 miles N of The Verne HM Prison, 3.3 miles SSE of Weymouth

FIRST serving as a Seaplane Station (sub-station for Calshot), Portland Harbour was opened in September 1916 for an RNAS War Flight, equipped with Wight seaplanes and later Short 184s. The site steadily expanded along the harbour wall within the Royal Navy base, but only ever featured a single Type G Seaplane Shed (90 by 60 feet), one Bessonneau, and a single slipway. Only occupying half an acre, the 29 officers, 11 SNCOs, four JNCOs, 113 other ranks and 32 women were all accommodated in Portland Castle and the Castle Inn.

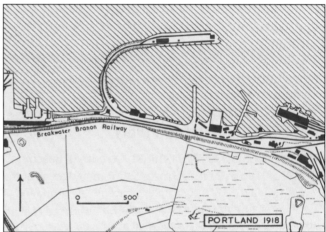

On 31 May 1918 the War Flight was redesignated as 416(S) and 417(S) Flights, both equipped with six aircraft. Priority for these two flights was anti-submarine patrols in the Channel, using the 184 and Campania. A further reorganisation saw the formation of 241 Squadron on 20 August, which encompassed 416 and 417 Flights and 513 Flight operating out of Chickerell. The end of the war did not bring an immediate closure to the seaplane station, which clung on until 18 June 1919, when 241 Squadron was disbanded. Aircraft returned to Portland in 1930 in the shape of several IIIF seaplanes, and continued on and off until July 1940.

Sandbanks (Poole Harbour)

50°41'26"N/01°56'56"W, SZ036882. Main Channel, N of Sandbanks, 2.4 miles SE of Poole

THIS was more like an area of water for seaplanes to land rather than a seaplane station, which would be established at Sandbanks during the Second World War. Aircraft that operated from here worked with the Marine Training Depot, which opened at Parkstone on 22 September 1918 and was disbanded on 24 October 1919.

Winton (Talbot Village)

50°44'37"N/01°53'07"W, SZ074936. In area of Bournemouth University, 2 miles NW of Bournemouth town centre

THE first aerodrome to be opened by the Bournemouth Aviation Co was Winton in 1915. Although not a military site, it was unofficially labelled as RFC Winton, because the company was mainly tasked with training future military pilots. Several never made it, including 2nd Lt Edward Rebbek, the son of a former Bournemouth mayor, whose aircraft crashed here. In 1917 the site was closed down and the Bournemouth Aviation Co moved to Kinson. Winton was briefly used by the USAAF in May and June 1944 as an ALG for a few Piper L-4s.

DURHAM

Bishopton

54°34'52"N/01°26'48"W, NZ358209. 0.5 miles SW of Bishopton, 5.5 miles from Stockton-on-Tees town centre

FIRST opened on 8 August 1916 as an HD NLG3, Bishopton was later expanded with much improved approaches and was upgraded to an HD NLG2 and DLG2 on 18 July 1917. In its final form the LG occupied 60 acres and measured 500 by 580 yards. The only unit to use the airfield was 36(HD) Squadron and, following its disbandment on 13 June 1919, Bishopton was relinquished on 13 August.

Catley Hill (Trimdon)

54°41'56"N/01°27'04"W, NZ354339. 0.75 miles W of Trimdon, 2 miles NNW of Fishburn

CATLEY HILL was opened as an NLG2 between October 1916 and June 1919, only serving 36(HD) Squadron during that time. The site took up 36 acres and measured 760 by 500 yards.

Cleadon (Sunderland/South Shields)

54°57'51"N/01°22'45"W, NZ398634. 0.64 miles NW of Whitburn near West Plantation, 1 mile NE of Cleadon

ONE of several LGs established for 36(HD) Squadron, it opened in April 1916 as an HD NLG3. 36 Squadron's Hylton Flight used Cleadon on several occasions for cooperation exercises with the local coastal batteries, including Frenchman Point Battery, which was only 2 miles away. The site was unused from December 1917 onwards.

Easington (Seaham Harbour)

54°46'33"N/01°21'17"W, NZ415425. On Mickle Hill, 0.6 miles SSW of Easington, 1.4 miles NW of Peterlee

AT 500 feet amsl and just 1.75 miles from the sea, Easington was susceptible to fog and mist but still gave good service between April 1916 and June 1919. The first and only occupant of this 39-acre HD NLG2 was 36(HD) Squadron. Measuring 600 by 350 yards, Easington was reclassified as an NLG3 and DLG2 on 18 July 1917.

Horsegate

54°55'43"N/01°48'49"W, NZ121596. NW of Broomfield Farm, 0.75 miles NNE of Chopwell, 2.65 miles SE of Prudhoe

HORSEGATE was the replacement for Currock Hill (1 mile to the west), and opened in May 1917 as an HD NLG3 for 36(HD) Squadron. Occupying 36 acres and measuring 450 by 560 yards, Horsegate remained open until May 1919.

Hylton (Usworth)

54°55'12"N/01°28'23"W, NZ340586. Bulk of site under Nissan car factory, due S of North East Aircraft Museum, 2.2 miles E of Usworth

IN the early summer of 1916 110 acres of land belonging to Cow Stand and South Moor farms were requisitioned for a new HD Flight Station to replace West Town Moor. The site measured 750 by 700 yards and was furnished with a pair of HD-pattern Aeroplane Sheds (120 by 60 feet), support buildings, including an armoury and a few huts for the 150 or so personnel that would, on average, occupy the aerodrome.

'B' Flight of 36(HD) Squadron was the first flying unit to arrive at Hylton from Cramlington in October 1916, mainly tasked with carrying out aerial co-operation with coastal batteries. 'B' Flight was redesignated as 'A' Flight on 10 August 1917, and on 1 July 1918 36(HD) Squadron moved its HQ here from Newcastle. On 15 July Hylton had its name changed to Usworth, although this was not adopted, locally at least, until November 1918. On 13 June 1919 36(HD) Squadron was disbanded, 'B' Flight arriving from Ashington and 'C' Flight travelling from Seaton Carew to disband with the main unit.

The site was returned to farmland by early 1920, but ten years later was reactivated as RAF Usworth, and from the early 1960s until 1984 became Sunderland Airport. The First World War site, together with the later airport, has been erased by the Nissan car factory, but the NEAM Museum keeps the aviation memories very much alive.

Sadberge

54°32'06, W01°28'58"W, NZ336157. Due W of Sadberge Hall Farm off Roman Road, 0.9 miles SW of Sadberge

ATYPICALLY basic LG occupying just 34 acres, it was first opened for the use of local RNAS units in 1917. The site was handed over to the RFC in March 1918 and from April served as an LG for 36(HD) Squadron until 1919, when it was closed down.

Seaton Carew I and Seaton Carew II (Tees Bay)

I: 54°38'48"N/01°11'25"W, NZ523283. Stephenson Industrial Estate off A178 Tees Road, 1 mile S of Seaton Carew

II: 54°37'59"N/01°10'36"W, NZ532267. On N edge of Seaton-on-Tees Channel, at SE corner of Hartlepool Nuclear Power Station, 2 miles SSE of Seaton Carew

THE first of two sites named Seaton Carew was opened as an HD Flight Station for 36(HD) Squadron in May 1916. Occupying 72 acres, the site measured 600 by 800 yards and was initially furnished with a pair of HD-pattern Aeroplane Sheds (139 by 69 feet) and a pair of Bessonneau hangars. With the formation of 495(LB) Flight in May 1918, equipped with the Blackburn Kangaroo, a further seven Bessonneau hangars were erected when the aerodrome became a Marine Operations (Aeroplane) Station. Known as Seaton Carew I, this aerodrome was closed down not long after 246 Squadron was disbanded here and at the seaplane site on 15 March 1919.

Seaton Carew II, a Marine Operations (Seaplane) Station, located less than a mile south of the aerodrome, was opened in September 1917. The site occupied just 7 acres but could handle up to twenty-four seaplanes and had one Seaplane Shed (60 by 120 feet), a pair of Bessonneau hangars and a single slipway. Station personnel strength was 28 officers, 9 SNCOs, 3 JNCOs and 80 other ranks. Aircraft operated from here were the Sopwith Baby and Short 184 for anti-submarine patrol duties. The site was closed down at the same time as the aerodrome.

While the bulk of the aerodrome has been swallowed up by an industrial estate, the technical site area is open land close to the edge of the Tees Road and, depending on conditions, the outlines of the several buildings can still be seen. The slipway of the seaplane station is still extant but all other traces have long disappeared, including a line of terraced houses called Snook Cottages, which were alongside the main access road.

Another aviation connection with Seaton Carew was that it was the home of 68th (Operations) Wing HQ in a house called 'The Gables' on Station Road. Formed on 11 July 1918 in 18 Group, the Wing controlled 246, 252, 256 and 274 Squadrons and stations at Ashington, New Haggerston, Redcar, Sea Houses, Seaton Carew I and II, and Tynemouth until it was disbanded on 1 August 1919.

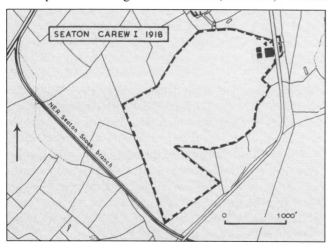

Seaton Carew I main units, 1916-19

36 Sqn 'A' Flt from Cramlington, May 1916;
to Hylton, 14 Aug 1917 (BE.2C/E, BE.12 and Scout)

36 Sqn 'C' Flt from Cramlington, 14 Aug 1917;
DB 13 Jun 1919 (BE.2C/E, BE.12 and Scout)

495(LB) Flt formed 30 May 1918;
absorbed into 246 Sqn, 15 Aug 1918 (Kangaroo)

246 Sqn, 15 Aug 1918;
DB 15 Mar 1919 (FE.2B and Kangaroo)

252 Sqn (detachment) from Tynemouth 1918;
to Killingholme, 31 Jan 1919 (DH.6)

274 Sqn formed Nov 1918; DB before aircraft arrived

Seaton Carew II main units, 1918-19

War Flt (detachment) from South Shields Sep 1917;
redesignated 451 and 452 Flts, 25 May 1918 (Baby)

451(BS) Flt formed 25 May 1918;
absorbed into 246 Sqn, 15 Aug 1918 (Baby)

452(BS) Flt formed 25 May 1918;
absorbed into 246 Sqn, 15 Aug 1918 (Baby)

402 (Seaplane) Flt formed 30 Jun 1918;
absorbed into 246 Sqn, 15 Aug 1918 (184)

246 Sqn (ex-402, 403, 451, 452 and 495 Flts),
15 Aug 1918; DB 15 Mar 1919 (184 & Baby)

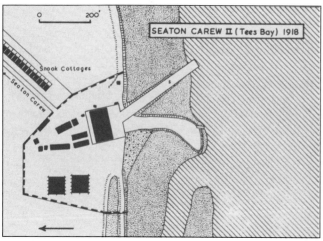

Spennymoor

54°41'11"N/01°37'47"W, NZ239325. On Binchester Moor off Clyde Terrace (Durham Road), 1.5 miles SW of Spennymoor, 3 miles NE of Bishops Auckland

OPENED in early April 1916, Spennymoor was another site for the use of 36(HD) Squadron. Classified as a DLG, Spennymoor occupied 38 acres and measured 450 by 480 yards. The site remained in military hands until June 1919 when it was returned to the original owners, and to this day is still farmland.

West Town Moor

54°55'10"N/01°27'30"W, NZ348584. E of A19 opposite Nissan car factory, 3.1 miles WNW of Sunderland railway station

NOT to be confused with its replacement only a few hundred yards to the west at Usworth (Hylton), West Town Moor was only active from May to October 1916. Used by 36(HD) Squadron, it occupied 33 acres and measured 400 by 480 yards. The site is covered by houses today.

EAST YORKSHIRE

Atwick (Hornsea)

53°57'01"N/00°11'07"W, TA185514. 0.5 miles NW of Atwick off Skipsea Road (B1242), 2.5 miles NNW of Hornsea

THE RNAS arrived at Atwick in 1915, establishing an HD War Flight equipped with TB.8s on the racecourse in August. Occupying 50 acres, the site measured 540 by 540 yards and was allocated Bessonneau hangars. From April 1916 Atwick was classified as an HD NLG1 for 33(HD) Squadron and later 76(HD) Squadron, the site being reclassified as an NLG2 from 5 January 1917.

Atwick became a Marine Operations (Aeroplane) Station on the formation of 504(SD) Flight on 31 May 1918, equipped with the DH.6. The unit served as 'B' Flight of 251 Squadron and carried out anti-submarine duties along the Yorkshire coast until the Armistice. Disbanded with the main squadron on 31 January 1919, Atwick was not relinquished until later that year and was completely clear of its RFC past by early 1920.

Barmby Moor (Pocklington)

53°56'04"N/00°50'01"W, SE765495. SW of Newfield Farm, 0.7 miles WNW of Barmby Moor of the A1079

ANOTHER LG for HD squadrons operating over East Yorkshire, Barmby Moor was opened as an NLG1 in April 1916. Its first occupant was 33(HD) Squadron, which rarely, if at all, made use of it, and in October 1916 control of the LG was transferred to 76(HD) Squadron. Reclassified as an NLG3 on 5 January 1917 and again as an NLG on 31 March, Barmby Moor remained in military hands until June 1919. The site occupied 56 acres and measured 580 by 430 yards.

Bellasize (Gilberdyke)

53°44'11"N/00°45'41"W, SE817274. 1.4 miles SW of Gilberdyke railway station, 5.3 miles NE of Goole

ORIGINALLY opened as an NLG1 in April 1916, Bellasize was reclassified as an NLG2 on 14 September 1917, but was restored to its original status in January 1918. Occupants were 33(HD) Squadron and 76(HD) Squadron, the latter from 11 October 1917. Despite the fact that the site was prone to flooding, it remained open until 15 May 1919, and was reopened as an RLG for 4 EFTS during the Second World War. The site occupied 33 acres and measured 420 by 380 yards.

Beverley (Racecourse)

53°50'36"N/00°27'31"W, TA015397. Current Beverley Racecourse off A1174, 1.5 miles W of Beverley railway station

LIKE all racecourse sites, Beverley required very little preparation to transform it into an aerodrome, beginning in March 1915 when it was classified as an HD Flight Station. By October it was classified as an NLG3 for the use of 33(HD) Squadron, which established its HQ here from March 1916.

Beverley photographed by an aircraft of 36(HD) Squadron on 7 May 1917.

Taking up 179 acres of the racecourse, the LG measured 1,150 by 600 yards. Being an HD station, Beverley had three 1915-pattern Flight Sheds (210 by 65 feet) and a technical site all concentrated around the area of the current grandstand.

Reclassified as an NLG2 on 31 March 1917, Beverley was classed as a Training Squadron Station from April 1916, which resulted in the arrival of several Canadian units, including 90 (Canadian) TS and later 36 TS, the latter remaining for the bulk of 1917. 72 TS, which arrived from Wyton in January 1918, was the main occupant until it was disbanded at Beverley in March 1919. The site remained as an NLG3 until June 1919, but notice of relinquishment was not issued until 18 March 1920. Placed under Care & Maintenance in November 1920, the military vacated soon after.

Beverley main units, 1916-19

47 Sqn formed 1 Mar 1916;
en route to Salonika, 6 Sep 1916
(504, BE.2C/D/E, FK.3 and BE.12)

34 Sqn from Castle Bromwich, 16 Mar 1916;
to Lilbourne, 15 Jun 1916 (BE.2C/E)

33 Sqn 'C' Flt formed 18 Mar 1916;
to Elsham, 3 Oct 1916 (BE.2C/D)

36 (Reserve) Sqn formed 5 Jul 1916;
redesignated 36 TS, 1 Jun 1917

78 (Canadian) Reserve Sqn formed Jan 1917;
to Canada, 15 Feb 1917 (no aircraft)

79 (Canadian) Reserve Sqn formed Jan 1917;
to Canada, 15 Feb 1917 (no aircraft)

82 Sqn from Doncaster, 6 Feb 1917;
to Waddington, 30 Mar 1917 (BE.2C/E, 504, RE.7 and RE.8)

82 (Canadian) Reserve Sqn from Montrose, 20 Feb 1917;
to Canada, 27 Feb 1917 (no aircraft)

83 (Canadian) Reserve Sqn from Catterick Mar 1917;
to Canada Mar 1917 (no aircraft)

60 (Reserve) Sqn formed 7 Apr 1917;
to Brattlebury (Scampton), 14 Apr 1917 (no aircraft)

89 (Canadian) Reserve Sqn from Turnhouse, 18 Apr 1917;
to Canada, May 1917 (no aircraft)

90 (Canadian) TS from Doncaster, 18 Apr 1917;
to Canada, May 1917 (no aircraft)

36 TS (ex-36 Reserve Sqn), 1 Jun 1917;
to Montrose, 27 Nov 1917 (504, FK.3, F.2B, BE.2C/E and RE.7)

80 Sqn from Montrose, 27 Nov 1917;
to Boisdinghem, 27 Jan 1918 (Camel)

72 TS from Wyton, 10 Jan 1918;
DB 1 Mar 1919 (504, SE.5A and Camel)

Brough

53°43'17"N/00°34'24"W, SE942259. Current BAE Systems Brough, on N bank of River Humber, 0.3 miles SE of Brough railway station

THIS is currently the world's oldest aircraft factory, which until recently has surpassed a stay of execution following a recent multi-billion-pound deal to supply both Hawks and Typhoons to the Omani Air Force.

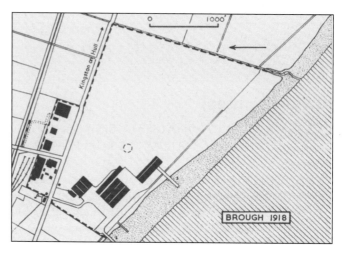

Brough was the home of the Blackburn Aeroplane & Motor Co Ltd, the site being discovered during a flight looking for suitable areas to flight-test seaplanes. Brough was located south-east of Ellerker Haven, and in the north-western corner a single steel hangar was erected, together with three slipways. The original aerodrome only covered an area of 44 acres and measured 550 by 390 yards when it became an HD NLG for 33(HD) Squadron in 1916.

As well as Blackburn, aircraft were produced by Brush Electrical Engineering, Dick Kerr, Phoenix Dynamo Manufacturing and Robey. All of these manufacturers tested their aircraft here, which brought about the formation of a No 2 (Northern) Marine Acceptance Park on 22 April 1918. With a sub-station at South Shields and a permanent detachment at Dundee, the unit prepared the bulk of all flying-boats and seaplanes that saw service with the RAF, until the unit was closed down in December 1919.

Blackburn was determined to remain in the aircraft industry, and this it successfully achieved at Brough until this famous name was absorbed by the Hawker Siddeley Group in 1961. Many famous aircraft have been constructed here over the years, including the Beverley, Buccaneer and, later, components for the Harrier, Hawk and Airbus.

Eastburn (Driffield)

53°59'29"N/00°29'02"W, SE995565. Current Army Cadet Centre, Driffield Camp, off A614, 1.7 miles WSW of Driffield

STILL in the hands of the military, the former RAF Driffield made a major contribution to the First and Second World Wars and the Cold War during its long history. A site north and south of the Goole to Bridlington road was

Looking west up the River Humber, Brough remained defiantly in the hands of Blackburn Aircraft until 1961 when this famous aircraft manufacturer was absorbed into the Hawker Siddeley Group.

surveyed for potential use as an aerodrome between Eastburn and Kellythorpe in 1916. The site opened with sparse facilities as an HD NLG for 33(HD) Squadron. It opened in October 1917 for the formation 2 SoAF, occupying 240 acres and measuring 1,200 by 1,050 yards. To the north of the A614 was the main technical site and flying field, while to the south was a large domestic site in the area now occupied by 'Four Winds'. The school was joined by a second unit, 2 SoAF&G, in May 1918, by which time the site was being heavily expanded by contractor H. Mathews & Sons Ltd, which was preparing the aerodrome for a TDS.

Seven 1918-pattern GS Sheds with Esavian doors (170 by 100 feet) were under construction when, on 15 July 1918, 3 TS arrived from Shoreham and 27 TS from London Colney to form 21 TDS the same day. Both aerial fighting schools had departed in May to make room for the new TDS, which was tasked with training pilots to fly single-seat fighters. A wide range of aircraft was on strength, but the main types were the 504 and the SE.5A.

The TDS continued its duties after the Armistice, but the aerodrome's buildings were not finally completed until February 1919. 21 TDS was redesignated 21 TS in July 1919 and did well to remain extant until February 1920. The site was placed under Care & Maintenance, but was closed down in late 1920. The buildings were systematically sold off and the site was completely cleared of its First World War roots.

Reopened in 1936 as RAF Driffield, the much larger airfield served as a bomber station throughout the Second World War and, after some to and froing with the Army, the last RAF personnel did not leave until 1996. Today the 1930s site is used for army cadet training, and the flying field is used for driver training.

Eastburn (Driffield) main units, 1917-20

2 SoAF formed 11 Oct 1917; absorbed into 2 SoAF&G at Marske, 6 May 1918 (M.1C, FK.8, DH.4, DH.9, 504, FK.3, Dolphin and Camel)

3 SoAF&G formed from 2 SoAF, 6 May 1918;
to Bircham Newton, May 1918 (unknown aircraft)

3 TS from Shoreham, 15 Jul 1918;
DB into 21 TDS, 15 Jul 1917

27 TS from London Colney, 15 Jul 1918;
DB into 21 TDS, 15 Jul 1918 (various aircraft)

21 TDS (ex-3 & 27 TS), 15 Jul 1918;
redesignated 21 TS, Jul 1919
(Pup, SE.5A, F.2B, DH.6, 504 and SPAD S.VII)

263rd Aero Sqn, USAAS, by 1918;
departed 17 Nov 1918

202 Sqn cadre from Varssenaere, 24 Mar 1919;
to Spittlegate, Dec 1919

217 Sqn cadre from Varssenaere, 19 Mar 1919;
DB 19 Oct 1919

21 TS reformed (ex-21 TDS), Jul 1919;
DB Feb 1920 (504K)

Flamborough

53°06'14"N/00°08'31"W, TA216691. Located at Dykes End where Danes Dyke reaches sea, 1 mile SW of Flamborough

A TEMPORARY seaplane refuelling station was placed here during 1918 under the control of 18 (Operations) Group, NE Area. The station would have been a convenient location for aircraft transiting up and down the East Coast to refuel.

Hedon (Hull)

53°44'39"N/00°13'22"W, TA175291. Salt End, W of Hedon off Hull Road (A1033), 4.7 miles E of Hull town centre

T HIS 80-acre site, originally a racecourse until 1914, was located on the northern side of the Hull to Hedon road and east of the Preston road junction. Measuring 800 by 500 yards, Hedon opened as an HD NLG1 in April 1916 for 33(HD) Squadron. The site was reclassified as an NLG2 by January 1917, and the later part of the LG's service was for 76(HD) Squadron until early 1919. By that year the military referred to the site as Hull, but by January 1920 the aerodrome had been relinquished. Reopened as Hull Municipal Airport in the 1920s, the site was also used by the ATC for gliding during the 1940s.

Sopwith Baby N1413 stands outside a Bessonneau hangar at Hornsea Mere in the summer of 1917. The aircraft was wrecked on the Mere on 9 October.

Hornsea Mere

53°54'26"N/00°10'40W, TA197472. Kirkholme Nab, E edge of Hornsea Mere, 0.3 miles WSW of Hornsea, 12 miles NE of Hull

T HE largest freshwater lake in Yorkshire, Hornsea Mere covers 467 acres, is 2 miles long and 0.75 miles wide, and is only 12 feet deep. Just over half a mile from the coast, the site was perfect for a Marine Operations (Seaplane) Station, which was opened in September 1917. The technical area occupied a small 6-acre peninsula called Kirkholme Nab, where a pair of Bessonneau hangars was erected with two slipways leading directly from them into the mere. Up to a dozen seaplanes could be operated from the mere, the first being FBA Type B flying-boats of an RNAS War Flight. They were later joined by Sopwith Babys and one, N1469, flown by Flt Sub Lt H. C. Lemon, dropped two 65lb bombs on a U-boat off Scarborough on 8 November. Further attacks were carried out in early 1918, including Flt Sub Lt G. Hyams in his personal Baby, N2078, named 'The Jabberwock', who spotted a U-boat on the surface off Scarborough on 26 March 1918. Lookouts spotted Hyams's high-speed low-level approach and the submarine just managed to crash dive to safety after Hyams bombed the foamy water.

The War Flight was redesignated 453(BS) Flight on 30 May 1918, and the same month 251 Squadron was formed here. Operating the DH.6, the unit only based its HQ at Hornsea while its aircraft were detached to various aerodromes. Short 184s began to arrive from June when 405(S) Flight was formed here, followed by 404(S) Flight from Killingholme in August. All three resident flights at Hornsea were then incorporated into 248 Squadron. Anti-

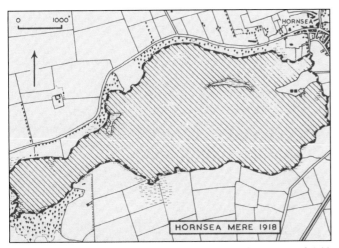

HORNSEA MERE 1918

submarine duties continued for the rest of the war and 248 Squadron remained until it was disbanded on 10 March 1919. The HQ of 79 (Operations) Wing, which was formed here on 26 August 1918, was the final unit to serve at Hornsea; it was disbanded on 1 August 1919.

Today Kirkholme Nab is occupied by the Hornsea Sailing Club, but the original seaplane station's pavilion, workshops, powerhouse and a boat house still survive, partly in use as café.

Hornsea Mere main units, 1918-19

RNAS War Flight formed Sep 1917;
redesignated 453 Flt, 30 May 1918 (FBA Type B)

251 Sqn formed 18 May;
to Killingholme as cadre, 31 Jan 1919
(DH.6 and DH.9 detached)

453 (BS) Flt formed 30 May 1918;
into 248 Sqn, 15 Aug 1918 (Baby)

405 (S) Flt formed 15 Jun 1918;
into 248 Sqn, 15 Aug 1918 (Short 184)

404 (S) Flt from Killingholme, 15 Aug 1918;
into 248 Sqn, 15 Aug 1918 (Short 184 and DH.6 detached)

248 Sqn (ex-404, 405 and 453 Flt), Aug 1918;
DB 10 Mar 1919 (Short 184, 320 and Baby)

Howden

53°47'11"N/00°51'52"W, SE750328. Boothferry Golf Club, NE of B1228, 2.2 miles SE of Breighton Airfield, 2.75 miles NNE of Howden

ONE of the largest airship stations in the country started as a small HD NLG for the use of 33(HD) Squadron in early 1916, approximately 50 acres in size. The site had already been surveyed by the Admiralty the previous year for potential use as an airship station, and from March 1916 a

Howden's two coastal airship sheds are under construction in early 1917; both survived until the early 1930s when they were reduced to scrap.

One of several Coastal Class airships that operated from Howden, nicknamed 'The Howden Pigs'. This C21 is being prepared for a sortie over the North Sea.

Class G Airship Station was established. With sub-stations at Kirkleatham and Lowthorpe, the site now occupied 400 acres, but by 1918 this had grown to 1,240 acres and measured 3,100 by 2,600 yards. Major expansion began from December 1916, when the site also became an airship station for rigid airships. Buildings on the site included one coastal Airship Shed of 333 by 111 by 80 feet, another measuring 320 by 110 by 80 feet, one rigid Airship Shed (704 by 149 by 101 feet), and two rigid Airship Sheds (750 by 150 by 130 feet).

A large number of non-rigid Coastal Class airships passed through Howden, the majority serving in the anti-submarine and convoy escort role over the North Sea. The huge rigid airships were also a common site, including the Beardmore-built 529-foot-long *R27*, which arrived in June 1918. However, its stay was destined to be short, because on 16 August a fire broke out in No 1 rigid shed, destroying the airship together with *SSZ38* and *SSZ54*.

Howden remained an active airship station after the war, its facilities being far too useful to relinquish straight away. The Directorate of Airships was formed here in 1919 and remained until 1 April 1920. On 16 March 1920 the former Airship Station (Howden) was redesignated RAF Airship Base (Home), and the School of Airship Training was established in April. Big rigid airships continued to visit Howden during the 1920s, including the ill-fated *R38* from Cardington in July 1921. Prepared for transfer to the US Navy as *ZR2*, the airship

left Howden on 23 August only to break up over the River Humber with the loss of 44 of the 49 crew on board. This loss marked the end of military airship development in Britain.

Closed to military airship operations in late 1921, the site was relinquished by the RAF in 1922, only to be reopened by the Airship Guarantee Co in 1924. By the 1930s the huge airship sheds were sold for scrap, but today the outline of one can still be seen to the north of the golf course, together with the bases of various buildings that have been demolished.

Lowthorpe

54°01'58"N/00°21'21"W, TA070610. On W edge of Church Wood, 0.75 miles NW of Lowthorpe village, 3.5 miles NE of Driffield railway station

IN an effort to reduce the airship traffic at Howden, several mooring-out stations were established in East Yorkshire, including one at Lowthorpe. Designed for non-rigid airships, the first examples, *SSZ32* and *SSZ38*, arrived in April 1918. *SSZ38*'s tenure was short-lived because it was blown into a tree on 10 May, and just nine days later *SSZ32* suffered a similar incident; both airships were deflated and returned to Howden by road.

A further four SSZ airships made use of Lowthorpe until the site was closed down in 1919.

Owthorne (Withernsea)

53°43'56"N/00°01'05"W, TA335285. 0.5 miles from centre of Withernsea, W of Withernsea High School off B1362, Hull Road

AN HD NLG3, Owthorne was opened in December 1916 for the use of 33(HD) and 76(HD) Squadrons. Originally 35 acres in size, the LG measured 500 by 250 yards. Designated as a Marine Operations (Aeroplane) Station from June 1918, 506(SD) Squadron was formed here the same month as part of 251 Squadron, flying the DH.6 and at least one Pup. As a result, Owthorne was expanded by 5 acres to the south-west. Several Bessonneau hangars were also erected; tents were pitched for the airmen, while officers enjoyed more comfortable accommodation in Withernsea.

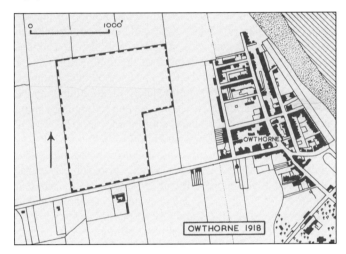

From November 1918 506(SD) re-equipped with the DH.9 and remained at Owthorne until June 1919, when the unit was disbanded at Killingholme. Owthorne was relinquished on 6 November 1919.

South Cave

53°47'46"N/00°37'15W, SE909343. E of Roman Road (A1034), 1 mile E of Hotham, 2 miles NNW of South Cave

IN an effort to defend the Humber Estuary several LGs appeared during 1916, including South Cave in April. The sole occupant was 33(HD) Squadron, which was called upon to respond to the massed Zeppelin raid on Hull on 9 August 1916, when at least one of the giant airships overflew South Cave. 76(HD) Squadron also operated a few machines from here in September 1916.

Laid out on 64 acres of land and measuring 660 by 480 yards, the LG remained under 33(HD) Squadron control until the unit was disbanded at Harpswell in June 1919.

ESSEX

Barking (Creekmouth), London Borough of Barking

51°31'27"N/00°05'39"W, TQ448831. Off River Road, next to Long Reach, 1.2 miles SE of Barking

BARKING was the location of the first Handley Page factory, which was opened in 1909. It was from here that the company's first powered machine, the H.P.1 'Blue Bird', made a few short hops from the nearby Barking marshes. By 1912 Handley Page began the first of several expansions, and Barking was no longer adequate, so the company moved to Cricklewood.

In June 1916 the site was taken over by the RNAS, with plans to build the MacMechan airship. Designed by Walter V. Kamp, this large rigid airship was a Zeppelin destroyer, but was never built. However, a single shed did reach an advanced stage of construction next to Creek Road (River Road today), east of Long Reach, and it is believed that it was still extant in 1920.

Barking (Longbridge Farm)

51°32'50"N/00°05'35"W, TQ452852. In playing-field off South Park Drive, 1 mile NE of Barking centre

THE HOME of 1 (Balloon) Squadron from 1917 to 1919, Barking was a Kite Balloon Station under the control of London Command from January 1918 and 7 Balloon Wing from November 1918.

Beaumont

51°52'18"N/01°09'46"W, TM178240. Due S of Beaumont Hall, 1 mile due N of Thorpe-le-Soken

QUICKLY established in a pair of fields known as Wood Field and Lower Wood Field, Beaumont was briefly an NLG between April and August 1916. Allocated to 37(HD) Squadron, very little activity would have taken place before it was closed down in favour of Plough Corner. Beaumont took up 43 acres of land and measured 450 by 350 yards.

Blackheath Common (Colchester)

51°51'18"N/00°54'38"W, TM006213. W of B1205, S of Cherry Tree Lane, 3 miles S of Colchester town centre

BELIEVED to have been established as early as March 1915, Blackheath was a 55-acre LG that measured 700 by 500 yards. With good approaches, it was classified as an HD NLG1, but was not assigned to a unit until February 1917 when 37(HD) Squadron, operating from Goldhangar, became the sole user.

While 37(HD) Squadron's collection of BE-type aircraft would have come and gone, it was only on the night of 19/20 October 1917 that an incident was recorded. That night the last major Zeppelin raid on Britain took place involving thirteen airships, all heading for targets in the North of England. Only eleven launched and, after facing strong headwinds, those ships that bombed did so randomly across southern England. One of the seventy-eight sorties flown that night was by a 2nd Lt Armstrong of 37(HD) Squadron who, after failing to make contact with the enemy, was forced to land at Blackheath following engine failure. Armstrong escaped injury in the incident but was destined to lose his life four months later on a similar sortie.

Blackheath Common was closed down in August 1919.

Bournes Green (Shoeburyness)

51°33'05"N/00°45'47"W, TQ917873. SE of Great Wakerling, 2 miles NW of Shoeburyness

THIS LG was opened on 30 April 1917 as a forward operating field for aircraft making use of the aerial gunnery facilities at nearby Shoeburyness. Laid out on land owned by the John Burgess Junior estate, Bournes Green only took up 35 acres and measured 425 by 325 yards.

Classified as a DLG2 because of the restrictive landing directions, the LG had no facilities other than a windsock and a few tents for crews staying overnight. However, after only a few weeks it was decided that air gunnery flights were being carried out far too close to the built-up areas of Thorpe Bay and Shoeburyness, and on 1 June 1917 the site was quickly relinquished and transferred to Marine Town, east of Sheerness.

Braintree

51°52'08"N/00°31'39"W, TL737216. N of Braintree suburban development of Great Notley, SE of Braintree, now dissected by A120 and A131

IN 1916 six fields were requisitioned from Stamfords Farm and two from Slamsley Farm, and once dividing hedges were removed a respectively sized LG of 60 acres was created in an area original known as Braintree Green. A level well-drained site of 700 by 400 yards could only be classed as an NLG2 when it was opened in January 1917 because of houses and woods in Queenborough Lane to the north.

The LG was allocated to 37(HD) Squadron, operating from Woodham Mortimer with a range of BE-type aircraft. Reclassified as an NLG3 on 14 September 1917, the LG was closed down in 1918.

Broomfield Court (Chelmsford)

51°46'29"N/00°27'10"W, TL693113. 1 mile NW of Broomfield, 3 miles N of Chelmsford town centre

SITED on land belonging to the Broomfield Court Estate, this HD NLG 2, covering 30 acres (later expanded to 45 acres) and measuring 700 by 500 yards, was opened for 37(HD) Squadron in April 1916. It was reclassified as an NLG3 on 5 January 1917, only to be changed back to an NLG2 from 31 March. The site was closed down in mid-1919, but was reopened in May 1932 as Broomfield/Chelmsford aerodrome. After an eventful few years the site was closed for good on 3 September 1939.

Broxted

51°55'16"N/00°16'45"W, TL568271. 0.6 miles W of Broxted, 1.9 miles ENE of Elsenham

THIS is a little-known HD NLG, which was only used by 39(HD) Squadron operating from Hounslow and/or Woodford Green in 1916. Broxted was most likely abandoned by the end of that year in favour of a more suitable location.

Burnham-on-Crouch

51°37'57"N/00°50'08"W, TQ962965. Between Dammer Wick Farm and Burnham Wick Farm, 1 mile ENE of Burnham-on-Crouch

ONE of the earliest military aviation sites in Essex, Burnham-on-Crouch was established as an RNAS 'branch station' in late 1914. With no preparation of the site whatsoever, a pair of TB.8s was placed here from Eastchurch to intercept the expected waves of Zeppelins. No interceptions were recorded before the defence of the nation from the air was placed in the hands of the RFC, which took over Burnham from April 1916. The RFC immediately set about making the site into an aerodrome by lifted hedges and felling trees along the eastern boundary. Once completed, the HD NLG2 occupied 102 acres and measured 750 by 600 yards. It was allocated to 37(HD) Squadron and had no facilities other than a few tents close to Dammer Wick Farm. The site was reclassified twice more, first on 5 January 1917 when it became an NLG3 and DLG2, and again on 31 March when it was upgraded to an NLG1 and DLG1, possibly after work on the site was completed. Burnham was relinquished in August 1919 and returned to the local farmers. Presumably access was from the northern boundary off Marsh Road; a military-type road leads to the site, although this could be later.

Chelmsford

51°43'28"N/00°26'49"W, TL691057. Industrial estate, Hanbury/Robjohns Road, 1.2 miles SW of Chelmsford town centre

FIRST surveyed in late 1914, this site was recommended as an RNAS 'branch station', but instead opened as an HD station in July 1915. The HD War Flight RNAS was based here until Chelmsford was abandoned in February 1916.

Chelmsford (Writtle)

51°43'59"N/00°25'58"W, TL680065. Off Lawford Lane, NE of Writtle, 1.5 miles W of Chelmsford town centre

ONE OF the earliest LGs specifically employed for HD duties in Essex, Writtle was opened in October 1914 for anti-Zeppelin patrols. No 1 RAS's HD detachment from Farnborough brought its BE.2Bs and Longhorns here on 19 December 1914. Very few if any patrols were flown from here during early 1915, and the RAS detachment returned to Farnborough. On 9 September 1915 the 5th Wing HD sent a detachment of BE.2Cs from Gosport after Zeppelin raids began to increase. Only one fruitless patrol was flown, looking in vain for Zeppelin *LZ.77*. 5th Wing returned to Gosport in September 1915 and Writtle was closed down the same month.

Chingford, London Borough of Waltham Forest

51°38'12"N/00°01'16"W, TQ370948. Now under William Girling Reservoir, technical site ran along S side of Lea Valley Road (A110), 0.6 miles ESE of Ponders Bridge railway station

A SITE at Chingford Marsh was first surveyed and selected as an RNAS HD 'branch station' on 27 December 1914, but there was little activity until April 1915 when the RNAS Preliminary Aeroplane School was formed here. The site occupied 150 acres and measured 1,500 by 400 yards, its odd shape dictated by a branch of the River Lea, which flowed up to the Pike & Anchor pub to the west. The fact that the Old River Lea ran across the middle of the site meant that a 200-foot-wide bridge had to be built at the northern end of the site for aircraft to taxi across.

From October 1917 the aerodrome was designated as an HD NLG2 for 39(HD) Squadron and later 44(HD) Squadron, by which time the site began to expand. Three Aeroplane Sheds of 180 by 50 feet, three 1916-pattern sheds (180 by 60 feet) and a single F Shed (200 by 100 feet) were erected, together with further technical and domestic buildings on the north-western boundary. Off-site, a Photographic Section was established at 'Whitehall', near Whitehall Road, and an SSQ at Sewardstone Lodge near Daws Hill on the Sewardstone Road. 'Whitehall', a large requisitioned house, was also the home of the 41st, 56th and 83rd Wing HQs.

This is Chingford not long after it was opened in May 1915, complete with a pristine line of white accommodation huts and various aeroplane sheds.

Armstrong Whitworth FK.8 B3354, during a visit to Chingford.

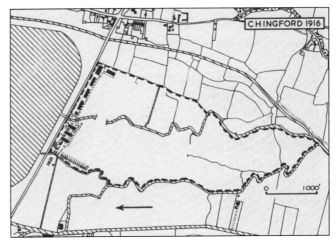

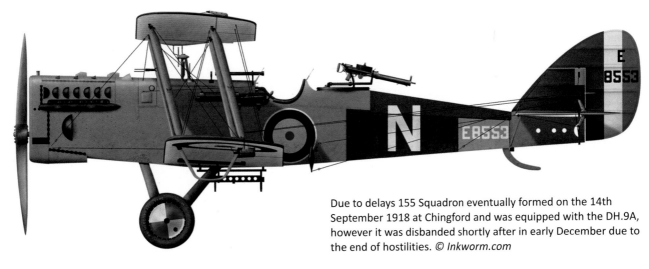

Due to delays 155 Squadron eventually formed on the 14th September 1918 at Chingford and was equipped with the DH.9A, however it was disbanded shortly after in early December due to the end of hostilities. © Inkworm.com

Chingford became the home of 207 TDS from 1 April 1918, which was redesignated as 54 TDS in July but had departed for Fairlop by early August. On 7 August Chingford became an RAF Mobilisation Station with 138, 154 and 155 Squadrons all being created from a range of TDSs. The site was surplus to requirements by February 1919 and was quickly closed down by the following month. Thirty-six acres of the old aerodrome briefly reopened to civilian flying in 1932 and 1933, but by 1935 the entire area began the long-protracted reincarnation as the William Girling Reservoir. This was not brought into use until September 1951, making Chingford a unique aerodrome site that today is under more than 40 feet of water.

Chingford main units, 1916-19

Preliminary Aeroplane School RNAS formed Apr 1915; redesignated 207 TDS Apr 1918

19 TS detached from Hounslow Feb 1, 1916; to Hounslow, 15 Apr 1916 (various)

2nd Balloon Wing formed in 2nd Brigade, 5 Dec 1916, comprising 1 to 8 Companies at Chingford; to Mont Rouge by 9 Apr 1917

3rd Balloon Wing formed in 3rd Brigade, 5 Dec 1916, comprising 9 to 12 Companies at Chingford; to Barly, 9 Apr 1917

4th Balloon Wing formed in 4th Brigade, 5 Dec 1916, comprising 13 to 16 Companies at Chingford; to Eterpigny by 9 Apr 1917

5th Balloon Wing formed in 5th Brigade, 5 Dec 1916, comprising 17 to 20 Companies at Chingford; to Contay by 9 Apr 1917

6th Balloon Wing at Chingford Oct 1917; to Egypt, 25 Nov 1917

207 TDS (ex-Prelim Aero School RNAS) formed 1 Apr 1918; redesignated 54 TDS, 20 Jul 1918 (504, Camel, RE.8, DH.6, Pup, Scout and Nieuport 17)

Photographic Flt from Farnborough, 9 Apr 1918; to Kenley, 21 May 1918

54 TDS detachment (remained in place), 20 Jul 1918; to Fairlop, Aug 1918 (Pup, Camel, DH.9 and 504)

154 Sqn formed (nucleus from 33, 37, 29 and 44 TDS), 7 Aug 1918; DB 11 Sep 1918

155 Sqn formed (nucleus from 1, 26, 55 and 57 TDS), 14 Sep 1918; DB 7 Dec 1918 (DH.9A)

138 Sqn formed (nucleus from 1, 5, 36 and 45 TDS), 30 Sep 1918; DB 1 Feb 1919 (F.2B)

8th Balloon Wing from Cyosing as cadre, 10 Feb 1919; DB 15 Feb 1919

1st Balloon Wing from Bruay as cadre, 10 Feb 1919; DB 15 Feb 1919

Clacton-on-Sea

51°46'59"N/01°08'50"W, TM172141. Along Marine Parade West, 0.5 miles SW of Clacton-on-Sea town centre

NO stranger to aviation prior to war, an 800-yard-long section of the West Beach was used as an RNAS seaplane station from August 1914 through to the autumn of 1916. Initially classified as a sub-station for RNAS Grain, Clacton was also a forward operating base and sub-station for Westgate.

East Hanningfield

51°40'37"N/00°32'53"W, TL763007. 0.5 miles SW of East Hanningfield, 3 miles SW of Danbury

THIS little-used HD NLG3 was located on one of the highest points of Essex, but it was destined only to be open from April to November 1916. Sixty-seven acres were relinquished for the LG, which was allocated to 39(HD) Squadron and possibly 37(HD) Squadron, but neither appears to have made much use of it.

Easthorpe

51°51'29"N/00°45'09"W, TL895214. Racecourse off Easthorpe Road, 2.2 miles SW of Marks Tey

THIS small 29-acre site was opened as an HD NLG2 in April 1916, the only facilities being a windsock, a few tents and a signals square. The latter was unusual for an LG of such stature and remnants of it were still extant up to the early 1970s.

Allocated to 39(HD) Squadron, Easthorpe was reclassified as an NLG3 on 5 January 1917 only to be changed back to an NLG2 on 31 March. Only one emergency landing has been recorded at Easthorpe, when Capt W. Sowrey of 'C' Flight suffered engine trouble in his BE.12A. Transferred to 37(HD) Squadron control, the site was closed down in December 1919.

Fairlop

51°36'02"N/00°06'03"W, TQ458914. Now playing-fields and a recreation ground off Forest Road, due N of Fairlop Waters

LOCATED less than half a mile away from Hainault Farm, Fairlop's duties would be that of training rather than of an operational nature. The site was first used for aviation in 1911, when engineers from Handley Page Ltd used the 30-acre Fairlop Oak playing-field for flight-testing until the following year. Fairlop then lay dormant until 1916, when it was opened as an LG and sub-station for the RNAS at Chingford. The site began to expand steadily until 1918, when a total of twenty-six buildings had been erected along the edge of Forest Road, the LG being occupied by an RNAS Flying School. By then the site took up 110 acres of land and measured 900 by 600 yards.

Fairlop was taken over by the RAF in April 1918 and on the first day of the month 207 TDS was formed here. The TDS had a wide variety of service types on strength, such as the 504, Camel, DH.9 and Pup. On 20 July 207 TDS was redesignated as 54 TDS, with its HQ at Chingford until 10 July 1919, when the unit was disbanded.

Post-war, the western side of the original site was renamed Forest Farm and used for civilian flying, while the eastern side was used by Alan Cobham for one of his circuses in 1935. Further east along Forest Road, past the Hainault road junction, was yet another airfield, named Chigwell, which was open for civilian flying during 1938 and 1939. To the south of Forest Road was the Second World War RAF Fairlop, which was open between 1940 and 1946 and, unlike its First World War cousin, has been completely wiped off the map!

Fyfield (Ongar)

51°43'37"N/00°14'57"W, TL554056. SE of Bundish Hall off Ongar Road, 1.3 miles SW of Fyfield

POSITIONED on land borrowed from the Eve family of Bundish Hall in October 1916, Fyfield was classified as an NLG3 for the use of 39(HD) Squadron. The site was only 25 acres in size and measured 370 by 350 yards. There were no permanent structures here, only tents that provided just enough wet weather protection for airmen who were tasked with lighting flares during night operations.

Fyfield was returned to the Eve family when it was relinquished in December 1919.

Goldhangar (Gardener's Farm, aka possibly Maldon)

51°44'26"N/00°44'24"W, TL892082. Between Gardener's Farm (originally in centre of LG) and Cobb's Farm off B1026, 3 miles ENE of Maldon

GOLDHANGAR'S life as an aerodrome began in August 1915 when it was classified as an HD NLG for the use of the RNAS. The site comprised five fields, totalling 77 acres, one owned by Cobb's Farm and the remainder by George Dobson of Gardener's Farm. The farm was in the middle of the site, not more than 200 yards from the landing circle. In June 1916 the RNAS moved out and Goldhangar was passed to the RFC; the only occupant during the summer was a detachment of 52 Squadron from Hounslow Heath flying the BE.2C.

In September 1916 Goldhangar was upgraded to an HD Flight Station, the only such example in the country under 100 acres. 'C' Flight of 37(HD) Squadron moved in from Woodford

Green on 15 September, and during this period the aerodrome was expanded with four HD-pattern Aeroplane Sheds (90 by 60 feet) built on the western edge of the site, close to the Maldon to Goldhangar road. A total of twenty-four wooden structures were erected at Goldhangar and a 75-foot-wide concrete apron was laid in front of the HD sheds.

The primary role of 37(HD) Squadron was to carry out cooperation duties with local anti-aircraft batteries and perform wireless telephony. However, anti-Zeppelin patrols were just as commonplace, but not all were successful, including one on 23/24 May 1917 when six enemy airships attacked London. Seven aircraft up from Goldhangar failed to intercept the intruders on this occasion, but on 16/17 June Lt L. P. Watkins in BE.12 6610 was more successful. Four Zeppelins were bound for London, including *L48*, which had already been attacked by two pilots from Orfordness before Watkins arrived. Pressing home his attack, the giant airship plunged to the ground at Holly Tree Farm, Theberton, Suffolk, killing the entire crew.

74 Squadron, en route to Northern Farm, made an unexpected arrival at Goldhangar on 25 March 1918 because of poor weather. The famous SE.5 unit left five days later and Goldhangar settled down with 37(HD) Squadron as the only resident, until it vacated to Biggin Hill on 17 March 1919. Closed down the same year, the Aeroplane Sheds were not dismantled until 1922, while the flying field, complete with Gardener's Farm, remains just the same.

Hainault Farm (Romford)

51°35'57"N/00°07'05"W, TQ468909. E of Hainault Road, S of Forest Road, 2.7 miles NW of Romford

THIS undulating site (from 90 to 140 feet amsl) for an aerodrome was first used by the RNAS as a DLG in October 1914. Named after the farm on the opposite side of Hainault Road, the original aerodrome occupied 60 acres belonging to Mr William Poulter, but by February 1915 the RNAS had moved on. The RFC did not leave the site begging for long, and from October 1915 classified the site as an NLG3 and expanded Hainault Farm to 950 by 750 yards, taking up a further 40 acres of land. Four HD-pattern Flight Sheds (90 by 60 feet) were erected, together with the usual array of supporting structures on both sides of Hainault Road, including a substantial MT shed.

A detachment from 5 Wing HD from Gosport were the first RFC machines here, but it was 'C' Flight of 39(HD) Squadron, arriving from Hounslow Heath in April 1916, that would put Hainault Farm on the map. Having already achieved success in its quest to shoot down as many Zeppelins

Hainault Farm was a perfect location for accommodating HD squadrons in defence of the capital. It was a brief home for 39, 151 and 153 Squadrons, but it was 44(HD) Squadron that served there the longest, firstly with the 1½ Strutter followed by the Camel.

A pair of HD-pattern flight sheds used by 'B' and 'C' Flight of 44(HD) Squadron at Hainault Farm; both buildings survive.
Via Stuart Leslie

as possible, Hainault Farm's day came on 23/24 September 1916. New Zealand-born 2nd Lt A. de B. Brandon flying a BE.2C spotted *L33* commanded by Kptlt Alouise Böcker just after midnight and, after making two attacks, the airship descended towards the village of Little Wigborough. After crash-landing close to New Hall Cottages, the crew, all of whom survived, tried to burn the airship before surrendering. The Zeppelin remained there for 14 weeks while engineers took every detail, and the subsequent British-built *R33*, which first flew in 1919, was based on the data taken from *L33*.

Hainault Farm was classified as an HD Flight Station from May 1916 through to 1919, and by 1918 was the home to the RAF's first true night fighter unit, 151 Squadron, flying the Camel. This unit was joined by 153 Squadron, in the same role, by late 1918. 44(HD) Squadron, which had been reformed here in July 1917 to deal with the Gotha threat, moved out to North Weald on 1 July 1919, and by the end of year Hainault Farm had been returned to the land.

The majority of the buildings were taken over by industry before the Second World War and the airfield itself, although not in use then, was classified as an ELG for RAF Hornchurch. All four hangars survived until 2013, and today, although heavily re-clad, 'B' and 'C' sheds are extant as well as the original MT shed.

Hainault Farm main units, 1915-19

5 Wing HD detached from Gosport, 3 Oct 1915;
to Hounslow, 1 Feb 1916

39 Sqn 'C' Flt from Hounslow Heath, 15 Apr 1916;
to North Weald, 9 Dec 1917 (BE.2C and Scout)

19 TS detached from Hounslow Heath, Apr 1916;
to Hounslow Heath 1917 (various aircraft)

44 Sqn reformed from 39 Sqn, 24 Jul 1917;
to North Weald, 1 Jul 1919 (1½ Strutter and Camel)

151 Sqn formed 12 Jun 1918;
to Marquise, 16 Jun 1918 (Camel)

153 Sqn formed 4 Nov 1918;
DB 13 Jun 1919 (Camel)

Sopwith Camel B2402 of 44(HD) Squadron is seen at Hainault Farm, and took part in the destruction of two Gothas in December 1917 and January 1918.

Horndon-on-the-Hill (Woodcock Field)

51°31'34"N/00°22'10"W, TQ645835. Off B188 between Conway's Farm and Gorwyn's Plantation, 0.75 miles NNE of Orsett

SELECTED for use by the RFC in April 1915, Horndon-on-the-Hill comprised four fields occupying 38 acres and measuring 525 by 425 yards. The site was not opened until April 1916 as an NLG for 39(HD) Squadron, but only remained open until the autumn, when its role was taken over by nearby Orsett. Several aircraft operating from Suttons Farm did land here in March 1917, after several sorties were carried out to pursue an unknown intruder. Children from a local school turned up to see the aircraft, all subsequently paying with a session or two of detention.

Loughton (Kings Oak Hotel, High Beech)

51°39'15"N/00°03'29"W, TQ424970. Due E of Woodbury Hollow, 0.5 miles WSW of Loughton centre

A BALLOON Training Centre was formed here as part of No 7 Balloon Wing in 1917, later redesignated as Balloon Experimental & Training Depot from 28 November 1917. In the meantime 7th Brigade was also formed at Kings Oak Hotel in preparation for service in Italy with the 14th and 51st Wings and No 9 and 20 Balloon Companies. The Brigade departed from Loughton over a ten-day period beginning on 16 November 1917.

The Balloon Experimental & Training Depot was redesignated as the Balloon Training Depot on 9 January 1918 and presumably remained at Loughton until the end of the war.

Mountnessing

51°39'23"N/00°22'41"W, TQ645970. 0.5 miles SSE of Heybridge, adjacent to Lodge Wood, N of Bellmans Farm

ESTABLISHED in a hurry in April 1916 on land belonging to the Petre Estate at Ingatestone House, Mountnessing was the smallest LG in Essex during the war, at just 21 acres. Classified as an HD NLG3, it was intended for 39(HD) Squadron, but was soon found to be far too dangerous to use because of several topographical features. Very few if any landings took place here and Mountnessing was closed down by December 1916, in favour of Palmers Farm located 2½ miles to the west.

North Benfleet (Sadlers Farm)

51°33'41"N/00°32'35"W, TQ763880. 1.3 miles SSE of North Benfleet, 2.5 miles ESE of Basildon town centre

LAID out on land owned by Charles Bayley of Sadlers Farm and James Buckenham of Jotmans Farm, North Benfleet was only a 37-acre LG. Opened as an HD NLG3 in April 1916, it was first used by 37(HD) Squadron based at Woodham Mortimer, although it was more likely only used by 'A' Flight, which operated from Rochford.

The site was redesignated as an NLG2 on 31 March 1917 and was later used by 61(HD) Squadron, before it was relinquished in March 1919.

North Ockendon

51°32'14"N/00°18'27"W, TQ601846. 0.6 miles SE of village, due S of Top Meadow Golf Club, 6 miles SE of Romford town centre

ALLOCATED to 39(HD) Squadron in April 1916, North Ockendon comprised nearly 40 acres of land requisitioned from the estate of John Henry Stewart. The HD NLG measured 500 by 325 yards and was closed down by October 1916 in favour of Orsett.

North Weald (Bassett)

51°43'17"N/00°08'56"W, TL485045. Current North Weald airfield, E of M11, 2.2 miles NE of Epping

IN early 1916 136 acres of open land to the west of the village of North Weald Bassett was requisitioned for an aerodrome. The site, which measured 900 by 850 yards, had four HD-pattern Aeroplane Sheds (two 80 by 60 feet and two 60 by 60 feet) and one Bessonneau located on the southern side, close to the Epping Road (B181). On the south side of Epping Road a busy domestic site was established.

Opened in April 1916 as an HD Flight Station, the first occupant was 'A' Flight of 39(HD) Squadron from Hounslow, flying the standard collection of BE types. Success came for the unit on 1 October 1916 when 2nd Lt W. J. Tempest stalked Zeppelin *L31* for almost 2 hours before shooting the airship down in flames over Potters Bar, earning the pilot an immediate DSO.

The rest of 39(HD) Squadron had joined 'A' Flight by December 1917 and was destined to remain at North Weald Bassett until disbanded in November 1918. 75(HD) Squadron saw out its days here, as did 44(HD) Squadron, which served here until disbanded on 31 December 1919.

The site lay dormant for several years only to reopen in 1927 as an RAF fighter station, a role in which it would remain until the mid-1960s. All evidence of the older aerodrome has been erased by the development of the airfield during the Second World War and post-war period.

North Weald Bassett main units, 1916-19

39 Sqn 'A' Flt from Hounslow, Aug 1916;
DB 16 Nov 1918 (BE.2C/E, BE.12 and F.2B)

39 Sqn 'B' Flt from Sutton's Farm, Sep 1917;
DB 16 Nov 1918

39 Sqn 'C' Flt from Hainault Farm, Sep 1917;
DB 16 Nov 1918

39 Sqn HQ from Woodford Green, 9 Dec 1917;
DB 16 Nov 1918

39 Sqn 'E' Flt formed Jan 1918;
to Gosport, Jan 1918

75 Sqn 'A' Flt from Hadleigh, 7 Nov 1918;
DB 13 Jun 1919 (Camel and F.2B)

75 Sqn HQ 'B' and 'C' Flt from Elmswell,
22 May 1919; DB 13 Jun 1919

44 Sqn from Hainault Farm, 1 Jul 1919;
DB 31 Dec 1919 (Camel)

Orsett I and II

51°31'01"N/00°23'10"W, TQ659809. SE of Cock Inn on old A13 road, now Orsett Golf Club

FIRST opened as an HD NLG for both 39(HD) and 75(HD) Squadrons in July 1916, this 80-acre site, measuring 650 by 250 yards, appears to have been closed down only a few weeks after it opened. However, the aerodrome was reopened as an HD NLG1 for the same units before the year was out, hence Orsett II. Orsett was not relinquished until 29 May 1919, and today is the site of a golf course.

Palmers Farm (Shenfield)

51°39'02"N/00°18'56"W, TQ603971. 1.3 miles W of Mountnessing, 2.2 miles NNE of Brentford town centre

A REPLACEMENT for Mountnessing, Palmers Farm was literally only a few fields away. Opened as an HD NLG3 for 39(HD) Squadron from September 1916, this small LG took up 40 acres with a landing area measuring 500 by 400 yards. Palmers Farm remained in used until June 1919.

Plough Corner (Little Clacton)

51°50'18"N/01°08'23"W, TM162203. 1.5 miles SW of Thorpe-le-Soken, 3.2 miles due N of Clacton-on-Sea town centre

PLOUGH CORNER was an HD NLG2 and DLG for the use of 37(HD) Squadron between October 1916 and July 1919, during which time the unit was based at Woodham Mortimer and Stow Maries. Due north of Little Clacton village, the site took up 53 acres and measured 650 by 420 yards.

Rochford (Eastwood)

51°35'11"N/00°42'12"W, TQ867890. Current London Southend Airport, 0.9 miles SSW of Rochford

WITH PASSENGER numbers now approaching one million per year and with high hopes of doubling that by 2020, London Southend is one of Britain's most successful airports. It was also one of the earliest military airfields, in Essex at least, and by far the largest when it opened in the spring of 1915 for an RNAS War Flight. An excellent site with open flat fields, it occupied 168 acres and measured 900 by 800 yards.

Initially classified as an HD station for the RNAS, the War Flight made its first sighting of a Zeppelin on 31 May/1 June 1915. Flt Sub-Lt R. H. Murlock in Blériot Parasol 1546 spotted *LZ38*, but had to force-land when his engine failed. The RNAS relinquished Rochford in April 1916 and from September the aerodrome became an HD Flight Station for 'A' Flight of 37(HD) Squadron. From this point the infrastructure of the site began to expand, including the construction of a pair of timber 1917-pattern GS Sheds (170 by 80 feet) and four HD-pattern Aeroplane Sheds (120 by 50 feet). By 1918, once construction had finally been completed, at least seventy-three buildings had been erected on two sites on the western and southern boundaries, occupying 35 acres.

From January 1917 Rochford was also classified as a Night Training Squadron Station for 11 RS, a night training squadron from Northolt. While night flying units were the main occupants until the end of war, 37(HD) Squadron retained a presence and was often alerted when daylight Gotha raids increased through 1917. One 37(HD) Squadron crew in 1½ Strutter A8271 were shot down by anti-aircraft fire on a defensive sortie during a large Gotha raid on London on 7 July 1917, killing both airmen.

Rochford remained a combined HD Flight Station and Night Training Squadron Station until mid-1919, then in early 1920 the site was closed down. The southern half of the aerodrome was taken over by housing, but by the mid-1930s Rochford was back as a municipal airport. Extensively used by the RAF during the Second World War, it returned to civilian aviation after the war and has continued to thrive ever since.

R.A.F. BE.2C 1164 served with 37(HD) Squadron at Rochford in 1917.

Rochford main units, 1915-18

RNAS War Flight formed May 1915;
DB Apr 1916

37 Sqn 'A' Flt from Woodham Mortimer, 29 Sep 1916;
to Stow Maries, May 1917 (BE.2C/D and BE.12/A)

11 RS from Northolt, 24 Jan 1917;
redesignated 98 DS, 8 Feb 1917 (various aircraft)

98 DS (ex-11 RS), 8 Feb 1917;
redesignated 198 DS, 27 Jun 1917 (various aircraft)

37 Sqn 'C' Flt from Woodham Mortimer, 23 May 1917
(BE.2C/D and BE.12/A)

99 DS formed 1 Jun 1917;
to East Retford, 23 Jun 1917 (various aircraft)

198 DS (ex-98 DS), 27 Jun 1917;
redesignated 198 NTS, 21 Dec 1917 (various aircraft)

56 Sqn 'A' Flt detached from Bekesbourne, Jun 1917;
to Estrée Blanche, 5 Jul 1917 (SE.5)

61 Sqn reformed 24 Jul 1917;
DB 13 Jun 1919 (Pup, SE.5A and Camel)

190 DS formed 24 Oct 1917;
redesignated 190 NTS, 21 Dec 1917
(DH.6, BE.2C/E and 504)

190 NTS (ex-190 DS), 21 Dec 1917;
to Newmarket, 14 Mar 1918 (DH.6, BE.2C/E and 504)

198 NTS (ex-198 DS), 21 Dec 1917;
DB May 1919 (various aircraft)

141 Sqn formed (from 'A' Flt, 61 Sqn) 1 Jan 1918;
to Biggin Hill, 9 Feb 1918 (BE.12 and Dolphin)

152 Sqn formed 1 Oct 1918;
to Carvin, 18 Oct 1918 (Camel)

Runwell

51°37'36"N/00°31'25"W, TQ747949. N of Church End Lane, 0.5 miles NW of St Marys Church, Runwell, 1.2 miles N of Wickford

FIRST proposed as an LG as early as May 1915, Runwell did not open until August 1917 as an NLG2 for the use of 61(HD) Squadron, whose HQ was at Rochford. Occupying 32 acres, partly owned by Thomas Kemble of Runwell Hall, this LG measured 400 by 500 yards.

Personnel working at Runwell had the luxury of more solid accommodation than was usually afforded to such an LG, in the shape of a bungalow off the southern border called 'Garden Mead', which belonged to Church End Farm. A timber building, the bungalow survived until the late 1970s.

'A' and 'B' Flights of 37(HD) Squadron took over Runwell from October 1917 as an emergency NLG, although the aerodrome was still available to 61(HD) Squadron if needed. Both squadrons had no further use for Runwell from October 1918, but the site remained in military hands until March 1919, and was not fully relinquished until a year later.

Sible Hedingham

51°57'21"N/00°33'51"W, TL763316. NW of Liston Hall Farm, due W of ex-RAF Gosfield, 3.2 miles WNW of Halstead

SIBLE HEDINGHAM took up 38 acres of land farmed by George Lewis of Liston Hall. Measuring 600 by 400 yards, this NLG2 opened in April 1916 for the use of 51(HD) Squadron until 29 December, when it was taken over by 37(HD) Squadron.

Reclassified as an NLG3, the site was occasionally used by 'B' Flight of 37(HD) Squadron, until control was handed over to 'C' Flight of 75(HD) Squadron from 31 March 1917. The same day, Sible Hedingham was reclassified again, back to an NLG2, and remained so until 75(HD) Squadron left the site in October 1918. The LG remained under military control until June 1919, when it was returned to farmland. During the Second World War RAF Gosfield swallowed up the land to the east and the airfield's bomb dump took over the northern half of the First World War LG.

Stow Maries

51°40'16"N/00°37'56"W, TL822002. Stow Maries Aerodrome, Hackmans Lane, 1.5 miles NE of South Woodham Ferrers

FIRST surveyed in August 1916, Stow Maries took up twelve fields belonging to Edwins Hall and Old Whitmans farms. Occupying 118 acres and measuring 850 by 650 yards, the aerodrome opened as an HD Flight Station for 37(HD) Squadron, whose 'B' Flight moved in from Woodford Green on 15 September 1916. The LG took a great deal of preparation before the first operational sorties were flown by a pair of BE.12As on 23 May 1917.

The aerodrome was well furnished with four Aeroplane Sheds (95 by 60 feet) and a wide range of technical and domestic buildings, the latter providing accommodation for up to 21 officers, 17 SNCOs, 16 JNCOs, 150 other ranks and 15 women.

'A' Flight 37(HD) Squadron arrived from Woodham Mortimer on 1 February 1918, and on 22 June the HQ moved here from the same aerodrome. By this time the squadron had a few SE.5s, 1½ Strutters and Pups on strength, but by June the main aircraft was the Camel. 'C' Flight from Goldhangar saw 37(HD) Squadron together as one for a few weeks, before the unit moved out to Biggin Hill on 17 March 1919.

Stow Maries closed down a few weeks after 37(HD) Squadron's departure and the land was quickly returned to the original farmers. However, rather than levelling the site or selling off the buildings, the site remained as the RFC had left it and, despite visits by Air Ministry surveyors during the Second World War, remained undeveloped. One of the original Aeroplane Sheds was demolished by a parachute mine, but the wreckage and the other sheds were not dismantled until 1946, leaving at least twenty First World War structures still standing. Those same structures remain to this day, which makes Stow Maries one of the best, if not *the* best, preserved HD Flight Stations in the country. Restoration work is current being sympathetically carried out by the owners and the site is open every week on Thursdays, Fridays and Sundays between 10am and 4pm.

Sutton's Farm

51°32'24"N/00°12'34"W, TQ533847. Hornchurch Country Park, 1.4 miles SSW of Hornchurch town centre

IN 1915 90 acres of land was purchased to the south of Sutton's Farm, followed by a further 15 acres before the site was officially opened as a flight station in October 1915. The main technical and domestic area of the aerodrome would grow around the farm, but at first only a couple of Bessonneau hangars and few tents would suffice.

The first occupants of Sutton's Farm were BE.2s of 13 and 23 Squadron detachments, the latter remaining until April 1916, by which time the site was classified as an NLG1. The LG was set up for night flying, complete with a petrol tin flare path approximately 300 yards long. 'B' Flight of 39(HD) Squadron moved in from 15 April 1916. One of the flight's pilots was Capt Arthur T. Harris, who described Sutton's Farm as 'one large field full of sheep'. 39(HD) Squadron had already contributed to the demise of Zeppelin *L15* in March, and on 16 May Lt W. Leefe Robinson attacked an unidentified Zeppelin without result. Leefe Robinson made history on the night of 2/3 September when he shot down Shutte-Lanz *L11* in flames over Cuffley in Hertfordshire, earning himself the VC. Two more Zeppelins were shot down by 'B' Flight, both on the night of 23/24 September; the first was *L33*, by 2nd Lt Brandon, followed by *L32* by 2nd Lt Sowrey, each pilot later awarded the DSO for their actions. 39(HD) Squadron moved to Woodford Green in September 1917, having firmly put Sutton's Farm on the map.

The aerodrome, which measured 800 by 750 yards, continued to expand around the farm in 1917, with four Aeroplane Sheds (90 by 60 feet) being erected, while the number of Bessonneaus rose to four and station buildings covered 20 acres of the site. From September 78(HD) Squadron was the main unit, charged with dealing with the increasing number of enemy Gothas passing over the region. 78(HD) was the last unit to serve here when it was disbanded on 31 December 1919, and by the following year the land was back in the hands of the local farmer. Virtually all of the buildings were demolished, but in late 1922 the original site and an area further south were surveyed again for a new RAF airfield. Reopened in 1928, the site was renamed RAF Hornchurch, which served until June 1962.

Sutton's Farm main units, 1915-19

13 Sqn detached from Gosport, 3 Oct 1915;
to Gosport, 7 Nov 1915 (BE.2C/D/E)

23 Sqn detached from Gosport, 3 Oct 1915;
to Gosport, 15 Apr 1916 (BE.2C, S.1 and FE.2B)

39 Sqn 'B' Flt from Hounslow, 15 Apr 1916;
to Woodford Green, Sep 1917 (BE.2C/E and BE.12/A)

46 Sqn from Bruay, 10 Jul 1917;
to Ste-Marie-Cappel, 30 Aug 1917 (Pup)

78 Sqn from Hove, 20 Sep 1917;
DB 31 Dec 1919 (1½ Strutter, FE.2D, BE.12B, Camel and Snipe)

189 NTS from Ripon, 1 Apr 1918;
DB 1 Mar 1919 (BE.12B, RE.8 and SE.5)

51 Sqn from Marham, 14 May 1919;
DB 13 Jun 1919 (Camel)

Thaxted

51°57'31"N/00°22'32"E, TL633316. 0.5 miles NE of Bardfield End Green, 1.5 miles ENE of Thaxted

FORTY-SEVEN acres of land belonging to the Franklin family of Terriers Farm were requisitioned in 1916 for an LG that measured 450 by 400 yards. Despite clear approaches, the site was classified as an NLG2 and allocated to 'A' Flight, 75(HD) Squadron, out of Yelling. Thaxted remained open until mid-1918 and the site was returned to the Franklins before the Armistice.

Widford

51°43'30"N/00°26'49"W, TL691057. Hanbury and Robjohns Road Industrial Estate, 1.2 miles SW of Chelmsford railway station

WIDFORD was selected in late December 1914 as one of five RNAS 'branch stations' in the South East of England to combat enemy floatplanes. Hemmed in by the River Wid on the western boundary and Widford Hall Lane to

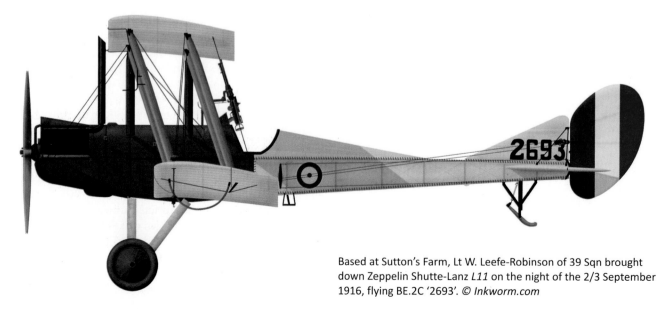

Based at Sutton's Farm, Lt W. Leefe-Robinson of 39 Sqn brought down Zeppelin Shutte-Lanz *L11* on the night of the 2/3 September 1916, flying BE.2C '2693'. © Inkworm.com

the east, the site measured 425 by 300 yards. A 7 Squadron Gunbus was the first aircraft to arrive on 6 January 1915, having taken off from Great Yarmouth 2hr 20min earlier, trying to reach Joyce Green in a strong headwind.

By March 1915 the Admiralty decided to change the role of its stations to Night ELGs, despite RNAS pilots having very little training in flying at night, let alone interceptions. By July at least three Caudron G.3s were based at Widford, two of which were wrecked on the night of 17/18 August chasing Zeppelin *L10*. One crashed on landing, while the other was completely destroyed when the Hale bombs it was carrying exploded, seriously injuring the crew.

The RNAS left Widford in September 1915, but aviation did make a brief return on 1 July 1936 when it was the location for Chelmsford's British Empire Air Display.

Woodford Green, London Borough of Redbridge

51°36′32″N/00°02′56″W, TQ420920. In the region of Ashton playing-fields, dissected by M11, 0.5 miles E of Woodford Green, 0.9 miles NE of Woodford

WOODFORD GREEN is the site of three aviation-related sites; one LG, one Balloon Squadron, and a Wing HQ. The first to be occupied was the LG, located east of Woodford Green, when 39(HD) Squadron moved in from Hounslow on 30 June 1916 with its BE.2Cs. It was joined by 37(HD) Squadron on 16 September 1916, which was reformed here from a nucleus provided by 39(HD) Squadron. 37(HD) Squadron moved to Woodham Mortimer on 29 September, where it was equipped with a variety of aircraft. 39(HD) Squadron departed from Woodford Green for North Weald on 9 December 1917, and it appears that the LG was then closed down.

The second site to be occupied at Woodford Green was Salway Lodge, which was requisitioned as the home for 49 HD Wing, formed here on 29 October 1917. The unit's occupancy was short-lived as it had moved to Upminster Hall by early 1918.

The third unit was part of the London Balloon Apron, 7 Balloon Wing, when No 2 Balloon Squadron was formed at 'Bon Avie', Broomhill Walk, Woodford Green, on 24 November 1917. The unit remained until 9 July 1919, when it was disbanded.

Woodham Mortimer

51°42′16″N/00°37′30″W, TL813039. Due E of Little Grange Farm, 0.5 miles S of Woodham Mortimer, 2 miles SE of Danbury

AFTER being reformed at Woodford Green on 15 September 1916, 37(HD) Squadron relocated to Woodham Mortimer on the 29th. The LG measured approximately 500 by 450 yards, and during the squadron's tenure here detachments were carried out to Goldhanger, Rochford and Stow Maries. The full range of service aircraft would have been seen here,

Sopwith 1½ Strutter A8274 of 37(HD) Squadron, seen at Woodham Mortimer in 1917, was one of many types operated by this unit.

such as the BE.2D, BE.12, BE.2E, BE.12A, 1½ Strutter, Pup, RE.7, BE.12B and SE.5A. 37(HD) Squadron moved to Stow Maries on 22 June 1918, and Woodham Mortimer appears to have been closed down. The field is much the same as it was almost 100 years ago, and aviation remains in the shape of a Jabiru microlight, which uses the same site.

Wormingford (Bures)

51°56′14″N/00°47′13″W, TL930302. W of Fordham Road, on E edge of WW2 airfield, 0.9 miles SSW of Wormingford

OPENED in December 1916 for the use of 'C' Flight, 37(HD) Squadron, Wormingford was classed as an NLG1; it occupied 74 acres and measured 750 by 450 yards. 75(HD) Squadron took over in January 1918 and remained until October, when it was open to all units until its closure in June 1919.

During the Second World War the LG became part of RAF Wormingford (Station 159) between 1942 and 1945.

FLINTSHIRE

North Shotwick

53°13′30″N/03°00′40″W, SJ332702. W of Welsh Road (A494), Deeside Industrial Park, 1 mile SSW of Shotwick, 1.5 miles WNW of Sealand

OPENED prematurely due to the pressures of war in October 1917, North Shotwick was initially a Training Squadron Station for the use 95 Squadron, which arrived in October, and 90 Squadron, which served here from 5 December. Together with Hooton Park, the aerodrome was under the control of the 37th (Training) Wing, which was established at The Oaks, Ledsham, Little Sutton, near Chester, on 10 October 1917. Construction of the hangars, which comprised seven 1917-pattern GS Sheds (170 by 100 feet), continued around the two squadrons, which had a wide selection of aircraft on strength, until early 1918. By this stage the site occupied 165 acres of land and measured 1,000 by 900 yards.

By July 1918 the two resident squadrons had worked up, but in the meantime the first of two training squadrons, 67 TS from Shawbury, had already arrived the previous April, joined by 55 TS from Lilbourne in July. The two units were disbanded into 51 TDS on 15 July, and North Shotwick's role

changed to that of a single-seat fighter training unit. 51 TDS plied its trade with up to seventy-two aircraft on strength until 14 March 1919, when it was redesignated 51 TS, and again to 4 TS on 31 May as the post-war RAF began to reorganise itself. Unlike hundreds of other training units across the country, 4 TS became one of several new specialist training schools; it became 5 FTS on 26 April 1920 and was destined to remain here until 1940. In the meantime this site, together with South Shotwick, slowly gelled into one aerodrome to become RAF Sealand in 1924.

Sealand remained open as an RAF station until 2006 and several areas are still in MoD hands. On the old North Shotwick site six of the original GS Sheds, accessed via the B5441, are extant and maintained in very good condition, if not quite in their original state, nestling next to a comparatively modern C Type hangar.

North Shotwick main units, 1917-20

95 Sqn from Ternhill, 30 Oct 1917;
DB 4 Jul 1918 (various aircraft)

90 Sqn from Shawbury, 5 Dec 1917;
to Brockworth, 5 Jul 1918 (various aircraft)

67 TS from Shawbury, 1 Apr 1918;
DB into 51 TDS, 15 Jul 1918 (Camel, Pup and 504)

55 TS from Lilbourne, Jul 1918;
DB into 51 TDS, 15 Jul 1918 (Camel, SE.5A and 504)

51 TDS (ex-55 and 67 TS), 15 Jul 1918;
redesignated 51 TS, 14 Mar 1919
(Dolphin, 504, SE.5A, Camel, Pup, DH.6 and BE.2E)

51 TS (ex-51 TDS), 14 Mar 1919;
redesignated 4 TS, 31 May 1919 (504K)

27 Sqn cadre from Bavay, 18 Mar 1919;
DB 22 Jan 1920 (no aircraft)

98 Sqn cadre from Alquines, 28 Mar 1919;
DB 24 Jun 1919 (no aircraft)

103 Sqn cadre from Maisoncelle, 26 Mar 1919;
DB 1 Oct 1919 (no aircraft)

4 TS (ex-51 TS) 31 May 1919;
redesignated 5 FTS, 26 Apr 1920 (504K and F.2B)

13 Group from Upton, 6 Aug 1919;
DB into No 3 (Training) Group, 18 Oct 1919

55 Sqn cadre from Renfrew, 30 Dec 1919;
DB 22 Jan 1920 (no aircraft)

South Shotwick (Chester/Queensferry)

53°13'14"N/03°00'14"W, SJ330696. W of Welsh Road (A494) opposite old Marsh Farm, 1.4 miles SSW of Shotwick, N of Garden City

TO the south of the already established North Shotwick slowly sprung up South Shotwick, which was under construction as an AAP for American-built aircraft from April 1918. Occupying 169 acres to the south of the railway line and measuring 1,500 by 700 yards, the AAP was not destined to be finished before the Armistice. Work ceased in June 1919, by which time nine Aeroplane Sheds (180 by 100 feet) had been completed. The site slowly gelled into the northern site to become part of RAF Sealand from 1924. Following the station's closure in 2006, this part of the old camp has been heavily redeveloped.

GREATER LONDON

Battersea Park,
London Borough of Wandsworth

51°28'49"N/00°09'32"W, TQ280776. Battersea Park, possibly half closer to river, 0.5 miles NW of Battersea Park railway station

ONLY active during 1914 and early 1915, it was a temporary ELG for the RNAS, and was replaced by Hyde Park.

Hackney Marshes,
London Borough of Hackney

51°33'25"N/00°01'47"W, TQ367860. Hackney Marsh (Recreation Ground), 0.9 miles NE of Homerton railway station

ONE of the largest areas of common land in Greater London, at more than 336 acres, Hackney Marshes made an ideal site for an HD NLG1. Opened in April 1916 for the use of 39(HD) Squadron, surprisingly the LG was abandoned by October 1917.

Hurlingham (Polo Ground),
London Borough of Kensington & Chelsea

51°28'08"N/00°12'05"W, TQ249761. 0.3 miles E of Putney Bridge railway station, 0.5 miles S of Parsons Green railway station

(NO 1) Free Balloon School was formed here on 15 April 1918, having absorbed the RFC Free Balloon Section at Kennington Oval. Under the command of SE Area, the balloon school left form Roehampton on 31 January 1919 and closed down not long after.

Hyde Park (Marble Arch & Rotten Row), London Borough of Westminster

Marble Arch: N51°30'33"N/00°09'33"W, TQ278805. 0.2 miles S of Speakers Corner

Rotten Row: N51°30'10"N/00°09'49"W, TQ275798. Between Rotten Row and New Ride

LITTLE more than half a mile apart, these two sites in Hyde Park were both designated as HD Night ELGs for the use of the RNAS during 1914 and 1915.

Kennington (The Oval), London Borough of Lambeth

51°29'01"N/00°06'54"W, TQ310778. The Oval cricket ground, 0.10 miles WNW of Oval underground station, 0.3 miles SSW of Kennington

THE Oval cricket ground briefly played host to the Free Balloon Training Section from early 1918, until it was disbanded on 11 May 1918. Just over half a mile to the north, in Walnut Tree Walk (N51°29'01"N/00°06'54"W, TQ311789), an earlier connection with the RFC was the formation of the Central Aircraft Repair Depot on 1 January 1917. The depot controlled several units until it was absorbed into the Western Aircraft Depot at Yate on 21 May 1917.

Kensington Gardens, London Borough of the City of Westminster

51°30'26"N/00°10'40"W, TQ265803. Between Round Pond and W end of Serpentine, 0.5 miles ENE of Kensington Palace

AN HD Night ELG was active here during 1914 for the use of the RNAS; it was replaced by Hyde Park.

Putney Heath

51°26'31"N/00°13'36"W, TQ233730. In clearing E of Ladies Mile, Putney Heath

PUTNEY HEATH was the home of the No 2 Balloon Training Wing and Free Balloon Section (later Free Balloon School) during 1918 and 1919. Balloon operations were carried out on the heath while the HQ may have been located at 331 Upper Richmond Road. It was here that the Free Balloon Section was formed in December 1918 and disbanded in September 1919.

Regent's Park, City of Westminster

51°31'53"N/00°09'14"W, TQ281830. 0.1 miles S of London Zoo, 0.9 miles W of Euston railway station

THE park served briefly in the capacity of an HD Night ELG during 1914 for RNAS Hendon.

Richmond Park (Beverley Brook), London Borough of Richmond-upon-Thames

51°26'57N/00°15'24W, TQ212737. E of park adjacent to Beverley Brook, NE of White Lodge Plantation, 2.2 miles ESE of Richmond centre

THIS 10-acre site was the home of a Kite Balloon Training Station and School from 1915 until 1919. The unit trained Army, RFC and later RAF personnel during its existence. In 1918 No 2 Balloon Training Depot also occupied the site until July 1919 when it moved to Rollestone.

Richmond Park (Kingston Hill), London Borough of Richmond-upon-Thames

51°25'54"N/00°16'03"W, TQ205717. E of large car park at Broomfield Hill, 0.25 miles NE of Kingston University, 1.5 miles NE of Kingston-upon-Thames railway station

THE second aviation site located within the confines of Richmond Park was established as a Kite Balloon Acceptance & Testing Depot for the RFC in 1915. This 25-acre site was also occupied by 5 Stores Depot Balloon Testing Section from April 1919, which moved from the Queen's Club, Barons Court. The depot was disbanded later in the year and the site was closed down.

Shooters Hill

51°28'00"N/00°04'08"W, TQ438762. Now Oxleas Café, Oxleas Wood, off A207, 1 mile NE of Eltham railway station

'WOOD LODGE' was requisitioned by the military in 1916 as part of London's air defence balloon apron. The building itself was taken over and a number of tents pitched around the outside for various personnel. Under the control of 7 Balloon Wing, Shooters Hill became the home of No 3 Balloon Squadron, and it was active here until at least November 1918.

'Wood Lodge' languished in a semi-derelict state for a number of years until it was pulled down in 1932.

GLOUCESTERSHIRE

Bristol (Filton/Patchway)

51°31'10"N/02°35'27"W, ST600804. W of Gloucester North Road (A38), 0.8 miles SW of Patchway railway station, 4.5 miles N of Bristol

THE British & Colonial Aeroplane Co Ltd, familiarly known as Bristol, was formed here by Sir George White in 1910. At first the company leased buildings from the Bristol Tramways Company and, by late 1910, Bristol Boxkites were being manufactured. Following the first of many War Office contracts, the company purchased land to the north of the tramway sheds as an aerodrome. Works offices and an array of buildings were erected as the company expanded in response to further orders for military aircraft from August 1914.

Braemar Mk II C4297 is pictured at Filton in late 1918 prior to its maiden flight in February 1919.

By 1915 the RFC arrived and Bristol became a training squadron station, by which time the site occupied 105 acres and measured 900 by 750 yards. The first of several units arrived from December 1915, 20 Squadron with its FE.2Bs being the first from Netheravon. Nos 33, 62 and 66 Squadrons were all formed here before the aerodrome began to expand again as an AAP.

The additional construction work for the AAP was carried out by P. W. Anderson in 1917 and involved the erection of thirteen 1917-pattern GS Sheds (170 by 80 feet) laid out as four triple units and one single, together with five 1915-pattern Flight Sheds (four 210 by 65 feet and one 140 by 65 feet). By October 1917 the site was known as No 5 (Bristol) AAP, tasked with accepting aircraft from local manufacturers. These of course included Bristol, which by this time was building the F.2B; Westland & Whitehead, which was supplying the DH.9 and DH.9A; and the Gloucestershire Aeroplane Company, which was also contracted to build the F.2B. One of the busiest aerodromes in the West Country, activity at Bristol began to slow down considerably when contracts were cancelled or reduced following the Armistice. The AAP wound down rapidly and was moved to Eastleigh in 1919, and by early 1920 the RAF had departed.

Of the three manufacturers who supplied the AAP, only the Whitehead Aircraft Company fell by the wayside, while Bristol, Gloster and Westland clung on through the 1920s and 1930s to revive again with more military orders during the Second World War. Bristol, or Filton by this stage, was once again a busy place and would remain so, witnessing the ever-changing post-war British aircraft industry, which saw the formation of BAC, British Aerospace and finally BAe Systems. Sadly it was in the hands of the latter that this historic site was closed down in 2013.

Today remnants of the First World War can still be found, including one triple unit of GS Sheds and the single 1915 Flight Shed (140 by 65 feet), both located on the northern side of the airfield. For decades both these buildings were far from the public eye but today, thanks to construction of Hayes Way, both can be seen up close.

Bristol main units, 1915-19

20 Sqn from Netheravon, 15 Dec 1915;
to St Omer, 16 Jan 1916 (FE.2B)

33 Sqn formed 12 Jan 1916;
to Tadcaster, 18 Mar 1916 (BE.2C)

42 Sqn from Netheravon, 1 Apr 1916;
to St Omer, 8 Aug 1916 (BE.2D/E)

19 Sqn from Netheravon, 4 Apr 1916;
to St Omer, 30 Jul 1916 (various aircraft)

66 Sqn formed 30 Jun 1916;
to Netheravon, 2 Jul 1916 (various aircraft)

66 Sqn from Netheravon, 27 Jul 1916;
to St Omer, 3 Mar 1917
(BE.2B/C/D, BE.12, 504K and Pup)

62 Sqn formed 8 Aug 1916;
to Rendcomb, 17 Jul 1917 (F.2B)

55 (Reserve) Sqn formed 15 Nov 1916;
to Yatesbury, 22 Nov 1916 (504 and DH.5)

51 (Reserve) Sqn formed 30 Dec 1916;
to Wye, 8 Jan 1917
(RE8, BE2C/E, DH4, DH6, DH9, Elephant and FE.2B)

35 (Reserve) Sqn formed 1 Feb 1917;
to Northolt, 16 Feb 1917 (504, F.2B and RE.7)

Bristol AAP opened 22 Mar 1917;
redesignated 5 AAP, 10 Dec 1917 (F.2B)

5 AAP (ex-Bristol AAP), 10 Dec 1917;
closed 11 Oct 1919 (F.2B, DH.9 and DH.9A)

121 Sqn from Narborough, 10 Aug 1918;
DB 17 Aug 1918 (DH.9)

101 Sqn from Morville, 16 Mar 1919;
DB 31 Dec 1919 (FE.2B/D)

Brockworth

51°50'43"N/02°10'23"W, SO881163. Gloucester Business Park, 1 mile SE of Hucclecote, 3 miles SE of Gloucester

IT always has to start with a field, and this was the case when H. H. Martyn & Co Ltd of Cheltenham chose such a place near Hucclecote in 1915 for flight-testing machines it had built for the Aircraft Manufacturing Co. By 1917 Martyn underwent a reorganisation and the aviation division was bought by the Gloucestershire Aircraft Co in June of that year. Aircraft built by the company were at first towed behind Ford lorries from the Sunningend factory, but by late 1917 the Air Board decided to build a new AAP, to be named Brockworth.

Work began on the AAP in early 1918, the site occupying 140 acres and measuring 1,100 by 600 yards, but it is not clear when the unit opened because it was still under construction when the Armistice was declared. The AAP consisted of five 1918-pattern GS Sheds (170 by 100 feet) and an impressive twenty-one Handley Page storage sheds (200 by 60 feet) presented as seven

triple units. In the meantime a couple of operational squadrons arrived, beginning with 90 Squadron from Shotwick on 5 July 1918, whose main equipment was the Dolphin. It was a short visit because the unit was disbanded on 29 July.

The AAP was still under construction in January 1919, by which time the RAF prepared to abandon the site, which was not fully relinquished until April 1920. The Air Board claimed the many assembly sheds, leaving the Gloucestershire Aircraft Co with drastically reduced orders, but the company persevered, remained in aviation and decided to expand the site; in 1926, as the Gloster Aircraft Co, it bought Brockworth/Hucclecote outright. Gloster remained until 1960, when the last Javelin fighter was flown out by chief test pilot Dicky Martin. In 1964 the site, then part of Hawker Siddeley, was sold off. Today the aerodrome is a typical outer-city business park with a combination of housing, supermarkets and services. While the later more complex airfield has been eradicated, the base of a coupled GS shed can be seen off the Hucclecote Road, behind the Tesco Extra supermarket – but for how long?

Cirencester

51°44'35"N/01°59'25"W, SP000051. Between Daglingworth and Ermin Way, S of Parson's Copses, 2 miles N of Cirencester

VERY little is known of the acreage and size of this LG. It was opened for 33 TS, AFC, which moved here from Ternhill on 12 January 1918. Operating the BE.12 and 504K, the move was only meant to be temporary, as 33 TS was intended for Minchinhampton, which was not yet ready. The unit was redesignated as 8 (Training) Squadron, AFC, on 14 January, and had departed from Cirencester on 18 February 1918, bound for Leighterton. The fact that this aerodrome was only active for just over a month would explain the lack of detail surrounding the site.

Further down the road, 21 (Training) Wing HQ moved into Cirencester Castle on 6 September 1916 from Filton, and remained until 7 September 1918, when it moved to Oxford.

Leighterton (Bowldown Farm)

51°37'50"N/02°14'57"W, ST828923. W of Bowldown Farm, E of A46, 1 mile NNE of Leighterton

BUILT specifically for the AFC, Leighterton was opened in January 1918 as a training squadron station. The site covered 202 acres and measured 1,150 by 900 yards, with hangars and a technical site located in the south-western corner, just north-east of Haymead Covert. A large domestic site was built in the north-western corner near Goss Covert. Five 1918-pattern GS Sheds (170 by 100 feet) were built, four of them coupled and the fifth serving as an ARS, complete with a pair of aeroplane stores all built by contractor Thomas Rowbotham Ltd.

The first two AFC training units arrived in 18 February 1918 in the shape of the 8th TS from Minchinhampton with varying numbers of 504s, Pups, Camels and Snipes, followed by the 7th TS, AFC, from Yatesbury five days later. Both units were tasked with training Australian pilots in the art of single-seat fighting and reconnaissance, and both squadrons

Capt A. H. Cobby (AFC) at the controls of Camel E7267 of the 8th TS (AFC) at Leighterton in 1918. *Via Ray Sturtivant*

continued this role until their disbandment in May 1919. No 1 ARS, AFC, briefly served here from January to June 1919, but it was a cadre of 66 Squadron from Yatesbury, disbanded on 25 October 1919, that was the last unit at Leighterton. The site was rapidly closed down and cleared by early 1920.

The LG is virtually unaltered and aircraft still operate from a pair of grass strips, 800 and 600 yards in length, located south-west of Bowldown Farm.

Leighterton main units, 1918-19

8th TS AFC from Minchinhampton, 18 Feb 1918;
DB May 1919 (504, Pup, Camel and Snipe)

7th TS AFC from Yatesbury, 23 Feb 1918;
DB May 1919
(504, DH.6, BE.2E, F.2B, RE.8, Camel and SE.5A)

No 1 Aircraft Repair Section AFC from Minchinhampton, Jan 1919;
DB Jun 1919

28 Sqn cadre from Yatesbury, 29 Mar 1919;
to Eastleigh, 20 Oct 1919

66 Sqn cadre from Yatesbury, 29 Mar 1919;
DB 25 Oct 1919

6 TS reformed Aug 1919; DB Sep 1919 (504K)

Minchinhampton

51°42'26"N/02°08'12"W, SO909009. Current Aston Down airfield, 2.4 miles E of Minchinhampton

ONE of several aerodromes allocated specifically for the use of the AFC, Minchinhampton was opened in late 1917 when 33 (Australian) TS moved in from Cirencester. The aerodrome was built south of the old Cirencester Road with a substantial domestic site to the north on 170 acres, measuring 950 by 800 yards.

By January 1918 the site was classified as a TSS, with an expanding technical site, built by Thomas Rowbotham Ltd, emerging on the south-western boundary, which included four 1918-pattern GS Sheds (170 by 100 feet). These were constructed alongside ten Bessonneau hangars, which served as temporary cover for the more than twenty-four 504s, dozen SE.5s and dozen Camels that were on site from the 5th and 6th TS, AFC, which arrived from Shawbury and Ternhill respectively in April 1918. The temporary Bessonneaus were destined to become permanent, as the GS Sheds were still not completed by the Armistice. The work was eventually completed just as the two TSs were disbanded in May and June 1919. Closed down in 1920, the site lay dormant for 18 years until reopened as RAF Aston Down, remaining in military hands until the early 1980s. Today much of the airfield site is owned by the Cotswold Gliding Club.

While little evidence of the First World War remains at the site, one gem survives at Much Marcle, 25 miles to the north-west. A single training hangar was purchased by Westons Cider in 1926 and relocated to Much Marcle, were it remains in superb condition in the hands of Jon Southall as Much Marcle Garage Ltd (51°59'49"N/02°30'08"W, SO655333).

Minchinhampton main units, 1917-19

33 (Australian) TS from Cirencester, Dec 1917;
redesignated 8th TS, AFC, 14 Jan 1918

8th TS AFC (ex-33 TS AFC) formed 14 Jan 1918;
to Leighterton 25 Feb 1918
(504, Pup, Camel and Snipe)

No 1 ARS (Training) Wing AFC from ARS Leighterton, Mar 1918;
DB 1919

5th TS AFC from Shawbury, 2 Apr 1918;
DB May 1919 (504, DH.6, Camel, Snipe and SE.5)

6th TS AFC from Ternhill, 25 Apr 1918;
DB Jun 1919 (504, DH.5, SE.5, Pup and Camel)

Storage Section formed 1919; DB 1919

Rendcomb

51°46'44"N/01°57'15"W, SP033089. E of White Way, W/SW of Chalkhill Wood, currently active aerodrome, 2.2 miles SW of Chedworth

IT is quite heart-warming that this old aerodrome is still presented as RFC Rendcomb by the operators of what is now a private airfield. Several original First World War buildings have been sympathetically restored and approximately a third of the original 226-acre site is still used by an array of light aircraft, including the Breitling Wingwalkers' Stearmans operated by AeroSuperBatics.

Opened in June 1916 as a training squadron station, the first resident was 48 Squadron with its BE.12s, which arrived from Netheravon on June 8. Before the squadron departed for action in northern France it provided the nucleus of Rendcomb's first training unit, 38 TS, formed on 1 August 1916 with an array of aircraft. This large unit brought in an influx of personnel and the site began to expand rapidly along the edge of White Way and along the northern boundary towards Chalkhill Wood, where a complex domestic site developed.

38 TS was disbanded into an even larger training unit in the shape of 45 TDS on 15 August 1918, by which time Rendcomb could boast six 1915-pattern Flight Sheds (210 by 65 feet) all aligned north to south on the eastern side of White Way. Each shed had its own concrete apron and short concrete taxiway extending towards the flying field, which measured 1,150 by 950 yards. With at least fifty aircraft on strength, 45 TDS became 45 TS in June 1919, but was disbanded on 8 July 1919. Rendcomb remained open but was considerably quieter with only cadres from 45 and 46 Squadrons in residence; the latter disbanded here on 31 December 1919. The site was closed down in 1920, but its First World War spirit remains to this day.

Rendcomb main units, 1916-19

48 Sqn from Netheravon 8 Jun 1916;
to La Bellevue, 8 Mar 1917 (BE.12)

38 TS formed (nucleus from 48 Sqn) 1 Aug 1916;
DB into 45 TDS, 15 Aug 1918
(504, F.2A/B, RE.8, BE.2C/E and RE.7)

62 Sqn from Filton, 17 Jul 1917;
to St Omer, 29 Jan 1918 (F.2B)

110 Sqn formed (nucleus from 38 TS) 1 Nov 1917;
to Dover (Swingate Down), 12 Nov 1917 (various aircraft)

59 TS from Lilbourne, 1 Feb 1918;
DB 15 Aug 1918
(DH.1, DH.6, FE.2B/D, BE.2C/E, BE.12A, F.2B and RE.8)

186th Aero Sqn, 'B', 'C' and 'D' Flts, USAAS,
by 17 Jul 1918

45 TDS (ex-38 and 71 TS) formed 15 Aug 1918;
redesignated 45 TS, Jun 1919 (BE.2E, F.2B and 504)

46 Sqn cadre from Baizieux, 10 Feb 1919;
DB 31 Dec 1919 (no aircraft)

45 Sqn cadre from Liettres, 17 Feb 1919;
to Eastleigh, 15 Sep 1919 (no aircraft)

45 TS (ex-45 TDS) reformed Jun 1919;
DB 8 Jul 1919 (504K)

Yate (Chipping Sodbury)

51°32'40"N/02°25'33"W, ST705830. Housing in Longs Drive passes through middle of site, 0.5 miles NW of Yate town centre

FIRST surveyed in 1916, work began on the construction of an ARD later in the year by contractor Robert McAlpine & Sons Ltd. The first unit to be formed at Yate was the Western ARD, which was created by absorbing the Central ARD at Kensington on 21 May 1917.

The infrastructure at Yate was typical of a wartime ARD with a variety of sheds, including a pair of erection sheds (210 by 70 feet), a salvage shed (200 by 100 feet), a workshop (220 by 90 feet), and a substantial engine workshop (240 by 70 feet). The site occupied 193 acres, 40 of which were taken up by buildings, and the aerodrome as a whole measured 1,100 by 800 yards.

On 12 October 1917 the ARD was redesignated as No 3 (Western) ARD, and at its peak in 1918 the unit comprised 48 officers, 104 SNCOs, 116 corporals, 1,028 other ranks, 452 women and a further 46 women employed as 'household'. Specialist sections of the ARD, such as the Engine Repair Section, handled Monosoupape, Le Clerget and Bentley aero engines. The Aeroplane Repair Section specialised in carrying out work on HD Camels, although Snipes and F.2Bs also passed through the unit in great numbers.

Only one flying unit is credited with serving at Yate, albeit without aircraft; this was the 840th Aero Squadron (USAAS), which arrived from the USA on 4 May 1918 and moved to France on 13 August 1918. No 3 (Western) ARD remained at Yate until 30 April 1920, when it was closed down. Yate became the home of Parnall Aircraft from 1930 until 1945, and today has been swept away by housing.

HAMPSHIRE

Aldershot (Balloon Square, Alison's Road, aka Stanhope Lines)

51°15'41"N/00°45'43"W, SU864521. Within the barrack area of Airborne Forces Depot and Regimental HQ of Parachute Regiment, Alison's Road, Aldershot

THIS historic location was where the Royal Engineers established a Balloon Factory and Balloon School in 1892. The unit was transferred to Farnborough Common during 1905 and 1906. A National Heritage memorial plaque is located at the site bearing the inscription: 'Balloon Square, The School of Ballooning which was then a branch of The Royal Engineers was founded in 1892.'

Andover (Weyhill)

51°12'26"N/01°31'45"W, SU329454. Technical site now known as Marlborough Lines, British Army HQ Land Forces, while LG is dominated by Tesco distribution centre, 1.6 miles W of Andover town centre

ANDOVER was opened as a TDS in August 1917 although, in a pattern similar to many wartime airfields, the infrastructure of the aerodrome was far from finished. Nestling between three major roads and with a railway line along the southern border, Andover had seven GS Sheds (170 by 10 feet), although several were still under construction in 1918. Initially, hangarage was provided by Bessonneaus and accommodation for the station's personnel was tents, eventually replaced by wooden huts. The aerodrome occupied 245 acres of land and measured 1,200 by 1,100 yards.

Andover's first role was to provide a place for new bomber squadrons to work up, beginning with 104, 105 and 106 Squadrons, which arrived in September and October 1917. These units were equipped with a variety of machines including the DH.6, DH.9 and RE.8; these made way for the

heavies of 207 and 215 Squadrons, which re-equipped from the O/100 to the O/400 at Andover. A great deal of night navigation training was carried out by O/400 crews in preparation for service in the Independent Air Force, which was cut off in its prime with the end of the war.

Seemingly unaffected by the Armistice, Andover remained an active RAF station until 10 June 1977, when the site was taken over by the Army, although the RAF retained a presence until 2009. The original GS Sheds remained a dominant feature at Andover and the last examples were not demolished until 2001.

Andover main units, 1917-18

104 Sqn from Wyton, 16 Sep 1917;
to St Omer, 19 May 1918 (DH.9)

105 Sqn from Waddington, 3 Oct 1917;
to Ayr, 16 May 1918 (DH.6; BE.2B; BE.2D and DH.9)

106 Sqn from Spittlegate, 3 Oct 1917;
to Ayr, 21 May 1918 (RE.8)

116 Sqn formed 1 Dec 1917;
to Netheravon, 31 Mar 1918 (various aircraft)

104th Aero Sqn, USAAS (detached), from Upavon;
to Old Sarum 24 Dec 1917 (no aircraft)

119 Sqn formed 1 Jan 1918;
to Duxford, 1 Mar 1918 (various aircraft)

148 Sqn formed 10 Feb 1918;
to Ford Junction, 1 Mar 1918 (FE.2B)

207 Sqn from Netheravon, 13 May 1918;
to Ligescourt, 7 Jun 1918 (O/400)

215 Sqn from Netheravon, 15 May 1918;
to Alquines, 4 Jul 1918 (O/400)

School of Instruction, Southern Training Brigade, from Old Sarum, 10 Jun 1918; DB 22 Jun 1918 (DH.9, RE.8 and BE.2E)

School of Aerial Navigation & Bomb Dropping formed 23 Jun 1918; absorbed into School of Air Pilotage, 23 Sep 1919 (O/400, DH.4, DH.6, DH.9 and FK.8)

169th Aero Sqn (USAAS) from USA, Jul 1918

This view of Andover, looking south-west, shows the flying field on the right and Handley Page O/400s of the School of Aerial Navigation & Bomb Dropping resting between training sorties. *Via Stuart Leslie*

The Moxton Road is clear heading towards Andover in this aerial view taken from 1,200 feet on 23 June 191? during an air display. *Via Stuart Leslie*

Beaulieu (East Boldre)

50°48'16"N/01°28'43"W, SU365005. On Bagshot Moor between Hatchet Lane (B3054) and East Boldre Road, 1.2 miles SW of Beaulieu

IN 1910 only the fifth flying school in the world to open was established here by William McArdle and American J. Armstrong-Drexel. Despite being refused permission for such an enterprise by the Office of Woods, the New Forest Flying School was created, complete with a pair of Aeroplane Sheds and a rudimentary LG. At its peak the flying school had ten aircraft at its disposal, and by 1911 the number of army officers wishing to be trained as aviators was on the increase. By 1912 the school was in decline and more flying schools around the country began to mushroom, forcing the site near East Boldre to close down.

It was not long before the site was viewed again with an aviation training purpose in mind, this time for the use of the RFC. On 15 December 1915 the site, now named Beaulieu, became a training squadron station and the home of 16 TS, which was formed here. Operating a variety of machines, the aerodrome continued in this capacity until it was expanded into a TDS in July 1918. Technical sites were built off East Boldre Road and Hatchet Lane, including six Aeroplane Sheds (four of 100 by 180 feet and two of 65 by 210 feet) and a single ARS Shed (65 by 210 feet). By now the aerodrome

occupied 213 acres (30 of which were covered by buildings) and measured 1,150 by 850 yards. Personnel strength by mid-1918 was 51 officers, 120 officer pupils, 60 NCO pupils, 47 SNCOs, 25 JNCOs, 320 other ranks, seven Forewomen, 155 women, and 54 'household' women. A large number of aircraft were stationed here, on average thirty-six Avro type and the same number of Dolphins during 1918.

Training of pilots continued at a reasonable pace after the Armistice, and it was not until March 1920 that 11 TS was disbanded. Closed down in late 1920, civilian flying returned between 1933 and 1938, then in 1942 on the western side of Hatchet Lane a much larger airfield was established, which was not disposed of until 1959.

Remnants on the ground can be seen off East Boldre Lane; the track south of the telephone box and almost opposite East Boldre Garage follows the road behind the hangar line, and if you look closely remains of the bases can still be seen. The village hall in East Boldre was used as the First World War officers' mess. The other interesting aviation link here is the Beaulieu letters (50°48'26"N/01°28'52"W, SU366009), which can be seen approximately 150 yards from the entrance to the Hatchet Lane car park; 15 feet high and extending for more than 110 feet, the letters are clearly visible from the air and were most likely placed to mark a turning point for the 1910 Bournemouth Air Show. Alternatively, they could have been placed there to mark the position of the original flying school.

Above: De Havilland DH.6 A9580 of 16 TS, a unit that served at Beaulieu from June to October 1917.

Left: Sopwith Camel B7376 of 73 TS at Beaulieu. This aircraft stalled and crashed over the airfield on 16 June 1918, killing 2nd Lt R. R. Brown. *Via Stuart Leslie*

Below: Camel B9280 during its brief service at Beaulieu with 73 TS between January and March 1918.

Beaulieu main units, 1915-19

16 TS formed 15 Dec 1915;
redesignated 16 TS, 1 Jun 1917
(504, BE.2C, JN.4 and BE.12)

23 TS formed Jun 1916; to Egypt, Aug 1916

84 Sqn formed from 16 (Reserve) Sqn, 7 Jan 1917;
to Lilbourne 22 Mar 1917 (various aircraft)

81 (Canadian) Reserve Sqn formed Jan 1917;
to Canada, 15 Feb 1917 (no aircraft)

87 (Canadian) Reserve Sqn from Gosport, Feb 1917;
to Canada 1917 (no aircraft)

16 TS (ex-16 (Reserve) Sqn), 1 Jun 1917;
to Yatesbury, 30 Oct 1917 (504, BE.2C, JN.4 and BE.12)

79 Sqn from Gosport, 8 Aug 1917;
to St Omer, 20 Feb 1918 (Dolphin from Dec 1917)

103 Sqn formed from 16 TS, 1 Sep 1917;
to Old Sarum, 8 Sep 1917 (various aircraft)

59 TS from Yatesbury, 30 Oct 1917;
to Netheravon, 20 Nov 1917
(DH.1/1A, DH.6, FE.2B/D, BE.2C/E, BE.12 and RE.8)

70 TS from Gosport, 20 Dec 1917;
absorbed into 28 TDS at Weston-on-Green, 27 Jul 1918
(Shorthorn, Pup, Camel, Dolphin, 504, RE.8 and BE.12)

1 TS from Port Meadow, Jan 1918;
absorbed into 29 TDS, 27 Jul 1918
(Camel, Dolphin, 504 and Pup)

93rd Aero Sqn (USAAS) from USA, 9 Jan 1918;
to Issoudun 24 Jun 1918 (no aircraft)

73 TS from Turnhouse, 20 Feb 1918;
absorbed into 29 TDS, 27 Jul 1918
(Camel, Pup, 504 and 1½ Strutter)

170th Aero Sqn (USAAS) from USA, 17 Jul 1918

177th Aero Sqn (USAAC) from USA, 17 Jul 1918

29 TDS (ex-1 and 73 TS), 27 Jul 1918;
DB 28 Mar 1919 (Camel, Dolphin, 504 and Pup)

43rd Aero Sqn (USAAC) detached from South Carlton,
24 Aug 1918;
to Codford (DH.4)

School of Instruction, Southern Training Brigade, formed 1918;
to Old Sarum, 1918 (BE.2E, RE.8 and DH.9)

11 TDS from Boscombe Down, Apr 1919;
redesignated 11 TS, Jul 1919
(DH.4, DH.6, DH.9, BE.2E, 504, Pup and Dolphin)

Wireless Telegraphy School from Winton, May 1919;
DD 1 Sep 1919
(FK.8, RE.8, BE.2C/D/E, F.2B, M.1C, Elephant and 1½ Strutter)

11 TS (ex-11 TDS) Jul 1919; DB Mar 1920 (504K)

Calshot

Seaplane Station: 50°49'06"N/01°18'30"W, SU487024.
End of Castle Spit, 0.9 miles NE of Calshot
Calshot Camp: 50°48'37"N/01°19'29"W, SU476014. In
Calshot village W of B3053

ONE of the first seaplane stations to be opened by the RNAS, on 29 March 1913, Calshot was an unusual layout that had its technical and flying site huddled around Calshot Castle, at the end of the spit, and its domestic site nearly a mile to the south-west in the village. Calshot Spit, which jutted out in the Solent, was an ideal location for operating seaplanes. It was initially used as an experimental station, but from the beginning of the war it became a seaplane training school.

The site progressively expanded to 80 acres and the spit was filled with hangars, including five seaplane and flying-boat sheds (one 104 by 90 feet, one 160 by 95 feet, one 140 by 91 feet, one 180 by 60 feet, and one 600 by 100 feet), together with four slipways. From 1915 Bembridge was allocated as a sub-station, and from 1917 Calshot was classified as a Flying Boat Base until June 1918, when the station became the home of 210 TDS. The TDS comprised two schools, one called the Float Seaplane Aerial Gunnery & Bomb Dropping School and the other the Boat Seaplane School. The former offered a three-week course on aerial firing, bomb dropping and general patrol work, while the latter taught pilots to fly flying-boats.

While the schools got into their stride, Calshot also became a Marine Operations (Seaplane) Station from August 1918 for 345 and 346(FB) Flights, which were now under the charge of 240 Squadron. Operating the big Curtiss H.12 and Felixstowe flying-boats, thirteen U-boats were sighted before the Armistice and eight were attacked by the two flights.

After the war, Calshot remained part of the RAF's plan, later becoming home of the High Speed Flight, which won the Schneider Trophy outright in 1931. All of the RAF's flying-boats from the Singapore through to the Sunderland operated from here, and the station was not closed down until 1961. Today the camp in the village, accessed by a light railway built in 1917 and nicknamed the 'Calshot Express', has long gone. However, at the spit three hangars still survive, named Schneider, Sunderland and Sopwith.

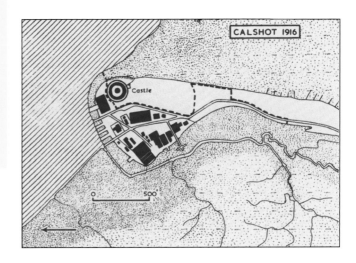

Norman Thompson NT.2B N1180 was delivered to the RNAS Seaplane School at Calshot on 8 June 1917. The NT.2B was the standard RNAS flying-boat trainer.

Although this vertical view of Calshot was taken in March 1935, the flying-boat station is the same as it would have appeared during the First World War. The entire spit was covered in military buildings leading virtually all the way back to the village, and could be accessed by a light railway.

Calshot main units, 1913-18

Naval Wing Seaplane Flts formed 1913;
became RNAS War Flts, Jul 1914

RNAS Seaplane School formed 1914;
DB into 210 TDS, Jun 1918

RNAS/RAF Seaplane War Flts formed Jul 1914;
redesignated 410 Flt, 31 May 1918

RNAS/RAF Flying-boat War Flts formed 1917;
redesignated 345 and 346 Flts

10 Group HQ formed 1 Apr 1918; to Warsash, Jun 1918

345(FB) and 346(FB) Flt (ex-FB War Flts), May 1918;
both into 240 Sqn, 20 Aug 1918 (H.12 and F.2A)

410(S) Flt formed 30 May 1918;
into 240 Sqn, 20 Aug 1918 (Short 184, 320 and Campania)

210 TDS formed Jun 1918;
DB into RAF & Naval Co-operation School, 15 May 1919
(Short 184, 320, FBA, F.2A, Campania and Wight seaplane)

'A' & 'B' Boat Seaplane Training Flts formed within 210 TDS,
8 Aug 1918;
DB Jan 1919

240 Sqn (from ex-345, 346 and 410 Flts), 20 Aug 1918;
DB 15 May 1919 (Short 320, 184, Campania and F.2A)

347(FB) Flt, 238 Sqn from Killingholme, 11 Dec 1918;
to Cattewater, 19 Dec 1918

Chattis Hill (Training Gallops/Stockbridge)

51°07'04"N/01°31'28"W, SU332357. N of A30, NW of
Houghton Down Farm, 1.9 miles W of Stockbridge

THE first of two airfields at Chattis Hill opened as a
training squadron station in August 1917 and was
occupied by 91, 92 and 93 Squadrons, which brought the
aerodrome alive in September and October. It occupied 150
acres of Houghton Down and measured 1,100 by 850 yards.
By March 1918 all three squadrons moved out to Tangmere,
as Chattis Hill was prepared to become a flying school and
eventual TDS. Six 1918-pattern GS Sheds (180 by 100 feet)
were erected by John Mowlem Ltd close to the main road, and
a seventh was built as an ARS Shed with a pair of plane stores
attached. Personnel, who numbered 51 officers, 120 officer
pupils, 60 NCO pupils, 47 SNCOs, 25 JNCOs and 320 other
ranks, were all accommodated on the north side of the main
road, east of the technical site. The only buildings on the south
side of the road were for the WAAF site.

34 and 43 TS were the first training units to arrive from
Ternhill in March 1918, but in July both were disbanded into
43 TDS, which continued to train Scout pilots until it was also
disbanded on 15 May 1919. Several buildings were still not
completed when the site was closed down in late 1919 and
returned to the original landowners in 1920.

Twenty years later Chattis Hill was selected as a dispersal
site for the Supermarine Spitfire, and several assembly sheds
were erected to the north of the First World War site in
Saddler's Plantation. The site was active from December 1940,
the first aircraft being delivered from here in March 1941. The
aircraft operated from the western side of Spitfire Lane until
1945, although the site was not fully relinquished by
Supermarine until 31 May 1948. There is no trace of the First
World War airfield, although the flying field is virtually extant
and hangar bases from the Second World War still remain.

A two-seat Sopwith Camel conversion, H823 only served with 43
TDS at Chattis Hill. *Via Ray Sturtivant*

Chattis Hill main units, 1917-18

91 Sqn from Spittlegate, 14 Sep 1917;
to Tangmere, 15 Mar 1918 (various aircraft)

92 Sqn from London Colney, 14 Sep 1917;
to Tangmere, 17 Mar 1918 (Pup)

93 Sqn from Croydon, 3 Oct 1917;
to Tangmere, 19 Mar 1918 (various aircraft)

34 TS from Ternhill, 18 Mar 1918;
DB into 43 TDS, 15 Jul 1918 (504 and Camel)

43 TS Ternhill, 20 Mar 1918;
DB into 43 TDS, 15 Jul 1918 (504 and Camel)

W/T School from Biggin Hill, 16 Apr 1918;
to Winton, 21 Nov 1918
(FK.8, RE.8, F.2B, BE.2C/D/E, Elephant, 1½ Strutter and M.1C)

43 TDS (ex-34 and 43 TS), 15 Jul 1918;
DB 15 May 1919 (504, Camel and FK.8)

171st Aero Sqn, USAAS, by 17 Jul 1918

Eastleigh (Southampton)

50°56'55"N/01°21'40"W, SU452168. Current
Southampton Airport, off M27, 3.3 miles NE of
Southampton

ALL other aviation events that have taken place at Eastleigh over the years will be forever overshadowed by the maiden flight of a small, pretty fighter designed by R. J. Mitchell on 5 March 1936. The Spitfire has remained an icon ever since, but it was back in 1910 that Rowland Moon first flew from here in a 20hp tractor monoplane. The land was owned by North Stoneham Farm, located between the River Itchen and Wide Lane (aka the A335). Grahame-White and Maurice Tetard also flew from here in 1910 and 1911, but it was not until 1917 that attention was shown by the military.

No 8 (Eastleigh) Stores Distributing Park was already established in Leigh Road, but the War Office wanted to expand the unit into a full AAP and the land at North Stoneham Farm appeared to be ideal. A 3-acre site, Leigh Road had one store shed (250 by 100 feet) with a large annexe (100 by 20 feet) for packing cases. With a stores capacity for 1,750 aircraft, Leigh remained active until May 1920.

In the meantime work began on an AAP to be named Eastleigh in late 1917, but construction was protracted and, by the time the site was offered to American forces in July 1918, it was still not completed. From 23 July 1918 the USN established a large depot here, renaming the site NAS Eastleigh or 'Base B'. The plan was to prepare American-built DH.4s, but these never arrived and instead a deal was struck with the British Government to supply DH.9s in exchange for Liberty engines. The DH.9s were shipped to Eastleigh in crates via rail, and offloaded direct into one of twenty-one storage sheds, each 200 by 60 feet. By now four 1917-pattern GS Sheds (170 by 100 feet) were nearing completion and an additional five storage sheds (150 by 50 feet) were also built on the site, which now occupied 158 acres and measured 1,000 by 750 yards.

Just as the USN unit was getting into its stride supplying aircraft to the 10th Northern Bombing Group, the Armistice arrived and all efforts now turned to dispatching aircraft back to the USA. The USN did not leave this busy aerodrome until 10 April 1920, when the depot was closed down. 5 AAP, which had moved in from Filton in 1919, was the final unit here when it disbanded in May 1920.

The same month Eastleigh was relinquished by the RAF, and the first chapter of this aerodrome's history was now over. However, the site remained an unlicensed LG and by late 1926 was a popular location for joyriding. In 1932 Eastleigh was officially reopened as a municipal airport and the site's rich history continued. Today Southampton Airport can boast more than 1.7 million passengers per year passing through its gates.

Eastleigh (Southampton) main units, 1918-19

AAP Eastleigh under construction by 1 Apr 1918;
still under construction 1 Jan 1919;
relinquished 6 May 1920.

USN Depot formed 1919; DB 10 Apr 1920

45 Sqn cadre from Rendcomb, 15 Sep 1919;
DB 31 Dec 1919 (no aircraft)

101 Sqn cadre from Filton, 12 Oct 1919;
DB 31 Dec 1919 (no aircraft)

28 Sqn cadre from Leighterton, 20 Oct 1919;
DB 20 Jan 1920 (no aircraft)

7 Sqn cadre from Old Sarum, 27 Oct 19;
to Farnborough, 19 Nov 1919 (no aircraft)

5 AAP from Filton 1919; DB May 1920

Eversley

51°21'17"N/00°53'45"W, SU770623. Between Eversley
and Lower Common, 2.6 miles NW of Blackbushe
Airport

THIS WAS only active as a temporary LG for two days, when 10 Squadron from Netheravon carried out a practice mobilisation with its BE.2Cs on 12-13 July 1915.

Farnborough

51°16'46"N/00°46'02"W, SU865542. Current
Farnborough airfield, 2.2 miles NNW of Aldershot

BY 1904 the Balloon Factory at Aldershot, under the command of Lt Col J. L. Templer, had outgrown its surroundings, and being ordered to build a 'balloon dirigible' forced the Army to look for an alternative site, preferably not too far away. It did not have to look far, as a suitable piece of land just 2 miles north was found on the north-eastern edge of Farnborough Common, west of Farnborough Road, although it was only meant to be a temporary location. A transportable Airship Shed (160 feet long and 72 feet high) was completed by May 1905 and, as the Farnborough site became less temporary, the majority of the remaining buildings at Aldershot were relocated. By this time a balloon school was formed and the unit was now under the command of Col J. E. Capper. The Army's first airships were built and flown from Farnborough, beginning with the *Nulli Secundus* on 10 September 1907, followed by the *Nulli Secundus II, Baby, Beta, Gamma* and *Delta*. The same shed in which these early airships were built also witnessed the work of Samuel F. Cody, who built his Wright-type aeroplane here in October 1907. After struggling to find a suitable engine, Cody began taxying trials on Jersey Brow in September 1908, and on 16 October flew the machine for the first time from Laffain's Plain to record the first sustained flight in Britain.

The Balloon Factory was renamed the HM Balloon Factory in 1908, and from October 1909 M. J. P. O'Gorman took charge, the first civilian to do so. Huge expansion took place all around the original Balloon Factory site, and even the original airship shed was extended to twice its original size. Originally unimpressed with Cody's aeroplane, it was not until 1911 that the Army realised its mistake, and in response the factory was renamed the Army Aircraft Factory on 1 April 1911. O'Gorman was also instrumental in encouraging aircraft design by offering to repair the Army's early aeroplanes. On 13 May 1912 the Royal Aircraft Factory (R.A.F.) was formed out of the Army Aircraft Factory and the first of many aircraft designs began to be created at Farnborough. Among the staff of the Factory was a young Geoffrey de Havilland, who worked as a test pilot before he branched out to create his own successful company.

Above right: Looking west, the original Balloon Factory site is already beginning to expand in 1912.

Right: Looking north-west from above the Farnborough Road, a pair of 1915-pattern Flight Sheds are in the foreground. The shed on the left (now painted all black) survives today.

Below: Until recently it was accepted that this 2 Squadron, BE.2C '347', was the first aircraft to cross the channel in WW1, flown by 1st Lt H.D. Harvey-Kelly, and landed at Amiens. However, it has recently been discovered that the aircraft Harvey-Kelly flew was in fact '471'.
© Inkworm.com

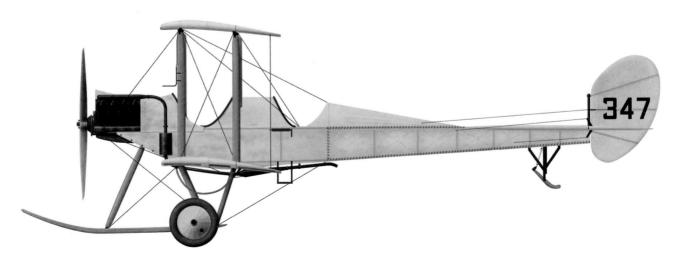

The Royal Aircraft Factory employed hundreds of people at the beginning of the war, and thousands by the end of it.

Farnborough during the early 1920s, long before the airfield we know today consumed Laffain's Plain and Cove Common to the west.

Farnborough continued to expand westwards, occupying Jersey Brow and later Cove Common and Laffain's Plain. A second site within the south-eastern boundary was referred to as South Farnborough, and was so isolated that it almost operated like a separate station. A huge range and number of units were either formed or served at Farnborough, and during its First World War period the aerodrome was a training squadron station, an HD station, school, depot, aircraft park, record office, ARD and ERD. Occupying 286 acres by 1918, early aeroplane hangarage consisted of ten 1912-pattern Aeroplane Sheds (70 by 65 feet), two 1915-pattern Flight Sheds, and various airship and ARD sheds, and a pair of wind tunnels were built during 1916 and 1917. Innumerable workshops and huts sprang up all around the site and several rows of workers' cottages were quickly built north of the factory. At the beginning of the war the factory employed 1,250 people, and by the Armistice this had risen to over 5,000.

With the formation of the Royal Air Force, the Royal Aircraft Factory became the Royal Aircraft Establishment (RAE) on 1 April 1918 and there was little doubt that a unit of this pedigree would continue to serve during the post-war period. In fact, the RAE continued its valuable work until 1988, when it became the Royal Aerospace Establishment, which subsequently merged into the Defence Research Agency in 1991.

Below: 70 Squadron and its Sopwith 1½ Strutters are seen at Jersey Brow (South Farnborough) not long after the unit was formed on 22 April 1916. *Via Aeroplane*

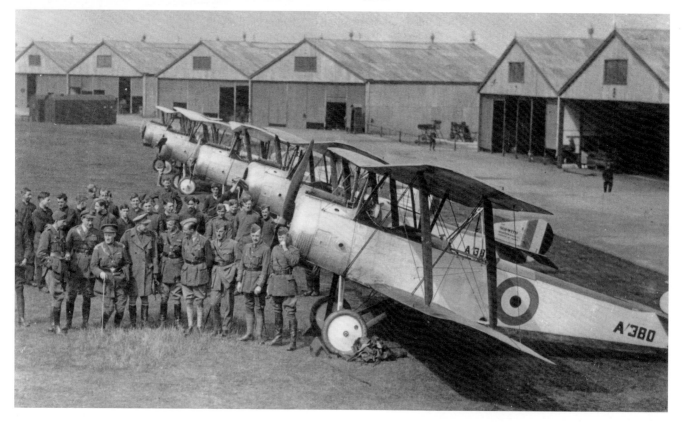

Farnborough main units, 1905-18

Balloon Factory from Aldershot, 30 Apr 1915;
redesignated HM Balloon Factory 1908

HM Balloon Factory 1908;
redesignated Army Aircraft Factory, 1 Apr 1911

Army Aircraft Factory 1 Apr 1911;
redesignated Royal Aircraft Factory, 13 May 1912

Royal Aircraft Factory 13 May 1912;
redesignated Royal Aircraft Establishment, 1 Apr 1918

1 Sqn formed 13 May 1912;
to Brooklands, 14 Aug 1914 (various aircraft)

2 Sqn formed 13 May 1912;
to Montrose, 26 Feb 1913 (various aircraft)

4 Sqn formed 16 Sep 1912;
to Netheravon, 14 Jun 1913 (various aircraft)

5 Sqn formed 16 Jul 1913;
to Netheravon 28 May 1914 (various aircraft)

6 Sqn formed 31 Jan 1914;
to Netheravon, 28 May 1914 (various aircraft)

7 Sqn formed 1 May 1914;
DB 8 Aug 1914 in various units to reinforce BEF

6 Sqn from Netheravon, 2 Jul 1914;
to Netheravon, 26 Sep 1914 (various aircraft)

2 Sqn from Montrose, 5 Aug 1914;
to Amiens, 13 Aug 1914 (various aircraft)

Wireless Flt formed Aug 1914;
to Dover 12 Aug 1914 (BE.2A)

Reserve Aeroplane Sqn formed Aug 1914;
redesignated 1 Reserve Sqn, 12 Nov 1914 (various aircraft)

7 Sqn reformed 29 Sep 1914;
to Netheravon, 22 Oct 1914 (various aircraft)

6 Sqn from Netheravon, 4 Oct 1914;
to Dover, 6 Oct 1914 (various aircraft)

30 Sqn formed Oct 1914;
to Egypt, 4 Nov 1914 (no aircraft)

1 (Reserve) Sqn (ex-Reserve Aeroplane Sqn)
12 Nov 1914;
to Gosport, 7 Apr 1916 (various aircraft)

10 Sqn formed 1 Jan 1915;
to Brooklands, 8 Jan 1915 (various aircraft)

4 (Reserve) Sqn formed 29 Jan 1915;
to Northolt, 1 Mar 1915 (various aircraft)

15 Sqn formed 1 Mar 1915;
to Hounslow, 13 Apr 1915 (BE.2C)

8 Sqn from Gosport, 6 Mar 1915;
to St Omer, 25 Apr 1915 (various aircraft)

31 Sqn formed 11 Oct 1915;
to India, 27 Nov 1915 (no aircraft)

70 Sqn formed 22 Apr 1916;
to Fienvillers from 31 May 1916 (1½ Strutter)

53 Sqn from Catterick, 11 Dec 1916;
to St Omer, 26 Dec 1916 (various aircraft)

58 TS formed late 1916;
to Egypt, 23 Jan 1917 (no aircraft)

100 Sqn from Hingham, 23 Feb 1917;
to St Andre aux Bois, 21 Mar 1917 (FE.2B and FE.2D)

101 Sqn formed 12 Jul 1917;
to St Andre aux Bois, 25 Jul 1917 (FE.2B and FE.2D)

104 Sqn from Wyton, 16 Sep 1917:
to St Omer, 19 May 1918 (DH.9)

105 Sqn from Waddington, 3 Oct 1917:
to Ayr, 16 May 1918 (DH.6, BE.2B, BE.2D and DH.9)

106 Sqn from Spittlegate, 3 Oct 1917:
to Ayr, 21 May 1918 (RE.8)

116 Sqn formed 1 Dec 1917;
to Netheravon, 31 Mar 1918 (various aircraft)

1 (Training) Wireless School formed 8 Nov 1917;
to Flowerdown, 8 Mar 1919 (FK.8 and F.2B)

104th Aero Sqn, USAAS (detached) from Upavon;
to Old Sarum, 24 Dec 1917 (no aircraft)

119 Sqn formed 1 Jan 1918;
to Duxford, 1 Mar 1918 (various aircraft)

148 Sqn formed 10 Feb 1918;
to Ford Junction, 1 Mar 1918 (FE.2B)

RAE (ex-Royal Aircraft Factory) 1 Apr 1918;
DB 23 Mar 1994 (various aircraft)

207 Sqn from Netheravon, 13 May 1918;
to Ligescourt, 7 Jun 1918 (O/400)

School of Instruction, Southern Training Brigade from Old
Sarum, 10 Jun 1918; DB 22 Jun 1918 (DH.9, RE.8 and BE.2E)

Fleet Pond

51°17'19"N/00°49'30"W, SU820550. SE of Fleet
railway station, 1 mile NE of Fleet town centre

THE RAE from Farnborough carried out early hydro-aeroplane experiments here during 1912. The pond offered clear stretches of water up to 400 yards long.

All six 1915-pattern Flight Sheds, which backed onto the Lee-on-Solent railway line, can be seen in this view with aircraft of 1 TS on display. *Via Stuart Leslie*

Gosport (Fort Grange and Fort Rowner)

50°48'09"N/01°09'52"W, SU589006. Current HMS Sultan, flying area bisected by Grange Road, 1.8 miles WNW of Gosport town centre

THE open land known as Grange Camp Field, to the west of Fort Grange and Fort Rowner, which were built in 1857, had been in the hands of the military for more than 100 years when the first flight was attempted here in November 1909. A pair of enthusiastic naval officers, Lts Cochrane and Stocks from the nearby Submarine Depot, built a pusher biplane, which was wrecked during its first attempt to take off. The Hampshire Aero Club followed in April 1910 after successfully negotiating with the War Office for use of the field for 'experiments in aeronautical science'. The club remained until early 1914, when an increasing military aviation presence, which first surveyed the site in November 1913, took over.

Gosport was established as a training squadron station and flying school for the RFC and RNAS from July 1914, the site

Instructors and mechanics of 1 School of Special Flying pose in front of an Avro 504 at Gosport in August 1918.

occupying 270 acres and measuring 1,450 by 800 yards. 5 Squadron was the first to arrive from Netheravon on 6 July 1914, but had departed to Dover (Swingate Down) by the following month. The site was then taken over by the RNAS, and on 15 October 1 Squadron RNAS was formed here with four Bristol Scouts. Not happy about the RNAS moving in while the RFC's back was turned, the War Office began to introduce more units to Gosport, and Fort Grange and Fort Rowner were also taken over as accommodation for the increasing number of personnel.

After a large number of squadrons were formed here, some semblance of order began to descend on the aerodrome, not only regarding the training of new units but also the infrastructure, which began to grow from May 1916. Until then only Bessonneau-type canvas hangars protected the aircraft, but these were complemented and replaced by six 1915-pattern Flight Sheds (210 by 65 feet), one 1916-pattern GS Shed (180 by 80 feet) and a pair of HD-pattern sheds (150 by 60 feet), all aligned to the west of Military Road between the two forts.

Gosport also served as an NLG1, first for 50(HD) Squadron from August to December 1916, then for 78(HD) Squadron from July to September 1917, and finally for 39(HD) Squadron until the end of the war. It was training where Gosport would make its mark, thanks to Major R. R. Smith-Barry who, after taking command of 1 TS, began to introduce a range of revolutionary ideas that would shape the flying training methods later adopted by the RAF. The result was the Special School of Flying (SSoF), which was created by disbanding 1, 25 and 55 TS into the service's first *ab initio* unit. During 39(HD) Squadron's tenure here, 'E' Flight was donated to create another influential unit, the School of Aerial Co-operation with Coastal Defence Batteries, with twelve BE.12s on strength. Subjects included experimental work with searchlights and sound locaters, working closely with the Royal Engineer School of Electric Lighting at Stokes Bay.

Fort Grange provides the backdrop for Camel B5157, which served with 'F' Flight of the School of Special Flying. *Via Ray Sturtivant*

The SSoF was redesignated No 1 SSoF in May 1918, then the Southwest Area FIS in July, by which time Smith-Barry had been posted out. However, what he had created laid the foundations of the syllabus for the RAF's CFS. Despite some doubt about the aerodrome's post-war future, Gosport grew from strength to strength and remained an active airfield until it was closed down in May 1956. The First World War structures were gone by the 1930s when the site was expanded and upgraded, and the hangars seen there today are of this vintage.

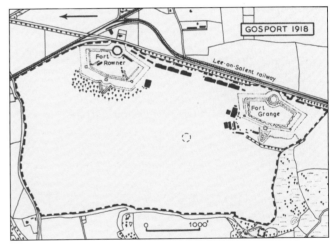

Serving with 28 Squadron, based at Gosport during 1916, this FE.2B most likely served in a training role, before being written off on 12th October 1916. © *Inkworm.com*

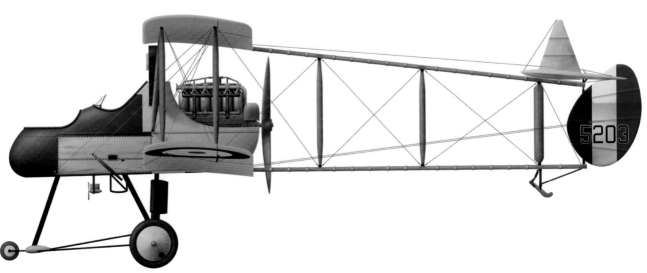

Gosport main units, 1914-20

5 Sqn from Netheravon, 6 Jul 1914;
to Dover (Swingate Down), 18 Aug 1914 (various aircraft)

1 Sqn RNAS reformed 15 Oct 1914;
to Dover (Guston Road), 28 Jan 1915 (various aircraft)

8 Sqn from Brooklands, 6 Jan 1915;
to St Omer, 15 Apr 1915 (BE.2A/B/C)

13 Sqn formed 10 Jan 1915;
to St Omer, 19 Oct 1915 (BE.2C and Scout)

17 Sqn formed 1 Feb 1915;
to Hounslow, 5 Aug 1915 (BE.2C)

14 Sqn from Hounslow, 5 Aug 1915;
en-route to Egypt, 7 Nov 1915 (BE.2C)

22 Sqn formed 1 Sep 1915;
to St Omer, 1 Apr 1916 (various aircraft)

23 Sqn formed 1 Sep 1915;
to St Omer, 15 Mar 1916 (various aircraft)

28 Sqn formed 7 Nov 1915;
to Yatesbury, 23 Jul 1917 (various aircraft)

29 Sqn formed 7 Nov 1915;
to St Omer, 25 Mar 1916 (various aircraft)

31 Sqn 'B' Flt formed from 22 Sqn, 18 Jan 1916;
to Risalpur, 1 Mar 1916 (BE.2C and F.27)

40 Sqn formed 26 Feb 1916;
to St Omer, 19 Aug 1916 (BE.2C, 504 and FE.8)

45 Sqn formed 1 Mar 1916;
to Thetford, 3 May 1916
(504, S.1, BE.2C, Scout and F.2B)

1 TS from Farnborough, 7 Apr 1916;
DB into SSoF, Gosport, 2 Aug 1917 (various aircraft)

41 Sqn formed 15 Apr 1916;
DB, renumbered 27 RS, 22 May 1916

31 Sqn 'C' Flt formed from HD Brigade, 10 May 1916;
to Murree, 4 Jul 1916 (BE.2C)

60 Sqn formed 16 May 1916;
to St Omer, 28 May 1916 (Morane H)

27 TS (ex-41 Sqn) formed 22 May 1916;
absorbed into SSoF, 2 Aug 1917
(Longhorn, Shorthorn, F.20 and FE.2B)

56 Sqn formed 9 Jun 1916;
to London Colney, 14 Jul 1916 (various aircraft)

41 Sqn reformed 14 Jul 1916;
to St Omer, 15 Oct 1916 (FB.5, DH.2 and FE.8)

81 Sqn formed 7 Jan 1917;
to Scampton, 1 Aug 1917 (various aircraft)

87 (Canadian) TS formed from 28 RS, 9 Feb 1917;
to Beaulieu, 28 Feb 1917 (JN.4)

59 TS formed 1 Feb 1917;
to Yatesbury, 30 Apr 1917 (DH.1, FE.2 and FE.2D)

91 (Canadian) TS formed from 27 RS, 15 Mar 1917;
to Armour Heights, 15 Jun 1917 (JN.3)

62 TS formed from 1 RS, 1 May 1917;
to Yatesbury, 10 May 1917 (various aircraft)

55 TS from Yatesbury 23 Jul 1917;
DB into SSoF, 2 Aug 1917
(504, Scout, DH.5, Pup and Nieuport)

88 Sqn formed from 1 TS, 24 Jul 1917;
to Harling Road, 2 Aug 1917 (various aircraft)

79 Sqn formed from 27 TS, 1 Aug 1917;
to Beaulieu, 8 Aug 1917 (various aircraft)

School of Special Flying formed 2 Aug 1917;
redesignated 1 SSoF, 18 May 1918
(Camel, Pup, Dolphin, F2.B, 504A/J/K, 1½ Strutter and DH.4)

70 TS from Netheravon, 20 Dec 1917;
to Beaulieu, 1 Jan 1918 (various aircraft)

39 Sqn 'E' Flt detached from North Weald, Jan 1918;
absorbed into School of Aerial Co-Operation with Coastal
defence Batteries, 31 Jan 1918 (F.2B)

School of Aerial Co-Operation with Coastal Artillery formed
31 Jan 1918;
to Cowes, Sep 1918 (BE.2E and BE.12)

1 SSoF (ex-SSoF) formed 1 May 1918;
redesignated SW Area FIS Camel, 1 Jul 1918
(Pup, Dolphin, F2.B, 504 and 1½ Stutter)

Special Experimental Flight formed 16 May 1918;
DB May 1919 (BE.2E, FK.8, F2.B, DH.4 and 504K)

South Western Area FIS formed 1 Jul 1918 from 3 flts of
1 SSoF in 8 Group;
DB 26 Feb 1919

Development Sqn formed 17 Aug 1918;
redesignated Development Flight RAF, Gosport,
Feb 1920 (Cuckoo and DH.4)

Special Duties Flt formed on/by 31 Aug 1918 (Cuckoo)

Special Defence Flt formed 5 Oct 1918;
DB 28 Dec 1918

HQ RAF Gosport formed 23 Oct 1918;
DB Jun 1919

10 TS from Lilbourne, 25 Jun 1918;
DB 24 Feb 1919 (various aircraft)

Gosport (Marine)

50°47'45"N/01°06'58"W, SU624000. King Charles Fort,
0.2 miles E of Gosport town centre

THIS was the location of slipways that were used by the
Gosport Aviation Co Ltd during 1918.

Hamble

Avro factory: 50°51'36"N/01°19'38"W, SU475068. In NE region of Ensign Way, 0.25 miles W of Hamble-le-Rice
MAD: 50°51'15"N/01°19'25"W, SU477062. SE corner of oil terminal, 0.4 miles SSW of Hamble-le-Rice

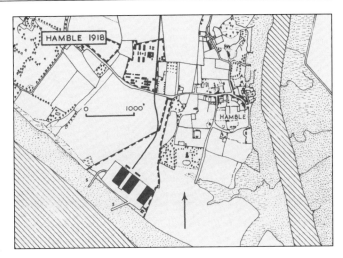

HAMBLE can trace its association with aircraft back to 1912, when experienced yacht-builders Hamble River Luke & Co designed and built the large 60-foot-span HL1 seaplane. However, it would not leave the water when tested by Gordon England in 1914, thanks to the floats being designed like yacht hulls.

In 1916 A. V. Roe expressed a wish to establish a new testing facility for seaplanes that would require a waterside location. Several different locations were visited in Lancashire, and at least one near Brighton, until an ideal site was found at Hamble on the edge of Southampton Water. Alliott had big plans for the Hamble site, which not only included a brand-new purpose-built works but also a garden city for Avro employees. The project progressed to the point of a few hangars and twenty-four houses before Alliott was forced to bring a halt to proceedings because of the demand for wartime building materials. Hamble would only aspire to being an experimental shop for the remainder of the war under the charge of General Manager R. J. Parrott, who joined Alliott in 1909 as an assistant and draughtsman. By 1919 aircraft production was moved to Manchester, but the site remained in Avro hands until 1934, when it was sold to Air Service Training.

In early 1918 construction work of a new site to the southeast of the Avro factory began in the shape of a new Marine Acceptance Depot. Twelve Seaplane Sheds (180 by 85 feet)

were built, together with two slipways, although it is possible that not all of the sheds were actually completed by the end of the war. Occupying 46 acres, the entire site measured 500 by 450 yards and was officially opened as 1 (Southern) MAD on 22 April 1918. The MAD was established to accept a wide range of seaplanes and flying boats from several companies such as Brush Electrical Engineering Co Ltd, S. E. Saunders Ltd (Short), May, Harden & May (Hythe) (F.2A), Supermarine Aviation Works, Norman Thompson (NT.2B), the Gosport Aviation Co (FBA), Robey & Co Ltd (Short), and White (NT.2B).

The MAD was disbanded on 17 November 1919, but the airfield, which later expanded on the north side of Hamble Lane, enjoyed a long and varied career that came to end in 1986.

Avro staff of at the Hamble Works smile for the camera in early 1917, in the first Avro 523 'The Pike'.

Two of only five B.E.2As, Nos 49 and 50, that served with the RNAS are pictured at Hilsea (Cosham) during the Royal Review in July 1914. *Via Stuart Leslie*

Hilsea (aka Cosham)

50°49'39"N/00°03'24"W, SU665035. In the region of the Admiral Park industrial area, SE of Hilsea railway station

THIS was a temporary LG for the use of RNAS flying machines taking part in the Naval Review at Spithead in July 1914.

Lee-on-Solent Seaplane Station is seen in its prime in early 1918 just before the seaplane school became 209 TDS. The group of larger Seaplane Sheds in the upper centre of this image are now the home of the Hovercraft Museum Trust. *Via Stuart Leslie*

Hythe (Southampton Water)

50°52'00"N/01°23'15"W, SU427076. Hythe Marine Park off Shore Road, 0.4 miles SE of Hythe

MAY, Harden & May established a large factory here in 1917 for the production of the large Felixstowe flying-boat, and a single slipway that could only be used at high tide. The company went on to build seventy-one Felixstowe F.2As, the first of which, N4510, was delivered in January 1918. A follow-up order for fifty F.5s was cancelled, but orders for twenty Porte Baby and two Phoenix hulls were also completed in 1918. The final task carried out by May, Harden & May was the construction of the Fairey Atalanta hull in 1919.

The site was later taken over by Supermarine, and served as a maintenance base for Imperial Airways and BOAC from 1937 until 1950. RAF Hythe was in the hands of the USAF from 1967 until 2006. Today all surviving buildings, which are many, are maintained in good condition.

Lee-on-Solent (Gosport)

50°48'28"N/01°12'30"W, SU558011. Off Marine Parade West, part of site occupied by Hovercraft Museum Trust, due S of ex-RNAS Lee-on-Solent (aka MCA Daedalus Aerodrome), 0.5 miles NW of Lee-on-Solent

OCCUPYING just 30 acres, Lee-on-Solent grew into one of the most famous RNAS, RAF and later FAA airfields, as it was expanded into a considerably larger site that remained active into the 21st century.

The site's history began in 1917 when it became a seaplane station complete with a sub-station at Calshot. The first unit here was the RNAS Seaplane School, formed on 30 July 1917. Hangarage was under canvas at first, but by the time the school

Looking down on the junction of Marine Parade West and Richmond Road, camouflaged Bessonneaus stand on the right. *Via Stuart Leslie*
A 209 TDS NT.2B is unceremoniously recovered after it crashed on landing off Lee-on-Solent.

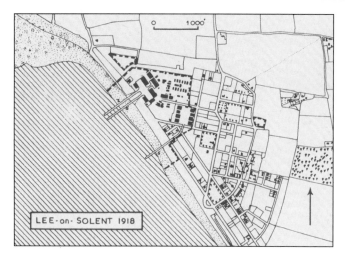

LEE-on-SOLENT 1918

had been redesignated as 209 TDS the site had two Type G Seaplane Sheds (180 by 60 feet), six Seaplane Sheds (60 by 48 feet) and three slipways. The TDS was made up of two training squadrons, one training pupils on seaplanes and the other on small flying-boats. The TDS could handle up to 100 pupils at any one time, and an average course lasted seven to eight weeks, which saw thirty to forty pupils passing out every month. Aircraft types at Lee-on-Solent included the Short 184, NT.2B, FBA and the sole Sage Type 4A, making on average up to forty-eight flying-boats and twenty-four seaplanes on strength.

209 TDS was redesignated as the RAF & Navy Co-operation School on 16 June 1919, then again to the RAF Seaplane Establishment on 14 July, before leaving for Calshot in December. The site was then placed under Care & Maintenance from December 1919 to June 1920, and rather than be closed down it was reopened and destined to remain in RAF and later Royal Navy hands, being commissioned HMS *Daedalus* in 1939. The site was given up by the Royal Navy in 1996, but today remains an active aerodrome. The First World War site was used by the Joint Service Hovercraft Unit in the 1960s, and today is appropriately occupied by the Hovercraft Museum Trust. Thanks to a long military occupation, both Type G sheds and at least two Seaplane Sheds are extant as part of the museum, together with several surviving early buildings around the site.

Lee-on-Solent main units, 1917-32

RNAS Seaplane School formed 30 Jul 1917;
redesignated 209 TDS, 1 Apr 1918

209 TDS (ex-RNAS Seaplane School) 1 Apr 1918;
redesignated RAF & Navy Co-operation School, 16 Jun 1919
(Short 184, NT.2B, FBA and Sage 4A)

RAF & Naval Co-operation School (ex-209 and 210 TDS),
16 Jun 1919;
redesignated RAF Seaplane Establishment, 14 Jul 1919
(Short 184 and NT.2B)

RAF Seaplane Establishment 14 Jul 1919;
to Calshot, Dec 1919

10 Group HQ from Warsash, 12 Jul 1920;
DB 18 Jan 1932

Lopcombe Corner

51°07'07"N/01°36'49"W, SU272354. E of Hollom Down Road, N of A30 at Testwood Farm, 1.3 miles E of Lopcombe Corner (Wiltshire)

CONSTRUCTED for training from the outset, Lopcombe Corner was opened for 3 TDS, formed here on 5 September 1917. Prior to this, the three flights that would form the nucleus of the new TDS arrived on 22 August 1917; these were 'A' Flight of 54 TS from Harlaxton, 'B' Flight of 28 Squadron from Yatesbury, and 'C' Flight of 62 TS from Dover.

The aerodrome occupied 228 acres and measured 1,250 by 850 yards, with buildings located on the western side of Hollom Down Road and the main technical site and flying field on the eastern side. Seven 1918-pattern GS Sheds (170 by 100 feet) were constructed, and this typically busy TDS site saw 29 acres of the aerodrome covered in various buildings. Tasked with carrying out single-seat fighter training, the TDS had thirty-six 504s and the same number of Camels on strength by 1918, and was staffed by more than 800 male and female personnel.

The TDS was redesignated 3 TS with only 504Ks on strength in May 1919, only to be disbanded on 20 June. Four squadrons, beginning with 74 Squadron in November, spent several months here as cadres, with the exception of 91 Squadron, which brought its Dolphins from Kenley in March, but was disbanded the same day as 3 TS. 52 Squadron cadre was Lopcombe's last unit when it was disbanded on 23 October 1919. Relinquished by early 1920, the site was briefly reused by a few US Army L-4s in 1944.

Today several First World War-era buildings survive on both sides of Hollom Down Road, and one GS Shed base is now used by Noons scrapyard.

Lopcombe Corner main units, 1917-19

3 TDS formed 5 Sep 1917;
redesignated 3 TS, 15 May 1919
(Camel, 504, Pup, DH.5, DH.6 and BE.2E)

154th Aero Sqn, USAAS, from Larkhill, 19 Mar 1918;
to Winchester, 30 Aug 1918

3 TS (ex-3 TDS), 15 May 1919;
DB 20 Jun 1919 (504K)

74 Sqn from Halluin as cadre, 30 Nov 1918;
DB 3 Jul 1919 (no aircraft)

85 Sqn from Ascq as cadre, 7 Dec 1918;
DB 3 Jul 1919 (no aircraft)

91 Sqn from Kenley, 7 Mar 1919;
DB 3 Jul 1919 (Dolphin)

52 Sqn from Netheravon as cadre, 28 Jun 1919;
DB 23 Oct 1919 (no aircraft)

Northam

50°54'47"N/01°22'55"W, SU435129. In general area of European Metal Recycling Ltd, 1 mile from Southampton town centre

THIS was the location of slipways once used by Camper & Nicolson and Gosport Aviation Ltd.

Tipner

50°49'N/01°05'W, SU63-03-. Close to Seamanship Training Centre, 1 mile NW of Portsmouth town centre

THE home of No 15 Balloon Base, formed here on 15 April 1918, Tipner occupied 12 acres on the eastern side of Portsmouth Harbour. Equipped with six Balloon Sheds (100 by 36 feet), this small station was run by 25 officers, 7 SNCOs, 15 JNCOs and 135 other ranks. The six balloons stationed here were employed for convoy patrol duties and general cooperation with the Royal Navy, all under the control of the C-in-C Portsmouth.

No 15 Balloon Base was disbanded on 16 October 1919, but the site remained in military hands and today is a rifle range and partly covered by the Seamanship Training Centre.

Woolston

50°53'58"N/01°22'58"W, SU435108. E of Victoria Road, 0.25 miles S of Itchen bridge, E of Woolston

THE name 'Supermarine' was created by Noel Pemberton Billing back in 1913, who, thankfully for the future of British aviation, made the wise decision to build 'boats that will fly, and not just aeroplanes with floats!'

The first flying-boat designed and built by Pemberton Billing was the P.B.1. The single-engined tractor-arrangement aircraft was very pleasing to the eye with its cigar-shaped hull, and made its first public appearance in March 1914.

On the outbreak of war Pemberton Billing responded to the national requirement for a single-seat fighting scout. The result was the P.B.9, an aircraft that was designed and built in a short period of time but not, as implied by its nickname, the 'Seven Day Bus'.

From 1914 Hubert Scott-Paine became the works manager, and from 1916, with Pemberton Billing concentrating on his political career, he became managing director. The same year the company was renamed the Supermarine Aviation Works Ltd, established on the banks of the River Itchen at Woolston, Southampton.

During the war, like so many other fledgling aircraft manufacturers, early aircraft orders were subcontracted from other companies that could not cope, including, in Supermarine's case, Short Brothers. The company also carried out experimental work for the Admiralty, including the Push-Proj in 1915, a single-seat pusher scout. The following year a pair of novel quadruplane landplanes was also designed to deal with the threat of the Zeppelin. 1916 also saw the arrival of the company's most influential aircraft designer, Reginald J. Mitchell, who was partly responsible for the N.1B Baby, Supermarine's most successful design of the First World War.

The Supermarine works on the River Itchen, at Woolston, Southampton, in early 1918. To the left is the Billing yacht basin and on the right an A.D. flying-boat is prepared for launching. *Aeroplane*

Worthy Down

51°06'56"N/01°19'55"W, SU468353. Due S of South Wonston, 3.75 miles NNW of Winchester

A SUBSTANTIAL aerodrome, Worthy Down was opened in January 1918 for the flying element of the Artillery & Infantry Co-Operation Squadron (ex-Wireless & Observers School) for the school of the same name that had been formed at Hursley Park on 12 October 1917. It was here that the RFC reconnaissance pilots graduated after passing through their TDS training. At Worthy Down the pilots received instruction in artillery and infantry cooperation, particularly map-reading and contact patrols over a two-to-three-week period. Future reconnaissance observers also passed through the squadron for a week's training.

Occupying 438 acres, Worthy Down measured 1,200 by 1,800 yards and was furnished with the same amount of technical and domestic buildings as a TDS. This included six Aeroplane Sheds (180 by 100 feet) and an ARS Shed with a pair of aeroplane stores (180 by 100 feet). Personnel strength was also large, including 123 officers, 432 officer pupils, 54 SNCOs, 27 JNCOS and 573 other ranks.

It was redesignated as the RAF & Army Co-Operation School, and again as the School of Army Co-Operation, until it was disbanded on 8 March 1920. Worthy Down was one of the few post-war survivors and would become instrumental as one of the centres where the RAF would grow again during the crucial pre-Second World War expansion period. The airfield passed to the Royal Navy during the post-war period, until its closure in 1960.

Worthy Down main units, 1918-19

Artillery & Infantry Co-Operation Squadron (flying element) from Hursley Park, Jan 1918;
redesignated RAF & Army Co-Operation School, 19 Sep 1918 (RE.8, 504, F.2B, BE.2D/E, FK.3, FK.8, DH.9 and Camel).

RAF & Army Co-Operation School
(ex-Army & Infantry Co-Operation School) 19 Sep 1918;
redesignated School of Army Co-Operation,
23 Dec 1919 (BE.2C, RE.8 and DH.9).

School of Army Co-Operation
(ex-RAF & Army Co-Operation School) 3 Dec 1919;
DB 8 Mar 1920 (BE.2, RE.8, F.2B, DH.4 and FK.8)

HERTFORDSHIRE

Bishops Hatfield

51°47'12"N/00°14'16"W, TL216112. 0.5 miles W of Stanborough off Green Lanes, 2 miles SW of Welwyn Garden City centre

A N HD NLG, the site of Bishops Hatfield was not well chosen for aviation and was only open from April to October 1916 because it was prone to fog. Allocated to 39(HD) Squadron and under the control of 18th Wing and HD Wing (Eastern) during 1918, there is little evidence of use.

Hertford (Ware)

51°48'03"N/00°02'50"W, TL347132. Pine Hurst Estate and Chadwell Springs Golf Club off Ware Road (A119), bisected by A10, 1.5 miles ENE of Hertford

H ERTFORD had its first tenuous connection with aviation when it was one of the turning points for the *Daily Mail* Air Races in 1913 and 1914. Whether the location was the same as the HD NLG 2 that was opened at Hertford on the eastern side of the town in October 1916 is unclear. Used by 39(HD) Squadron, the site was reclassified as an NLG3 in January 1917, but was abandoned by mid-1918 in favour of Stanstead Abbots. Today the site is split by the A10, part covered by a golf course to the north-east and housing to the south-west.

London Colney

51°42'22"N/00°17'40"W, TL178021. Due E of Harperbury Hospital, W of B5378, 1.4 miles E of Colney Street

N ESTLING between heavy woodland and with an undulating flying field, London Colney was not one of best locations for an aerodrome. Later finished with three 1915-pattern Flight Sheds (210 by 65 feet) and two 1917-pattern GS Sheds (170 by 100 feet), London Colney occupied 212 acres and measured 1,050 by 1,000 yards. Opened as an HD NLG2 for the use of 36(HD) Squadron and later 44(HD) Squadron in April 1916, the site was first occupied by one of the RFC's famous units, 56 Squadron, which moved in from Gosport on 14 July. Another well-known unit, 54 Squadron, also passed through in December, bound for St Omer and a busy war in Northern France. 56 Squadron, which was operating a variety of aircraft until March 1917, was not moulded into a fighter unit until February when, among others, Capt Albert Ball arrived. Already the RFC's leading ace, Ball departed with the squadron on 5 April 1917, but sadly the VC-winner was killed one month later.

This panorama of London Colney during 56 TS's tenure in October 1917 shows all three of the aerodrome's 1915-pattern Flight Sheds.

Just before 56 Squadron's departure, 56 TS was formed here on 7 February with a typical mix of aircraft ranging from the BE.2 to the Camel. The aerodrome was now classified as a TSS, but London Colney would grow into a TDS, thanks to 56 TS providing the core for 41 TDS on 15 July 1918. The TDS was tasked with training pilots to fly single-seat fighters, and the main equipment was twenty-four Avro 504s and the same number of Snipes, although a variety of other types also appeared on the unit's inventory. 41 TDS remained at London Colney until it was disbanded in November 1919, having been redesignated as 41 TS only the previous month. Relinquished in early 1920, the site was quickly run down that same year.

Considering that the site is within the M25 today, virtually all of it is undeveloped. Only 1.5 miles to the north-west is the old Handley Page airfield at Radlett, and 1 mile to the east sits Salisbury Hall, the birthplace of one of the greatest combat aircraft of all time, the Mosquito.

This often-published photo shows Capt Albert Ball VC, DSO**, MC in R.A.F. SE.5 A4850 of 56 Squadron at London Colney; note the immaculate and well-constructed Flight Sheds in the background.

London Colney main units, 1916-19

56 Sqn from Gosport, 14 Jul 1916;
to St Omer, 5 Apr 1917 (various aircraft and SE.5)

45 TS formed 2 Nov 1916;
to South Carlton, 13 Nov 1916
(Henry Farman, FB.5/9, DH.5 and FE.8)

54 Sqn from Castle Bromwich, 22 Dec 1916;
to St Omer, 24 Dec 1916 (Pup)

56 TS formed 7 Feb 1917;
DB into 41 TDS, 15 Jun 1918
(BE.2/E, 504, SPAD, Pup, SE.5A, Camel and Scout D)

74 Sqn from Northolt, 10 Jul 1917;
to Goldhangar, 25 Mar 1918 (various aircraft)

92 Sqn formed (nucleus from 56 TS), 1 Sep 1917;
to Chattis Hill, 14 Sep 1917 (Pup)

24th Aero Sqn, USAAS, detached from Wye, 31 Jan 1918;
to Wye, 7 Mar 1918

27 TS reformed, 22 Mar 1918;
DB into 21 TDS, 15 Jul 1918
(Dolphin, 504A/J, Pup, SPAD S.VII and SE.5A)

41 TDS (ex-56 TS) formed 15 Jul 1918;
redesignated 41 TS, Oct 1919
(Snipe, 504J/K, SE.5A, Pup, DH.6, DH.9, Camel and SPAD S.VII)

24 Sqn cadre from Bisseghem, 12 Feb 1919;
to Uxbridge, 19 Sep 1919

1 Sqn cadre from Izel-le-Hameau, 1 Mar 1919;
to Uxbridge, 10 Sep 1919

41 TS (ex-41 TDS) reformed Oct 1919;
DB Nov 1919 (504K)

Sawbridgeworth I

51°49'04"N/00°08'45"W, TL480154. W of Cambridge Road (A1184), N of West Road, Sawbridgeworth

ON the immediate north-western edge of the village, the first Sawbridgeworth aerodrome opened as an HD NLG for 39(HD) Squadron in April 1916. Its premature closure in the autumn of that year may have been because of its close proximity to the village, and an alternative site was surveyed north-east of Tharbies Farm (51°49'38"N/00°08'20"W), but was not taken up. Sawbridgeworth occupied 57 acres and measured 500 by 400 yards, and was abandoned when a better alternative was found west of Shingle Hall.

Sawbridgeworth II

51°50'15"N/00°07'04"W, TL459177. W of Shingle Hall, S of Parsonage Lane, 2.2 miles NW of Sawbridgeworth

THE second aerodrome to be named Sawbridgeworth was quickly opened in the autumn of 1916, replacing the site much closer to the village. Occupying 31 acres and measuring 450 by 300 yards, the main occupant was once again 39(HD) Squadron. Classified as an HD NLG2, the site remained open until June 1919 and was later swallowed up by RAF Sawbridgeworth, which was active from 1937 to 1947.

Stanstead Abbots (Stanstead St Margarets)

51°46'56"N/00°01'09"W, TL393112. SE of Netherfield House off B181, 0.85 miles SE of St Margarets railway station

CLASSIFIED as an NLG2, Stanstead Abbots was established during early 1918 for the use of 39(HD) Squadron operating out of North Weald with the F.2B; it occupied 48 acres and measured 500 by 450 yards. 39(HD) Squadron would have stopped using the site from November 1918 following its disbandment, and the site was later relinquished in May 1919.

Therfield (Heath Farm/Baldock)

52°01'00"N/00°05'59"W, TL304371. SE of Heath Farm off Chain Walk, 2 miles W of Therfield, 4.3 miles NE of Baldock

A DETACHMENT from 75(HD) Squadron made use of this small LG from 1917, initially with the BE.2C, the BE.12 and, before the unit relocated to Elmswell, the BE.2E. Measuring approximately 500 by 350 yards, Therfield was relinquished before the end of the war.

Willian (Hitchin)

51°58'05"N/00°13'15"W, SE066355. Off Wymondley Road, 0.75 miles S of Willian, 1 mile NE of Great Wymondley

T HE name of Willian gained its first aviation connection on 6 September 1912 when Capt P. Hamilton and Lt A. W. Stuart of 3 Squadron RFC crashed their Deperdussin Monoplane close to the Wymondley Road. Sadly the duo was killed, but an impressive memorial can be seen on the side of the road, close to where the aircraft fell.

Willian opened as a DLG, but by 1916 had been reclassified as a DLG2 because of an incident that took place on the night of 1 October. Eleven Zeppelins set out that day to attack various targets from Lincolnshire down to London, including *L24*, which crossed the Norfolk coast at 1005hrs. By 0100hrs *L24* had decided to attack London, but not before the airship was drawn to the lit flares at Willian, where the Zeppelin dropped its first bomb at 0114hrs. Twenty-six high-explosive and twenty-six incendiaries were dropped along a line 2.5 miles long from Willian to Weston before the airship made its escape. Very little damage was done, but one man was killed, Private William Hawkes of the Royal Defence Corps; he was buried in his home village of Stopsley. One of the potential reasons why the captain of the *L24* dropped his bombs where he did may have been influenced by the loss of *L31* that night near Potters Bar; rather than suffer a similar fate, *L24* chose Willian as a target of opportunity and fled!

Willian occupied 46 acres and measured 480 by 410 yards. It was closed down by early 1919.

KENT

All Hallows (Sheerness)

51°28'13"N/00°38'20"W, TQ831775. 0.3 miles due W of All Hallows (All Saints) church, S of Radcliffe Highway

T HIS NLG2 (later NLG3) was located west of the small village of All Hallows and was opened in October 1916. The LG was allocated to 50(HD) Squadron, which had just moved to Harrietsham with the BE.2C, BE.12 and Vickers ES.1. Under the control of Eastern Group Command by 1917, All Hallows took up 32 acres and measured 530 by 530 yards.

On 1 February 1918 control of All Hallows was passed to the FK.8-equipped 143 Squadron at Throwley, which moved to Detling on 14 February, where it re-equipped with the SE.5A.

Overall control of the LG passed to 53rd (HD) Wing, and expansion took place to accommodate No 1 Balloon Training Base, which was formed on 14 April 1918. Operating under No 1 Balloon Training Wing, the unit worked closely with local Royal Navy units, until it moved to Merifield on 31 July 1919. Notification prior to this date of All Hallows's impending closure came in May 1919, making No 1 Balloon Training Base the last unit to operate from this small LG.

Bekesbourne

51°15'17"N/01°09'28"W, TR202553. Between Adisham Road and Canterbury to Dover railway line, 0.75 miles ESE of Bekesbourne, 3.75 miles SE of Canterbury

B EKESBOURNE was built as an HD Flight Station, complete with a pair of coupled HD-pattern Aeroplane Sheds (60 by 135 feet). With the arrival of 50(HD) Squadron from Swingate Down in September 1916, accommodation for this large unit's inventory of aircraft was found lacking and a further 1918-pattern GS Shed (170 by 100 feet), complete with office annex, was erected.

A Sopwith Camel of 50(HD) Squadron at Bekesbourne in 1918.

When first opened in April 1916, Bekesbourne was classified as an NLG1, taking up 98 acres and measuring 1,160 by 450 yards. 50(HD) Squadron was the main unit throughout the aerodrome's existence, although 56 Squadron also passed through in April and May 1917, destined for fame and success over Northern France.

Closed down in June 1919, today the technical site has been taken over by housing on what is now known as Aerodrome Road. A memorial to RFC/RAF Bekesbourne has been erected off this road, very close to where the HD-pattern sheds were located. The flying field, which still remains today, was briefly used by the Lysanders of 13 Squadron in May 1940 when they returned from a mauling in France.

Bekesbourne main units, 1916-19

50 (HD) Sqn 'B' Flt from Dover (Swingate Downs),
1 Sep 1916; DB 13 Jun 1919 (various aircraft)

56 Sqn HQ, 'B' and 'C' Flts from Liettres, 21 Jun 1917;
to Estrée Blanche, 5 Jul 1917 (SE.5A)

56 Sqn 'A' Flt from Rochford, 4 Jul 1917;
to Estrée Blanche, 5 Jul 1917 (BE.12, SE.5A and Camel)

50 (HD) Sqn 'C' Flt from Harrietsham, 8 Feb 1918;
DB 13 Jun 1919 (BE.12A/B, SE.5A and Camel)

50 (HD) Sqn 'A' Flt from Detling, 8 Feb 1918;
DB 13 Jun 1919 (BE.12A/B, SE.5A and Camel)

50 (HD) Sqn from Harrietsham, 5 Mar 1918;
DB 13 Jun 1919 (BE.12A/B, SE.5A and Camel)

Biggin Hill (Westerham)

51°19'42"N/00°01'44"W, TQ415607. On current London Biggin Hill Airport site, 1.2 miles NNW of Biggin Hill, 4.3 miles SW of Orpington

THIS famous airfield started out as an 80-acre HD NLG1 for the use of 50(HD) Squadron from April 1916, but was soon expanded to 115 acres when it was upgraded to HD Flight Station and Squadron Station status from December 1917. Hangars were erected on the north-western and southern boundaries in the shape of three 1918-pattern GS Sheds (170 by 80 feet), one 1917-pattern GS Shed (170 by 80 feet) and a single Aeroplane Shed (135 by 60 feet). By this stage 35 acres of the site were covered in buildings and the aerodrome measured 1,120 by 560 yards.

One of the earliest permanent units stationed here was the Wireless Testing Park, which arrived from Joyce Green in January 1917. Biggin Hill would be at the centre of wireless telephony experiments into the 1920s, and a specialist RFC, later RAF, Radio Signals Unit was established here. Under Air Ministry control, the unit was renamed the Wireless Experimental Establishment, and was tasked with all experimental work for wireless telegraphy and telephony equipment for the RAF.

141 Squadron brought its F.2Bs here from Rochford on 8 February 1918, the unit being tasked with wireless telephony and anti-aircraft co-operation duties. It was joined by 140 Squadron, which was formed here on 1 May 1918, bringing the total number of F.2Bs on station to twenty-four. Station strength was now 40 officers, 19 SNCOs, 18 JNCOs, 166 other ranks and 29 women. 140 Squadron was disbanded on 4 July 1918, but 141 Squadron remained until 1 March 1919, when it moved across the Irish Sea to Tallaght.

R.A.F. RE.8 C7001 of the Wireless Experimental Establishment at Biggin Hill in early 1918.

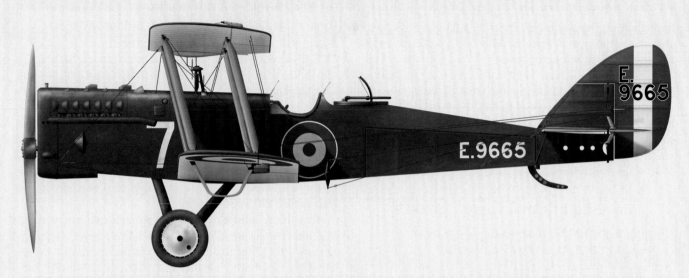

One of a batch of 100 DH.9A constructed by Mann Egerton & Co. Ltd, Norwich, 'E9665' was supplied to the Wireless Experimental Establishment at Biggin Hill in September 1918 and used for trials. © *Inkworm.com*

This interesting collection of uniforms includes remnants of the RFC, the new RAF, the Royal Navy (ex-RNAS) and the Army, represented by these officers of the W/T Establishment at Biggin Hill.

RAF Biggin Hill's rich history continued until 1958, when it ceased to be an operational station, but the RAF remained until 1992, when the Aircrew Selection Centre moved to Cranwell. Following Croydon's closure in 1959, civilian aircraft began to make use of the airfield, which has bloomed into London Biggin Hill Airport.

Biggin Hill main units, 1917-18

Wireless Testing Park from Joyce Green, 1 Jan 1917; redesignated Wireless Experimental Establishment (BE.2E, 1½ Strutter, F.K.8, RE.7 and Pup)

39 Sqn 'D' Flt from Woodford Green, 1 Dec 1917; redesignated 78 Sqn, 11 Dec 1917 (BE.2C/E, BE.12 and F.2B)

78 Sqn (ex-39 Sqn 'D' Flt) 11 Dec 1917; absorbed into 141 Sqn (possibly 1½ Strutter)

Wireless Experimental Establishment (ex-Wireless Testing Park) 14 Dec 1917; redesignated W/T Establishment, 2 Apr 1918 (various aircraft)

141 Sqn from Rochford, 8 Feb 1918; to Tallaght, 1 Mar 1919 (Dolphin, BE.2E, BE.12, Pup, FB.26 and F.2B)

W/T Establishment formed 2 Apr 1918; redesignated Instrument Design Establishment, 1 Nov 1919 (various aircraft)

140 Sqn formed 1 May 1918; DB 4 Jul 1918 (F.2B)

The interior of one of Capel's Airship Sheds, which was designed to accommodate a *Beta*-Type airship rather than the larger SS-Type. As a result a trench had to be dug down the middle of the shed for the SS-Type's gondola to fit into! *Via Stuart Leslie*

Broad Salts (Sandwich)

51°17'13"N/01°21'36"W, TR345594. 0.5 miles E of Stonar Lake, 1.2 miles NE of Sandwich

UNSURPRISINGLY prone to flooding because of its salt marsh environment, Broad Salts still managed to remain open from October 1916 through to late 1918. An HD NLG2, the aerodrome measured 700 by 400 yards and was solely used by 50(HD) Squadron based at Harrietsham.

Broomfield (Herne Bay)

51°21'29"N/01°09'57"W, TR204668. 0.6 miles E of Broomfield, 2 miles from Herne Bay town centre S of A299, Thanet Way

THIS 30-acre HD NLG3 was another aerodrome allocated to 50(HD) Squadron, between October 1916 and June 1919. The landing area was initially recorded as 550 by 350 yards when first laid out, but a 53rd Wing report in 1918 reduced this to 400 by 300 yards. Broomfield was relinquished on 13 August 1919.

Capel (Capel-le-Ferne/Folkestone)

51°06'17"N/01°13'30"W, TR259389. Bisected by New Dover Road (B2011), part covered by Blue Channel Caravan Park, between Satmar and Abbot's Farm, 2.75 miles NE of Folkestone

BUILT quickly in response to the increasing German U-boat threat to shipping passing through the Dover Straits, Capel was opened as a Class C Airship Station on 8 May 1915. With sub-stations at Boulogne, Godmersham Park and Wittersham, operations were first carried out by ex-Army *Beta*, *Delta* and *Gamma* airships, but Capel would later become one of the biggest assembly stations for the successful SS-Type airships.

A portable Airship Shed under construction at Capel in October 1915, after it was moved from Dunkerque. *Via Stuart Leslie*

Capel grew rapidly, the entire site occupying 124 acres and measuring 960 by 780 yards. Three Airship Sheds were built: No 1 was 306 by 39 by 48 feet, No 2 was 311 by 44 by 51 feet, and No 3 measured 322 by 70 by 60 feet. As the site grew, a large hutted domestic site was built close to the Royal Oak Inn.

While Capel was an excellent location for airship operations, it was also found to be exposed to the enemy. This was proven on 23 January 1916 when a German seaplane dropped five bombs, narrowly missing one of the airship sheds. Intensive airship patrols were flown from Capel and its sub-stations, although very rarely was a U-boat spotted, which can be credited to the continuous presence of the airships. Attacks were made, but the only confirmed success was achieved by *SSZ1* on 16 September 1918, which sank *UB-103*.

By August 1920 the site was run down and in the hands of the Disposal Board. One of the airship sheds remained until the beginning of the Second World War, the giant structure proving to be an excellent turning point for many pre-war air races.

143(HD) Squadron on parade at Detling after the unit converted to the Sopwith Camel.

Detling

51°18'08"N/00°35'46"W, TQ810592. Off A249, NE of Kent County Showground, 1.3 miles NE of Detling

ANOTHER famous name associated with the Battle of Britain in 1940, aviation first arrived at Detling in April 1915 with the formation of an RNAS War Flight. Detling was classified as an HD NLG and later as a Flight Station, when 50(HD) Squadron brought its BE.2Cs here from Dover in April 1917. Prior to the squadron's arrival, the site had been placed under Care & Maintenance. By this time the aerodrome occupied 95 acres and measured 1,200 by 500 yards and was furnished with a pair of HD-pattern Aeroplane Sheds (135 by 60 feet), one Aeroplane Shed (70 by 70 feet) and several buildings, all lined alongside the main road, which ran along the eastern and southern edge of the LG.

112 Squadron was formed here from 'B' Flight of 50(HD) Squadron in July 1917, by which time Detling was classified as an HD Flight Station and Squadron Station, with an ever-increasing number of personnel on site. This reached a peak in February 1918 when 143 Squadron arrived from Throwley, 112 Squadron having provided a nucleus for its formation.

R.A.F. SE.5A D5995 of 143(HD) Squadron at Detling in 1918.

A pair of 1916-pattern HD Flight Sheds are under repair at Detling in 1918. *Via Stuart Leslie*

Equipped with the SE.5A, which was replaced by the Camel in August, the Sopwith fighter was joined by the Snipe in June 1919. Disbanded on 31 October 1919, Detling was placed under Care & Maintenance again until early 1920, when it was quickly returned to agriculture.

Despite becoming a much larger airfield in the 1930s, the original site was in the southern half of the later one, and today the flying area remains undeveloped. The services on the western side of the A249 are roughly situated close to the position of the two HD Aeroplane Sheds.

Detling main units, 1915-19

War Flt RNAS formed May 1915;
redesignated Strategic Bombing Wing RNAS, Feb 1916

Strategic Bombing Wg (ex-War Flt RNAS) Feb 1916;
redesignated 3 Wg RNAS, Apr 1916

3 Wg RNAS (ex-Strategic Bombing Wg) Apr 1916;
to Manston, 29 May 1916

50 Sqn 'A' Flt from Dover (Swingate Down),
3 Apr 1917; to Bekesbourne 15 Feb 1918 (BE.2C and BE.12)

112 Sqn formed (ex-50 Sqn 'B' Flt) 25 Jul 1917;
to Throwley, 30 Jul 1917 (Pup, BE.12 and 504)

50 Sqn 'B' Flt from Throwley by 12 Aug 1917;
to Bekesbourne by 22 Aug 1917 (BE.12)

143 Sqn from Throwley 14 Feb 1918;
DB 31 Oct 1919 (SE.5A, Camel and Snipe)

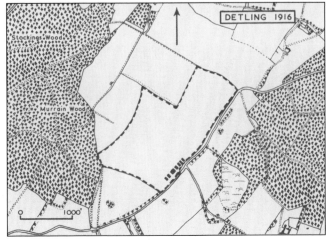

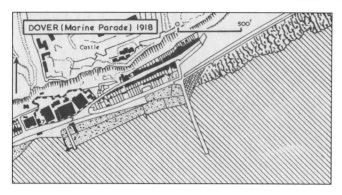

Dover (Dover Harbour/Marine Parade)

51°21'29"N/01°09'57"W, TR326414. Between Marine Parade and Townhall Street (A20), 0.75 miles E of Dover railway station

A SEAPLANE station was established on Marine Parade in November 1914, and the first occupant formed there was the RNAS Seaplane War Flight on the 21st. Occupying just 2 acres of land, Dover was progressively developed throughout the war, and by early 1918 boasted two slipways and three Seaplane Sheds (two 100 by 90 feet and one 146 by 74 feet). A plethora of technical buildings were also crammed into the site, including a detonator store, ammunition store (both of these were in caves), various workshops, a smithy and a torpedo store, to name a few. By this time the station could handle all types of waterborne aircraft and was recognised as a fully fledged flying-boat base.

On 30 May 1918 the War Flight was redesignated as 407(S) Flight equipped with Short 184s and Babys. Dover was then designated as a Marine Operations (Seaplane) Station under 5 (Operations) Group, tasked with carrying out anti-submarine patrol duties over the Channel. 407 Flight then became part of 233 Squadron, formed here and at Guston Road on 31 August 1918. The flight continued to operate from Dover until 31 March 1919, when it was disbanded, and the flying-boat base was closed down by May.

This poor but rare aerial view of Dover (Guston Road) in 1916 clearly shows the Dover Road heading south towards the town and the collection of Flight Sheds to the left of it. Fort Burgoyne is just under the wing.

Dover (Guston Road)

51°08'19"N/01°19'23"W, TR325429. Due N of Fort Burgoyne, S of S boundary of Duke of York's Royal Military School recreation ground, 0.9 miles NE of Dover

O NE of several air stations planned by the Admiralty in November 1912, Dover (Guston Road) was chosen to protect the new naval base being prepared in Dover harbour. The exact location of the new aerodrome was not confirmed until June 1913. The site, occupying 55 acres and measuring 600 by 400 yards, was not ideal, but was located on Government-owned land.

On the outbreak of war the site was still not complete, but work did hasten and before the year was over Guston Road had seven Aeroplane Sheds (two 180 by 60 feet, one 140 by 60 feet, one 80 by 80 feet, and three 70 by 60 feet) and at least three Bessonneau-type canvas hangars. Opened in December 1914 as an HD Station RNAS, the first occupants were detachments from 1 and 2 Squadrons, RNAS, from Gosport and Eastchurch respectively, both flying the TB.8. From July 1915 the site hosted the RNAS Aeroplane School, which was destined to remain until the formation of the RAF on 1 April 1918.

On 10 February 1915 thirty aircraft were assembled at Guston Road for a raid on the German submarine base at Zeebrugge. Setting off the next day, poor weather prevented all but one aircraft reaching the target, but the exercise was repeated on the 17th, when seven floatplanes and seventeen aircraft attacked installations at Ostend and Zeebrugge. Operations were flown from Guston Road in July 1916 in preparation for an attack on the Tirpitz battery, which used a 12-inch Dominion gun. During the attack, Dover-based aircraft protected the observation machines that were plotting the fall of shot.

On 31 August 1918 233 Squadron was formed here as a dedicated anti-submarine unit flying the DH.4 and DH.9. Concentrating on the Straits of Dover, the squadron's efforts helped to virtually eliminate the submarine threat in the region. With 233 Squadron's departure to Walmer in January 1919, Guston Road began to quieten and in August 1919 the site was slowly wound down before closing in early 1920. The bulk of the aerodrome became military married quarters during the 1970s, although a large percentage remains open land, now used as a sports field.

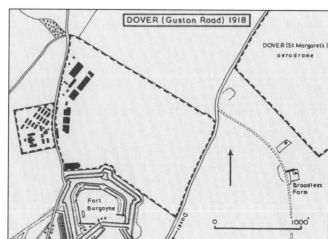

Dover (Guston Road) main units, 1914-19

2 Sqn RNAS detached from Eastchurch, 24 Dec 1914;
to Eastchurch 2 Jan 1915 (TB.8)

1 Sqn RNAS detached from Gosport, Dec 1914;
to St Pol, 26 Feb 1915 (TB.8)

2 Sqn RNAS detached from Eastchurch, 10 Feb 1915;
to St Pol, Aug 1915 (Blériot Parasol)

3 Sqn RNAS from St Pol, Feb 1915;
to Dardanelles, 26 Feb 1915

Detached Flt RNAS formed Mar 1915;
redesignated 4 Sqn RNAS, 25 Mar 1915

4 Sqn RNAS (ex-detached Flt RNAS) 25 Mar 1915;
redesignated 4 Wg RNAS, Jun 1915

4 Wg RNAS (ex-4 Sqn RNAS) Jun 1915;
to Eastchurch 3 Aug 1915 (various aircraft)

RNAS Aeroplane School formed 14 Jul 1915;
DB 1 Apr 1918 (various aircraft)

5 Sqn RNAS formed 2 Aug 1915; DB Oct 1915 (504)

Machine Gun School formed 3 Oct 1915;
to Hythe, 27 Nov 1915

5 Wg 'B' Flt RNAS formed 1 Mar 1916;
to Coudekerque, Mar 1916 (various aircraft)

15 Flt RNAS formed Jul 1916;
DB Aug 1916 (various aircraft)

6 Sqn RNAS formed 1 Nov 1916;
to Petite Synthe, 12 Dec 1916 (no aircraft)

7 Sqn RNAS from Middle Aerodrome, 10 Dec 1917;
to Teteghem, 14 Feb 1918 (Camel)

6 Sqn RNAS reformed 1 Jan 1918;
to Petite Synthe, 14 Jan 1918 (DH.4)

9 Sqn RNAS from Middle Aerodrome, 8 Feb 1918;
to Middle Aerodrome, 20 Mar 1918 (Camel)

218 Sqn formed 24 Apr 1918;
to Petite Synthe, 23 May 1918 (DH.9)

491 Flt formed 16 Jun 1918;
into 233 Sqn, 31 Aug 1918 (DH.9 and 1½ Strutter)

233 Sqn formed 31 Aug 1918;
to Walmer, 21 Jan 1919 (DH.4, DH.9 and Camel)

School for Marine Operational Pilots formed
15 Oct 1918;
DB 1 Feb 1919 (DH.9)

217 Sqn from Varssenaere, 20 Feb 1919;
to Dunkerque, Mar 1919 (DH.9)

217 Sqn from Dunkerque 27 Mar 1919;
to Driffield, 28 Mar 1919 (no aircraft)

Dover (Swingate Down/St Margaret's, aka Langdon)

51°08'15"N/01°20'22"W, TR336429. N of Upper Road,
E of Jubilee Way (A2), 1.3 miles NE of Dover

LOCATED only a few hundred yards north-east of where Louis Blériot famously landed after crossing the Channel in 1909, Swingate Down (aka St Margaret's) was used by pre-war aviators. As war approached in the summer of 1914, the RFC did not have to look far for a convenient aerodrome that could be used to cross the Channel at its narrowest point. When the war broke out it was the personnel of 6 Squadron RFC who arrived first, without their aircraft, to prepare Swingate Down as a military aerodrome. By 12 August fuel supplies were organised and a workshop had been built, before the aircraft of 2, 3 and 4 Squadrons arrived with orders to leave for France the following day. On 14 August at 0625hrs the first aircraft, a BE.2A of 2 Squadron flown by Lt H. D. Harvey-Kelly, became the first to land in France, arriving at Amiens 2 hours later.

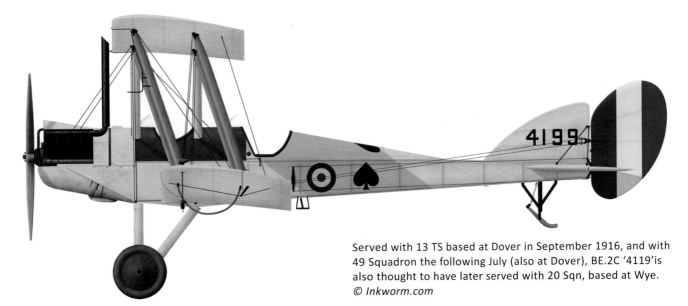

Served with 13 TS based at Dover in September 1916, and with 49 Squadron the following July (also at Dover), BE.2C '4119' is also thought to have later served with 20 Sqn, based at Wye.
© Inkworm.com

It was not until May 1915 that Swingate Down, now officially named Dover St Margaret's, could class itself as a proper aerodrome; by then it occupied 219 acres and measured 1,200 by 800 yards. The infrastructure took up 33 acres of land and included six 1915-pattern Flight Sheds (210 by 65 feet), which were aligned along the southern boundary beside Upper Road. Throughout its existence the aerodrome was classified as a transit station for obvious reasons, but it was also labelled as a training squadron station and an HD Flight Station, serving initially as an NLG1 for 50(HD) Squadron, later downgraded to an NLG2 on 31 May 1917. Equipped with the wholly inadequate BE.2C for its role of anti-Zeppelin operations, only once did a 50(HD) Squadron machine come close to an enemy airship, on 24 August 1916. Despite being held for quite some time in Dover's searchlights, Capt T. W. Woodhouse tried to attack *L32*, only to see his bullets fall short as the giant airship slipped away 2,000 feet above him.

A variety of units came and went throughout 1917, including 65 TS from Sedgeford, which would provide the nucleus for 53 TDS, formed here on 15 July 1918. A large unit, the TDS became the School of Marine Operational Pilots (SMOP) in October 1918, specialising in training pilots in the art of anti-submarine and convoy patrol duties.

Activity at Dover St Margaret's began to slow from early 1919, beginning with the disbandment of the SMOP in February 1919; later in the year the aerodrome was open for emergency use only. Closed completely by early 1920, the six Flight Sheds were retained for many years for storage, and by the Second World War three still remained. The site was taken over as one of the first Chain Radar stations in 1940, and two of these famous landmarks remain to this day. Two of the Flight Shed bases survive off Upper Road, and next to them is an RFC memorial, one of the first to be erected in the country.

Dover (Swingate Down/St Margaret's) main units, 1914-19

4 Sqn 'C' Flt from Eastchurch, 30 Jul 1914;
to Fère-en-Tardenois, 20 Sep 1914 (various aircraft)

4 Sqn detached from Amiens, 13 Aug 1914;
to Maubeuge, 16 Aug 1914 (various aircraft)

15 Sqn from Hounslow, 11 May 1915;
to St Omer, 5 Jan 1916 (BE.2C)

9 Sqn from Brooklands, 23 Jul 1915;
to St Omer, 12 Dec 1915 (504, BE.8A and Martinsyde S.I)

12 TS formed 15 Nov 1915;
to Thetford, 16 Nov 1915 (no aircraft)

13 TS formed 27 Nov 1915;
to Yatesbury, 1 Jun 1917 (504, BE.2C and RE.8)

27 Sqn from Hounslow, 10 Dec 1915;
to St Omer, 1 Jan 1916 (Martinsyde G.100)

20 TS formed 1 Feb 1916;
to Wye, 24 Jul 1916 (504, BE.2C and RE.8)

49 Sqn formed (nucleus from 13 TS) 15 Apr 1916;
to La Bellevue, 12 Nov 1917 (BE.2C and RE.7)

50 Sqn formed (nucleus from 20 TS) 15 May 1916;
to Harrietsham, 23 Oct 1916
(BE.2C/E, BE.12/A/B and FB.19)

50 Sqn 'A' Flt formed 15 May 1916;
to Detling, 3 Apr 1917 (various aircraft)

64 TS formed 7 Apr 1917;
to Narborough, 14 Apr 1917 (no aircraft)

110 Sqn from Rendcomb, 12 Nov 1917;
to Sedgeford, 26 Nov 1917 (various aircraft)

65 TS from Sedgeford, 25 Nov 1917;
DB into 53 TDS, 15 Jul 1918 (various aircraft)

58 Sqn from Cramlington, 22 Dec 1917;
to St Omer, 10 Jan 1918 (FE.2B)

53 TDS (ex-65 TS) 15 Jul 1918;
redesignated SMOP, 15 Oct 1918
(Camel, 504 and DH.9)

141st Aero Sqn, USAAS, by 17 Jul 1918

154th Aero Sqn detachment, USAAS, from Stockbridge, 16 Aug 1918

SMOP (ex-53 TDS) 15 Oct 1918;
DB 1 Feb 1919

212 Sqn from Great Yarmouth, 7 Mar 1919;
DB 9 Feb 1920 (DH.9 and DH.9A)

3 Sqn cadre from Wye, 2 May 1919;
to Croydon, 15 Oct 1919 (no aircraft)

Dymchurch (Hythe/Palmarsh)

51°03'19"N/01°02'18"W, TR128330. Off Dymchurch Road (A359); site is now Nickolls Quarry, 0.5 miles NNE of Dymchurch Redoubt, 2.2 miles WSW of Hythe

LOCATED on the edge of Romney Marsh on 131 acres of land originally known as Palmarsh, Dymchurch (Hythe) opened on 27 November 1915 when the RFC Machine Gun School relocated from Dover. Taking advantage of the good range facilities nearby, the school established its HQ in the Imperial Hotel, Hythe, while the BE.2C, RE.7 and FB.5 aircraft allocated to the unit operated from nearby Lympne.

A plan to move the Machine Gun School, by then renamed the School of Aerial Gunnery (SoAG), to Loch Doon was shelved when work on the Scottish station was abandoned. Renamed again to No 1 (Aux) SoAG, the unit specialised in training observers over a two-week course. By early 1917 the use of Lympne was stopped and the site was expanded into an LG measuring 700 by 500 yards, equipped with eight Bessonneau hangars and a collection of more permanent technical and domestic buildings, the bulk of them huddled close to the Dymchurch Road. Personnel accommodation was still sparse and many who served at Dymchurch joined their colleagues in the Redoubt.

By March 1918 the school was renamed yet again to 1 (Observers) SoAG, which was a more accurate description of the unit's speciality. On 1 November 1918 the school left Dymchurch, which by then was classified as an ELG for aircraft using the Hythe ranges. However, this role was short-lived and the site was closed down in 1919 and cleared by 1920.

Dymchurch (Hythe) main units, 1915-18

Machine Gun School from Dover (Swingate Down)
27 Nov 1915;
redesignated SoAG, 13 Sep 1916 (aircraft at Lympne)

SoAG formed (ex-MGS) 13 Sep 1916;
redesignated 1 (Aux) SoAG, Jan 1917

1 (Aux) SoAG formed (ex-SoAG) Jan 1917;
redesignated 1 (Observers) SoAG

1 (Aux) SoAG detached from Lympne, Jan 1917;
joined parent unit, Jan 1917

1 (Observers) SoAG detachment formed (ex-1 and 3 (Aux) SoAG), 9 Mar 1918;
to New Romney, 1 Nov 1918

Dymchurch (Redoubt)

51°02'56"N/01°02'11"W, TR125319. Dymchurch Redoubt off Dymchurch Road (A259), 1.9 miles SSE of Lympne

DYMCHURCH Redoubt opened as a kite balloon base in November 1915, with one section carrying observation duties for the nearby Hythe gunnery range. An annual rent of £1 per acre was provisionally agreed with the farmer, and a pair of Balloon Sheds and a winch were quickly installed.

However, by the time the War Office had finalised the lease for the site, the cheeky farmer decided that £1 per acre was not enough and raised the rent to 30 shillings an acre (plus rates), which the military paid without even quibbling. The Redoubt was used for accommodation for the personnel. A machine gun school HQ, which eventually changed into an observers' school, also operated from here from November 1915 through to November 1918. The kite balloon section was wound up in 1919.

Dymchurch (Redoubt) main units, 1915-18

Kite Balloon Section formed Nov 1915; DB 1919

Machine Gun School HQ from Dover Swingate Down,
27 Nov 1915;
redesignated School of Aerial Gunnery HQ, 13 Sep 1916

School of Aerial Gunnery HQ 13 Sep 1916;
redesignated 1 (Aux) SoAG HQ, Jan 1917

1 (Aux) SoAG HQ Jan 1917;
redesignated 1 (Observers) SoAG HQ, 9 Mar 1918

1 (Observers) SoAG HQ 9 Mar 1918;
to New Romney, 1 Nov 1918

Eastchurch (HMS *Pembroke II*)

51°23'19"N/00°50'51"W, TQ982693. HMP Elmley, Standford Hill and Swaleside, either side of Brabazon Road, 1 mile SSW of Eastchurch

FLYING began at Eastchurch when C. S. Rolls tested his Short-built glider at Stamford Hill in July 1909. The land, 400 acres in total, had been purchased by Francis McLean, who gave the Royal Aero Club full rights to use it for the token sum of £1 in rent per year. By 1910 Eastchurch became a manufacturer's aerodrome for Short Brothers, and from February 1911 also served as a naval flying school until February 1912. The aerodrome was expanded to 600 acres and a number of Aeroplane Sheds began appear, including one of 90 by 70 feet, six 70 by 61 feet, and a dozen 50 by 55 feet.

The military first arrived in March 1911 in the shape of the Naval Pilots Training Unit, and from November Eastchurch was classified as Flying School and HD Station

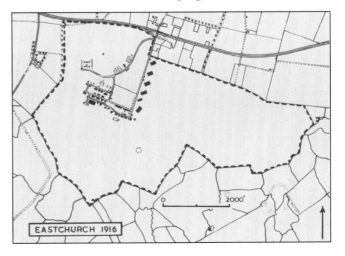

EASTCHURCH 1916

RFC (Naval Wing) & RNAS Station, known as HMS *Pembroke II* from 1913. In August 1914 the first of many units began to pass through Eastchurch, which by then measured a healthy 2,000 by 1,600 yards. The infrastructure increased, with two further Aeroplane Sheds (180 by 60 feet), six F-Type sheds (200 by 100 feet), and two other sheds (70 by 65 feet), not to mention an increasing number of technical and domestic buildings as personnel strength quickly rose.

Various RNAS units came and went during the early stages of the war, but permanent units, including the Wireless Experimental Section, served from 1914 to May 1916, and the Gunners & Observers School was formed here in March 1916. Eastchurch's remoteness lent itself to flying training and ground training, the latter including a Boy Mechanics Training School formed in June 1918, which catered for 600 mechanics of all trades on a nine-month-long course. 1 Observers School

was also formed in January 1918; later redesignated as 2 Marine Observers School in December, the unit incorporated a Ground Armament School and was the parent unit of the Boy Mechanics School. Observer School instruction included bomb-dropping, Lewis machine gun training, navigation, naval codes, signalling and ship recognition training in a course lasting from twelve to sixteen weeks.

Eastchurch's post-war future was bright, as it became the Armament & Gunnery School during the inter-war years. It went on to play its part in the Battle of Britain and remained in RAF hands until 1947. Three years later, the Home Office took over and converted the site into an open prison, which today has evolved into three prisons, nicknamed the 'Sheppey Prisons Cluster'. One F-Type shed is extant on the western side of the original technical site, while 'the home of British aviation' is recognised with several memorials in the region.

Eastchurch in 1914, viewed from Standford Hill. *Via Stuart Leslie*

A 75hp Maurice Farman of the Gunnery Flight, Gunners & Observers School at Eastchurch in 1916.

Eastchurch main units, 1911-20

Naval Pilots TU formed 1 Mar 1911;
DB 3 Aug 1911 (Short triplane)

Naval FS formed Aug 1911;
DB Jul 1914 (Short triplane)

RNAS Defence Flights formed Jul 1914;
DB 1914

4 Sqn from Netheravon 21 July 1914;
to Dover, 12 Aug 1914 (various aircraft)

Eastchurch (Mobile) Sqn formed 8 Aug 1914;
to Immingham, 9 Aug 1914 (various aircraft)

Eastchurch (Mobile) Sqn from Skegness, 24 Aug 1914;
to Ostend, 27 Aug 1914 (various aircraft)

2 Sqn RNAS formed 10 Sep 1914;
to Dunkirk, 16 Sep 1914 (various aircraft)

2 Sqn RNAS reformed 17 Oct 1914;
redesignated 2 Wg RNAS 21 Jun 1915 (various aircraft)

Wireless Experimental Section formed 1914;
to Cranwell, May 1916

2 Wg RNAS (ex-2 Sqn RNAS) 21 Jun 1915;
to St Pol, 4 Aug 1915 (various aircraft)

4 Wg RNAS from Dover, 3 Aug 1915;
to Petite Synthe, 11 Apr 1916 (various aircraft)

7 Sqn RNAS formed Aug 1915;
to Petite Synthe, Apr 1916 (various aircraft)

Gunners & Observers School formed Mar 1916;
to Leysdown, 25 Apr 1917

War Flight formed (ex-4 Wg RNAS) 16 Apr 1916;
DB 1917

Design Flt formed 14 Aug 1916;
to Grain, 17 Mar 1917

204 TDS (ex-Naval FS) 1 Apr 1918;
DB Mar 1919 (various aircraft)

Boy Mechanics School Jun 1918;
to Halton Camp, 9 Oct 1919

1 Observers School formed in SE Area Jul 1918;
redesignated 2 Marine Observers School, 28 Dec 1918 (DH.9)

2 Marine Observers (ex-1 OS) 28 Dec 1918;
DB Jun 1919 (DH.6, DH.9, 504 and F.2B)

No 3 Boys Training Centre formed (ex-Boys TS) Aug 1919;
redesignated School of Technical Training (Men), 18 Feb 1920

Farningham

51°24'00"N/00°14'03"W, TQ555690. 0.65 miles NW of Horton Kirby, due S of Farningham Road railway station, 1.5 miles NNE of Farningham

THIS small HD Flight Station was opened in October 1915, and the first occupant was 10 RAS HD detachment from Joyce Green, which did not arrive until 31 January 1916. 10 RAS returned to Joyce Green on 1 February, to be replaced by 19 RAS HD detachment from Hounslow, which remained until 15 April.

Farningham was then classified as an HD NLG2 for the use of 50(HD) Squadron, until it was closed down on 1 May 1917.

Frinsted (Harrietsham)

51°16'40"N/00°42'28"W, TQ889556. Yokes Court fields, 0.35 miles S of Frinsted, 4.5 miles S of Sittingbourne

ONE of the highest LGs in Kent at 530 feet amsl, Frinsted was opened for 50(HD) Squadron in January 1917, occupying 48 acres and measuring 600 by 400 yards. Later transferred to 112(HD) Squadron, which operated a collection of Pups, Camels and Snipes, the only significant event to take place involving this LG occurred during the early hours of 20 May 1918. While returning from a successful raid on London, Gotha G.V 979/16 was caught trying to make its escape to the coast by the CO of 143(HD) Squadron, Major F. Sowrey, in his SE.5A, and Lts E. E. Turner and H. B. Barwise in their 141(HD) Squadron F.2B Fighter. Sowrey attacked the bomber first, but his guns jammed before he could press home his attack. The pilot of the Gotha, Lt J. Flathow, was wounded during Sowrey's attack and decided to make for the lit flarepath at Frinsted. Very close to the LG, Lt Turner manoeuvred behind the big bomber, not realising that it was attempting to land, and delivered a final, fatal burst of fire. The Gotha plunged to the ground, killing Flathow and observer Vize-Feld A. Sachter, but the gunner, Uffz H. Tasche, survived to become a POW.

The two German airmen were interned in St Dunstan's churchyard, Frinsted, but were later moved, together with another Gotha crew killed that night, to Cannock Chase during the early 1960s. Frinsted NLG was close down in June 1919; today the site is a private airfield with a main grass runway approximately 760 yards long.

Right: One of many types flown by 50(HD) Squadron out of Harrietsham was the R.A.F. BE.12A.

Below: The wreckage of Gotha G.V 979/16, which attempted to land at Harrietsham on 20 May 1918.

Lt E. E. Turner, the pilot of the 143(HD) F.2B Fighter that carried out the final, fatal attack on Gotha G.V 979/16 on 20 May 1918.

Godmersham Park

51°12'59"N/00°55'59"W, TR049504. SW end of Godmersham Park towards North Downs Way, 0.8 miles W of Godmersham Park Heritage Centre

A SUB-STATION for Capel-le-Ferne, Godmersham Park was only open from 1918 until February 1919, under the charge of 5(Operations) Group, SE Area.

Grain and Port Victoria, Isle of Grain

51°26'14"N/00°42'44"W, TQ885745. House Fleet, 0.9 miles SSE of Isle of Grain village, access by Port Victoria Road

THIS remote site was surveyed in 1912 by the Admiralty, as the location for one of the first RNAS seaplane stations, which was established by December of the same year. A large area of the foreshore was purchased and, because the marshy area was so low-lying, a gap in the sea wall had to be made to access the slipway. Commissioned on 30 December 1912 under the command of Lt J. W. Seddon, the first unit here was a Seaplane War Flight equipped with Maurice Farmans. Serious money was invested in the station in 1913, resulting in six Seaplane Sheds and four Aeroplane Sheds.

By 1914 the site was expanded into an aerodrome (900 by 500 yards), the rough fields on the inside of the sea wall had their dykes boarded over, and several Bessonneau hangars complemented the permanent structures. In 1915 the Royal Naval Aeroplane Repair Depot (ARD) was commissioned just west of the original seaplane station, under the name Port Victoria. In 1915 the Armament Experimental Section and later the Seaplane Testing Flight was formed alongside the ARD. These units were the first stages of the RNAS gaining its own

With an experimental hook trailing underneath, Sopwith Pup prototype N9497 is pictured taking part in early arrester gear trials on a dummy flight deck at Grain.

This Blackburn Baby looks impressive with five Le Prier rockets mounted on each wing during trials at Grain.

The RAF Isle of Grain fire section was well-equipped, including its own engine, pictured on 8 May 1918.

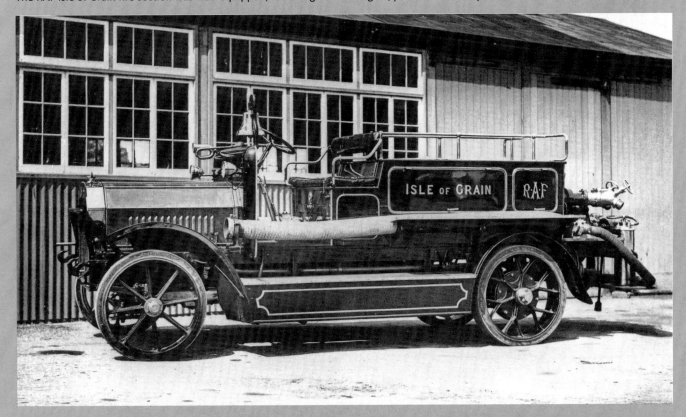

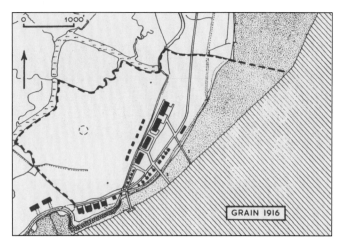

GRAIN 1916

'Farnborough', which would later create, in April 1918, the Marine Experimental Aircraft Depot (MEAD). By then the depot had expanded and the two sites merged into one, the MEAD being divided into three sections. These sections covered all experimental work with marine-type aircraft from performance trials and armament trials to methods of operating aircraft from ships of the fleet. The site grew in complexity and at least fifteen permanent sheds/hangars and three slipways served the now combined Grain and Port Victoria. A large accommodation camp was established south of Isle of Grain village for up to 1,500 personnel. In March 1920 the MEAD became the MAEE, which remained until 17 March 1924, when it was moved to Felixstowe.

Grain was closed down after the MAEE's departure, but remained in military hands until after the Second World War. The original buildings had long been dismantled by then, leaving only their bases behind. At least five hangar bases can still be seen today, on land that is now in the hands of the National Grid, which operates the huge power station that overlooks this once important experimental aerodrome.

Grain and Port Victoria main units, 1912-24

Seaplane War Flight formed Dec 1912;
DB into SP&AES 1917

ARD formed 1915;
DB into SP&AES 1917

Seaplane Testing Flight formed 1915;
DB into SP&AES 1917

Armament Experimental Section formed 1915;
DB into SP&AES 1917

SP&AES formed 1917;
DB into MEAD Apr 1918

MEAD formed Apr 1918;
redesignated MAEE, Mar 1920

Meteorological Station formed 1919;
DB 1924

Wireless Station formed 1919;
DB 1924

MAEE formed Mar 1920;
to Felixstowe, 17 Mar 1924

Grove Park, London Borough of Bromley

51°25'26"N/00°01'05"W, TQ404714. W of Burnt Ash Lane (A2212), E of Southover Road, 0.5 miles SSW of Grove Park railway station

THIS HD NLG2 was opened for 39(HD) Squadron from 30 June 1917, which was replaced by 78(HD) Squadron from December 1917. Grove Park occupied 51 acres of land, measured 450 by 500 yards, and remained in use until May 1919. This prime building land was quickly engulfed by housing during the post-war period, but the large playing field, south-east of the Launcelot Junior and Infants School, represents a large portion of the original aerodrome.

Guilton (Ash)

51°16'38"N/01°15'42"W, TR275581. Between Guilton and Durlock Road, 0.75 miles W of Ash, 3.5 miles W of Sandwich railway station

GUILTON was introduced late in the war as an HD NLG2 for 50(HD) Squadron, between 1918 and June 1919. The small site only covered 25 acres and measured 490 by 350 yards.

Harty

51°22'19"N/00°54'47"W, TR028676. NE of Elliott's Farm, 1.75 miles S of Leysdown-on-Sea, Isle of Harty

THIS small LG, positioned on the eastern side of the Isle of Sheppey, was opened as an NLG3 in December 1917. Both 50(HD) and 143(HD) Squadrons used Harty, which occupied just 27 acres and measured 520 by 250 yards, until it was closed down in October 1919.

Hawkinge (Folkestone)

51°06'46"N/01°09'12"W, TR208395. Off Aerodrome Road, Kent Battle of Britain Museum, on SW edge of original WWI technical site, 2.2 miles NNW of Folkestone

IT was in 1912 that aviation arrived at one of the country's most famous airfields near Hawkinge. A Dutchman by the name of W. B. Megone rented a corrugated-iron shed in the corner of a field at Barnhouse to build a flying machine. Apparently his aircraft could only manage a few hops and by September 1914 the shed was abandoned and the Dutch aviator had disappeared. By then the country was at war and the War Office began searching Kent for suitable aerodromes, especially those close to the coast that would effectively shorten the flight across the Channel. Guided by the postmaster in Hawkinge, officials were steered towards Megone's old flying field and before long the site was approved and 166 acres of land were requisitioned.

The site was used as a stepping stone by units posted to France, including 12 Squadron, which was one of the first to use Hawkinge in September 1915. A few months later the Examination Ground was formed in April 1916 to handle and dispatch aircraft in transit for the BEF. Tents and several Bessonneau hangars appeared, and to assist pilots across the Channel to St Omer a pair of large circles were cut in the turf;

once lined up, they pointed directly at the French aerodrome. More structures appeared from later in 1916 when the Aircraft Dispatch Section was formed, a unit that would eventually create 12 (Hawkinge) AAP, established on 12 October 1917.

Within months the site expanded to nine 1918-pattern GS Sheds (170 by 100 feet) and the site measured 900 by 800 yards (landing runs of 2,400 feet E/W and 2,000 feet N/S) with a personnel strength of 30 officers, 28 SNCOs, 41 JNCOs, 425 other ranks and 131 women. The AAP was still under construction when the Armistice arrived but, unlike hundreds of other sites across the country, Hawkinge was set to remain firmly in the hands of the military, despite the main unit closing down in 1919. Much of the wartime infrastructure remained until the early stages of the Second World War, when the Luftwaffe saw fit to level the bulk of it. The site remained an RAF station until 1962, and today it is slowly succumbing to modern housing, although the Kent Battle of Britain Museum is located in the middle on one of the original shed bases, reminding those who visit how rich the airfield's aviation past was.

Hawkinge main units, 1915-20

12 Sqn from Netheravon 5 Sep 1915;
to St Omer, 6 Sep 1915 (504 and BE.2C)

Examination Ground formed Apr 1916;
absorbed into 8 AAP, 1917

ADS formed Dec 1916;
redesignated AAP, 1917

¼ ARS formed 1916;
to Lympne Feb, 1917

AAP formed (ex-Dispatch Section & Examination Ground) 1917;
redesignated 12 (Hawkinge) AAP, 12 Oct 1917

12 (Hawkinge) AAP formed 12 Oct 1917;
DB 1919

38 Sqn cadre from Serny, 14 Feb 1919;
DB 4 Jul 1919

83 Sqn cadre from Serny, 14 Feb 1919;
to Croydon, 15 Oct 1919 (FE.2B/D)

120 Sqn from Wyton, 20 Feb 1919;
to Lympne, 17 Jul 1919 (DH.9)

Hunton (Maidstone)

51°13'03"N/00°26'30"W, TQ706493. 0.3 miles S of Cheveney, 0.65 miles SE of Yalding, 5 miles SW of Maidstone

FIRST surveyed in October 1915, Hunton (named Hanton in the survey report) did not open until August 1916. Classified as an NLG3, only 50(HD) Squadron made limited use of the site until it was closed down in October 1917.

Kings Hill (West Malling)

51°16'31"N/00°24'16"W, TQ678556. E of Tower View Road, 0.25 miles NE of ex-RAF West Malling control tower, 0.7 miles SSE of St Leonard's Street

AS of 2014 a large proportion of the 47 acres that was occupied by King Hill HD NLG2 is still undeveloped, compared with the later and more extensive RAF West Malling, which has now succumbed to the sprawl of Kings Hill. Opened in March 1917, Kings Hill measured 650 by 380 yards and its first occupant was 50(HD) Squadron, followed by 143 Squadron from February 1918. The site was closed down in August 1919, but was reopened as a much larger aerodrome from 1930 and was not fully closed down to aviation until the early 1990s.

Joyce Green

51°28'27"N/00°13'01"W, TQ540773. E of River Darent as it joins Thames at Dartford Marshes, 1 mile ENE of Slade Green

ONE of the most unlikely choices for an aerodrome was first established by Vickers in 1911, when the company purchased a section of Franks Farm to flight-test aircraft from its Erith factory. Nothing more than a marsh covered in wide ditches, nevertheless the site was prepared for flying with hangars and workshops located at the southern boundary and the ditches boarded over with railway sleepers. The only serious flying that Vickers undertook here during the pre-war period was when Herbert F. Wood tested the company's REP Monoplanes.

From October 1914 Joyce Green was partly taken over by the military, which extended the northern end of the site into an HD NLG for the RNAS and an HD Advanced Base for the

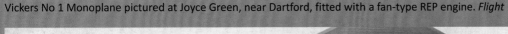
Vickers No 1 Monoplane pictured at Joyce Green, near Dartford, fitted with a fan-type REP engine. *Flight*

R.A.F. FB.9 A8612 was built by Vickers at Weybridge, but served briefly with 10 TS at Joyce Green.

RFC. Six Aeroplane Sheds, workshops and domestic buildings were erected close to the Longreach Tavern. The aerodrome now covered 121 acres and measured 1,200 by 1,000 yards.

In 1916 Joyce Green became part of the complex anti-Zeppelin defence of the capital, and the aerodrome was classified as an HD NLG1 for 39(HD), 50(HD) and later 112(HD) Squadrons. From October 1916 it was also a Wireless Testing Park until January 1917, when this large unit settled at Biggin Hill. Training units were the main residents at Joyce Green, including 10 TS, one of whose instructors was Lt J. B. McCudden, who checked out thirty pupils before leaving for Dover in May 1917. 63 TS, which served here from June 1917 to October 1918, was a typical training unit with a dozen 504s and a dozen Camels on strength, tasked with carrying out single-seat training. 63 TS was replaced by the Scout School, Pool of Pilots, which arrived from Manston in October 1918 to convert experienced pilots on new types. Up to fifty officer pupils would be catered for, all of whom were held at Joyce Green before being posted for tours overseas.

Vickers retained a presence here until 1919, and it was from Joyce Green that the Vimy bomber made its first flight on 30 November 1917. Vickers moved its operation to Brooklands, and when the Pool of Pilots disbanded in November 1919 the aerodrome was closed down the following month. The local farmer made use of the buildings during the inter-war period, but the bulk had gone by the Second World War.

Joyce Green main units, 1914-19

1 Sqn detached from Brooklands Oct 1914;
to Brooklands, Nov 1914

1 TS detached from Farnborough, 19 Dec 1914;
to Farnborough, Dec 1914

7 Sqn detached from Netheravon, 22 Dec 1914;
to Netheravon, Dec 1914 (various aircraft)

2 TS detached from Brooklands, Jul 1915;
absorbed into 10 TS, 1 Sep 1915 (various aircraft)

10 TS formed 1 Sep 1915;
to Ternhill, 1 Jun 1917 (FE.8, FB.5/9 and Farman)

Wireless Test Park from Brooklands, 21 Oct 1916;
to Biggin Hill, 1 Jan 1917
(BE.2E, FK.8, RE.7, Pup and 1½ Strutter)

63 TS from Ternhill, 1 Jun 1917;
to Redcar, 5 Oct 1918 (504, DH.5, Pup and Camel)

8th Aero Sqn, USAAS, from Flower Down, 24 Dec 1917;
to Thetford, 1 May 1918

162nd Aero Sqn, USAAS, from Flower Down by 17 Jul 1918

Scout School, Pool of Pilots, from Manston, 5 Oct 1918;
DB 23 Nov 1919
(Snipe, F.2B, SPAD, DH.4, DH.9, 504, Camel and SE.5A)

Kingsnorth (Hoo/Chatham)

51°25'25"N/00°35'54"W, TQ806726. Due N of decommissioned Kingsnorth Power Station and part covered by industrial estate to N, 1.5 miles ENE of Hoo

ONE of only a few Class G Airship Stations built in Britain before the war, Kingsnorth occupied 570 acres of land and measured 2,566 by 1,700 yards. It was opened in March 1914 for the construction and assembly of non-rigid airships for the RNAS, the site progressively expanding right up to its closure in 1921.

Among the many technical and domestic buildings constructed here, the skyline was dominated by a pair of Airship Sheds, one of which (No 2) was made of wood and measured 700 by 150 by 98 feet, and the other smaller shed (No 1) was constructed of steel, and was 555 by 109 by 100 feet. The first permanent military unit based here was the RNAS/RAF Airship Section, which arrived from Farnborough in March 1915 and was destined to remain at Kingsnorth until its disbandment in 1920. The Airship School was formed in March 1915 but was disbanded on 1 February 1916, while 5 (Balloon) Stores was also formed in 1918. Redesignated as the Balloon Stores Depot, this unit was the last to serve at Kingsnorth, being disbanded in 1921. Relinquished by the middle of the year, the site was quickly closed down by late 1921.

Several military-type building bases are extant on the western and south-western sides of the industrial estate, while the area where the two large hangars once stood is still open ground.

Leigh (Tonbridge)

51°12'16"N/00°11'28"W, TQ531473. SW of Leigh Park Farm, 0.6 miles E of Charcott, 1 mile NW of Leigh railway station

A SHORT-LIVED LG, Leigh was opened as an HD NLG for 50(HD) Squadron in October 1916. Just two months later it was closed down in favour of Penshurst (Chiddingstone Causeway), located a mere half a mile to the south-west.

Leigh Green (Tenterden)

51°04'40"N/00°42'09"W, TQ893333. Off Appledore Road (B2080), E of Tenterden, 9 miles SW of Ashford

THIS 30-acre site ran along the south side of the Appledore road and was opened as an HD NLG2 in October 1916 for the use of 50(HD) Squadron. Reclassified as an NLG3 on 5 January 1917, the 800-by-250-yard aerodrome saw out its operational days with 112(HD) Squadron, until it was closed down in June 1919. The field the LG occupied it now filled with houses to its borders.

Looking east across Kingsnorth's technical site, the station's gas plant is in the centre and to the right the steel Airship Shed No 2, which was 555 feet long. *Via Stuart Leslie and author*

Leysdown (Shellbeach)

51°23'19"N/00°56'03"W, TR040698. Off Shellness Road, now Leysdown Country and Coastal Park, 0.5 miles SE of Leysdown-on-Sea, Isle of Sheppey

IT was at Leysdown on 2 May 1909 that the first powered flight was made by J. T. C. Moor-Brabazon, so it seems logical that the military's association began not long after. In the meantime the site became the home of the Royal Aero Club and Short Brothers from 1909 until May 1910 (the latter continued seaplane experimental work here until 1913).

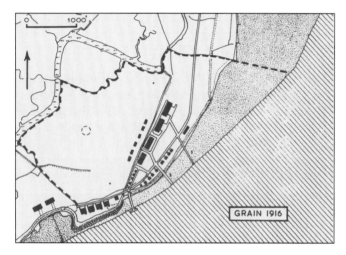

The RNAS used the LG from 1911, the most common visitors being aircraft from the Naval Flying School at Eastchurch. It was a number of years before the site was developed into the home of the Gunners & Observers School. Opened in 1917, the site now occupied 115 acres, measured 1,100 by 700 yards, and was furnished with three Aeroplane Sheds (one 180 by 60 feet and the other 120 by 96 feet); 'Mussel House' was requisitioned as the officers' mess.

On 1 April 1918 the school was redesignated as the Pilots & Observers Aerial Gunnery & Aerial Fighting School under the control of the Eastchurch Ground Armament School; the former operated a dozen 504s and at least six DH.4s and/or DH.9s. All classroom work was carried out at Eastchurch while the practical, including aerial gunnery and bomb-dropping, was performed at Leysdown. As well as aircrew cadets, wireless telegraphy operators and flying-boat engineer mechanics were also trained at Leysdown in the art of aerial gunnery. The Marine Observers School was formed in August 1918, operating a collection of aircraft including the RE.8, Pup, 1½ Strutter and DH.9. The Aerial Gunnery School was closed down in late 1918, while the Marine Observers School remained until September 1919. The site was quickly run down and was fully relinquished by early 1920.

Today the historical importance is fully recognised with several memorials, marking Brabazon's flight, Short Brothers, a blue plaque on 'Mussel House', and a 'century of flight' memorial close by; even the village sign celebrates the 'Birthplace of Aviation'.

Lidsing (Chatham)

51°19'50"N/00°33'41"W, TQ785622. W side of Ivy Farm off Lidsing Road, 0.65 miles W of Bredhurst, 3.8 miles SE of Chatham

LIDSING was the site of a balloon equipping store and a free balloon training ground for the Royal Engineers.

Lydd

50°57'16"N/00°54'03"W, TR038212. W edge of cricket ground off Dennes Lane, 0.3 miles NW of Lydd

NO 2 Balloon School of Instruction was formed here in July 1916 and remained until disbanded in September 1918. It was replaced by No 2 Balloon Training School, which remained until July 1919.

Lydd (Dering Farm)

50°57'08"N/00°53'47"W, TR032208. Dering Farm, past cricket ground off Dennes Lane, 0.5 miles WNW of Lydd

THIS was a temporary aerodrome during 1913 and 1914 for the use of two early RFC units. 3 Squadron was detached here with a variety of aircraft from Larkhill on 1 June 1913 for gunnery training and trials. The squadron left Dering Farm on 27 June for Netheravon, the main unit having relocated on the 16th. The site was unused until the arrival of 2 Reserve Aeroplane School (HD) on detachment from Brooklands on 19 December 1914. Before the year was out the school had returned to Brooklands and Dering Farm was never used again.

Lydd

50°56'44"N/00°53'46"W, TR015230. 0.4 miles NW of Newland Farm, 1.75 miles SW of Old Romney, 2 miles NW of Lydd

THE third aviation site that used the name of Lydd was a 60-acre aerodrome, measuring 600 by 600 yards, which opened in January 1917 for co-operation with the guns at the Hythe ranges. The first unit was the Artillery Co-operation Flight, which was disbanded into the Artillery Co-operation Squadron only days after forming. The aerodrome, which only had a few Bessonneau hangars, was classified as an HD NLG2 for the use of 112(HD) Squadron in August 1917, and remained in this role until December 1918. The Artillery Co-operation Flight was reformed in 1919 and, together with the squadron, was disbanded by October 1919. The site was closed down soon after and quickly returned to agriculture.

Lydd Camp

50°56'44"N/00°53'46"W, TR035202. Within confines of current Lydd Camp, 0.6 miles SW of Lydd

ONE of the older aviation sights within this book is Lydd Camp, which had a balloon station allocated to it from 1886 to 1914. The balloons were tested by the Royal Engineers for artillery observation duties.

Lympne

51°04′28″N/01°02′40″W, TR136351. Due S of Folks Wood off Aldington Road, 0.9 miles E of Lympne, 1.7 miles W of Hythe

THE first of two aerodromes by the name of Lympne was opened in 1915 as a flying field for the Machine Gun School, Hythe. The school arrived from Dover (Swingate Down) on 27 November 1915 with its HQ established at Dymchurch. Heavy rain over the winter exposed a severe drainage problem on the southern side of the field, along the edge of Aldington Road, and rather than spend a huge amount of money on the problem the War Office abandoned the site on March 1916 and chose a new location to the north-west of Lympne village.

With seventeen aircraft sheds, Lympne was one of the largest aerodromes in the South East of England, but this amazing view only lasted until the Second World War, when the Luftwaffe virtually bombed the history out of the place.

Lympne (Hythe)

51°04′38″N/01°00′53″W, TR112352. Off Aldington Road and Otterpool Lane, E of Lympne, 3 miles W of Hythe

OPENED in September 1916 as a replacement for the site east of the village, the first unit here was the former Machine Gun School, which had been redesignated as the School of Aerial Gunnery (SoAG). Occupying 205 acres and measuring 1,050 by 850 yards, Lympne (Hythe) was established as a school aerodrome with Bessonneau hangars lined along Aldington Road and a rapidly expanding tented camp on the western side of the village. By late 1916 Lympne Castle was being used as the officers' mess, while the tents were replaced by wooden huts built on allotments, much to the chagrin of the local villagers. By January 1917 the SoAG was redesignated again to No 1 (Auxiliary) SoAG and was very busy supporting a wide range of aircraft coming and going from the nearby ranges.

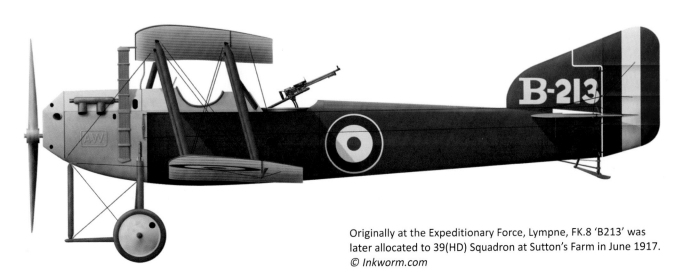

Originally at the Expeditionary Force, Lympne, FK.8 'B213' was later allocated to 39(HD) Squadron at Sutton's Farm in June 1917.
© Inkworm.com

As early as 1916 an Aircraft Erection Section was established, which evolved into the Aircraft Erection Park in January 1917. The seeds were now sown for Lympne to become an AAP, and it became No 8 (Lympne) AAP on 10 October 1918. Lympne continued to expand when the Bessonneaus made way for six 1918-pattern GS Sheds (with sliding doors) of 180 by 100 feet, nine 1916-pattern GS Sheds (170 by 80 feet), one Aeroplane Shed (150 by 80 feet), and a single Running Shed (160 by 80 feet). The usual collection of technical and domestic buildings continued to grow, mainly along the southern edge of the site, close to the village. During the construction of the hangars, on 25 May 1917, the aerodrome came under attack from several Gothas of Kagohl 3, which had been unable to bomb London because of poor weather.

In early 1918 No 8 AAP handled all types of aircraft destined to serve with the Expeditionary Force in France, and it was not long before the unit was outputting more than forty aircraft per month. 1918 also saw Lympne classified as an NLG1 for the use of 50(HD) Squadron until November. Several RAF squadrons passed through the aerodrome in 1919 and, remaining firmly under Air Ministry control, No 8 AAP was not closed down until November 1921. The airfield remained in military hands and an RAF presence began to return from the late 1920s onwards, by which time the majority of the buildings close to the village and Aldington Road had been dismantled, although the GS Sheds off Otterpool Lane remained. The airfield was destined to enjoy a busy career during the Second World War, but thanks to a few Luftwaffe raids during the Battle of Britain the last vestiges of the earlier site were razed to the ground. In civilian hands after the war, Lympne enjoyed another busy period as Ashford Airport, until the site was finally closed down in the 1970s.

Lympne (Hythe) main units, 1916-19

Aeronautical Inspection, Lympne, formed April 1916 in 8th Wing and Northern Command to handle aircraft in transit to/from BEF; redesignated 8 (Lympne) AAP, 10 Dec 1917

SoAG formed (ex-Machine Gun School) from original Lympne site, 13 Sep 1916; redesignated 1 (Aux) SoAG

Aircraft Erection Section formed 1916; redesignated Aircraft Erection Park, 1 Jan 1917

Aircraft Erection Park formed 20 Jan 1917 in place of Aircraft Park, Hurst Park, under Inspector of Repair Depots; redesignated AAP Lympne, 1 Sep 1917

1 (Aux) SoAG detachment (ex-SoAG) Jan 1917; to Dymchurch, Feb 1917

OC Ferry Pilots from South Farnborough, 30 Apr 1917; at Lympne came under control of Directorate of Air Organisation and attached to Aircraft Erection Park; fate unknown

8 (Lympne) AAP formed (ex-Aircraft Erection Park) 10 Oct 1917; DB Nov 1921

98 Sqn from Old Sarum, 1 Mar 1918; to St Omer, 1 Apr 1918 (DH.9)

108 Sqn cadre from Gondecourt, 16 Feb 1919; DB 3 Jul 1919

102 Sqn cadre from Serny, 26 Mar 1919; DB 3 Jul 1919

120 Sqn from Hawkinge, 17 Jul 1919; DB 21 Oct 1919 (DH.9)

83 Sqn cadre from Hawkinge, Sep 1919; to Croydon, 15 Oct 1919

Manston (Manstone)

51°20'43"N/01°21'13"W, TR337660. Former Kent International Airport and RAF Manston (DFTDC), 2.75 miles W of Ramsgate

THE colossal sprawl that became Kent International Airport began life in 1915 as a humble NLG of 20 acres for RNAS aircraft operating out of Westgate. A pair of duty Air Mechanics, operating from a converted packing case equipped with a telephone and two bunks, would run the field, lighting gooseneck flares to mark it out. By February 1916 the site was known as Manstone LG and facilities had improved to a pair of wooden huts and a single temporary hangar. A few months later the nucleus of 3 Wing RNAS moved in from Detling, followed by the RNAS War Flight from Westgate, marking the point at which the aerodrome began to rapidly expand.

Now known as Manston, the aerodrome was classified as an HD Flight Station of 40 acres, but would grow to occupy 680 acres and measure 2,000 by 2,000 yards, and its infrastructure would expand continually until late 1918. It was not until 1917 that it was decided to make Manston a permanent station, which, together with Cranwell, would

MANSTON 1918

Manston aerodrome covered 680 acres of land spread across a pair of well-furnished sites. The tightly packed hutted area to the north is the location of the modern-day fire training area.

Camel B3834 of the Manston War Flight; in the hands of Flt Lt A. F. Brandon it contributed to the destruction of a Gotha over Margate on 22 August 1917.

become one of the main instructional units for the RNAS. As well as the original technical site on the eastern boundary, the aerodrome expanded on the western side by some margin. Rows and rows of accommodation huts, workshops and classrooms sprang up, and by mid-1918 more than 2,500 personnel (of which 750 were pupils) were on strength. By now 100 acres of aerodrome was covered in buildings, including new hangars made up of four F-Type Aeroplane Sheds (200 by 100 feet), five Aeroplane Sheds (three 200 by 106 feet, one 180 by 60 feet and one 70 by 70 feet), and twenty-two Bessonneaus. Four underground hangars were commissioned in 1917, but by the end of war only two were finished on the very edge of the northern boundary.

Manston became a Marine Operations (Aeroplane) Station from May 1918 with one flight of Camels and two of DH.9s,

which later came under the control of 219 Squadron. The half-dozen Camels of 470(F) Flight carried out seaplane escort duties while the DH.9s of 555 and 556 Flights were employed on anti-aircraft patrols. 2 (Observers) School was also formed here in September 1918 to teach aerial gunnery, map-reading and aerial photography during a six-week training course.

With so much invested in Manston, it was unsurprisingly retained after the war and was destined to remain in RAF hands until 1996; even today it retains an RAF presence. The bulk of the airfield was sold off by the RAF in 1989 to become Kent International Airport, which only recently closed to passenger operations on 15 May 2014. A large number of First World War huts still survive as part of the original RAF camp and fire training area; the future for the airfield itself, though, is now in doubt.

Manston main units, 1916-22

3 Wing RNAS (nucleus) from Detling, 29 May 1915; to Luxeuil, Oct 1916 (O/100 and 1½ Strutter)	DH.9, Pup and 504)
War Flight RNAS from Westgate 27 Jun 1916; redesignated 470 Flt, 27 May 1918	470(F) Flt formed 27 May 1918; absorbed into 219 Sqn, 22 Jul 1918 (Camel)
HP Sqn formed 1916; to Luxeuil, 21 Dec 1916 (O/100)	555 and 556 (LB) Flts formed 26 Jun 1918; absorbed into 219 Sqn, 22 Jul 1919 (DH.9 and DH.9A)
HP Training Flt formed 4 Dec 1916; to Stonehenge, Jan 1918 (O/100)	55 TDS formed (ex-203 TDS) 14 Jul 1918; to Narborough, 12 Sep 1918 (DH.4, DH.6. BE.2E, Dolphin, Camel, 504, DH.9 and SE.5A)
War School RNAS formed 11 Sep 1917; redesignated Pool of Pilots, 1 Apr 1918 (Scout)	219 Sqn formed (470, 555 and 556 Flts) 22 Jul 1918; DB 7 Feb 1920 (Hamble, Baby, DH.9, Camel, 184 and IIIB)
DH.4 School RNAS formed 1917; DB into 203 TDS, 1 Apr 1918	2 OS formed 14 Sep 1918; DB into 1(O)SoAG, New Romney, Sep 1919 (DH.4 and 504)
Pool of Pilots (ex-War School RNAS) formed 1 Apr 1918; to Joyce Green, 5 Oct 1918 (various aircraft)	1(O)SoAG from New Romney, Sep 1919; DB Dec 1919
203 TDS (ex-DH.4 RNAS School) 1 Apr 1918; redesignated 55 TDS, 14 Jul 1918 (BE.2C/E, RE.8, DH.4, DH.6,	

Marden (Staplehurst)

51°09′56″N/00°31′15″W, TQ764438. 1.4 miles ESE of Marden village, 1.4 miles W of Staplehurst village

MARDEN was opened in October 1916 as an HD NLG2 for 50(HD) Squadron, which had recently moved to Harrietsham with a collection of BE.2Cs, BE.12s and a few Vickers ES.1s. A generous LG occupying 65 acres and measuring 900 by 440 yards made Marden one of the more inviting options to land in the event of an emergency. Facilities only included a single Bessonneau hangar, but word soon spread that the food at the nearby Station Hotel in Staplehurst was excellent, and many aircrew, especially those from 141 Squadron at Biggin Hill, made a regular habit of making 'precautionary' landings at Marden.

Marden's size saw the establishment of an Aeroplane Despatch Section from October 1916 under the control of Aircraft Park, Farnborough. The section only remained until March 1917 when the new, larger and more organised AAPs were formed.

143(HD) Squadron operated from Marden from February 1918, flying the SE.5A at first, then the Camel from August 1918.

The aerodrome remained in military hands until October 1919, but continued to enjoy a busy civilian period until its final closure on 24 June 1935.

New Romney (Littlestone)

Aerodrome: 51°00′51″N/00°58′25″W, TR087292. Bisected by Romney, Hythe & Dymchurch Railway (laid in 1925), N of Jefferstone Lane, St Mary's Bay
South Camp: 51°00′28″N/00°58′27″W, TR088285. S of Jefferstone Lane, N of New Sewer (Drain), St Mary's Bay

NOW virtually erased by the expanding coastal village of St Mary's Bay, New Romney was opened on 1 August 1917 for the newly formed 3 (Auxiliary) SoAG. It was a sprawling site of 450 acres on both sides of Jefferstone Lane up to the Dymchurch Road (A259) on the water's edge. Permanent hangars included two Aeroplane Sheds (90 by 70 feet and 80 by 60 feet), at least a dozen Bessonneau hangars, and more than fifty supporting structures mainly built south of Jefferstone Lane.

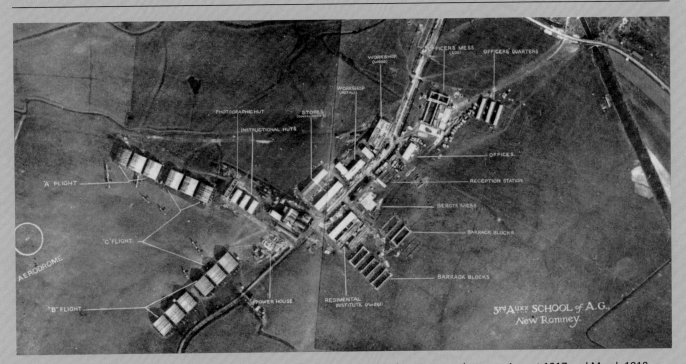

This aerial view shows New Romney during the tenure of 3 (Auxiliary) School of Air Gunnery, between August 1917 and March 1918, when it became 1 (Observers) School of Gunnery. The labels give an idea of how a typical site was segregated from the locations of individual aircraft flights, the barrack blocks and messes.

After being redesignated as 1 (Observers) SoAG, the unit remained until 1919, leaving for Dymchurch (Hythe), only to reform in September of that year and depart again for Manston. By November service pilots were told not to land at New Romney, and soon afterwards the aerodrome was in the hands of the Government Surplus Property Disposal Board. New Romney was then selected as an ELG for civilian aircraft crossing the Channel from the mid-1920s until the mid-1930s. Many of the buildings, especially on the southern side of site, were still extant during the Second World War.

New Romney main units, 1917-19

3 (Aux) SoAG formed 1 Aug 1917;
redesignated 1 (Observers) SoAG detachment, 9 Mar 1918

1 (Observers) SoAG (ex-3 (Aux) SoAG) detached 9 Mar 1918; absorbed into parent, 1 Nov 1918

120th Aero Sqn, USAAS, from USA 9 Mar 1918;
to Wittering (Stamford), 10 Aug 1918 (no aircraft)

1 (Observers) SoAG from Dymchurch (Hythe), 1 Nov 1918;
to Dymchurch (Hythe), 1919
(504, F.2B, Pup, DH.4, FK.3 and O/400)

1 (Observers) SoAG reformed (absorbed 2 OS from Manston) Sep 1919;
to Manston, Sep 1919

Old Romney

50°59'26"N/00°53'06"W, TR032254. NW of Old Romney village, 2 miles W of New Romney

THIS small site was opened between 1917 and 1918 as a kite balloon station for balloon and artillery co-operation, presumably with both RFC and, later, RAF units.

Penshurst (Chiddingstone Causeway)

51°12'00"N/00°10'46"W, TQ523468. Due N of Chiddingstone Causeway, W of Blackhoath Wood, 4 miles W of Tonbridge

FIRST opened as an HD Flight Station for a detachment of 'C' and 'B' Flights of 78(HD) Squadron from Hove on 25 December 1916, Penshurst was better known as the home of No 2 Wireless School. Classified as an NLG2 and later an NLG1, the site occupied 73 acres, measured 800 by 500 yards, and was furnished with a pair of Aeroplane Sheds (130 by 60 feet). 'B' Flight of 78(HD) Squadron left the aerodrome for Gosport on 20 September 1917, although Penshurst retained its HD Flight Station status for the benefit of 39(HD) Squadron, which remained until November 1918.

No 2 Wireless School was formed here on 8 November 1918 with a mix of aircraft including the 504, BE.2C/E, Snipe, Camel and DH.6; eighteen of the latter made it the most common type in use. The school was tasked with training aircrew in the art of wireless work, specifically in co-operation with Coast Defence Artillery, anti-aircraft guns and any Allied force engaged in HD against enemy aircraft. Subjects taught included the following:

1 Wireless officers in higher technical wireless work; 2 Wireless operators and mechanics in wireless telephony, continuous wave and tonic train; 3 Scout pilots in wireless telephony, formation flying and reception of orders at a range of 100 miles, from ground stations in the London Defence Area; 4 Pilots and observers in aircraft reception of tonic train and spark wireless observing for coast defence guns against hostile naval surface craft; 5 Special training for home defence troops as directed by home forces; 6 Inter-communication schemes between VI Brigade, RAF units and home divisional and corps HQs; 7 Depot for wireless stores, repair of apparatus and testing.

The average course length was a week for a scout pilot and four weeks for wireless operators. On 23 March 1919 the Wireless School was disbanded and the airfield was closed. Civilian flying returned in the 1930s and in 1942 the site was reopened under the control of 35 Wing, Army Co-Operation Command. A variety of communications squadrons passed through, mainly with Austers, until the site was closed down for good in March 1945.

Pluckley

51°10'23"N/00°44'16"W, TQ914452. 0.6 miles due W of Pluckley village, 6.3 miles WNW of Ashford railway station

THIS 61-acre site opened as an HD NLG2 in January 1917 for the use of 50(HD) Squadron based at Harrietsham. This unit operated a wide range of aircraft, although the most common would be the ubiquitous BE.2C and later 'E', until the squadron moved to Bekesbourne in March 1918. Pluckley, which measured 900 by 360 yards, was then taken over by the Camels of 112(HD) Squadron until the end of the war. Pluckley was relinquished on 25 May 1919.

Plumstead Marshes, London Borough of Bexley

51°30'01"N/00°07'51"W, TQ480800. On playing fields (Southmere Park) on E edge of Earith Marshes, 0.75 miles NE of Abbey Wood railway station

THIS small HD NLG3 only served 39(HD) Squadron between April 1916 and May 1917 while the parent unit was based at Woodford Green.

Queenborough

51°24'39"N/00°43'30"W, TQ893716. On W side of Ladies Hole Point, 0.9 miles WSW of Queenborough, Isle of Sheppey

SHORT Brothers built at least one slipway on Ladies Hole Point, on Long Reach, for its own seaplanes in 1917.

Ramsgate

51°19'46"N/01°25'11"W, TR383644. Ramsgate's Royal Harbour

SEAPLANES are known to have operated from Ramsgate from as early as 1914, but beyond 1915 is unlikely. An RNAS 'branch station' was also planned to be established outside the town for a pair of HD aircraft, but there is no evidence that this station was ever established.

The one and only Short S.81, No 126, is pictured in Ramsgate Harbour circa 1914. The aircraft's main armament can be seen protruding from the front of the machine; this varied from a 1½ Vickers to a 6lb Davis.

Rochester (Chatham)

51°23'03"N/01°21'17"W, TQ737678. Off the Esplanade on E bank of River Medway, 0.6 miles SW of Rochester town centre

THE site of at least one slipway, which is extant, was built by Short Brothers for its seaplanes in 1913.

Sheerness I, Isle of Sheppey

51°25'59"N/00°44'58"W, TQ912741. Bisected by New Road, E of Brielle Way (A249), 0.75 miles SW of Sheerness

THE landscape has changed a great deal over the years around Sheerness, and the kite balloon training station established here in 1917 has long disappeared under houses and industry. Opened as Kite Balloon Station Sheerness, the site occupied 75 acres on the water's edge, but required no jetties, as its balloons would not be embarked on ships. Redesignated as 1 Balloon Training Base on 17 April 1918, the unit moved to Merifield in July 1919 and the site was closed down.

Sheerness II, Isle of Sheppey

51°25'57"N/00°46'20"W, TQ932744. Sheerness Holiday Park off Hallway Road, 0.7 miles SE of Sheerness

ALL 50 acres of this DLG are now occupied by a holiday park, but its original purpose was to serve artillery co-operation units. Measuring 400 by 400 yards, the LG was allocated to 39(HD) Squadron from May 1917 until 1919, when the site was abandoned.

Sole Street (Crundale)

51°12'N/00°59'W. Between the villages of Sole Street and Crundale

A 1918 survey of VI Brigade LGs describes Sole Street's location as simply 4.5 miles from Wye. The exact location of this NLG3 is unclear, but it is known that it was used by 50(HD) Squadron, occupied 21 acres, measured 350 by 400 yards, and was open between February 1917 and June 1919.

South Ash (Wrotham)

51°20'46"N/00°18'01"W, TQ603633. Between Rumney Farm and Bakers Wood, 0.6 miles S of Ash, 1.6 miles E of West Kingsdown

IN operation from December 1916, the main occupant of South Ash was 141(HD) Squadron, which did not use the site until early 1918. Occupying 35 acres and measuring 500 by 350 yards, South Ash was classified as an NLG2 and would most likely have been closed down by March 1919.

Swingfield

51°09'43"N/01°12'06"W, TR239452. Between Park Wood and Swanton Court Farm, 0.9 miles NE of Swingfield, 5.5 miles NW of Dover

FIRST opened as an unmanned ELG, by late 1916 the site was reclassified as an NLG2 for the use of 50(HD) Squadron. Rectangular in shape, Swingfield occupied 50 acres of land and measured 450 by 550 yards. Returned to the plough by 1919, the site was resurrected during the Second World War and, among other things, served as an ALG until it was closed down for good in 1945.

Throwley (Faversham)

51°14'48"N/00°51'02"W, TQ991535. W of Bell's Forstal, E of Dodds Willows, S of Throwley Forstal

THROWLEY began its association with aviation in October 1915 when it was opened as an NLG for 'C' Flight of 50(HD) Squadron. It was a bleak site at first, with only a few tents and a single requisitioned cottage. However, it was in a good position to deal with enemy raiders, and by mid-1917 had been elevated in status to that of a squadron station. By then the site occupied 87 acres, measured 900 by 550 yards, and was equipped with four Aeroplane Sheds (two 130 by 60 feet and two 180 by 100 feet) and three Bessonneau hangars. Trees were cut down in Dodds Willows to make room for a large hutted camp and several workshops, and at least three MT sheds were built.

An example of a Camel Night Fighter of 112(HD) Squadron, which served at Throwley during the later stages of the war.

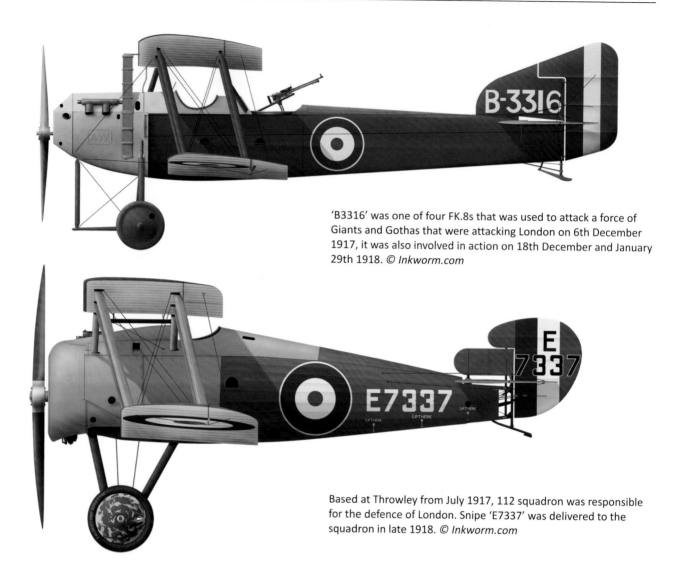

'B3316' was one of four FK.8s that was used to attack a force of Giants and Gothas that were attacking London on 6th December 1917, it was also involved in action on 18th December and January 29th 1918. © Inkworm.com

Based at Throwley from July 1917, 112 squadron was responsible for the defence of London. Snipe 'E7337' was delivered to the squadron in late 1918. © Inkworm.com

112 Squadron was formed here in July 1917 from 'B' Flight of 50(HD) Squadron, initially equipped with the Pup, which was later replaced by the Camel. It was with the latter that the squadron felt it had a decent machine capable of taking on the enemy, which by 1918 was the Gotha heavy bomber. By April 1918 the increasingly crowded aerodrome was also home to 186 NTS and 188 NTS, which moved in from East Retford. 112 Squadron had been frustrated on many occasions, but its day would come when the Germans launched an all-out forty-strong Gotha raid on the capital on the evening of 19 May 1918. On that day eighty-four defending fighters were in the air ready to greet the enemy, including 112 Squadron's Capt C. J. Q. Brand, who spotting a Gotha G.IV trapped in a searchlight beam at 8,700 feet over Canterbury. Brand's first burst of fire disabled one of the bomber's engines, forcing the Gotha to try and make a break for it. Brand stayed with the bomber and gave it a second burst of fire, which sent it crashing in flames near Harty Ferry on the Isle of Sheppey. Only thirteen of the forty made it to London and six were shot down; one of them by Capt Brand, who scored 112 Squadron's first and last success of the war.

The units at Throwley continued to fly defensive patrols until the Armistice, with an increasing number of fighters. 112

Squadron was the final unit here when it was disbanded in June 1919. By October the site was in the hands of the Ministry of Munitions, but appears not to have been used for any further military purpose and was quickly returned to the land. The site was classified as a dispersal ELG for RAF Detling during the Second World War, but whether it was used, despite the number of raids suffered by the Battle of Britain station, is doubtful.

Throwley main units, 1917-19

50 Sqn 'C' Flt from Harrietsham Oct 1916;
to Bekesbourne 1918 (BE.2C/E and BE12/A)

112 Sqn from Detling, 30 Jul 1917;
DB 13 Jun 1919 (Pup, Camel and Snipe)

143 Sqn formed 1 Feb 1918;
to Detling, 14 Feb 1918 (FK.8)

186 NTS (ex-112 Sqn) 1 Apr 1918;
to East Retford, May 1918 (DH.6 and 504J/K)

188 NTS from East Retford, 5 May 1918;
DB 1 Mar 1919 (DH.6, 504, Pup and Camel)

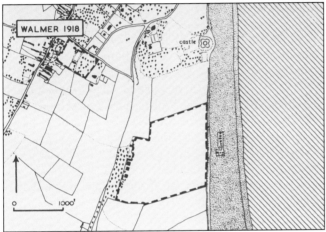

Camel B6242, named 'Fidgety Phil', served with 3 (Naval) Squadron and later the Walmer Defence Flight. *Via Stuart Leslie*

Operating half a dozen Camels, the flight was tasked with anti-seaplane operations, seaplane escort duties and aerial defence of the port of Dover. 491(LB) Squadron, operating DH.9s, also moved into Walmer on 31 August while 471 Flight left for Stahille, Belgium, on 28 October 1918. 491 Flight was disbanded in March 1919, leaving a detachment of 2 OS from Manston with DH.4s, which disbanded here in September 1919.

Quickly closed down, Walmer's wartime efforts were acknowledged by a memorial placed on the edge of the aerodrome, sponsored by the Countess Beauchamp on 8 August 1920. Walmer was used by the RAF during the Second World War as a station for MT. The site today is occupied by the Hawkshill Activity Centre, and the memorial, which was rededicated on 7 July 1952, is now looked after by the local RAFA.

Walmer

51°11'36"N/01°23'55"W, TR239452. On Hawkshill Down, W of Kingsdown Road, 0.9 miles SSE of Walmer

ONLY occupying 57 acres and measuring 550 by 550 yards, Walmer may have been small, but its excellent location on the Kent coast put it in the thick of action not long after it was opened in May 1917. The main resident unit was called the Walmer Defence Flight, equipped with the BE.2C, Scout and Pup. The aircraft were accommodated in three Aeroplane Sheds (65 by 60 feet) and a single Bessonneau lined up along the eastern edge of the Firs. Personnel were initially accommodated in tents, later replaced by wooden huts, while the officers stayed at Mayes Farm, then later 'Leelands' in Grange Road.

First success came for a Walmer-based aircraft when Canadian Flt Lt H. S. Kerby in a Pup attacked a formation of Gothas of Kagol 3 on 8 August 1917. After firing several rounds at the formation he spotted a straggler below, which he managed to force down into the sea. The German bombers returned two weeks later and Kerby claimed another Gotha, which was not confirmed, although the attacking force did lose nine aircraft, convincing them not to return again.

Walmer became a Marine Operations (Aeroplane) Station from June 1918 specifically for 471(F) Flight, which was under the charge of 233 Squadron based at Dover (Guston Road).

Walmer main units, 1917-19

Walmer Defence Flight formed May 1917;
became 6 (Naval) Sqn at Dover, 1 Jan 1918
(BE.2C, Scout and Pup)

3 (Naval) Sqn from Bray Dunes (Middle) from 27 Oct 1917;
to Bray Dunes, 3 Jan 1918 (Scout)

4 (Naval) Sqn from Bray Dunes (Frontier), 2 Jan 1918;
to Bray Dunes, 1 Mar 1918 (BE.8 and Nieuport 10)

8 (Naval) Sqn from Bray Dunes (Middle), 3 Mar 1918;
to Bray Dunes, 28 Mar 1918 (Camel)

471(F) Flight formed 14 Jun 1918;
joined 233 Sqn, 31 Aug 1918;
to Stalhille, 28 Oct 1918 (Camel)

491(LB) Flight from Dover (Guston Road) to join 233 Sqn, 31 Aug 1918;
DB 1 Mar 1919 (DH.9 and 1½ Strutter)

2 Observers School detached from Manston from Sep 1918;
DB by Sep 1919 (DH.4)

Westgate
(St Mildred's Bay and Mutrix Farm)

Seaplane: 51°23'05"N/01°20'42"W, TR328704. E edge of St Mildred's Bay, off St Mildred's Gardens, 0.5 miles ENE of Westgate-on-Sea town centre

Landplane: 51°23'03"N/01°21'17"W, TR334703. Due S of Sunken Garden, S of Royal Esplanade

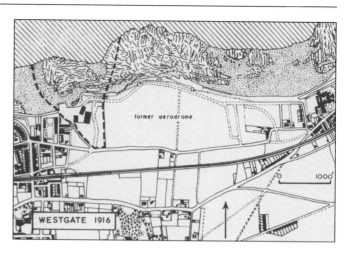

SEAPLANE operations first took place from St Mildred's Bay on 1 August 1914, and not long after a permanent seaplane station was established on the edge of the bay, built by Holland, Hannen & Cubitt. Large enough to accommodate a dozen seaplanes, Westgate had two Seaplane Sheds (60 by 180 feet and 100 by 200 feet) and two slipways. Twenty-three acres in size, the station was run by 16 officers, 9 SNCOs, 13 JNCOs and 73 other ranks. The station also had its own Wireless Station.

In 1915 the site was expanded when land at Mutrix Farm was requisitioned above the cliffs to the east for an aerodrome, which measured approximately 900 by 300 yards. Several huts and at least one Bessonneau hangar were built for the aerodrome, which operated a small War Flight until it was moved to Manston in July 1916 following several accidents.

On 25 May 1918 406(S) Flight was formed at Westgate with at least six 184s on strength, which were later joined by Baby and Hamble Baby seaplanes. The flight became part of 219 Squadron when it was formed at Manston on 22 July 1918, and it is possible that Camels from this unit occasionally used the aerodrome. This theory is reinforced by a detachment of Camels from 273 Squadron at Burgh Castle, which used Westgate aerodrome during the late summer of 1918. 442(S) Flight moved its IIIBs from Felixstowe to Westgate in November 1918 and remained until the unit was disbanded in February 1920. 406 Flight had already been disbanded in September 1919, and Westgate was closed down in March 1920.

One slipway from the seaplane station is extant, while the aerodrome site has disappeared under housing.

Westgate main units, 1918-20

406(S) Flt formed 25 May 1918;
DB Sep 1919 (184, Baby and Hamble Baby)

219 Sqn formed (seaplanes at Westgate, landplanes at Manston) 18 Aug 1918;
DB 7 Feb 1920
(184, Hamble Baby, Baby, DH.9, Camel and IIIB)

273 Sqn (detachment) from Burgh Castle summer 1918 (Camel)

442(S) Flt from Felixstowe 18 Nov 1918;
DB 7 Feb 1920 (IIIB)

Storage Section formed 1918;
closed Mar 1920

Acceptance Park, Killingholme, from Killingholme 11 May 1918;
closed down after arrival

Wittersham

51°01'18"N/00°41'17"W, TQ886281. Sheepwash Plantation, 1 mile NW of Wittersham, 5.75 miles NNW of Rye

ESTABLISHED as a sub-station for SS-Type airships operating out of Capel, Wittersham was operational from 1918 up to the Armistice. The site was little more than a clearing in Sheepwash Plantation, but proved useful as a place of shelter during poor weather conditions, to which the parent station at Capel was regularly exposed. Wittersham was slowly closed down after the Armistice and was officially relinquished on 31 March 1919.

Wye

51°11'37"N/00°55'22"W, TR044478. Between Boughton Corner and Maiden Wood off A28, 1 mile NW of Wye

ON the surface, Wye was a pleasant spot to locate an aerodrome, but the nearby wooded North Downs would catch out many an airmen when weather conditions took a turn for the worse. Regardless, the first of several training units arrived on 1 June 1916 when 20 TS made the short hop from Dover (Swingate Down). Occupying 86 acres and measuring 700 by 600 yards, facilities at Wye were basic at first, with all aircraft and personnel living under canvas, a situation that would remain for at least a further twelve months.

R.A.F. BE.2B 2774 is pictured at Wye possibly while in service with 20 TS in the summer of 1916.

Despite the poor facilities and conditions, 50 TS was formed here in December 1916, and 51 TS moved in from Filton in January 1917. By late 1917 the aerodrome was reorganised, leaving just 42 TS in situ, which had moved in from Hounslow in December. More permanent buildings were now erected at Wye, mainly concentrated near Maiden Wood. These additional buildings included three hangars, storage sheds and workshops for the use of an Anglo-American training unit. Three USAAS units eventually arrived at Wye from early 1918, but the main occupant was still 42 TS, which tirelessly produced as many trained single-seat fighter pilots for units in Northern France as it could. One of the tasks performed by 42 TS was air-to-ground firing, which was carried out on a steep hillside east of the town of Wye called 'The Crown' (51°10'52"N/00°57'45"W).

By the Armistice the Americans had left, leaving 42 TS to steadily wind down until it was disbanded on 1 February 1919. A few days later 3 Squadron cadre arrived from Inchy, remaining here until 2 May 1919, when it made the short journey to Dover (Swingate Down), and the process of closing down Wye began. By October the site was vacated, and in early 1920 fully relinquished.

Wye main units, 1916-18

20 TS from Dover (Swingate Down) 1 Jun 1916;
to Wyton 1 Jun 1917 (BE.2B/C, RE.8 and 504)

50 TS formed 7 Dec 1916;
to Narborough, 14 Dec 1916 (FK.3 and FK.8)

51 TS from Filton, 8 Jan 1917;
to Waddington, 14 May 1917 (BE.2C/E)

66 TS formed (out of 20 TS) 1 May 1917;
to Yatesbury, 20 May 1917
(BE.2C/E, BE.12, RE.8, Pup and DH.6)

86 Sqn from Shoreham, 17 Sep 1917;
to Northolt, 16 Dec 1917 (various aircraft)

42 TS from Hounslow 16 Dec 1917;
DB 1 Feb 1919 (FK.3, BE.2E, RE.8, Pup, Camel, JN.4 and 504)

24th Aero Sqn (USAAS) from USA, 31 Jan 1918;
to Narborough, 1 May 1918 (DH.4)

153rd Aero Sqn, 'C' Flt (USAAS) from USA by Jul 1918

165th Aero Sqn, 'B' Flt (USAAS) from USA by Jul 1918

3 Sqn from Inchy as cadre, 1 Feb 1919;
to Dover (Swingate Down), 2 May 1919

LANCASHIRE

Aintree Racecourse, Merseyside

53°28'41"N/02°56'39"W, SJ374983. On site of current Aintree Racecourse, Ormskirk Road, Aintree, Liverpool, L9 5AS

THE flat open surface of Aintree Racecourse was first used as a natural aerodrome in 1909 and, presumably, on and off until the outbreak of war. The military made use of Aintree from 1916, when the RFC established an examination ground under the control of 8th Wing, Western Group Command. From 1917 Aintree became the home of National Aircraft Factory No 3. The factory was operated by the Cunard Steamship Co Ltd, which manufactured the Bristol F.2B Fighter until late 1918. By then Factory No 3 was redesignated as No 4 Aircraft Salvage Depot, its tasking changing from production to reclamation within a short space of time. 1918 also saw the formation of No 4 Aircraft Storage Unit, which would have worked closely with the salvage unit, storing surplus airframes and engines. A final name change for the main unit to No 4 National Aircraft (Salvage) Depot came on 9 January 1919, but by the end of the year all resident units had been disbanded and the racecourse returned to its original intended equestrian role.

Barrow-in-Furness (Cavendish Dock)

54°06'13"N/03°12'45"W, SD208681. SW side of Cavendish Dock, 1.25 miles SSE of Barrow-in-Furness railway station

THIS dual site was used as an airship construction station by Vickers Sons & Maxim, and for hydro-aeroplane experiments, under the guise of the HMS *Hermione* Flying Club. Occupying a 142-acre area, this was the infamous location were HMA *Mayfly* broke her back before her maiden flight on 24 September 1911.

Above: The ill-fated airship HMA *Mayfly* at Cavendish Dock not long before she broke her back before her maiden flight in September 1911.

Left: A two-seat Camel conversion, B9140 was a presentation aircraft titled 'Jonathan. Presented by the Paramount Chief and Basuto Nation'. The aircraft is pictured in service with 42 TS in early 1918. *Via Stuart Leslie*

Barrow-in-Furness (Walney Island)

54°06'57"N/03°15'50"W, SD174696. Between West Shore Road and Cows Tarn Lane, 0.5 miles W of North Scarle, 0.75 miles SSW of Walney Island Airport

THIS airship construction station took up 325 acres of land in an area that is now known as North Walney. Measuring 1,730 by 1,186 yards, one shed (539 by 148 by 95 feet) was built, which was joined by a single portable Airship Shed (300 by 45 by 52 feet). Several technical buildings were also constructed, and a property off Mill, 'Longland House' (since demolished), was requisitioned as the officers' quarters. The site was large enough for an LG, which was located north-north-east of the sheds.

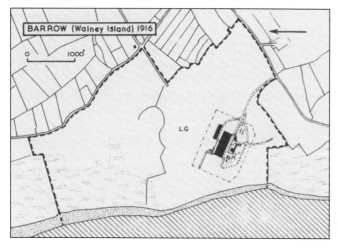

Opened in June 1914, the station was leased to Vickers Ltd, which was contracted to build rigid airships. The sheds drew the attention of German submarine *U-21* on 29 January 1915, which managed to fire a couple of rounds at the structure before being driven off by coastal guns at Walney Fort.

Two military units briefly served here, beginning with Aeroplane Detachment RNAS and the Rigid Airship Trials Flight RNAS. Barrow remained open until April 1921 and the site was relinquished on 8 August 1925.

Blackpool Sands

53°48'26"N/03°03'27"W, SD302350A. 0.25 miles S of Central Pier, 1 miles SSW of Blackpool railway station

A COMBINED manufacturer's aerodrome and LG, it was used occasionally by the RFC.

Didsbury (Manchester/Alexandra Park)

53°26'13"N/02°15'27"W, SJ834935. W side of Hough End Fields, Chorlton-cum-Hardy, 2.2 miles NNW of Didsbury railway station

ESTABLISHED in 1917, Didsbury was a substantial site covering 212 acres and measuring 1,400 by 500 yards. Its role was an Aircraft Acceptance Park for all locally built Avro aircraft, constructed by several manufacturers in the Manchester area. Six GS-pattern sheds (170 by 100 feet) were erected, all joined as three triple units, together with six storage sheds (150 by 60 feet).

The AAP became 15 (Manchester) AAP on 10 July 1918, only to be renamed Manchester Storage Park on 21 July 1919, although the latter role was brief, as it was closed down by the end of the year.

Flookburgh

54°10'05"N/02°57'44"W, SD372751. At Nun's Hill, due N of Cark airfield, 0.5 miles SE of Flookburgh

IN 1916 the airship station at Cavendish Dock was declared to be vulnerable to attacks by U-boats and the Admiralty set to work looking for an alternative location. Ten miles to the east a suitable site was found south-east of Flookburgh for the use of Vickers Ltd. However, thanks to shortages of steel and rising costs the project was abandoned in July 1917. During the Second World War the site became the home of Cark airfield.

Lytham

53°44'16"N/02°56'43"W, SD377272. Off Preston Road, 0.5 miles due S of Saltcotes

LYTHAM was the location of the manufacturer's sheds and slipways for the military flying-boats built by Dick Kerr and the Phoenix Dynamo Company. Up to 2000 the bases of two large seaplane hangars were extant; the site is now covered by housing.

Manchester (Burnage)

53°25'24"N/02°13'10"W, SJ855919. W of Parrs Wood Road, area of Fog Lane Park recreation ground, 0.2 miles NW of Burnage railway station

AN aerodrome that was used occasionally throughout the First World War, the site was first used by Louis Paulhan during the *Daily Mail* Air Race in 1910, which he subsequently won.

Manchester (Miles Platting)

53°29'39"N/02°12'23"W, SJ861996. W of Hulme Hall Lane (A6010), 0.75 miles NNW of Manchester City football ground

THIS was used by A. V. Roe & Company Ltd as a manufacturer's aerodrome throughout the war.

Manchester (Trafford Park)

53°28'20"N/02°19'14"W, SJ787973. Area of S. Norton & Co Ltd, W of Mellors Road, 1.3 miles NW of Manchester United football ground

FIRST opened for the Manchester Aero Club in 1911, the aerodrome saw limited use during the war.

Oldham (Chadderton/Hollinwood)

Aeroplane factory: 53°31'48"N/02°09'31"W, SD884039. Off Broadway, on N side of Rochdale Canal
LG: 53°31'49"N/02°10'38"W, SD884039. Due W of BAE Systems factory at Chadderton

THIS ambitious and complex site was spread over three locations taking up 212 acres of land. Named Aircraft Acceptance Park Oldham, construction began on 1 April 1918, with the intention of flight-testing American-built Handley Page O/400s for the USAAC, which had been assembled at Gorse Mill, Chadderton, and Lilac Mill, Shaw. Due west of the main factory site, six erecting shops (500 by 120 feet) were built, and west of the railway a further eight Aeroplane Sheds (280 by 150 feet) were constructed around the edge of an LG measuring 1,100 by 1,200 yards.

Construction was halted on 11 November 1918 when at an advanced stage and before it became operational. Twenty years later the same site was selected, west of the railway, by Avro for its Chadderton plant.

Scale Hall (Lancaster/Morecombe)

54°03'34"N/02°49'45"W, SD457628. S of A683 and A589, NE of White Lund Trading Estate, 1.8 miles ESE of Morecombe railway station

ESTABLISHED as a DLG for local units, Scale Hall occupied 49 acres and measured 476 by 500 yards.

LEICESTERSHIRE

Blaston (Uppingham)

52°33'30"N/00°46'19"W, SP829962. Due E of Belchers Hill crossroads off B664, 3.3 miles SW of Uppingham

DESPITE dense woodland located to the north and east of this site, an LG at Blaston was opened in December 1916 for 38(HD) Squadron. Classified as an HD NLG1, the LG was transferred to 90(HD) Squadron during the latter stages of the war. Blaston was relinquished in June 1919.

Brentingby (Melton Mowbray)

52°45'24"N/00°50'24"W, SK784184. 0.3 miles due S of Brentingby, 2 miles E of Melton Mowbray town centre

THE airfield at Brentingby was only open from April to October 1916 as an HD NLG2 for 38(HD) Squadron. This unit only moved to Melton Mowbray on 1 October 1916, and the squadron is believed to have used Scalford instead.

Burton on the Wolds (Loughborough)

52°47'07"N/01°05'11"W, SK609212. 1.3 miles due E of village centre, S of Melton Road

AN HD NLG3 opened in October 1916 for 38(HD) Squadron based at Melton Mowbray, Burton on the Wolds was a 27-acre LG measuring 500 by 100 yards. Reclassified as an HD NLG2 on 5 January 1917 and again as a DLG2 from 6 June 1917, the aerodrome was also used by 90(HD) Squadron, operating from Buckminster, from the summer of 1918. Burton would have been abandoned by early 1919.

Castle Donington

52°49'35"N/01°19'59"W, SK450257. Terminal 1, East Midlands Airport, 1 mile SSE of Castle Donington, 2.3 miles WSW of Kegworth

The first airfield on this site occupied just 18 acres and measured a mere 320 by 310 yards. It was classified as an HD NLG2 and opened on 1 October 1916 for 38(HD) Squadron. Reclassified as a DLG2 from 14 September 1917, Castle Donington remained open until August 1918. The site was obliterated by a much larger airfield during the Second World War and the original site is virtually covered by East Midlands Airport main terminal.

Loughborough Meadows

52°46'54"N/01°11'17"W, SK542212. 0.4 miles W of Cotes, N of A60, 0.3 miles E of current Brush Turbogenerators works

THE Brush Electrical Engineering Company can trace its roots back to the late 1870s with Francis Brush, the American inventor of the Brush arc lamp and dynamo. Brush was first associated with Loughborough in 1889 when, after a merger with the Falcon Engine & Car Works Ltd, the company moved to the Leicestershire town from London.

Brush's association with aviation began in 1915 when Winston Churchill, First Sea Lord of the Admiralty, announced that the RNAS was to be expanded. This led to the need for civilian factories, and Brush was one of the many organisations with the necessary skills to produce aircraft for the RNAS and, later, the RFC. Between 1915 and April 1919 the company produced more than 650 aircraft, including the Avro 504, Short Seaplane and Maurice Farman

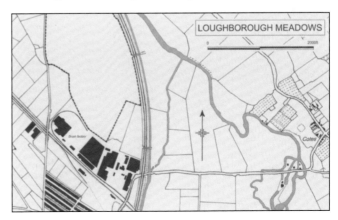

Longhorn. All this led to the first of two airfields being built in Loughborough, and Brush was fortunate that a suitable site was found near the factory. Loughborough Meadows was a large flat piece of land that was used by the company for test flying and delivery flights.

The LG was located to the north of factory between Meadow Land and the railway line. When aircraft production ended in 1919, the LG fell into disuse and was later used for many years as a racecourse, and flying never returned.

Peckleton (Desford)

52°36'49"N/01°17'39"W, SK479022. Halfway between Peckleton and Desford

USED exclusively by 38(HD) Squadron from October 1916 through to August 1918, Peckleton was an HD NLG2. It only saw occasional use by the squadron's aircraft and was quickly restored to farmland when relinquished. It was reactivated as Desford airfield in 1929.

Queniborough

52°41'44"N/01°01'58"W, SK654113. N of Ridgemere Lane, 0.6 mile SE of Queniborough village centre

THIS small HD NLG2 opened in the spring of 1916, but on 30 June was reclassified as an NLG3 and DLG before the arrival of 38(HD) Squadron in October. Queniborough was relinquished by August 1918.

Scalford (Melton Mowbray)

52°47'12"N/01°54'03"W, SK74228. N of Nottingham Road (A606), E of Sysonby Lodge Farm, 1.4 miles NNW of Melton Mowbray town centre

SCALFORD was brought into use to replace Brentingby by late 1916 as an NLG2. At 49 acres and measuring 700 by 600 yards, this new aerodrome was twice the size of Brentingby and its location must have influenced the move of 38 Squadron HQ here on 1 October 1916. Scalford was regularly used until May 1918, when 38(HD) Squadron departed for its first tour in France. With the formation of 90(HD) Squadron at Buckminster, responsibility for Scalford was taken over by that Lincolnshire airfield until the end of the war, when it was no longer required.

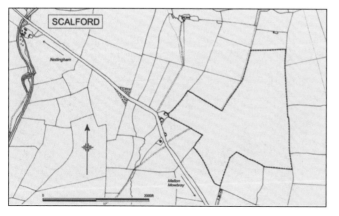

Welham

52°31'56"N/00°52'03"W, SP770933. W of Slawston Road, 0.9 miles SSW of Slawston, 4 miles NNE of Market Harborough railway station

MOST likely established for the use of 38(HD) Squadron, which moved into Melton Mowbray on 1 October 1916, Welham was a small LG that occupied 38 acres. It does not appear that the squadron made much, if any, use of the site, as it was closed down a few months later in favour of the much larger LG at Blaston. The same area was encompassed by a large parachute training zone during the Second World War.

LINCOLNSHIRE

Anwick/Ruskington Fen (Sleaford)

53°02'51"N/00°21'00"W, TF110515. SE of Poplar Farm, 0.75 miles N of Anwick, 2 miles E of Ruskington

ANWICK was in operation from September 1916 until June 1919 as an NLG2 for the use of 33(HD), 38(HD) and 90(HD) Squadrons. The site occupied 54 acres and measured 530 by 550 yards. During the Second World War the same site was used as a decoy airfield for nearby Digby between September 1939 and August 1942.

Blyborough

53°25'53"N/00°34'04"W, SK953937. 1 mile ESE of Blyborough village, 2 miles of SSE of Kirton-in-Lindsey airfield

A LARGE site, Blyborough occupied 101 acres of land and as such was classified as an HD NLG1. Opened in October 1916, the only user of the LG was 33(HD) Squadron until February 1918.

Bracebridge Heath (Robey's Aerodrome)

53°11'32"N/00°31'37"W, SK985673. Off Sleaford Road (A15) behind petrol station, 1.5 miles N of RAF Waddington, 2.7 miles SSE of Lincoln city centre

IN 1915 Lincoln-based Robey & Co Ltd won an Admiralty contract to build thirty Sopwith Type 806 Gunbuses. By the time the first examples were ready for flight-testing Robey had purchased several acres of land south of Lincoln at Bracebridge Heath. Here, two aeroplane workshops were built and a drawing office, which was run by Mr J. A. Peters. Only seventeen Gunbuses were built by Robey, the remainder being supplied as spare parts, although in the meantime Peters began to design Robey's first aircraft, a single-seat scout biplane. Neither this nor a subsequent design for a pusher biplane left the drawing board, but an anti-Zeppelin machine designed to an Admiralty specification did. Two prototypes of the Robey-Peters fighting machine (aka Davis Gun Machine) were built; the first crashed onto a nearby hospital and the second stalled on take-off and was wrecked in January 1917. Not long afterwards Peters left the company, and the design office was closed down.

Robey-Peters Davis Gun Machine 9498 at Bracebridge Heath.

All seven GS Sheds were still extant at Bracebridge Heath in 1995.

Bracebridge began a lengthy period of expansion from 1916, the site now occupying 111 acres and measuring 950 by 600 yards. That same year the site was classified as an HD NLG and AAP for the RFC, and the first of many Bessonneau hangars were erected. By late 1917/early 1918 these were joined by seven 1918-pattern GS Sheds (170 by 100 feet) and, later in the year, two Handley Page Sheds (540 by 170 feet), built along the hedgeline behind the current Bracebridge Heath Recreation Ground.

The site also became the home of National Aircraft Factory No 4, which was opened on 2 October 1917 but did not accept its first aircraft until 10 April 1918. Bracebridge became very busy very quickly, as the production rate of local manufacturers, such as Clayton & Shuttleworth, Dick Kerr, Marshall Sons and Ruston Proctor, increased and they delivered their aircraft for acceptance.

The LG also served a couple of RAF units: 120 Squadron came from Cramlington on 3 August 1918, and 121 Squadron was reformed on 14 October. By November 120 Squadron had moved out to Wyton, and 121 Squadron disbanded before an aircraft was received. The same month Bracebridge got busier when 4 (Lincoln) AAP moved in from West Common. The AAP was disbanded in March 1920 and the aircraft factory was closed down the following month, leaving Bracebridge in a state of Care & Maintenance.

In 1941 the site was requisitioned by the Ministry of Supply and placed in the hands of Avro as part of a repair organisation for the Lancaster. After the war Lancasters, Lincolns and Yorks passed through for repair, all being towed down the A15 with their outer wings missing, for final assembly and flight-testing from nearby RAF Waddington. The two-seat Avro 707C was also built at Bracebridge and, with the gradual changes in the aviation industry, the site passed through the Hawker Siddeley days to British Aerospace, which closed down the site in 1982. A single GS Shed is immaculately presented by classic car specialists Rimmer Brothers, and opposite is a triple GS Shed, although all but the furthest from the road now have pitched, rather than curved, roofs.

Braceby

52°54'36"N/00°29'23"W, TF016358. 0.6 miles NNE of Braceby, 6.5 miles E of Grantham town centre, S of the A52

OPENED as an HD NLG2 for 33(HD) Squadron in October 1916, Braceby only took up 38 acres and measured 500 by 540 yards. The squadron gave up Braceby in May 1918, but in August 90(HD) Squadron took over until the site was relinquished in June 1919.

Buckminster

52°48"16"N/00°40'27"W, SK893235. Due S of Aerodrome Farm off Crabtree Road, 1.1 miles NE of Buckminster, 2.4 miles W of Colsterworth

ARTHUR Harris is a name more synonymous with Bomber Command during the Second World War. However, during the First World War he was a young officer

tasked with travelling the area to look for suitable sites for HD airfields. With the increase in German Zeppelin activity in late 1915 and early 1916, several new squadrons were formed for the protection of the industrial Midlands.

Harris chose a site near Buckminster, which lay to the north-east of the village (located in Leicestershire), and was just a few yards over Lincolnshire border. The aerodrome was first occupied by 'B' Flight, 38(HD) Squadron, from 1 September 1916, the site opening as an HD Flight Station.

The aerodrome occupied 196 acres and measured 1,300 by 750 yards and was initially furnished with a pair of HD-pattern Flight Sheds (80 by 65 feet). By mid-1918 38(HD) Squadron made way for 90(HD) Squadron, which was reformed on 14 August 1918, the unit's HQ being located in Buckminster Hall on the northern edge of the village.

In the meantime, Buckminster was chosen as a site for an AAP, the protracted construction beginning in early 1918. To help the process along, a large number of German POWs were drafted in to help with the building work. Buckminster expanded rapidly on both sides of Crabtree Road, including the erection of seven 1918-pattern GS Sheds (170 by 100 feet). Still under construction at the time of the Armistice, rather than carrying out its intended role of accepting locally built aircraft the AAP was used for storage and was closed down by 1919. By later that year the site was rapidly wound down and fully closed by early 1920, although the buildings lingered on for many years.

Buckminster main units, 1916-19

38 Sqn 'B' Flt from Castle Bromwich, 1 Sep 1916;
to Cappelle-la-Grande, 29 May 1918
(BE.2C/E, BE.12 and FE.2B)

38 Sqn 'C' Flt from Melton Mowbray, 1 Sep 1916;
DB 29 May 1918 (various aircraft)

Storage AAP formed Feb 1918;
DB 1919

38 Sqn Depot detached by 29 May 1918;
absorbed into 90 Sqn, 14 Aug 1918

92nd Aero Sqn, 'B' Flt, USAAS, by 17 Jul 1918;
to Ford Junction

90 Sqn reformed 14 Aug 1918;
DB 13 Jun 1919 (504K)

1 POW MT Repair Depot formed 14 Oct 1918;
DB 1919

Bucknall (Horncastle)

53°12'37"N/01°14'33"W, TF174696. 1 mile W of Waddingworth, 1 mile due N of Bucknall

THIS 32-acre LG, measuring 600 by 300 yards, was opened in October 1916 following 33(HD) Squadron's move from Tadcaster to Gainsborough. Initially classed as an HD NLG2, Bucknall was reclassified as an NLG3 from 14 September 1917, before it was closed down in June 1919.

Cranwell's North aerodrome was dominated by a 700-foot-long Rigid Airship Shed, which dwarfs the accompanying Coastal Patrol and single SS Airship Sheds.

Cranwell (North and South)

South airfield: 53°01'49"N/00°29'00"W, TF010510;
North airfield: N53°02'32"N/00°29'32"W, TF015490.
Current RAF Cranwell, N of A17, 4 miles NW of Sleaford

IT was 1914 when an Admiralty survey party first visited an area of open land west of Cranwell village. Under the Defence of the Realm Act, the land was requisitioned for an aerodrome to train pilots, not only to fly aircraft but also kite balloons, free balloons and dirigible airships. Additional instruction would also be given in the art of bomb-dropping, gunnery and torpedo delivery, and wireless and navigation training.

Frederick Sage-built Avro 504K (F8759) fronts this line-up on the South aerodrome at Cranwell, with a pair of F-Type sheds in the background. Two F-Types remain in use to this day.

Work began on 28 December 1915 on this huge aerodrome, occupying 2,466 acres and measuring 4,200 by 2,800 yards, bisected by Cranwell Avenue, which conveniently separated the site into North and South aerodromes. Construction began on the south side of Cranwell Avenue, where four Type-F sheds (200 by 100 feet) and two 1916-pattern Aeroplane Sheds (180 by 60 feet) were built. On the north side were one Rigid Airship Shed (700 by 150 feet), one Coastal Patrol Airship Shed (220 by 70 feet) and one SS Airship Shed (151ft 9in by 44ft 10in). A large number of technical and accommodation huts were erected and the station was linked to Sleaford via a new branch railway line.

On 1 April 1916 Cranwell was officially opened as HMS *Daedalus* supporting the following units: the Aeroplane School (Central Training Establishment); the Kite Balloon Training Depot; the Free Balloon Training Depot; a Class G Airship Training Station; a Boys Training Wing; a Physical Training School; and a Boy Apprentices School.

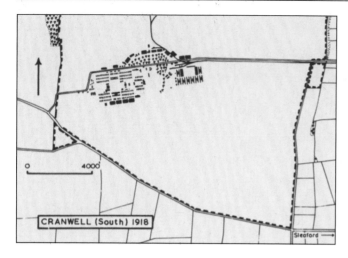

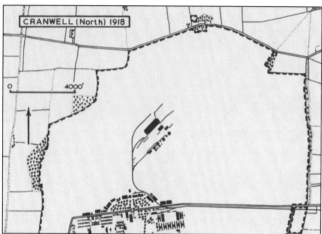

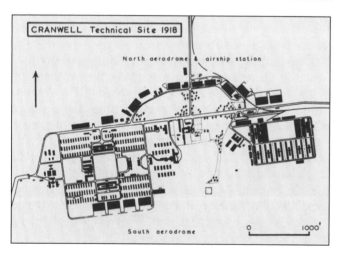

Trenchard, Chief of Air Staff, the site was chosen as a location for a new RAF Cadet College, and has remained so ever since.

Two of the original F-Type sheds are still in use on the South aerodrome, which remains fully active, and while the Airship Sheds have long gone the North aerodrome is equally active as a glider field.

Cranwell main units, 1916-29

RNAS Central Training Establishment formed Apr 1916; redesignated 201 and 202 TDS 1 Apr 1918 (various aircraft)

Kite Balloon Training Depot formed Apr 1916; DB 1919

Free Balloon Training Depot formed Apr 1916; DB 1919

Wireless Experimental Section from Eastchurch, May 1916

Airship Training Wing formed Nov 1916; DB after May 1919

Wireless School formed 1917; DB 1918

201 TDS formed 1 Apr 1918; redesignated 56 TDS, 27 Jul 1918 (Camel, 504, RE.7, Pup and Scout)

202 TDS formed 1 Apr 1918; redesignated 57 TDS, 27 Jul 1918 (DH.4, DH.9, BE.2C/E, O/400 and RE.8)

12 Group HQ formed 1 Apr 1918; DB 1 Nov 1918

213 TDS formed 17 Jun 1918; redesignated 58 TDS, 27 Jul 1918 (O/400)

157 Sqn 'C' Flt nucleus formed Jul 1918; to Upper Heyford, 15 Jul 1918

58 TDS (ex-213 TDS) 8 Jul 1918; DB 13 Mar 1919 (O/400, FE.2B, 504, DH.6 and BE.2C/E)

56 TDS (ex-201 TDS) 27 Jul 1918; DB 13 Mar 1919 (Camel, 504, DH.9, Snipe and Pup)

57 TDS (ex-202 TDS) 27 Jul 1918; DB 13 Mar 1919 (BE.2C, DH.4, DH.6, DH.9, Camel and 504)

155 Sqn nucleus flt formed Sep 1918; to Chingford, 14 Sep 1918

RAF Cadet College formed 20 Feb 1919; redesignated RAF College 1 Feb 1929 (various aircraft)

From April 1918 flying training was carried out on a grand scale from the South aerodrome, when Cranwell started to form a three-unit-strong TDS. 201 and 201 TDS were formed here on 1 April for single-seat fighter training and day bombing training. They were joined by 213 TDS on 17 June, which was formed to train O/400 crews. All three were redesignated as 56, 57 and 58 TDS in July, and by then the three units had more than 120 aircraft on strength, including 504s, Camels, DH.4s, DH.9s and O/400s.

After the war, as with so many aerodromes across the country, Cranwell's future hung in the balance, but thanks to the efforts of Winston Churchill and Major General Sir Hugh

Cockthorne (Market Rasen)

53°22'31"N/01°22'12"W, TF076873. Off A46, 1.2 miles SW of Middle Rasen, 2.4 miles SW of Market Rasen

COCKTHORNE opened as an HD NLG2 in October 1916, taking up 56 acres and measuring 600 by 400 yards. Used solely by 77(HD) Squadron for its operations over Northern Lincolnshire, Cockthorne remained open until June 1919.

Cuxwold

53°29'27"N/01°13'18"W, TA181009. 0.5 miles ESE of Cuxwold, 3.75 miles E of Caistor

THIS large 80-acre HD NLG2, measuring 750 by 750 yards, was opened for 33(HD) Squadron in October 1916. On the night of 24/25 September 1917 the LG received the full attention of Zeppelin *Z46* while the runways were being lit by gooseneck flares. The airship's entire bomb load was dropped, but all fell harmlessly into surrounding fields. The LG was closed down by June 1919.

Elsham

53°36'36"N/00°24'33"W, TA055138. Due E of WW2 airfield, 1.5 miles NE of Elsham, 5.2 miles NE of Brigg

THE industrial importance of the Humber Estuary did not passed unnoticed by the Germans during the First World War. The new aerial threat in the guise of the feared Zeppelin began to make frequent visits over the area from 1916. Several Home Defence (HD) units were formed to defend against such attacks, including 33(HD) Squadron. After a few moves the squadron settled its HQ at Gainsborough on 3 October 1916. Several LGs were surveyed for its use throughout the county, including Manton (Kirton-in-Lindsey), Scampton and Elsham. The latter was located to the south-west of the crossroads where Wold Road and Race Lane meet.

Approximately 120 acres in size and measuring 800 by 600 yards, facilities would have been limited, but it is known that at least two HD-pattern Aeroplane Sheds (130 by 60 feet) were constructed. A small practice bombing range was also set up on one edge of the LG. From early 1917 'C' Flight of 33(HD) Squadron operated approximately eight R.A.F. FE.2Bs and FE.2Ds. While Zeppelin activity was high and encounters frequent, none were shot down, but several were claimed as being seen off. One notable pilot who served briefly at Elsham was Lt William Leefe Robinson VC.

On 12 June 1918 33(HD) Squadron moved its HQ to Kirton-in-Lindsey and the same month gained the capable F.2B Fighter. This was to be brief, however, because by August both detachments at Scampton and Elsham were brought to an end, as the Zeppelin threat had diminished. By late August 1918 Elsham was abandoned and, like so many other LGs, was returned to agriculture.

Freiston

52°56'58N/00°03'42"W, TF388408. 0.75 miles North Sea Camp (HM Prison), 4 miles ESE of Boston

FREISTON had a varied career that began in 1916 following the establishment of a range on the nearby mud flats, where a variety of targets, including at least one redundant aircraft, had been laid out. To cut down the time it was taking to fly to the range from Cranwell (approximately 40 minutes each way) it was decided to establish an ALG just over the sea wall from the range. The site occupied 90 acres and measured 500 by 500 yards. From late 1916 the RNAS Gunnery School had a detachment at Freiston, equipped with a variety of types including the BE.2, 504 and Camel.

The officer commanding No 4 SoAF&G, Cdr Harold Kerby DSC (left), stands in front of a Sopwith Camel at Freiston in 1918.

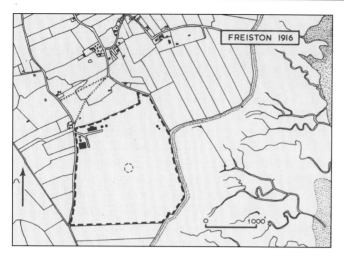

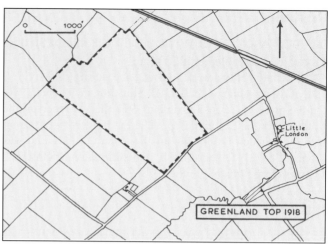

On 1 April 1918 the RNAS Gunnery School was redesignated the SoAF&BD. On 6 May the unit was renamed No 4 SoAF&G and finally to No 4 FS on 29 May 1918, now only equipped with the 504J/K, Camel, Snipe and Pup. Around this time a flight of Bristol Scouts tasked for anti-Zeppelin duties was attached to the Gunnery School, which may explain why Freiston was classified as an NLG2 between August 1918 and June 1919. No 4 FS was disbanded on 18 March 1920, and Freiston closed down shortly afterwards, but not before a serious storm demolished hangars and several wooden buildings. All that remained on the LG was subsequently sold off in a public auction and scattered to the four winds; remnants are very likely still to be found in farms and gardens in the locality.

Gosberton (Spalding)

52°51'07"N/00°16'05"W, TF167297. E of South Forty Foot Drain, 3 miles W of Gosberton Risegate, 6.3 miles NW of Spalding town centre

DESPITE being such a remote location, it only took a few gooseneck flares to expose the location of the HD NLG2 at Gosberton to the unwelcome attentions of a Zeppelin. Several bombs were dropped, their locations being occasionally exposed, from the air at least, when the conditions are right.

Opened in October 1916 for the use of 38(HD) Squadron, Gosberton occupied 55 acres and measured 400 by 640 yards. The squadron moved out in May 1918 and 90(HD) Squadron took over from August and remained until the site was closed down in June 1919.

Goxhill

53°40'55"N/00°18'57"W, TA113219. N edge of WW2 airfield off Ruard Road, 0.75 miles NE of Goxhill village

IN situ by 30 April 1916, thanks to information gleaned from a War Office map, Goxhill was opened as an HD NLG for 33(HD) Squadron. The unit's stay was short, as it had vacated by the autumn in favour of New Holland, and it was not until the establishment of the much larger Second World War airfield in 1941 that aviation returned. The First World War site was only yards from the later RAF Goxhill memorial.

Greenland Top (Stallingborough)

53°35'28"N/00°13'12"W, TA178120. Off Keelby Road, W of Little London, 1.5 miles WNW of Stallingborough railway station

GREENLAND TOP first came into use in December 1916 as an HD NLG1 for 33(HD) Squadron, a role that continued, albeit secondary, until June 1919. The threat of the Zeppelin was replaced by the U-boat during 1918, and Greenland Top, covering 112 acres and measuring 900 by 530 yards, was upgraded to a Marine Operations (Aeroplane) Station from May. Facilities remained sparse but 505(SD) Flight, which was formed here on 31 May with DH.6s, was provided with a few Bessonneau hangars for the aircraft and Armstrong huts for its personnel. 505(SD) Flight moved to West Ayton on 27 August, leaving Greenland Top virtually unused until it was designated as an RLG for Killingholme's land-based aircraft. This remained the state of affairs until 29 May 1919, when the relinquishment notification was issued, later confirming the closure of the aerodrome on 22 January 1920.

Harlaxton

52°52'58"N/00°39'33"W, SK905325. E of Gorse Lane, E of Warren Farm, 0.5 miles ENE of Harlaxton College, 2 miles SE of Grantham

FROM humble beginnings as an HD NLG1, opened in November 1916, Harlaxton grew quickly into a large TSS and TDS, occupying 386 acres and measuring 1,350 by 1,200 yards, with buildings on both sides of Gorse Lane. The site was originally allocated to 38(HD) and 90(HD) Squadrons for their local activities, but visits by aircraft from these units were rare.

Flying training would be the main focus here for the next two years, but the first unit was 68 Squadron, formed with DH.5s on 30 January 1917, the unit leaving for France in September. Several TSs passed through Harlaxton during 1917, including 20 TS from Spittlegate and 53 TS from Narborough in November and December respectively. In the meantime, construction work at Harlaxton was gaining momentum, including six 1917-pattern GS Sheds (170 by 80 feet) and an increasing number of supporting buildings, which now stretched along the western side of Gorse Lane within yards of Harlaxton Manor (the college

Two of the six GS Sheds under construction at Harlaxton not only expose the amount of timber needed but also the intricate and strong Belfast trusses that gave a span of 80 feet.
Via Stuart Leslie

A view of Harlaxton from the western side of Gorse Lane, looking north-east towards the GS Sheds in the distance.
Via Stuart Leslie

today). On 15 August 1918 20 and 53 TS were disbanded to create 40 TDS with an average strength of more than seventy aircraft and more than 600 personnel on station. The unit was tasked with training pilots for the reconnaissance role, and remained at Harlaxton until disbandment on 8 May 1919.

By early 1920 Harlaxton was closed down but, unlike many other similar sites, the buildings languished for many years. Several of the hangars remained until 1931, when they were finally sold off; one of them was dismantled and moved to Boston, were it served as a vehicle store for Holland Brothers until the mid-1970s. The airfield was reopened during the Second World War and remained in military hands until 1958.

Harlaxton main units, 1916-19

44 TS from Lilbourne, 13 Nov 1916;
to Waddington, 24 Nov 1917 (RE.7 and DH.4)

68 Sqn formed 30 Jan 1917;
to Baizieux, 21 Sep 1917 (DH.5)

54 TS from Wyton, 17 Mar 1917;
to Castle Bromwich, 12 Dec 1917 (DH.5 and Avro)

98 Sqn formed 15 Aug 1917;
to Old Sarum, 31 Aug 1917 (various aircraft)

26 TS from Turnhouse, 22 Sep 1917;
to Narborough, 3 Feb 1918 (various aircraft)

20 TS from Spittlegate, 27 Nov 1917;
DB into 40 TDS, 15 Aug 1918 (various aircraft)

53 TS from Narborough, 12 Dec 1917;
DB into 40 TDS, 15 Aug 1918 (various aircraft)

64 TS from Marham, 12 Dec 1917;
DB 15 Aug 1918 (Nieuport, Shorthorn, RE.8, BE.2E, DH.6 and 504)

85th Aero Sqn, USAAS, by July 1918

159th Aero Sqn, 'D' Flt, USAAS, by July 1918

40 TDS (ex-20 and 53 TS) 15 Aug 1918;
DB 8 May 1919 (DH.6. RE.8, FK.8 and 504)

Harpswell (Hemswell)

53°24'17"N/00°35'33"W, SK936906. E of Hemswell
village off B1398, on W edge of ex-RAF Hemswell

THE first of two airfields destined to be built on Hemswell
Cliff, 220 feet amsl, was opened in December 1916 as an
NLG1 for 33(HD) Squadron. By mid-1917 a decision was
made to enlarge the LG to an area of 152 acres and develop
Harpswell into a Night Training Squadron Station, which was
duly opened in June 1918. By then the LG had become more
established, with a brick-built operations room, four GS Sheds
(100 by 170 feet) and three more under construction, including
an ARS Shed; it now measured 950 by 800 yards.

The first training unit to move in was 199 NTS from East
Retford on 26 June 1918, equipped with the FE.2B and 1½
Strutter. It was joined on 10 November by 200 NTS, also from
East Retford with FE.2Bs and Avro 504Js and Ks. When the
war came to an end, all building and expansion work ceased,
but 199 NTS served on until 1 May 1919 and 200 NTS was
disbanded on 13 June 1919.

Harpswell was closed down in early 1920, although the
buildings lingered on for a few more years, the brick
operations room going on to survive the Second World War
expansion and be re-employed as a farm store.

Immingham (Aerodrome)

53°36'47"N/00°12'35"W, TA184145. Area of Oasis
Academy, off Pelham Road, 0.25 miles ESE of
Immingham town centre

A TEMPORARY aerodrome was operated on the eastern
side of Immingham between 28 July and 2 September
1914 for a detachment of RNAS Eastchurch Squadron (mobile).

Immingham (Kite Balloon Base)

53°37'29"N/00°11'11"W, TA199157. SE end of
Immingham Dock in area of Simon Storage, off
Alexandra Road South

ONE of several kite balloon stations established near
important ports, work began on 26 acres of land
belonging to the Great Central Railway at the south-eastern
end of the main dock in November 1917. A pair of canvas
Balloon Sheds (100 by 36 feet) and a dozen huts were erected.
On 15 April 1918 the site was renamed No 8 Balloon Base,
and by August four balloons were on strength, numbered
AM154, AM155, AM176 and AM219. Several vessels were
used to move the balloons offshore for their patrols, AM154
being the only casualty when it burst into flames on 2
September 1918. By January 1919 the three remaining
balloons were deflated and placed into storage, and No 8
Balloon Base was disbanded on 30 March 1919. The site was
quickly de-requisitioned and handed back to the Great Central.

Kelstern (Louth)

53°24'00"N/00°07'37"W, TF247908. 0.6 miles NW of
Kelstern, 1.25 miles SW of ex-RAF Kelstern, 5.8 miles
WNW of Louth

AT 400 feet amsl, the HD NLG1 at Kelstern was by far the
highest of its type used during the war. First surveyed in
1916, by December of that year 90 acres of land belonging to

A very rare aircraft and image of Albatros B.II No 890, spotted at
Immingham after it was impressed into RNAS service on 5 August
1914. The aircraft gave good service and was not deleted until
April 1918.

Mill Farm was requisitioned for use by the RFC. Located north of the village, the site measured 750 by 650 yards and was allocated to 33(HD) Squadron. As well as a safe haven, Kelstern provided a convenient refuelling point in the north of the county in support of efforts to defend against Zeppelin attacks.

The most common aircraft to use the LG would have been the FE.2B, FE.2D and, briefly, the F.2B. It was one FE.2B pilot, Lt A. R. Kingsford of 33(HD) Squadron, who recorded the following: 'October 18, 1917 – crashed on forced landing at emergency landing ground in fog, FE.2B 5636. Got teeth knocked out, Observer minor injuries. I left him with two mechanics and went to a farmer's home nearby, he was irate, being wakened at 3am, offered no help!' Kingsford went on to comment how he thought he had landed in 'No Man's Land' because of the bleakness of the LG.

Despite the war ending in November 1918 and the Zeppelin threat long gone, 33(HD) Squadron retained Kelstern until June 1919. It was then quickly cleared of all RFC traces and equally as quickly returned to the irate farmer.

More than 20 years later a much larger site to the north-east became a heavy bomber station between 1943 and 1945.

Killingholme

53°40'09"N/00°14'43"W, TA116203. N expansion of Humber Sea Terminal, 1.2 miles ENE of East Halton, 2 miles NE of North Killingholme

FIRST surveyed in late 1912 as one of a chain of new air stations along Britain's coastline, a small strip of land close to the Admiralty Oil Depot was selected for an LG. The site was originally named RNAS Immingham (not to be confused with the temporary aerodrome), but was renamed RNAS Killingholme when it opened in 1914. Hangarage was at first a single Bessonneau, which was supplemented by four Seaplane Sheds (77 by 66 feet) in September 1914.

The very first aircraft at Killingholme were a single Bristol TB.8, a pair of S.38s and a single DFW biplane, all under the command of Sqn Cdr Courtney, RMLI. These four primitive machines were tasked with defending the nearby oil depot,

At 800 feet long and 220 feet wide, the giant Seaplane Shed at Killingholme was one of the largest, if not the largest, buildings in the country. The huge structure was used by the USN to assemble a batch of Curtiss H.16 flying-boats that had been delivered by sea from the USA. Via Stuart Leslie

only armed at the time with twelve Hales grenades between them! As improved aircraft steadily arrived, Killingholme could expand its ability to perform coastal patrol duties as the presence of U-boats began to increase along the East Coast.

During 1915 a Preliminary Aeroplane School and a Seaplane War Flight were formed, giving Killingholme a dual role. The site grew to 142 acres, 60 of which were taken up by the original aerodrome, while the remainder became a seaplane station and later a seaplane school. Three slipways were constructed, one 700 by 60 feet and two at 850 by 35 feet; their above-average length was needed to reach the edge of the deeper water of the River Humber. Resident flying-boats began to increase in size from the manageable NT.4As through to the much larger Porte Babies, F.2As and H.16s. To accommodate these larger aircraft more hangars were required, including three Seaplane Sheds (one of 177 by 56 feet and two of 200 by 100 feet) and a huge Seaplane Shed (800 by 220 feet); the latter was the largest built in the country to date.

Killingholme became a Marine Operations (Seaplane) Station on 20 July 1918 and was now under the charge of the US Navy. Twenty-three Curtiss H.16s had been delivered in crates by the USS *Jason* in June for assembly in Killingholme's main hangar. The US Navy remained at Killingholme until January 1919, when the station was handed back to the RAF. Several squadrons returned from the continent to disband until the station was closed down in 1920. The site has had a number uses ever since, but today the modern terminal has erased all signs of the station with the exception of one rapidly deteriorating slipway.

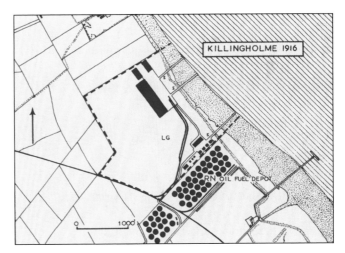

A batch of Pemberton Billing PB.25 'Push-Proj' pusher biplanes at Killingholme in 1917. Only twenty examples were built, the majority of them being stored at Killingholme until most were deleted by late 1917. *Via Stuart Leslie*

Short Type 320 (aka 310-A4) N1400 at Killingholme after its arrival on 16 February 1918.

Killingholme main units, 1914-19

Eastchurch Sqn (Mobile) RNAS detached from Eastchurch, 9 Aug 1914;
to Immingham, 23 Aug 1914

Preliminary Aeroplane School RNAS formed 1915;
DB 1915

Seaplane War Flight RNAS/RAF formed 1916;
redesignated 403 and 404 Flts, 30 May 1918

Acceptance Park (Killingholme) formed 1916;
DB Jul 1918

Seaplane School formed Apr 1916;
DB 20 Jul 1918

Flying-boat War Flight RNAS/RAF formed 1917;
redesignated 320, 321 and 322 Flts, 30 May 1918

320, 321 and 322(FB) Flts formed 30 May 1918;
DB 20 Jul 1918, aircraft to USNAS

403 Flt formed 30 May 1918;
to Seaton Carew (246 Sqn), 15 Aug 1918

404 Flt formed 30 May 1918;
to Hornsea Mere (248 Sqn), 15 Aug 1918

USNAS Flying-boat Flts (ex-320-322 Flts) formed 20 Jul 1918;
DB 6 Jan 1919

347 Flt, 238 Sqn from Cattewater, 5 Nov 1918;

to Holy Island, 11 Nov 1918

347 Flt, 238 Sqn from Holy Island, 19 Nov 1918;
to Calshot, 11 Dec 1918

Meteorological Station formed 5 Dec 1918;
DB 1919

251 Sqn cadre from Hornsea, 31 Jan 1919;
DB 30 Jun 1919 (no aircraft)

252 Sqn cadre from Tynemouth, 31 Jan 1919;
DB 30 Jun 1919 (no aircraft)

256 Sqn cadre from Seahouses, 31 Jan 1919;
DB 30 Jun 1919 (no aircraft)

229 Sqn cadre from Great Yarmouth, 3 Mar 1919;
DB 31 Dec 1919 (no aircraft)

249 Sqn cadre from Dundee, 3 Mar 1919;
DB 8 Oct 1919 (no aircraft)

228 Sqn cadre from Great Yarmouth, 5 Jun 1919;
DB 30 Jun 1919 (no aircraft)

Seaplane Flt, Murmansk, formed Jul 1919;
to HMS *Argus*, RAF Mission, Northern Russia, 23 Jul 1919

Seaplane Flt, Archangel, formed Jul 1919;
to HMS *Argus*, RAF Mission, Northern Russia, 23 Jul 1919

Kirton Lindsey (Manton)

53°30'39"N/00°34'41"W, SE949019. Due S of Newlands Farm, half of aerodrome now a quarry, 0.8 miles ESE of Manton, 2.3 miles NNE of Kirton-in-Lindsey

THIS large HD Flight Station was opened for 33(HD) Squadron in October, the unit's 'B' Flight moving in its FE.2B/Ds from Gainsborough on the 3rd. The site occupied 119 acres and measured 1,000 by 600 yards; 10 acres of the site was covered in buildings, including a pair of HD-pattern Aeroplane Sheds (140 by 65 feet) coupled together as a single unit, and one Bessonneau.

'B' Flight was joined by the rest of the squadron, also from Gainsborough, on 12 June 1918. Detachments were carried out to Scampton and Elsham before the Armistice, the squadron remaining at Kirton until 2 June 1919, when it made the short journey 7 miles south to Harpswell. Relinquished by mid-1919, the aerodrome was closed down in 1920 and today only half of the flying field remains to the east, the western half having since been quarried.

An Avro 50K of 33(HD) Squadron is pictured at Kirton Lindsey (Manton) in 1918.

Leadenham

53°03'33"N/00°33'29"W, SK967523. Off Pottergate Road, 1 mile E of Leadenham, 3 miles NW of RAF Cranwell

LEADENHAM was declared open with the arrival of 'C' Flight, 38(HD) Squadron and its four FE.2Bs (although BE.12s and BE.2Es were still on squadron strength) from Castle Bromwich on 1 September 1916. They were joined by four more FE.2Bs of 'A' Flight from Melton Mowbray on 2 October. Despite responding to every Zeppelin raid carried out over Lincolnshire, no success or even contact was made by the unit's aircraft.

By 1918 the role of 38(HD) Squadron was changed to bombing and, in preparation, the main unit moved from Melton Mowbray to Buckminster on 25 May. A few days later the squadron was on its way to France, and a depot detachment left behind at Leadenham was absorbed into 90(HD) Squadron, 'A' Flight, having moved in on 14 August. Equipped with the 504K(NF), 90(HD) Squadron retained a presence at Leadenham until its disbandment on 13 June 1919.

A pair of HD-pattern sheds (130 by 80 feet) were erected at Leadenham and several technical brick buildings, the aerodrome itself occupying 86 acres and measuring 800 by 600 yards. At least one of the latter buildings survives today, accessed by a period road off Pottergate Road.

Lincoln (Handley Page Field)

53°13'42"N/00°30'36"W, SK995711. Old factory site now home of Bifrangi UK Ltd, Tower Works, Spa Road, Lincoln

IN 1916 the established Lincoln engineering firm of Clayton & Shuttleworth expanded its skills into aircraft production, building a new factory east of its Stamp End Works. The new site was named the Abbey and Tower Works, and to the east of the new factory there was a reasonably sized LG. In October 1917 the company won a contract to build fifty Handley Page O/400s, and from that point the site was known by locals as Handley Page Field. The huge O/400s were far too large to be delivered by road to Lincoln (West Common), where they would be flight-tested. So, as lightly loaded as possible, the bombers were flown out of Handley Page Field and, after a short circuit, were back down on the ground a few minutes later on the other side of the city. The company was also contracted to build the Vickers Vimy, but few left the Tower Works before the contract was cancelled at the end of the war.

The site of the Abbey and Tower Works is now part of Bifrangi UK and is contained within the original factory's boundaries, leaving the original LG extant. The original Stamp End Works (SK984709) is also extant, complete with the letters C&S on the western end. The factory was named 'The Titanic Works' because it was the same length as the ship; the building is now called Witham Park House.

Lincoln (West Common Racecourse)

53°14'07"N/00°33'40"W, SK960719. West Common (aka Carholme), E of Saxilby Road (A57), 1 mile NW of Lincoln city centre

ONE of the country's most vibrant early centres for aircraft production, it was inevitable that Lincoln would house one of the busiest AAPs as the war gained momentum. The wide-open space of West Common Racecourse was first used as a manufacturer's aerodrome from 1915 by Clayton & Shuttleworth, Ruston Proctor & Co, Robey & Co and Marshall & Sons.

The military established itself here from April 1916 when the Aeronautical Inspection, Lincoln, was formed to accept new aircraft from local manufacturers. The aerodrome by this stage measured 1,000 by 700 yards and covered 129 acres, but it was already noted that the site was prone to flooding. Regardless, construction continued including two Aircraft

Sheds (140 by 60 feet) and two 1916-pattern GS Sheds (170 by 80 feet), and use was made of the existing racecourse buildings, including the grandstand.

On 22 March 1917 AAP (Lincoln) was formed to accept new aircraft from Leeds and Lincoln; these were from Blackburn (Kangaroo), Marshall & Sons (F.2B), Clayton & Shuttleworth (Camel and Handley Page), Marsh, Jones & Cribb (Camel), and Ruston Proctor (Camel).

Redesignated as 4 (Lincoln) AAP on 12 October 1917, the unit moved out to Bracebridge Heath in November 1918, by which time the demand for new aircraft had passed. The site was wound down in late 1919 and relinquished in early 1920. The aerodrome site is still much as it was during the First World War, including the officers' mess, which is now a tennis and bowls club. Another gem within the grandstand building is a large RFC mural over a fireplace, dated 1917.

Market Deeping

52°41′02″N/00°16′05″W, TF171110. 0.6 miles NE of Frognall, 2.2 miles E of Market Deeping town centre

KNOWN to locals as 'The 90 acres', the HD NLG1 established at Market Deeping actually occupied 75 acres and measured 850 by 650 yards. Reclassified as an NLG2 on 28 February 1917, the first occupant was 38(HD) Squadron, closely followed by 90(HD) Squadron from Buckminster. Operating the FE.2B and 504K(NF), 90(HD) Squadron made use of Market Deeping until it was closed down in June 1919.

Moorby (Horncastle)

53°10′12″N/01°03′19″W, TF312654. 1 mile NE of Moorby village, 3.5 miles SE of Horncastle town centre

THE remote LG at Moorby was opened in October 1916 for 38(HD) Squadron as an HD NLG1. Larger than most HD-type LGs at 82 acres, Moorby had open approaches and measured 700 by 570 yards. By 1918 the LG was being operated by 90(HD) Squadron. Located more than half a mile from the nearest public road, the site was relinquished in June 1919.

New Holland

53°41′57″N/00°22′02″W, TA078235. 0.3 miles due W of New Holland village, dissected by B1206 (Lincoln Castle Way)

WELL placed on the southern edge of the Humber Estuary, New Holland was brought into use from October 1916 in place of Goxhill. Large enough at 83 acres, and 700 by 550 yards in size, New Holland warranted a higher classification, but was only an HD NLG2. This classification possibly reflected its proximity to a brickworks, warehousing and the nearby village.

The only occupant of the LG was 33(HD) Squadron from its opening until January 1919. Relinquished by the military on 21 August 1919, the LG was under consideration for civilian use from early 1919. Unfortunately, no further aviation use of New Holland came to fruition.

North Coates Fitties (North Coates)

53°30′06″N/00°04′24″W, TA375025. Next to sea bank, 0.5 miles due E of WW2 airfield, 2.2 miles ENE of North Coates village

RAF North Coates enjoyed a long and illustrious career that did not come to end until the finale of the Cold War. The original aerodrome, then known as North Coates Fitties, was opened in 1916 as an NLG3 for 33(HD) Squadron operating from Gainsborough and later Kirton-in-Lindsey. The site during those early years was little more than 22 acres in size and measured 500 by 210 yards.

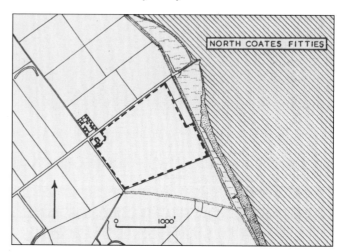

By 1918 the aerodrome began to expand up to flight station status under 18 (Operations) Group, which would set the tone of the coastal site's useful position so close to the North Sea. By this time the site had grown to 88 acres. North Coates Fitties then became the home of 404 Flight; originally equipped with seaplanes, the unit re-equipped with the DH.6 on arrival on 26 September 1918. A number of anti-submarine operations were flown from the aerodrome before the Armistice, but with no peacetime role the unit was disbanded, with its parent unit, 248 Squadron, at Hornsea on 6 March 1919. By 1920 the site was abandoned. However, in 1927 the same area of land was requisitioned again and the airfield grew westwards; taking advantage of the coastal ranges nearby, it quickly became one of the busiest stations in the county.

Scampton (Brattleby)

53°18′08″N/00°32′58″W, SK966794. Current RAF Scampton, 4.5 miles N of Lincoln

LONG since swept away by the much larger RAF Scampton and the equally impressive history that came with it, the original site, called Brattleby until mid-1917, was established as an HD Flight Station from October 1916. Scampton's long history began when a searchlight unit positioned itself on land belonging to Aisthorpe Farm, accompanied by 'A' Flight of 33(HD) Squadron from Bramham Moor (Tadcaster). A large site from the outset, Scampton occupied 287 acres and measured 1,450 by 1,000 yards, but its infrastructure would continue to expand when the aerodrome was classified as a training squadron station and finally as a TDS.

Looking east across Scampton on 23 November 1917, Ermine Street can be seen running behind the station. Closed down in 1920, virtually all of the First World War structures had been removed before the site was reopened in 1936.

The work to expand Scampton into a TDS was awarded to contractors Trollop & Colls and Dick Kerr & Co Ltd, the latter making a name for itself as an aircraft manufacturer in nearby Lincoln. Six 1917-pattern GS Sheds (170 by 80 feet), made of timber, were built alongside two HD-pattern Aeroplane Sheds (140 by 60 feet), the latter being built for 33(HD) Squadron. 34 TDS, tasked with single-seat fighter training, was formed here in July 1918, equipped with the 504 and Dolphin. The unit was disbanded into 46 TDS at neighbouring South Carlton in March 1919 and, after a period of Care & Maintenance, Scampton was closed down in March 1920.

Reopened as a bomber station in 1936, all trace of the original site had already been cleared, as Scampton grew into one of Britain's best-known airfields. In recent years its future has been in doubt, but today it is still the home of the Red Arrows, a Control and Reporting Centre, 1 Air Control Centre and a Mobile Met Unit.

Bristol Scout 'D' A1785 of 34 TDS inside one of Scampton's GS Sheds in late 1918.

Scampton (Brattleby) main units, 1916-18

33(HD) Sqn 'A' Flt from Gainsborough, 3 Oct 1916;
to Harpswell, 13 Jun 1919 (BE.2C/E and RE.8)

49 TS from Norwich (Mousewold), 16 Oct 1916;
to Spittlegate, 14 Nov 1916
(Shorthorn, Longhorn, 504, FK.3, RE.8, BE.2E and DH.4)

37 TS from Catterick, 13 Nov 1916;
to Spittlegate, 15 Sep 1917 (FK.3, 504 and RE.8)

33(HD) Sqn 'A' Flt from Gainsborough, 27 Nov 1916
(BE.2C, BE12 and Scout);
departed?

81 Sqn from Gosport, 15 Jan 1917;
absorbed into 34 TDS, 4 Jul 1918 (various aircraft)

60 TS from Beverley, 14 Apr 1917;
absorbed into 34 TDS, 15 Jul 1918 (various aircraft)

33(HD) Sqn 'A' Flt from Gainsborough, 21 Aug 1917;
to Kirton-in-Lindsey Nov 1918 (FE.2B/D and FE.2B)

11 TS from Spittlegate, 15 Sep 1917;
absorbed into 34 TDS, 15 Jul 1918 (various aircraft)

135th Aero Sqn, USAAS, detached from Waddington,
8 Jan 1918 (DH.4)

34 TDS formed 15 Jul 1918;
DB into 46 TDS (South Carlton), 5 Mar 1919
(Pup, Dolphin, Camel, Scout and 504)

During the 1930s RAF Digby underwent expansion-period development but still retained its complete First World War infrastructure. Only the Type-C hangar on the right of this image still survives at RAF Digby today.

Scopwick

53°05'53"N/00°26'21"W, TF043569. Current RAF Digby, 6 miles N of Sleaford

IT has been suggested that a field was used south-west of the village of Scopwick as an RLG for Cranwell a long time before the site was surveyed to become an established aerodrome in its own right. Work on the site officially began in late 1917, the main contractor being P. & W. Anderson, which was contracted to build a TDS. The main technical and domestic area was located in the south-eastern corner of the site, off Cuckoo and Heath Road, the same as it is today.

The main unit was 59 TDS, which moved in from Portholme Meadow on 15 October 1918 with a variety of aircraft. These included up to thirty Avro 504s, approximately eighteen F.2Bs and an allocation of up to ten Handley Page O/400s; the latter were destined never to arrive. The aerodrome was a good size, occupying 250 acres and measuring 1,400 by 1,000 yards. Facilities included seven 1918-pattern GS Sheds (170 by 100 feet) and enough smaller buildings to cover 30 acres. 59 TDS was redesignated 59 TS and in turn became part of the RAF's main post-war training units in the shape of 3 FTS. To avoid confusion with Shotwick (aka RAF Sealand), the site was renamed RAF Digby in July 1920. Digby went onto enjoy a rich military history, which continues to this day, as the airfield is now the home of HQ JSSO and JSSU (Digby) and looks to remain an RAF station for the foreseeable future.

Scopwick main units, 1918-22

59 TDS from Portholme Meadow, 15 Oct 1918; redesignated 59 TS, 14 Mar 1919
(DH.6, DH.9, F.2B, BE.2E and 504J/K)

209 Sqn cadre from Froidmont, 14 Feb 1919; DB 24 Jun 1919 (no aircraft)

210 Sqn cadre from Boussieres, 17 Feb 1919; DB 24 Jun 1919 (no aircraft)

59 TS (ex-59 TDS) 14 Mar 1919; redesignated 3 FTS, 26 Apr 1920 (504K)

213 Sqn cadre from Stalhille, 19 Mar 1919; DB 31 Dec 1919 (no aircraft)

11 Sqn cadre from Spich, 3 Sep 1919; DB 31 Dec 1919 (no aircraft)

25 Sqn cadre from South Carlton, 3 Dec 1919; DB 31 Jan 1920 (no aircraft)

203 Sqn cadre from Waddington, Dec 1919; DB 21 Jan 1920 (no aircraft)

3 FTS 26 Apr 1920; DB 1 Apr 1922 (F.2B and 504K)

Skegness (Burgh Road)

53°09'11"N/00°19'37"W, TF557643. S of Burgh Road, 0.75 miles NNW of Skegness railway station

ON the outbreak of war in August 1914 there was an immediate fear that Germany would unleash its Zeppelin force against the civilian population, especially along the East Coast. To reassure local people, aircraft were positioned at strategic points on temporary LGs, including one on the western edge of Skegness off Burgh Road. A group of seven aircraft of various types, led by Sqn Cdr Samson from Eastchurch, descended upon Skegness, although two were wrecked on arrival. On 25 August 1915 Samson was ordered to London for new orders and, with no imminent Zeppelin threat on the horizon, the aircraft had all returned to Eastchurch by the end of the month.

The first of four airfields to be established on the edge of the seaside town, the Burgh Road site has been under houses for many years.

South Carlton

53°16'30"N/00°33'11"W, SK965763. Cliff Farm, N of Hallifirs, between Middle Street (B1398) and A15, 0.7 miles E of South Carlton, 2.5 miles NNW of Lincoln city centre

A BUSY training aerodrome from the outset, South Carlton was surveyed in late 1915 and was opened in time for the arrival of 45 TS in November 1916. Occupying 198 acres and measuring 1,000 by 1,000 yards, the technical and domestic site was extensive, taking up 40 acres. Seven Aeroplane Sheds were erected, six being 170 by 60 feet, together with the usual array of supporting buildings, which extended to the northern edge of Hallifirs.

Several units passed through South Carlton during 1916 and 1917, including the former 2 Squadron (AFC), which reformed as 69 Squadron and 96 and 109 Squadrons, both of which had moved on by late 1917. 39 TS brought a large number of aircraft from Montrose in September 1917 and this unit, together with 45 TS, was absorbed into 46 TDS, formed on 27 July 1918. Tasked with carrying out single-seat fighter training, the TDS operated more than seventy aircraft, consisting mainly of 504s and Dolphins. 46 TDS became 46 TS from July 1919, equipped with the 504K, until it was disbanded on 26 April 1920.

Closed down later that year, the aerodrome returned to the plough, while many buildings lingered on for years afterwards. A few still survive to this day, clustered around Cliff Farm, including one Aeroplane Shed and the station cinema, the former in use, the latter deteriorating. The local church has a memorial, erected in 1920 in the shape of a carved pulpit, to the many RFC and RAF personnel who served at South Carlton.

An RAF truck at South Carlton in 1918.

Still in use today, one Aeroplane Shed survives at South Carlton, although the brick piers have gone and the roof is now pitched.

An official photograph of the senior staff of 39 TS, which arrived at South Carlton from Montrose in September 1917 but was absorbed into 46 TDS in July 1918.

South Carlton main units, 1916-19

45 TS from London Colney, 13 Nov 1916;
absorbed into 46 TDS, 27 Jul 1918 (various aircraft)

69 Sqn (2 Sqn AFC renumbered) formed 28 Dec 1916;
to Lympne, 24 Aug 1917 (various aircraft)

61 TS from Cramlington, 10 May 1917;
absorbed into 28 TDS, 27 Jul 1918 (various aircraft)

39 TS from Montrose, 3 Sep 1917;
absorbed into 46 TDS, 27 Jul 1918 (various aircraft)

96 Sqn formed (nucleus from 45 TS) 8 Oct 1917;
to Shotwick, 30 Oct 1917 (various aircraft)

109 Sqn formed (nucleus from 61 TS) 1 Nov 1917;
to Stonehenge, 12 Nov 1917 (various aircraft)

135th Aero Sqn, USAAS, detached from Waddington,
8 Jan 1918;

to Waddington, 27 Feb 1918 (DH.4)

43rd Aero Sqn, USAAS, by 16 Mar 1918;
to Codford, 14 Oct 1918 (DH.4)

158th Aero Sqn, USAAS, detached from Cramlington by
17 Jul 1918

46 TDS formed 27 Jul 1918;
redesignated 46 TS, Jul 1919 (Camel, Dolphin, Pup and 504)

46 TS (ex-46 TDS) Jul 1919;
DB 26 Apr 1920 (504K)

57 Sqn from Morville, 4 Aug 1919;
DB 31 Dec 1919 (DH.9A)

25 Sqn from Merheim, 6 Sep 1919;
to Scopwick as cadre, 3 Dec 1919 (DH.9A)

Spittlegate

52°54'06"N/00°35'19"W, SK939342. Current Prince
William of Gloucester Barracks, 1.6 miles SE of Grantham

AN LG had been in use at Spittlegate Hill for quite some time before the site was surveyed in 1916 as a potential training aerodrome for the RFC. The land was cleared to the north of Spittlegate Heath Farm and Somerby Hill Road (A52) to an extent of 199 acres, and the site measured 1,250 by 750 yards. Seven 1915-pattern Aeroplane Sheds (170 by 80 feet) were erected, one of them serving as an Aeroplane Repair Section (ARS).

49 TS from Scampton, with a large collection of machines, was the first to arrive on 14 November 1916, later sharing the aerodrome with 11 TS from Montrose. Several units came and went during 1917, but it was 15 and 37 TS from Doncaster and Brattleby respectively that would be later disbanded to form Spittlegate's largest unit, 39 TDS, on 15 August 1918. Tasked with training crews for reconnaissance duties, the unit was under the charge of 24th Wing, whose HQ moved to Spittlegate in March 1917 and on to Mille House in Grantham

in October 1918. The main equipment of 39 TDS was the 504 and the F.2B, thirty-six of each being the establishment, until the unit was redesignated as 39 TS in March 1919.

39 TS, now only equipped with the 504K, continued training pilots until November 1919, and during that year 29, 43 and 70 Squadrons all returned from the continent to disband. 70 Squadron, flying the Snipe, was the last when it was disbanded on 22 January 1920. Spittlegate, renamed Grantham in 1928 and Spitalgate in 1944, remained an RAF station until 1975, when it was transferred to the Army.

Spittlegate main units, 1916-20

49 TS from Scampton, 14 Nov 1916;
to Doncaster, 15 Sep 1917 (various aircraft)

83 Sqn from Montrose, 15 Jan 1917;
to Wyton, 15 Sep 1917 (various aircraft)

86 (Canadian) TS formed 9 Feb 1917;
to Canada, 16 Apr 1917 (no aircraft)

11 TS from Montrose, 14 Apr 1917;
to Scampton, 15 Sep 1917 (various aircraft)

106 Sqn formed 12 Sep 1917;
to Andover, 3 Oct 1917 (RE.8)

15 TS from Doncaster, 15 Sep 1917;
DB into 39 TDS, 1 Aug 1918 (504, RE.8 and FK.3)

20 TS from Wyton, 15 Sep 1917;
to Harlaxton, 27 Nov 1917 (various aircraft)

37 TS from Brattleby, 15 Sep 1917;
DB into 39 TDS, 15 Aug 1918 (various aircraft)

9th Aero Sqn, USAAS, from Winchester, 28 Dec 1917;
departed by 7 Aug 1918 (DH.4 and FE.2)

50th Aero Sqn, USAAS, from Romsey, 4 Feb 1918;
to Winchester, 3 Jul 1918

174th Aero Sqn, USAAS, by 17 Jul 1918

39 TDS (ex-15 and 37 TS) 15 Aug 1918;
redesignated 39 TS, 14 Mar 1919 (FK.8, BE.2E, F.2B and 504)

43rd Aero Sqn, USAAS, detached from South Carlton,
24 Aug 1918;
to Codford, 14 Oct 1918 (DH.4)

39 TS (ex-39 TDS) 14 Mar 1919;
DB 24 Nov 1919 (504)

29 Sqn cadre from Bickendorf, 10 Aug 1919;
DB 31 Dec 1919 (no aircraft)

43 Sqn from Eil, 25 Aug 1919;
DB 31 Dec 1919 (Snipe)

70 Sqn from Bickendorf, 3 Sep 1919;
DB 22 Jan 1920 (Snipe)

More than twenty aircraft are visible on the flying field and in front of the GS Sheds at Spittlegate in 1918, viewed from the south-west. The GS Shed not coupled is the ARS.

Swinstead (Grimsthorpe)

52°47'09"N/00°30'13"W, TF013220. 0.65 miles SW of Swinstead off B1176, 5.3 miles W of Bourne town centre

THIS NLG2 was laid out in an L-shape, covered 64 acres and measuring 730 by 600 yards. Swinstead was occupied by a few 38(HD) Squadron BE and later FE types from 1 October 1916 until May 1918. With 38(HD) Squadron's departure to France, Swinstead was taken over by 90(HD) Squadron in August 1918 until its closure in July 1919.

Tydd St Mary (Wisbech)

52°43'03"N/00°09'42"W, TF460192. 1.1 miles ENE of Tydd St Mary, 1.75 miles SW of Sutton Bridge

NESTLED in the bottom right-hand corner of Lincolnshire, close to the Norfolk and Cambridgeshire borders, Tydd St Mary was opened as a DLG1 (later an NLG1 and HD Station) in the summer of 1916. Bordered by a railway line to the east and the South Holland Main Drain to the north, Tydd was 125 acres in size and measured 700 by 650 yards, and was furnished with a pair of Flight Sheds (130 by 60 feet). On average, personnel strength at Tydd was 7 officers, 3 SNCOs, 2 JNCOs and 39 other ranks. Tydd's first occupants were the FE.2Bs of 'B' Flight, 51(HD) Squadron, operating from Marham.

Equipped with eight FE.2Bs, 'B' Flight was called to arms on the night of 12/13 April 1918 when Zeppelin *L62* dropped several bombs to the east of the LG. Despite the efforts of 'B' Flight, the giant raider managed to slip away to the south unharassed.

The 92nd Aero Squadron, USAAC, arrived at Tydd on 17 July 1918 equipped with a variety of aircraft, including the DH.6 and a selection of Avros and BEs. Using the LG for training, the 92nd left for Ford in September, destined never to see action in France.

One of two Flight Sheds survived at Tydd St Mary until 1987, when it was destroyed in a severe gale. *Alastair Goodrum*

By late 1918 'B' Flight had re-equipped with the 504K(NF) and retained a small presence at Tydd until it was closed down in June 1919. At least one brick-built structure, originally used as the LG HQ, was pressed into use as a farm office, and one hangar was used as a farm store. The latter remained a local landmark until 1987, when it was destroyed in high winds, while the farm office has since been demolished. The site is now a wind farm.

Waddington

53°10'05"N/00°31'28"W, SK988645. Current RAF Waddington, 4 miles S of Lincoln

ONE of several sites across the country that had been considered as a potential aerodrome since 1912, Waddington did not open as a training squadron station until November 1916 when 47 TS and 48 TS arrived from Cramlington and Narborough respectively. Large numbers of aircraft soon filled the skies around Waddington and within a short period of time a variety of TSs came and went, until those remaining were absorbed into 48 TDS in July 1918. By then nine GS Sheds (170 by 80 feet) and a single ARS (180 by 170 feet) had been erected, spread over two separate sites.

Waddington grew to an area of 350 acres measuring 1,650 by 1,250 yards and, as well as the large TDS, a healthy number of USAAS servicemen served here with the 11th and later the 157th Aero Squadron, flying the DH.4, DH.9 and RE.8. The TDS operated up to seventy-two aircraft at its peak, and the resident TS had at least a dozen 504s and another dozen DH.4s and DH.9s to its name, making Waddington a very busy place. By early 1919 several squadrons returning from France arrived to disband, the last of them, 203 Squadron, in December 1919, which marked the end for Waddington. With the bulk of the First World War infrastructure still in place, the RAF returned in 1926 and it was not until the mid-1930s that the older sheds and buildings made way for the expansion-period bomber station. Since then RAF Waddington has been a busy station, which today is the home of 34 Expeditionary Wing, comprising intelligence-gathering, surveillance and reconnaissance units.

USAAS and RFC personnel pose next to Bristol Scout 'C' 3051, with one of Waddington's GS Sheds providing the backdrop.

Waddington main units, 1916-19

47 TS from Cramlington, 13 Nov 1916;
redesignated 47 TS, 1 Jun 1917 (Shorthorn)

48 TS from Narborough, 13 Nov 1916;
redesignated 48 TS, 11 Jun 1917 (Grahame-White)

82 Sqn from Beverley, 20 Mar 1917;
to St Omer, 17 Nov 1917 (FK.8)

51 TS from Wye, 14 May 1917;
redesignated 51 TS, 1 Jun 1917 (RE.8 and BE.2)

47 TS (ex-47 RS) 1 Jun 1917;
absorbed into 48 TDS, 4 Jul 1918 (Shorthorn, RE.8 and DH.9)

48 TS (ex-48 RS) 1 Jun 1917;
absorbed into 48 TDS, 4 Jul 1918 (Shorthorn, RE.8 and DH.6)

51 TS (ex-51 RS) 1 Jun 1917;
to Baldonnel, 4 Oct 1918
(Elephant, DH.4, DH.9, BE.2C and FE.2B)

5 TDS 'B' Flt formed 15 Sep 1917;
to Easton-on-the-Hill, 24 Sep 1917

105 Sqn formed (nucleus from 51 TS) 23 Sep 1917;
to Andover, 3 Oct 1917 (various aircraft)

6 TDS 'A' Flt formed 1 Oct 1917;
to Boscombe Down, 1 Nov 1917

44 TS from Harlaxton, Nov 1917;
DB 1919 (DH.4 and DH.9)

75 TS formed 14 Nov 1917;
to Cramlington, 22 Dec 1917 (DH.4 and DH.9)

97 Sqn formed (nucleus from 51 TS) 1 Dec 1917;

to Stonehenge, 21 Jan 1918 (various aircraft)

117 Sqn formed 1 Jan 1918;
to Hucknall, 3 Apr 1918 (various aircraft)

135th Aero Sqn, USAAS, from Garden City, NY, 8 Jan 1918;
to Issoudun, 24 Jun 1918 (DH.4)

123 Sqn formed 1 Feb 1918;
to Duxford, 1 Mar 1918 (DH.9)

Photographic Flight from South Farnborough, 9 Apr 1918;
temporary unit accommodation at Kenley;
became Photographic Experimental Section at Kenley,
21 May 1918

11th Aero Sqn, USAAS, from Stamford, Feltwell and Harling
Road, 24 Jun 1918;
to Delouze, 7 Aug 1918 (DH.4, DH.9 and RE.8)

48 TDS formed 4 Jul 1918;
redesignated 48 TS, Apr 1919 (DH.9, RE.8 and FK.3)

157th Aero Sqn, USAAS, by 17 Jul 1918

204 Sqn cadre from Heule, 7 Feb 1919;
DB 31 Dec 1919 (no aircraft)

48 TS (ex-48 TDS) Apr 1919;
DB 4 Nov 1919 (DH.9)

23 Sqn from Clermont, 15 Mar 1919;
DB 31 Dec 1919 (Dolphin)

203 Sqn cadre from Boisdinghem, 27 Mar 1919;
to Scopwick, Dec 1919 (no aircraft)

Wellingore

53°05'N/00°30'W, TF00?57?. Most likely E of Wellingore village, W of the A15

THE exact location of an LG for the use of RNAS machines from nearby Cranwell still remains vague to this day. Active from mid-1917, the LG was in the region of Graves Farm, and types using it would have included the BE.2, Camel and 504. The site was apparently reactivated as a RLG for Cranwell in the 1930s.

Willoughby Hills

52°59'21"N/00°01'04"W, TF355455. N of Johnson's Garden Centre off A52, 2 miles NE of Boston town centre

ANOTHER small LG of 25 acres for 38(HD) Squadron, Willoughby Hills opened as a DLG2 in September 1916 but was later upgraded to an NLG2. With 38(HD) Squadron's posting to Northern France in May 1918, the LG was closed down the following month.

Winterton (Roxby)

53°39'51"N/00°34'12"W, SE945197. E of Eastfield Farm, 1.4 miles NE of Winterton, 5 miles WSW of Barton-on-Humber

OPENED in December 1916 as an NLG2 for 33(HD) Squadron, Winterton occupied 55 acres and measured 600 by 400 yards. Only BE and FE types would have used the site on occasions, but it still remained open until June 1919.

MERSEYSIDE

Southport (Hesketh Park Sands)

53°39'59"N/02°59'33"W, SD345192. Close to junction of Hesketh Road and Marine Drive, 1.4 miles NE of Southport railway station

AN aerodrome was established at Southport in the summer of 1910 by Woodhead and Gaunt, the location of the site being described as 'at the top end of Hesketh Road'. At least one hangar was erected and the aerodrome was described as '40 square miles' of hard sand. Gaunt Aircraft operated its Baby from here from 1911 until 22 August 1912.

The site remained quiet until it was selected as the home of No 11 AAP, which was formed here on 15 September 1917 specifically for the acceptance of locally built aircraft by the Vulcan Motor & Engineering Company, located at Crossens, 1.5 miles east-north-east of the aerodrome. The company received several contracts during the war, including 100 DH.4s, 100 DH.9s, 225 DH.9As and 300 BE.2C/D/Es, all of which would have passed through the AAP before being delivered to RFC units. Redesignated as No 11 (Southport) AAP on 12 October 1917, the site remained open until 11 January 1919.

Waterloo Sands (Blundellsands/Bootle)

52°29'13"N/03°03'06"W*, SJ302994*. On beach between Blundellsands and Brighton le Sands

IN 1911 Mr Henry Melly established the Liverpool Aviation School at Waterloo Sands in 1911 with the main office in Sandheys Avenue, Waterloo. Equipped with one single-seat and one two-seat Blériot, the school advertised itself with 'flying rights over several miles of hard smooth beach, very broad (probably the best flying ground in England)'. A pair of wooden hangars was also offered to rent as well as providing cover for the school's own machines. A third Blériot with an Anzani engine was also assembled by Mr Melly. The site was also later used by the Avro Transport Company as one of many operating bases for its 504Ks. It is possible that the site was requisitioned by the RFC and later the RAF, but very little, if any, military activity is recorded, and the site was closed down by 1920.

* Both positions approximate

MIDDLESEX

Acton (Ealing/Hangar Hill/Hanger Hill Garden Estate/London Aviation Ground)

51°31'28"N/00°16'42"W, TQ195820. Site is today Westwood Park Trading Estate, 0.3 miles SE of Park Royal underground station

ACTON was opened as a private flying school aerodrome for Ruffy Bauman in 1917, until it was taken over by the Alliance Aeroplane Company in July 1918. Alliance was joined by Waring & Gillow in 1919, both companies being committed to the production of DH.9s.

Cricklewood, London Borough of Brent

51°34'07"N/00°12'51"W, TQ238870

ORIGINALLY used by aircraft manufacturer Beatty Aviation Company Limited in 1916, the site was taken over by Handley Page from 1917. It was from this period that the site was known as 'Cricklewood Aerodrome', until the factory was sold Oswald Stoll in 1920, to become Cricklewood Studios.

Handley Page continued aircraft production at Cricklewood until 1964.

Handley Page staff at Cricklewood pause momentarily for the camera from their work of producing the rear nacelle/cowling for the O/400's Eagle VIII engines.
Via Stuart Leslie

Below: More famous as being the home of de Havilland's first aircraft factory from 1920 to 1934, Stag Lane also served as MLG during the First World War. These DH.9s were part of the de Havilland School of Flying.

Edgware (Stag Lane), London Borough of Brent

51°35'52"N/00°16'88"W, TQ200920. Stag Lane, 0.5 miles SW of Burnt Oak underground station, 0.6 miles ENE of Queensbury underground station, 1.4 miles W of RAF Museum

EDGWARE was sited in open fields north of London as a private airfield for the use of London & Provincial and its flying school. At 83 acres in size, and with generous dimensions of 920 by 820 yards, Edgware first drew the attention of the military in June 1917. Designated as an HD NLG2, the site was used jointly by 39(HD) and 44(HD) Squadrons until December 1918.

Several Bessonneau hangars were erected and the school, run by London & Provincial, was also in charge of the 18th Wing School of Instruction from nearby Hendon during 1918. 29 TS also made use of Edgware between 6 August and 14 December 1918. Edgware's location saw aviation remain after the war, and from 1920 the site was renamed Stag Lane, destined to become de Havilland's first aircraft factory. Expanded beyond recognition, the airfield remained busy until de Havilland relocated to Hatfield and the land-hungry property developers snapped up every square inch from 1934.

The interior of the Whitehead works at Feltham during the First World War.

Feltham, London Borough of Hounslow

51°26'29"N/00°24'13"W, TQ110725. E of Hounslow Road (A244); centre of technical area was centred on Air Park Way and Bowell's Lane, 0.5 miles SSE of Feltham railway station

ORIGINALLY established as a private aerodrome for Whitehead Aircraft Co Ltd. and the Whitehead Flying School from 1915, Feltham occupied 142 acres and measured 1,150 by 850 yards. The flying field utilised Hanworth Park to the east, taking up all of the land around Hanworth Park House and gardens.

An Experimental Works was formed on 8 July 1916, but from 1917 the site was chosen as an AAP designed to accept Handley Page bombers. The Experimental Works was disbanded into the Southern ARD at Farnborough in September 1917, giving the future AAP the freedom of the site, which was extensively expanded on the western side. Twelve 1918-pattern GS Sheds (170 by 100 feet) made up as four treble units and twenty-one HP Storage Sheds (200 by 60 feet) were erected as seven treble units.

On 1 April 1918 AAP Feltham was formed to handle Whitehead-built aircraft such as the BE.2B, Pup, SE.5A and DH.9. The role of handling large bombers began on 28 September 1918 when 116 Squadron brought its Handley Page O/400s here from Kenley, making Feltham a Mobilisation Station. 116 Squadron's time at Feltham was cut short with

the Armistice and the unit was disbanded on 20 November. The AAP was closed down in March 1919 and all of the buildings were cleared from the site very quickly.

The aerodrome was resurrected in 1929, known locally as Hanworth Park, but it was also known as London Air Park. During the 1930s it was the centre for many light aircraft manufacturers. Used by 5 EFTS at the outbreak of war, the unit was moved north to the safety of Weir, but the site continued to be used by General Aircraft Ltd, which carried out light aircraft repairs on Hamilcar and Hadrian gliders until the site was closed down in 1948.

Hayes (Harlington), London Borough of Hillingdon

51°30'06"N/00°25'37"W, TQ092791. S of North Hyde Road (A437), site now called Westlands Estate, 0.3 miles SW of Hayes & Harlington railway station

FAIREY began production of its very first aircraft contract as a sub-tenant in a factory at Clayton Road, and further expansion took place when a flying field was purchased at Harlington, close to the GWR railway line to Reading. A hangar was erected for Short 827 assembly, and this site was destined to become the main Fairey factory, built along the North Hyde Road during 1917 and 1918. However, the site was found to be unsuitable for flight testing and all flying was transferred to Northolt.

The Fairey N.9 with a Falcon I engine and large upper mainplane, pictured at Hayes before it was transferred to the Isle of Grain for trials.

Hendon

51°35'54"N/00°14'39"W, TQ215905. Area of Grahame Park and location of RAF Museum, 1.3 miles N of Hendon railway station

SEVERAL years before the outbreak of war Hendon had well and truly established itself as 'The London Aerodrome', its rich history beginning in 1909. Two gentlemen by the name of Everett and Edgcumbe constructed a small shed at the end of Colindale Avenue for a monoplane of their own design. The aircraft was ultimately unsuccessful, but the field from which the duo attempted to fly soon drew the attention of many pioneering aviators. One of the latter was Claude Grahame-White, who tested a Farman in January 1910, and by October the field had become an aerodrome with eight sheds along the western boundary. It quickly became a centre for a large number of flying schools, including Grahame-White's own, and by the beginning of the war the five that were still solvent were contracted to train pilots for the military. Grahame-White's flying school alone trained 490 pilots, including Albert Ball, Mick Mannock and Reginald Warneford, all destined to win the VC.

From August 1914 the RNAS used Hendon as a HD Station and flying school until 1916, when it became an HD NLG1 for the RFC. By then the site occupied 192 acres and measured 1,200 by 1,200 yards.

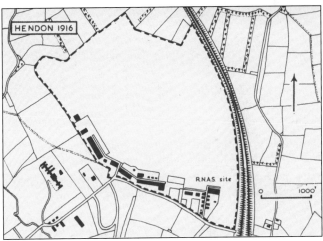

From September 1916 Hendon was classified as an RFC Flying School for the benefit of 18th Wing School of Instruction. The aerodrome saw increased expansion when No 2 AAP was formed on 22 March 1917 for the acceptance of new aircraft from local manufacturers. These included Airco (DH.4/5/6/9/9A and 10), Alliance (DH.9 and 10), Berwick (DH.4/9 and 9A), British Caudron (DH.5), Darracq (DH.5), Glendower (DH.4), Grahame-White (504 and DH.6), Handley Page (O/400), Hewlett & Blondeau (504), Hooper (Camel), Kingsbury (DH.5 and Dolphin), Nieuport (Camel), Palladium (DH.4), and Waring & Gillow (DH.9). This busy unit was redesignated as No 2 (Hendon) AAP on 10 December 1917 and was closed down on 10 January 1919. As result of the AAP's occupation, the number of sheds rose dramatically, to include six 1917-pattern timber GS Sheds (170 by 80 feet), two RNAS Aeroplane Sheds, and eight storage sheds (three 480 by 100 feet, two 200 by 100 feet, one 540 by 100 feet, one 550 by 55 feet, and one 180 by 100 feet). Buildings used by the AAP took up 40 acres of the entire site.

The interior of the Grahame-White factory at Hendon presents us with several different types under construction simultaneously. Aircraft evident are Maurice Farmans, Henry Farman HF.20s (foreground), DH.6s and the Grahame-White Type 20 prototype.

The prototype Handley O/100 first flew from Hendon at 1.51pm on 17 December 1915, reaching 50mph with Lt Cdr John Babbington at the controls and Lt Cdr Steadman as observer.

Aircraft manufacturing, which was first established by Grahame-White Co Ltd before the war, was also prevalent at Hendon. Nieuport & General Aircraft Co Ltd, Aircraft Manufacturing Ltd and Handley Page Ltd also built aircraft here. The latter built a factory at Kingsbury to assemble O/100 and O/400 bombers, and it was from here that the O/100 prototype made its maiden flight on 17 December 1915.

Hendon was classified as a training squadron station from August 1918, by which time it had become the home of the Medical Flight and 1 (Communications) Flight. The former became 29 Training (Control) Squadron from 1 August, a title that did little give away this unit's unique role of reintroducing pilots injured both physically and psychologically to flying duties.

With the war over, the huge Grahame-White plant began producing cars rather than aircraft, and from 1920 the aerodrome was in civilian hands. An RAF station again from 1925, Hendon became famous for its inter-war RAF Displays. It remained active until 1957, when it succumbed to the ever-encroaching demand for housing. In 1963 the RAF Museum was established, making use of a pair of original GS Sheds. Officially opened by the Queen in 1973, the aerodrome has long been erased by urban development.

Hendon main units, 1914-19

War Flight RNAS formed Aug 1914;
DB Feb 1916

Aeroplane School RNAS formed 1914;
DB 1916

17 TS detached from Croydon, 31 Jan 1916;
to Croydon, 1 Feb 1916

19 TS detached from Hounslow by 1 Feb 1916;
to Hounslow, 15 Apr 1916 (various aircraft)

18th Wing School of Instruction, Hendon, formed 22 Sep 1916;
DB 12 Oct 1918

2 AAP opened 22 Mar 1917;
redesignated 2 (Hendon) AAP, 12 Oct 1917

Hendon Air Station Flt formed 1917;
redesignated Comms Sqn, 23 Jul 1917

2 (Hendon) AAP 12 Oct 1917;
closed down, 1 Jan 1919

6 Stores Depot detachment formed Apr 1918;
DB 1918

The Medical Flt formed 1918;
redesignated 29 T(C)S, 1 Aug 1918

1 Aircraft Salvage Depot formed 1918;
DB 1918

Comms Sqn 23 Jul 1918;
redesignated 1 (Comms) Sqn 26 Jul 1918

1 (Comms) Sqn formed 23 Jul 1918;
to Kenley, May 1919
(DH.4, DH.9, 1½ Strutter, BE.2C, Scout, 504, F.2B and O/400)

29 T(C)S (ex-Medical Flt) 1 Aug 1918;
to Edgware (Stag Lane), 6 Aug 1918 (various aircraft)

86th (Comms) Wing HQ formed 4 Feb 1919;
to Kenley, 17 Apr 1919

Hounslow Heath, London Borough of Hounslow

51°27'27"N/00°23'13"W, TQ121743. Hounslow Heath, between A315 to N and A314 to SE, 3 miles SE of Heathrow Airport

IT was in 1909 that the very first landing took place at Hounslow Heath, and by the following year a hangar was erected. Up to this time the heath was used by cavalry units based at the nearby Hounslow Barracks for general manoeuvres and exercises.

On the outbreak of war the heath was taken over by the RFC, and from October 1 Sqn HD detachment from Brooklands was here with a variety of machines, all ready to take on the Zeppelin threat. Little more than a show of force to keep Londoners happy, the detachment returned to Brooklands after only a few weeks. During 1915 Hounslow began to receive a steady flow of squadrons, six in all; two of them, 24 and 27 Squadrons, were formed in September and November respectively. By then Hounslow occupied 266 acres and measured 1,100 by 1,100 yards, but being so hemmed in by buildings and trees it was not the easiest from which to operate.

The first dedicated training unit to serve at Hounslow was 19 TS, formed on 29 January 1916. From 19 TS was created 39 Squadron in April 1916, and in turn this unit helped to form 52 Squadron in May. Both squadrons left by the end of 1916, 39 Squadron for HD duties while 52 Squadron headed for France. By this time three 1915-pattern Flight Sheds (220 by 60 feet), one 1916-pattern GS Shed (180 by 80 feet), and a single salvage shed (80 by 30 feet) had been erected in the north-eastern corner of the aerodrome.

The arrival of 62 TS from Dover in May and 28 TS from Castle Bromwich in July 1918 marked the beginning of a large reorganisation at Hounslow. On 15 July 1918 the two TSs simultaneously disbanded to create 42 TDS, tasked with training pilots to fly single-seat fighters. The TDS had up to forty-eight aircraft on strength, made up of 504s and Snipes. The TDS carried out its duties until disbandment claimed it in July 1919. In the meantime, a communications unit was briefly formed here in early 1919, and the Demonstration Squadron, which had at least one captured Fokker D.VII on strength. Several wartime aces took the chance to see what one of the enemy's machines was really like, including Major W. G. 'Billy' Barker VC, DSO*, MC**.

One of only a handful of R.A.F. FE.9s built was A4818, pictured during a visit to Hounslow in 1917.

After the war Hounslow's future looked bright, and when the RAF closed down the site in August 1919 the aerodrome switched immediately to civilian operations. However, the Army was having none of it, and by March 1920 the site had been claimed back by the military. Today, most likely thanks to its return to military ownership, the old aerodrome site is open, undeveloped land, but it is very hard to imagine how busy Hounslow Heath once was.

Hounslow main units, 1914-19

1 Sqn HD detached from Brooklands, Oct 1914;
to Brooklands, Nov 1914 (various aircraft)

10 Sqn from Brooklands, 1 Apr 1915;
to Netheravon, 7 Apr 1915 (various aircraft)

15 Sqn from Farnborough, 13 Apr 1915;
to Dover (Swingate Down), 11 May 1915 (BE.2C)

14 Sqn from Shoreham, 11 May 1915;
to Gosport (Fort Grange), 5 Aug 1915 (BE.2C)

17 Sqn from Gosport (Fort Grange), 5 Aug 1915;
en route to Egypt, 15 Nov 1915 (BE.2C)

24 Sqn formed (nucleus from 17 Sqn) 1 Sep 1915;
to St Omer, 7 Feb 1916 (various aircraft)

27 Sqn formed (nucleus from 24 Sqn) 5 Nov 1915;
to Dover (Swingate Down), 10 Dec 1915 (G.100/102)

19 TS formed 29 Jan 1916;
to Fermoy, Dec 1917 (Farman, DH.1, DH.4, BE.2B/C/E, FE.2B, FB.5, BE.12, 504, RE.8 and Elephant)

39 Sqn formed (from 19 TS) 15 Apr 1916;
to Woodford Green, 30 Jun 1916 (BE.2C/E and Scout)

52 Sqn formed (nucleus from 39 Sqn) 15 May 1916;
to St Omer, 17 Nov 1916 (BE.2C, BE.12 and RE.8)

42 TS formed 2 Nov 1916;
to Wye, 16 Dec 1917 (504, FK.3, RE.7, RE.8, BE.2E, BE.12, JN.4, Pup, Camel, DH.6 and M.1C)

85 Sqn from Norwich, 10 Aug 1917;
to Marquise, 22 May 1918 (SE.5A)

87 Sqn from Sedgeford, 19 Dec 1917;
to St Omer, 24 Apr 1918 (various aircraft)

62 TS from Dover, 5 May 1918;
DB into 42 TDS, 15 Jul 1918 (Camel, 1½ Strutter, DH.5, BE.2E, 504, Pup, F.2B and Elephant)

28 TS from Castle Bromwich, 1 Jul 1918;
DB into 42 TDS, 15 Jul 1918 (Scout, 1½ Strutter, RE.7, 504, RE.8, SE.5, Pup, FE.2B and Farman)

42 TDS formed (ex-28 and 62 TS) 15 Jul 1918;
DB Jul 1919 (Snipe, Camel, 504 and M.1C)

149th Aero Sqn, USAAS, by 17 Jul 1918

3 (Comm) Sqn formed Feb 1919;
DB Mar 1919

107 Sqn cadre from Maubeuge, 18 Mar 1919;
DB 13 Aug 1919 (no aircraft)

Demonstration Sqn formed Mar 1919;
DB 1919 (504, Snipe and Fokker D.VII)

Kingsbury (Church Lane), London Borough of Brent

51°34'44"N/00°15'35"W, TQ208881. E of Church Lane in area of current Church Lane recreation ground, 0.9 miles SE of Kingsbury underground station

THIS was the home of the Kingsbury Aviation Co Ltd, which built the DH.6, Snipe and Vimy. The manufacturer's aerodrome was only active during 1917 and 1918.

Kingsbury (Grove Park), London Borough of Brent

51°35'23"N/00°15'41"W, TQ205893. Centre of aerodrome in region of St George's Avenue, 0.8 miles ENE of Kingsbury underground station

THIS was a manufacturer's aerodrome for the use of the Aircraft Manufacturing Company (Airco) between 1916 and 1919.

Northolt

51°33'19"N/00°24'59"W, TQ099852. Current RAF Northolt, N of A40, 0.6 miles W of South Ruislip railway station

THE site that we know as RAF Northolt was surveyed a number of times from 1910, until the current location was settled upon in 1914. Work began in early 1915, under the name of the 'RFC Military School, Ruislip', later changed to Northolt (after the nearby Northolt railway junction, now named South Ruislip) prior to opening on 1 March 1915. The first occupant of the aerodrome, now classified as a training squadron station, was 4 RAS (later RS, then TS), which moved in from Farnborough. On 11 May 18 Squadron was formed out of 4 RAS for HD duties, and Northolt also became an HD NLG1 for this purpose. 18 Squadron flew its first anti-Zeppelin operation on 4/5 June 1915.

By the end of 1915 the aerodrome was extended to 401 acres and measured 1,800 by 850 yards. Six 1915-pattern Flight Sheds (210 by 65 feet) were erected, later joined by one timber 1917-pattern GS Shed (170 by 80 feet) and one twin Aeroplane Shed with units measuring 100 by 53 feet.

From late 1916 Northolt became a manufacturer's aerodrome for the Fairey Aviation Co Ltd located at nearby Hayes. Fairey was a major Sopwith sub-contractor at the time, including production of the 1½ Strutter. 43 Squadron re-equipped with Fairey-built Strutters when it passed through Northolt from 8 December 1916, then on to France on 17 January 1917. Another famous fighter unit, 74 Squadron, was formed here with 504s on 1 July 1917, and would make way for Camels at London Colney a few days later.

Northolt's final Great War role was as a TDS, which began on 15 July 1918 with the formation of 30 TDS, created by disbanding 2 and 4 TS. Tasked with carrying out single-seat fighter training, the unit became 30 TS in May 1919 and was disbanded in April 1920. Northolt's subsequent aviation history has not skipped a beat since, and today it remains defiantly as one of the RAF's remaining active stations.

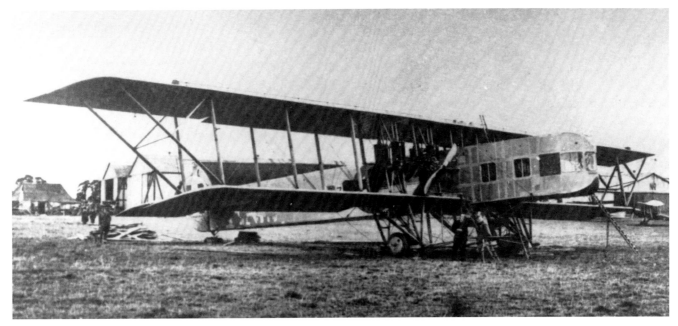

The incredible Kennedy Giant, designed by J. C. H. MacKenzie Kennedy, was so large that it had to be assembled out in the open. This view presents us with a tantalising glimpse of Northolt's rare twin Aeroplane Sheds.

Northolt main units, 1915-20

4 TS from Farnborough, 1 Mar 1915; DB into 30 TDS 15 Jul 1918 (various aircraft)

18 Sqn formed 11 May 1915;
to Mousehold Heath, 16 Aug 1915
(S.1, Shorthorn, Scout and FB.5)

13 Sqn detached from Gosport, 3 Oct 1915;
to Gosport, 29 Jan 1916 (BE.2C/D/E)

23 Sqn detached from Gosport, 3 Oct 1915;
to Gosport, 15 Apr 1916 (various aircraft)

11 TS formed 12 Oct 1915;
to Rochford, 24 Jan 1917 (various aircraft)

40 TS formed 5 Jul 1916;
to Port Meadow, 21 Aug 1916 (various aircraft)

43 Sqn from Netheravon, 9 Dec 1916;
to St Omer, Jan 17 1917 (Scout, BE.2C and 1½ Strutter)

2 TS from Brooklands, 31 Jan 1917;
DB 15 Jul 1918 into 30 TDS (various aircraft)

35 TS from Filton, 16 Feb 1917;
to Port Meadow, 16 Dec 1917 (various aircraft)

74 Sqn formed 1 Jul 1917;
to London Colney, 10 Jul 1917 (various aircraft)

8th Aero Sqn, USAAS, detached from Joyce Green, 1917;
to Thetford, 1917

30 TDS (ex-2 and 4 TS) 15 Jul 1918;
redesignated 30 TS, May 1919
(Snipe, SE.5A, Dolphin, 504 and SPAD)

4 Sqn cadre from Linselles, 13 Feb1919;
to Uxbridge, 20 Sep 1919 (no aircraft)

SE Area Comm Flt formed May 1919;
redesignated Inland Area Comm Flt, 1 Apr 1920 (504)

30 TS (ex-30 TDS) May 1919;
DB 15 Mar 1920 (504K and F.2B)

North Wembley, London Borough of Brent

51°33'54"N/00°17'57"W, TQ180865. 0.3 miles NE of North Wembley underground station

THIS 40-acre aerodrome was adjacent to Messrs F. W. Hooper & Co Ltd, not far from North Wembley underground station. Initially tasked with building aircraft components, it was not long before Hooper was building Camels, at a rate of three per day by 1918.

Westpole Farm

51°38'21"N/00°09'02"W, TQ280950. Oak Hill Park, due W of Oak Hill College, 1 mile SE of New Barnet railway station

POTENTIALLY opened as early as 1914, Westpole Farm (or West Pole) was a 42-acre LG measuring 600 by 420 yards. It was classified as an NLG3 by 1916, allocated to 39(HD) Squadron whose main aerodrome was Woodfood Green. Surrounded by trees and houses, not much different from how it is today, Westpole was a tricky LG from which to fly, and had a poor surface. The site was relinquished in 1919.

Wormwood Scrubs (HMS *President*), London Borough of Hammersmith & Fulham

51°31'18"N/00°14'06"W, TQ225818. 0.3 miles NE of prison, 0.75 miles SW of Kensal Green underground station

WORMWOOD SCRUBS began life in April 1915 as a Stores Depot for the RNAS, but within months was earmarked as an airship training school and construction site for non-rigid airships. During the Stores Depot occupation, which came to an end in October 1915, construction began on a pair of Airship Sheds (354 by 75 by 98 feet and 300 by 45 by 55 feet). Buildings occupied 5 acres of this 30-acre site when the Airship Pilots School and Airship Constructional Station was formed in October 1915.

On 9 May 1918 No 10 (Mechanical Transport) Repair Depot was also established here, and with the end of the First World War the Admiralty considering taking over this unit as part of the airship factory. This never came to fruition, and No 10 (MT)RD continued until December 1919, by which time the pilots school had closed. The site was closed down in 1921 and much of the area occupied by the station remains undeveloped as sports fields today.

NORFOLK

Bacton

52°50'17"N/01°28'34"W, TG341325. 0.5 miles due S of Broomholm, W boundary accessible via Pollard Street off North Walsham Road

Bacton was brought into use as an NLG from August 1915, serving as a sub-station to Yarmouth for both RNAS and later RAF operations. Buildings on the site slowly expanded, including an Aeroplane Shed (66 by 42 feet), which together with several other structures was located in the north-eastern corner of the airfield, although the latter development only amounted to a few huts. Occupying 120 acres, the average personnel strength was 2 officers and 30 other ranks.

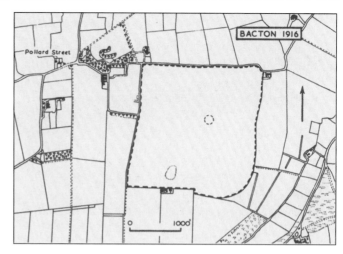

The first unit to arrive at Bacton was the RNAS HD Flight in April 1916, which occupied the airfield until its disbandment in April 1918. From August 1918 the DH.9s of 557 Flight were in residence until they were moved to Dover (St Margaret's) in March 1919. The Armistice saw a detachment of three Camels from 470(F) Flight, which was part of 273 Squadron. This move marked the beginning of a four-month period when Bacton became a Marine & HD Operations (Aeroplane) Station operating under the 73rd (Operations) Wing based at Yarmouth. A final detachment from 219 Squadron in March 1919 from Manston brought Bacton's short yet busy existence to an end.

Bexwell

52°35'37"N/00°24'12"W, TF628022A. NE of Stonehill Farm, N of Stonehills Wood, 1.5 miles ESE of Downham Market

OPENED as an HD ELG in 1915, very little is known about this LG, including its use or units allocated, although 51(HD) Squadron is the favourite.

De Havilland DH.4 A7459, seen at Bacton in 1917, was given the name 'Allo Lédeé Bird'. The aircraft was lost in the North Sea on 5 September 1917. *Via Stuart Leslie*

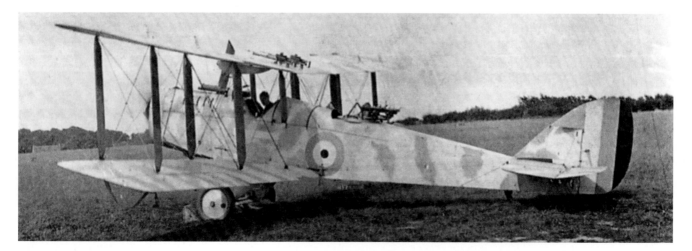

Bircham Newton

52°52'29"N/00°39'28"W, TF789341. Bircham Newton Training Centre, 1.3 miles E of Bircham Newton village, 2.25 miles SE of Docking

CONSTRUCTION at Bircham Newton began in 1917 with the intention of using it as a TDS. Instead it opened as a training squadron station for 3 SoAF&G from Eastburn in May 1918. Being built as a TDS, Bircham Newton was well furnished with hangars, including seven 1918-pattern GS Sheds (170 by 100 feet). A generous site, the aerodrome occupied 297 acres and measured 1,100 by 900 yards.

Bircham Newton was destined to have a much bigger role to play when it was selected as the first mobilisation station for 27 Group under the command of Lt Col R. H. Mulock. This was the early stages of the RAF's new Independent Air Force, equipped partly with long-range Handley Page V/1500 bombers capable of attacking Berlin. The first examples of this huge 126-foot-span bomber were planned to join 166 Squadron, formed at Bircham in June 1918, but initially the crews had to make do with considerably smaller FE.2Bs. By October 1918 only three V/1500s had been delivered, and with the Armistice just days away Germany escaped the potentially destructive power of the Independent Air Force.

November 1918 saw Bircham designated as an Experimental Meteorological Station, and a second V/1500 unit in the shape of 167 Squadron was formed on the 18th. The third and final V/1500 unit to be created, 274 Squadron, was formed on 15 June 1919, securing Bircham's post-war future as a bomber station, a role that it carried through to the Second World War. Expanded during the 1920s and 1930s, much of Bircham's later building history remains intact, but its First World War existence has been virtually erased. The RAF left the site in 1966 and today the old airfield is the home to the Construction Industry Training Board.

Bircham Newton main units, 1918-19

3 SoAF&G from Eastburn, May 1918;
redesignated 3 FS, 19 May 1918
(DH.5, SE.5A, Pup, Dolphin and Snipe)

3 FS (ex-3 SoAF&G) 29 May 1918;
to Sedgeford, Oct 1918
(DH.5, SE.5A, Pup, Dolphin, Snipe and Camel)

166 Sqn formed 13 Jun 1918;
redesignated 3 (Comms) Sqn, 31 May 1919 (FE.2B and V/1500)

86 Wing HQ formed 29 Sep 1918;
DB 10 Dec 1918

87 Wing HQ formed 29 Sep 1918;
DB 10 Dec 1918

27 (Ops) Group from Room 230, 11 Oct 1918;
reorganised to concentrate mainly on long-distance communication flights with 5 to 8 (Comms Sqns), 12 Feb 1919;
DB 19 May 1919

167 Sqn formed 18 Nov 1918;
redesignated 5 (Comms) Sqn, 21 May 1919 (V/1500)

Earsham

52°26'43"N/01°23'50"W, TM309885. 0.7 miles N of Norfolk & Suffolk Aviation Museum, 2 miles WSW of Bungay

OPENED in April 1916 for 51(HD) Squadron, Earsham was a 45-acre site measuring 750 by 400 yards. Classified as an HD NLG3, 75(HD) Squadron also operated from here until it was closed down in June 1919.

Feltwell

52°28'25"N/00°31'34"W, TL716892. W of Feltwell Road (B1112), bulk of original site within boundary of current RAF Feltwell

THE first of two airfields to be located at Feltwell was opened on 1 November 1917 for 7 TDS. The unit was created from the nucleus flights of 'A' Flight, 18 TS, from Montrose, 'B' Flight, 63 TS, from Joyce Green, and 'C' Flight, 28 TS, from Castle Bromwich. The main technical and domestic areas occupied the same area in the south-eastern corner of the aerodrome off the Feltwell Road, south of the village. As a TDS, the site was well facilitated with seven 1918-pattern GS Sheds (170 by 100 feet), but one aerial photograph taken in May 1918 shows at least sixteen Bessonneau hangars in use. The aerodrome occupied 208 acres and measured 1,100 by 800 yards and once the TDS was fully worked up, at least seventy-two aircraft were on strength, the main type being the SE.5A, even though the TDS was tasked with training day bomber crews. From April 1918 the main type was, appropriately, the DH.9.

The TDS was disbanded on 22 April 1919, the same day that the Midland Area FIS arrived from Lilbourne with an array of aircraft types including the 504/J/K, Snipe, DH.4 and DH.9. The unit was redesignated the Northern Area FIS on 18 October 1919, but this was short-lived, as the unit was disbanded on 27 November. By early 1920 the site was de-requisitioned and the majority of the buildings were dismantled and removed.

The RAF expansion airfield that followed in the 1930s occupied the same flying area, but the more complex technical and domestic area was located much closer to Feltwell village on the northern side of the site. Still in RAF hands, the site has been occupied by the USAFE for many years and looks to remain so for the foreseeable future. Six buildings from the First World War remain on the western side of the Feltwell Road, south of the golf course.

Freethorpe

52°35'40N/01°33'41W, TG414056. 0.25 miles NE of Freethorpe off Palmer's Lane, 2.2 miles NE of Cantley railway station

ONE of the most easterly of 51(HD) Squadron's NLGs, Freethorpe was located on the edge of the Broads, and was in military hands from April 1916 until June 1919. Classified as an NLG1, Freethorpe took up 43 acres and measured 550 by 500 yards.

Frettenham

52°43'01N/01°20'19W, TG255185. NE of Clamp Wood off Frettenham Road, 1.3 miles SE of Coltishall village

THIS 55-acre NLG2, measuring 500 by 480 yards, was opened in August 1916 and occupied by 51(HD) Squadron while serving at Hingham and later Marham. The site was closed down in June 1919, and the same month 51(HD) Squadron was disbanded at Suttons Farm.

Gooderstone (Warren Farm)

52°35'02"N/00°38'18"W, TF787016. W of Warren Farm, 1.6 miles E of Gooderstone, 4.6 miles SSW of Swaffham

ANOTHER element of 51(HD) Squadron's network of LGs across East Anglia was Gooderstone, which came into use from August 1916 as an HD NLG3. A 65-acre field measuring 700 by 450 yards, the site was redesignated as an NLG2 on 3 March 1917, and remained under the charge of the squadron until it was closed down in June 1919.

Harling Road (Roudham)

52°27'02"N/00°54'28"W, TL979873. Roudham Park Industrial Estate on either side of Hereward Way, 1.25 miles NW of East Harling

HARLING ROAD'S time as an aerodrome began in September 1916 when it was opened as an HD Flight Station for 51(HD) Squadron. Operating a collection of BE.2Cs, BE.12s and later FE.2Bs, the HD unit moved out in August 1917 to make way for a flurry of units made up of the 151st Aero Squadron and 88, 89 and 94 Squadrons, all of which had arrived from early August 1917. The site was slowly upgraded to an NLG1 for 75(HD) Squadron from September 1917, by which time Harling Road was a training squadron station.

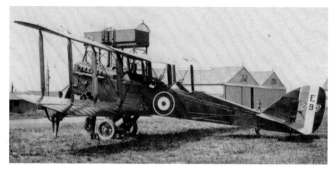

De Havilland DH.9A E797 was modified with dual controls at Harling Road and continued to serve the RAF until 1926.

By early 1918 Harling Road was being prepared as a TDS and had grown to 245 acres, measuring 1,100 by 1,100 yards, with a technical and domestic site growing on the north side of Hereward Way and an expanding hangar area with further technical buildings on the south side of the road. Several 1917-pattern GS Sheds (170 by 80 feet) and a single ARS Shed were in place by the time 10 TDS was formed on 15 April 1918. Personnel were well catered for, although other ranks were generally under canvas; the officers and SNCOs had their own messes, and 52 staff officers and up to 90 pupil officers were accommodated in permanent huts.

10 TDS was under the control of 39 (Training) Wing established locally at 79 London Road, Brandon, where it remained until 4 April 1919. 10 TDS became 10 TS on 14 March 1920 and continued to train pilots until the 19th. Presumably the aerodrome was closed down soon after and many buildings were sold off. One survivor today is the single ARS Shed, which remains in use and the flying field is pretty much undisturbed. During the Second World War the site was taken over by the US Army and the many military huts on the site are remnants from that period.

Avro 504A A8515 is seen during a visit to Harling Road.

Harling Road main units, 1916-20

51 Sqn from Hingham, 23 Sep 1916;
to Marham, Aug 1917 (BE.2C/E, BE.12 and FE.2B)

151st Aero Sqn, 'C' and 'D' Flts, USAAS, by 17 Jul 1918

94 Sqn from Gosport, 3 Aug 1917;
to Shoreham, 27 Jul 1918 (various aircraft)

88 Sqn from Gosport, 2 Aug 1917;
to Kenley, 2 Apr 1918 (F.2B)

89 Sqn from Catterick, 7 Aug 1917;
to Upper Heyford, 17 Jul 1918 (various aircraft)

75 Sqn 'A' and 'B' Flts from Elmswell by 24 Sep 1917;
to Elmswell by 12 Apr 1918 (BE.2C/E and BE.12)

10 TDS formed 15 Apr 1918;
redesignated 10 TS, 14 Mar 1919 (DH4, DH.9/9A, Dolphin, Camel, Martinsyde, DH.6, BE.2E, RE.8 and 504)

10 TS (ex-10 TDS) 14 Mar 1919;
DB Mar 1920 (504K and F.2B)

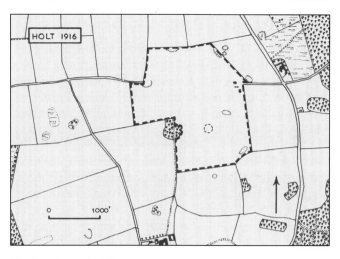

Hickling Broad

52°44'47"N/01°34'21"W, TG410225. Whispering Reeds (Hoseasons) and Heron Way off Staithe Road, E of Hickling Heath, 1.75 miles N of Potter Heigham

THE Marine Operations (Seaplane) Station at Hickling Broad was a sub-station to Great Yarmouth from 22 October 1918. The site only occupied 4 acres split between two sites, within 250 yards of each other. The flying site is the current Hoseasons moorings, while the domestic site was built where Heron Way is today, both off Staithe road. A single slipway, a pair of boathouses and two Bessonneau hangars were erected next to the seaplane moorings. The Heron Way site was made up of Armstrong huts and a few technical buildings, while all take-offs and landings were carried out on the northern half of the broad.

Hickling sub-station was employed as a calm-water diversion for the seaplanes of 228 Squadron at Great Yarmouth until April 1919, when the unit moved north to Brough as a cadre.

Hingham

52°34'42"N/00°57'20"W, TG004019*. W of village off B1108, between Tollgate Farm and Frost Row

INFORMATION as to the exact location of this Norfolk LG is a little sketchy. What can be confirmed is that 51(HD) Squadron arrived here from Thetford on 23 September 1916 with BE.2Cs and BE.12s and, after re-equipping with the FE.2B and BE.2E, moved to Marham on 7 August 1917. Two important squadrons were also formed here, beginning with 100 Squadron, the nucleus provided by 51(HD) Squadron on 11 February 1917; the squadron moved to Farnborough on the 23rd. The second unit to be formed was 102 Squadron on 9 August 1917, which moved to St Andre-aux Bois on 24 September.

* Approximate location

Holt (Bayfield)

52°55'54"N/01°04'09"W, TG065415. W of Cley Road, between Swan Lodge and Majors Clump, 1.7 miles NNW of Holt

A 90-ACRE HD Flight Station, measuring 600 by 700 yards, was established north of Holt in August 1915 as another sub-station for Great Yarmouth. The War Flight RNAS was formed here and remained until September 1917. In August 1918 the site was upgraded to a Marine Operations (Aeroplane) Station and a single Aeroplane Shed (66 by 42 feet) was erected to protect the half-dozen DH.9s operated by 558(LB) Flight, which was part of 212 Squadron. The flight only operated from Holt in August 1918, although the aerodrome would remain a marine station until March 1919.

King's Lynn

52°45'46"N/01°24'02"W, TF620210. Between Edward Benefer Way (A1078) and Old East sea bank, in region of Netto supermarket, 0.6 miles N of King's Lynn town centre

THIS was a manufacturer's aerodrome for the use of Savage Ltd, which built DH.1s in the nearby St Nicholas Works. A manufacturer of fairground equipment, Savage initially struggled with building aircraft and only five had been delivered to the RFC by 1915. Seventy were eventually built, followed by orders for the Voisin LA, 504K and DH.6; however, the vast majority of these machines were more likely built at Savage's Stroud factory. The works were demolished in 1973 and the site has been slowly developed ever since.

King's Lynn was also the home of 7 Wing, which moved from Norwich to Belgrave House, St Johns Terrace, on 8 January 1918. Controlling various flying units across Norfolk, 7 Wing joined 3 Group in May 1918 and was disbanded on 12 September 1918.

Marham

52°38'47"N/00°33'06"W, TF725084. Centre of current RAF Marham, 5.8 miles W of Swaffham

ONE of the busiest RAF stations in the country, supporting three Tornado squadrons, RAF Marham began its association with aviation with a much humbler 80-acre site, which today is little more than open ground located between its triangle of runways. Measuring no more than 740 by 550 yards, land to the east of Field House was requisitioned for an aerodrome in August 1916, and by the following month became the home of 'C' Flight, 51(HD) Squadron, from neighbouring Narborough. Opened as an HD Flight Station, the aerodrome was initially furnished with a pair of HD-pattern Aeroplane Sheds (130 by 60 feet), with sliding doors, surrounded by a few huts and tented accommodation.

With 51(HD) Squadron from Hingham in place from August 1917, the site became overcrowded when it became a night training squadron station from November, thanks to the formation of 191 DS (later 191 NTS). Four Bessonneau hangars were hastily erected to accommodate the unit's collection of aircraft, which included the FE.2B/D, DH.6 and FE.2B. The night training unit left for Upwood in July 1918, leaving 51(HD) Squadron with considerably more space, remaining here until it moved to Sutton's Farm on 14 May 1919. Closed down in 1920, the RAF was destined to return here in 1935 when work began on a considerably larger expansion airfield, which has remained busy ever since.

Marham main units, 1916-18

51 Sqn 'C' Flt from Narborough, 23 Sep 1916;
to Mattishall, 7 Aug 1917 (BE.2C/E, BE.12, FE.2B and Camel)

51 Sqn HQ from Hingham, 7 Aug 1917;
to Sutton's Farm, 14 May 1919 (FE.2B, G.100 and Camel)

192 DS from East Retford, 10 Oct 1917;
to Newmarket, 14 Nov 1917 (FE.2B/D and BE.2C/D/E)

191 DS formed 6 Nov 1917;
redesignated 191 NTS, 21 Dec 1917 (BE.2D/E, DH.6 and FE.2B)

191 NTS (ex-192 DS) 21 Dec 1917;
to Upwood, 1 Jul 1918 (BE.2D/E, DH.6 and FE.2B)

Marsham

52°45'56"N/01°15'22"W, TG195236. 150 yards SW of Marsham All Saints Church, 2.2 miles S of Aylsham town centre

THIS small LG on the very edge of Marsham village was only open from April to October 1916, during which time it was occasionally used by 51(HD) Squadron. The site was shut down in favour of Saxthorpe.

Mattishall

52°39'39"N/01°03'27"W, TG069114. Due N of Tollgate Farm, off Mattishall Road, 0.6 miles WNW of East Tuddenham

ANOTHER aerodrome catering for 51(HD) Squadron was Mattishall, located in the heart of Norfolk, which opened as an NLG1 in April 1916. The unit was slow in making use of the site, which was upgraded to an HD Flight Station from September 1916, complete with two HD-pattern Aeroplane Sheds (130 by 60 feet) coupled together, and several smaller buildings, nestling along the side of Mattishall Road. The site measured 600 by 500 yards and occupied 61 acres, six of them covered by buildings.

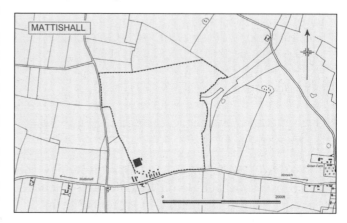

'B' Flight, 51(HD) Squadron, moved in from Thetford on 16 September 1916 and remained until 7 July 1917, when it made the short hop to Marham. 'C' Flight, also from Thetford, made use of Mattishall from the same day until April 1918, being relieved by 'A' Flight from Tydd St Mary, which remained until 14 May 1919, leaving for Sutton's Farm. Like many old LGs in Norfolk, the site is much the same as it was when the RAF departed in 1920.

Methwold

52°30'39"N/00°32'56"W, TL729933. Centre of WW2 airfield site, 1 mile due S of Methwold, 5.5 miles NW of Brandon town centre

AN HD NLG, Methwold only remained open from April to October 1916 for 51(HD) Squadron. All duties were taken over by Gooderstone, but considerably more use would be made of the location during the Second World War.

Narborough
(The Great Government Aerodrome)

52°39'42"N/00°34'51"W, TF746102. Bisected by Chalk Lane, S of Marham Road, 0.6 miles from end of RAF Marham's runway 06 (approach lighting straddles site)

NARBOROUGH grew into one of the country's largest aerodromes, which by 1917 occupied 908 acres and measured 2,930 by 1,870 yards, while its near neighbour Marham paled into insignificance. Opened in August 1915 as

an HD LG for the RNAS, the site was taken over by the RFC from April 1916, expanded eastwards and was classified as an NLG1 (NLG from September 1916) for 'C' Flight, 51(HD) Squadron, which moved in from Norwich (Mousehold Heath) in June. The site was expanded throughout 1916 and in May was also classified as a training squadron station, a title it would retain until its closure.

The main hangar line, which consisted of six 1916-pattern GS Sheds (170 by 80 feet), was along the southern edge of Marham Road, with technical buildings behind (messes included). Two large domestic sites were built on the eastern side of Chalk Lane, heading north towards Narborough village, on the southern edge of the Contract Plantation.

Narborough became the home of 55 TDS from September 1918 and, like so many aerodromes, received a number of squadron cadres returning from the continent to disband in early 1919. The TDS was redesignated 55 TS in March 1919, the unit remaining until November, when the site was wound down. Closed down completely in 1920, it was the much smaller Marham site to the west that was later expanded, while

A line of R.A.F. BE.2Es, including A1276 of 53 TS in the foreground, is seen at Narborough in 1917.

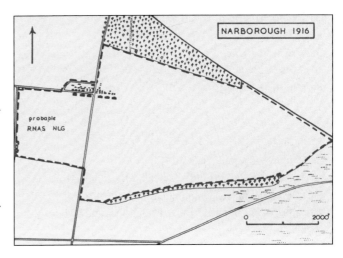

A vertical view of Narborough (orientated north) on 5 November 1918, during the tenure of 55 TDS. A chalk line is visible through the middle of the photograph.

Narborough returned to the plough. One hangar lingered on into the 1970s and the land around the Marham Road/Chalk Lane junction still bears the scars of hangar bases and

buildings. The modern sheds at Battles Farm are built on the base of a 1918-pattern GS Shed (180 by 100 feet), which was erected later on in the war.

Narborough main units, 1915-19

RNAS HD detached from Great Yarmouth Aug 1915;
to Great Yarmouth, Apr 1916

51 Sqn 'C' Flt from Norwich (Mousehold Heath) by 1 Jun 1916;
to Marham, 23 Sep 1916 (BE.2C and BE.12)

35 Sqn from Thetford, 16 Jun 1916;
to St Omer, 26 Jan 1917 (various aircraft)

59 Sqn formed 1 Aug 1916;
to St Omer, 13 Feb 1917 (RE.8)

48 TS formed 2 Nov 1916;
to Waddington, 13 Nov 1916 (DH6, Shorthorn and RE.8)

50 TS from Wye, 14 Dec 1916;
to Spittlegate, 30 Nov 1917 (FK.3 and FK.8)

53 TS from Sedgeford, 14 Feb 1917;
to Harlaxton, 6 Dec 1917 (RE.8, BE.2E, DH.6 and 504)

64 TS from Dover (Swingate Down), 14 Apr 1917;
to Harlaxton, 12 Dec 1917 (RE.8, BE.2E, DH.6 and 504)

1 TS reformed 1 Oct 1917;
to Port Meadow, 10 Oct 1917 (Camel, 504 and Pup)

69 TS from Cramlington, 9 Dec 1917;
DB into 22 TDS (DH.4, DH.6 and DH.9)

83 Sqn from Wyton, 12 Dec 1917;
to St Omer, 6 Mar 1918 (FE.2B)

121 Sqn formed 1 Jan 1918;
to Filton, 10 Aug 1918 (various aircraft)

20th Aero Sqn, USAAS, detached from USA, 8 Jan 1918;
to Easton-on-the-Hill, 1 May 1918

26 TS from Harlaxton, 3 Feb 1918;
DB into 22 TDS, 1 Aug 1918 (various aircraft)

24th Aero Sqn, USAAS, from Wye, Croydon, Sedgeford and Winchester, 1 May 1918;
to St Maxent, 19 Jul 1918 (no aircraft)

55 TDS from Manston, 12 Sep 1918;
redesignated 55 TS, 14 Mar 1919 (DH.4, DH.6, BE.2E, Dolphin, FB.9, Camel, 504, DH.9, SPAD and SE.5A)

64 Sqn cadre from Froidment, 14 Feb 1919;
DB 31 Dec 1919 (no aircraft)

56 Sqn cadre from Bethencourt, 15 Feb 1919;
to Bircham Newton, 30 Dec 1919 (no aircraft)

60 Sqn cadre from Inchy, 28 Feb 1919;
to Bircham Newton, 1 Jan 1920 (no aircraft)

55 TS 14 Mar 1919;
DB Nov 1919

North Elmham (Dereham)

52°44'42"N/00°56'22"W, TF985205A. Most likely on land adjacent to King's Head Farm S of B1145, 1.5 miles NW of Swanton Morley airfield

THIS HD NLG 3 was open during February and March 1917 for 51(HD) Squadron. Its actual use would have been negligible.

Norwich (Aylsham Road)

52°39'30"N/01°16'30"W, TG213120. Between Reepham and Cromer, former Aylsham, Roads (A140), 2.25 miles NNW of Norwich city centre

A 60-ACRE manufacturer's aerodrome was shoehorned between the Reepham and Cromer roads from 1915 to 1919 to serve the Mann Egerton & Co Ltd factory, which was located at the southern end of the site towards the Boundary Road junction. The company received a 'war loan' of £30,000 to buy the land and contribute towards the cost of establishing an aircraft factory on the site. Six major buildings were constructed; the largest, at 200 by 100 feet, was begun in March 1916, by which time aircraft manufacture in the shape of the Short 184 had already commenced. Mann Egerton went on to build the 1½ Strutter, DH.9 and DH.10, until the site was closed down in 1919.

Norwich (Mousehold Heath)

52°38'41"N/01°19'47"W, TG255104. Both sides of Salhouse Road, E of Heartsease Lane and W of Woodside Road, 1.75 miles NE of Norwich city centre

TAKING its name from the heath that lies to the west, this aerodrome has succumbed, unlike the heath, to the urban sprawl of Norwich, but some original buildings have been incorporated into an industrial park.

A large site at 263 acres, Norwich (Mousehold Heath) measured 1,100 by 1,000 yards and was opened in July 1915 for 9 TS, which was equipped with a large variety of aircraft. This unit went on to help create 37 and 51 Squadrons, the latter being forever remembered as one of the main HD units employed to protect Norfolk from the Zeppelin threat. 51(HD) Squadron operated two flights from here until June 1916, and during this period the aerodrome was classified as an NLG1 and a training squadron station.

The main flying field was located south of Salhouse Road, and on the northern edge three 1915-pattern sheds (210 by 60 feet) were erected, while on the edge of Heartsease Lane a 1915-pattern Flight Shed (140 by 60 feet) stood on its own. To the north of Salhouse Road, two more 1915-pattern sheds (210 by 60 feet) were located at the Mousehold Lane/Gurney Road junction, and further along the road, again to the north, stood nine 1916-pattern GS Sheds (170 by 80 feet) and

An early production DH.9, D1716, stands outside the Mann Egerton shed at Norwich (Aylsham Road) circa May 1918. The building behind was the main 200-by-100-foot factory.

Norwich (Mousehold Heath) is captured at 1130hrs on 5 June 1917 looking eastwards over the heath, with Salhouse Road disappearing into the distance. The heath in the foreground was used as an army camp, training camp and rifle range, and today has escaped the developers, while across Heartsease Lane the aerodrome has been consumed by industry and housing.

twenty-one storage sheds (200 by 60 feet). The bulk of the latter served 3 (Norwich) AAP (originally 3 AAP), which was formed on 22 March 1917 to handle aircraft built by local manufacturers. The latter included Boulton Paul Ltd (Camel), Mann Egerton & Co (DH.9), Portholme Aerodrome Ltd (Camel), and Ransomes Simms & Jeffries (FE.2B).

From April 1918 the aerodrome was officially known as RAF Mousehold Heath, but it was the AAP that dominated until its closure on 26 July 1919. 3 Group had its HQ here from 1 July to 10 November 1919 but, rather than being completely abandoned after the war, civilian aviation began to take over. The Norwich & Norfolk Aero Club was formed here in 1927, and by 1933 Mousehold served as the first Norwich Airport, long before the site at Horsham St Faith. Several ex-3 AAP hangars survive in harmony with more modern buildings on the industrial estate north of Salhouse Road.

Airship Sheds Nos 1 and 2 under the construction, with the much smaller Coastal Patrol Shed already in operation beyond, at Pulham St Mary in 1917.

Norwich (Mousehold Heath) main units, 1915-19

9 TS formed 27 Jul 1915;
became Advanced Training Squadron, to Sedgeford, 10 Jan 1918 (FE.2B, Farman, 504, BE.2C, Longhorn, Caudron, Martinsyde Scout, F.2B, Camel and Pup)

18 Sqn from Northolt, 16 Aug 1915;
to St Omer, 19 Nov 1915 (S.1, Shorthorn and Scout)

37 Sqn formed (nucleus from 9 TS) 15 Apr 1916;
to Orfordness, 16 Apr 1916 (no aircraft)

51 Sqn formed (nucleus from 9 TS) 15 May 1916;
to Thetford, 1 Jun 1916 (BE.2C and BE.12)

49 TS formed 23 Sep 1916;
to Brattleby, 16 Oct 1916 (Shorthorn and Longhorn)

3 (Norwich) AAP formed 22 Mar 1917;
DB 26 Jul 1919 (handled Camel, FE.2B and DH.9)

85 Sqn from Upavon, 10 Aug 1917;
to Hounslow, 27 Nov 1917 (SE.5A)

117 Sqn from Hucknall, 15 Jul 1918;
to Wyton, 30 Nov 1918 (DH.9)

Non-rigid airships based at Pulham included *C17*, *C26*, *C27*, *SS14*, *SSE1* and *SSZ3*, but from February 1918 the station was redesignated as an airship experimental station and normal military operations began to decrease. Much larger rigid airships were based at Pulham from late 1917, including at least two R23 class airships, and the *R34* settled here after crossing the Atlantic and back in July 1919. Pulham remained an experimental station until October 1920, the site remaining in military hands. Experiments still continued during the 1920s, especially air-launch trials when one, or often two, aircraft were carried aloft and dropped.

In 1928 the largest of the Airship Sheds was dismantled and moved to Cardington, where it can be seen to this day. The site became the home to several MUs during the Second World War and was not fully relinquished by the RAF until 1958. The second large Airship Shed survived until 1948, and today the remnants of those airship days can still be clearly seen. Both large shed bases are still visible and the bases of the four gas tanks are still in place.

Pulham St Mary

52°24'23"N/01°13'37"W, TM194836. NW of Airstation Farm, NW of Rushall, 0.3 miles SW of Pulham St Mary

THIS once famous site was the location for a Class G Airship Station for the operation of non-rigid airships from February 1916. A large site, which occupied 920 acres and measured 2,600 by 2,330 yards, Pulham also served as an RNAS and later RAF Marine Operations (Aeroplane) Station. Three Airship Sheds were built here, one Non-rigid Airship Shed or Coastal Airship Shed (223 by 69 by 70 feet), one much larger Rigid Airship Shed (No 1) (711 by 150 by 100 feet), and another even larger shed (No 2) (758 by 180 by 110 feet), together with a large permanent mooring mast in the middle of the field. The technical site was covered by the usual array of buildings associated with airship operations, including a four-tank gas plant, which would not have been out of place on the edge of a city.

Saxthorpe (Aylsham)

52°49'58"N/01°08'59"W, TG122309. SW of Mossymere Wood, 0.5 miles NE of Saxthorpe, 5 miles NW of Aylsham

AN NLG2 for 51(HD) Squadron, Saxthorpe occupied 37 acres and measured 550 by 320 yards. The LG would have been open from August 1917 until the end of the war.

Scoulton

52°34'14"N/01°55'30"W, TF983009. N of Norwich Road (B1108), SW of Mere Road, NW of Scoulton

LITTLE is known about this site other than it was opened as an HD NLG3 for 51(HD) Squadron between January and October 1917.

Sedgeford

52°53'43"N/00°34'36"W, TF732360. Due N of Fring, 1.5 miles E of Sedgeford

ASITE that continued to expand during its four-year existence, Sedgeford was opened as an HD NLG for the RNAS in August 1915. A single Aeroplane Shed (70 by 65 feet) together with a few huts and tents were all that gave the site away as an aerodrome, until the RFC took over in May 1916 with the arrival of 45 Squadron from Thetford. More hangarage was erected in the shape of two 1917-pattern GS Sheds (170 by 80 feet), made of timber, and eight corrugated-iron Aeroplane Sheds (100 by 46 feet) joined as four coupled units. The aerodrome grew to 170 acres and measured 1,150 by 700 yards, and from 1916 also served as an HD NLG1 for 51(HD) Squadron.

From February 1917 the first of several training squadrons made Sedgeford its home, the aerodrome being classified as a training squadron station and, from September 1918, a temporary mobilisation station for 3 FS from Bircham Newton. The busy FS became 7 TS, which was disbanded in October 1919. The site was run down during late 1919 and had closed by early 1920.

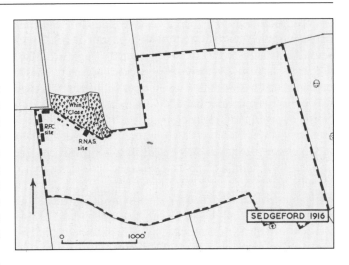

Sedgeford main units, 1916-19

45 Sqn from Thetford, 21 May 1916;
to St Omer, 8 Oct 1916 (F.20 and 1½ Strutter)

64 Sqn formed 1 Aug 1916;
to St Omer, 14 Oct 1917 (F.20, BE.2C, FE.2B, Pup, 504 and DH.5)

53 TS formed (out of 64 Sqn) 1 Feb 1917;
to Narborough, 14 Feb 1917 (RE.8 and BE.2C)

65 TS from Croydon, 10 May 1917;
to Dover, 25 Nov 1917 (various aircraft)

87 Sqn from Upavon, 15 Sep 1917;
to Hounslow (various aircraft)

72 Sqn from Netheravon, 1 Nov 1917;
en route to Persian Gulf, 25 Dec 1917 (504 and Pup)

110 Sqn from Dover (Swingate Down), 26 Nov 1917;
to Kenley, 15 Jun 1918 (various aircraft)

9 TS from Norwich, 10 Jan 1918;
to Tallaught, Aug 1918 (various aircraft)

24th Aero Sqn (USAAC) from Wye, 31 Jan 1918;
to Narborough, 1 May 1918 (DH.4)

159th Aero Sqn (USAAC) from ? by mid-Jul 1918;
to ? (aircraft unknown)

122 Sqn formed 1 Jan 1918;
DB 17 Aug 1918 (planned DH.9;
various aircraft)

3 FS from Bircham Newton, 21 Sep 1918;
redesignated 7 TS, 14 Mar 1919 (various aircraft)

7 TS (ex-3 FS) 14 Mar 1919;
DB Oct 1919 (504K)

13 Sqn cadre from St Omer, 27 Mar 1919;
DB 31 Dec 1919

Sporle

52°40'32"N/00°44'31"W, TF855121. 0.6 miles NW of Sporle, S of Sporle Road, 2 miles NW of Necton

OCCUPYING just 40 acres and measuring 520 by 430 yards, Sporle was another LG for 51(HD) Squadron. Classified as an NLG3, the site was only in military hands from the spring of 1918 until June 1919.

Taverham

52°41'41"N/01°11'49"E, TG161156. NW of Breck Farm, E of Fir Covert Road, 0.6 miles N of Taverham centre

AN HD NLG is recorded as being located north of the village of Taverham by late 1916 for the use of 51(HD) Squadron.

Thetford (Snarehill)

52°23'33"N/00°47'15"W. E of A1088, S of Great Snarehill Belt, N of Little Ouse, 2.2 miles SE of Thetford

ESTABLISHED in late 1915, Thetford's sole purpose from the outset was to train pilots and create squadrons, which it did until early 1918. Its first resident was 12 TS, which arrived from Dover on 16 November 1915 with a collection of already antiquated aircraft.

A DH.9 of 25 TS is seen at Thetford circa early 1918. *Via Stuart Leslie*

The aerodrome was large, occupying 414 acres and measuring 1,900 by 1,050 yards. It was also well furnished with seven Aeroplane Sheds (210 by 65 feet) and a single ARS Shed (170 by 80 feet), together with a range of technical and domestic buildings that by 1918 took up 30 acres of the site. Thetford was a busy aerodrome that also served as an HD NLG for Norfolk's own 51(HD) Squadron for a spell in 1916. But it was training that was Thetford's main role, and this came to a peak in September 1918 when No 4 SoN&BD was formed here. The unit acted as a finishing school for pilots and observers who had already graduated, and subjects taught included aerial navigation, map-reading and the art of flying in formation with a fully loaded aircraft. Up to seventy-two DH.9s and DH.9As were on strength, and on average forty-five pilots and forty-five observers passed through the school during a two-week course. The bombing school was closed down in April 1919 and the aerodrome soon after. The relationship between Thetford and bombing would continue when the site was reactivated as Rushford bombing range in the 1930s.

Thetford main units, 1915-18

12 TS from Dover (Swingate Down), 16 Nov 1915;
DB into 35 TDS, 15 Jul 1918
(Blériot, Shorthorn, Longhorn, BE.2 and RE.8)

15 TS formed 15 Dec 1915;
to Doncaster, 1 Jun 1917 (various aircraft)

25 Sqn from Montrose, 31 Dec 1915;
to St Omer, 20 Feb 1916 (various aircraft)

35 Sqn formed (from 9 TS) 1 Feb 1916;
to Narborough, 16 Jun 1916 (various aircraft)

38 Sqn formed (from 12 TS) 1 Apr 1916;
redesignated 25 TS, 22 May 1916 (BE.2C/E)

45 Sqn from Gosport, 3 May 1916;
to Sedgeford, 21 May 1916 (various aircraft)

51 Sqn from Norwich, 1 Jun 1916;
to Hingham, 23 Sep 1916 (BE.2C and BE.12)

25 TS (ex-38 Sqn) 22 May 1916;
DB into 35 TDS, 15 Jul 1918 (Shorthorn, Longhorn, DH.4, DH.6, DH.9, BE.2E, RE.8, Camel, 504 and FE.2B)

73 TS formed 7 Jul 1917;
to Turnhouse, 17 Jul 1917 (1½ Strutter, Camel and Pup)

128 Sqn formed 1 Feb 1918;
DB 4 Jul 1918 (various aircraft)

8th Aero Sqn, USAAS, detached from Joyce Green, 1 May 1918;
to France, 11 Jul 1918 (no aircraft)

35 TDS (ex-12 and 25 TS) 15 Jul 1918;
to Duxford, 21 Aug 1918 (DH.4, DH.6, DH.9, RE.8 and 504)

23rd Aero Sqn, USAAS, from USA, 25 Jul 1918;
to Duxford, 2 Sep 1918 (DH.4)

119 Sqn from Duxford, 19 Aug 1918;
to Wyton, 26 Sep 1918 (various aircraft)

4 SoN&BD formed Sep 1918;
DB 26 Apr 1919 (DH.4, DH.6, DH.9 and FE.2B)

Tibenham

52°27'06"N/01°07'13"W, TM122883. NE of Tibenham Farm off Heath Road (B1134), 1 mile SW of Pristow Green, 1.75 miles W of Tibenham airfield

THIS NLG2 was first allocated to 51(HD) Squadron from October 1916 and later to 75(HD) Squadron until its closure in late 1918. The site occupied 30 acres and measured 500 by 400 yards.

Tottenhill

52°39'47"N/00°24'41"W. W of Lynn Road (A10), E of Watlington Road, 0.65 miles NW of Tottenhill

CONTINUING 51(HD) Squadron's network of LGs, Tottenhill was opened in late 1916 as an NLG3 close to the hamlet at Tottenhill Row. The site occupied 45 acres and measured 575 by 450 yards, and parish records indicate that the aerodrome was still in RFC hands in 1918. Today the site is a gravel works.

West Rudham

52°47'53"N/00°41'26"W, SZ642887. Largest fields that could accommodate size of aerodrome would be due E of West Rudham Grange, 1.75 miles W of ex-RAF West Raynham

OPENED in December 1916 as an NLG2 for 51(HD) Squadron based at Higham, West Rudham occupied 62 acres and measured 900 by 550 yards. The LG was relinquished at the end of the war.

Yarmouth (South Denes I and II)

52°34'47"N/01°44'10"W. At South Denes, opposite Great Yarmouth Outer Harbour, 0.9 miles S of Pleasure Beach

THE thin strip of land that protects the River Ware and the port of Great Yarmouth was opened for seaplane operations on 15 April 1913. The small station would expand on the outbreak of war with a pair of slipways, three Seaplane Sheds and an LG to the rear, amounting to 85 acres and measuring 1,200 by 300 yards.

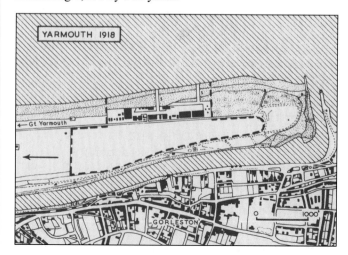

The Sopwith Admiralty Type 880 'Circuit of Britain' served at Yarmouth from August 1914 through to May 1915. *Via Stuart Leslie*

Yarmouth's role was to carry out coastal reconnaissance, anti-submarine operations and counter the Zeppelin, which not only approached the Norfolk coast on many occasions en route to its targets, but also often tried to make its escape the same way. As a result a large number of Zeppelins were attacked by Yarmouth-based units, including *LZ61* on 27 November 1916. Bound for Leeds, but deterred by accurate anti-aircraft fire, *LZ61* bombed several targets before it was intercepted by three RNAS pilots, Flt Lt E. Cadbury and Flt Sub-Lts G. W. R. Fane and E. L. Pulling, all flying BE.2Cs out of Yarmouth. The airship burst into flames after an exchange of fire and came down in the sea 8 miles east of Lowestoft. Further success came on 17 June 1917 when *LZ95*

Delivered to Yarmouth in late 1917 for 'special service', DH.4 A7848 later became part of 490 (Light Bomber) Flight, displaying the code 'II'. The aircraft was transferred to 'B' Flight, 1 (Comms) Squadron, at Kenley in June 1919.

was shot down off the coast near Leiston, and again on 1 July 1918 when Major E. Cadbury and Capt R. Leckie in a DH.4 brought down *LZ112* over the North Sea.

Yarmouth became a Marine Operations (Aeroplane and Seaplane) Station on 20 August 1918, and the large number of flights now based here were brought together under the banners of 212, 228 and 229 Squadrons. 212 Squadron, operating the DH.9 and DH.9A, was tasked with attacking any hostile aircraft and escort duties, while 228 Squadron, equipped with the F.2A, carried out long-range reconnaissance. 229 Squadron, equipped with a range of seaplanes, performed anti-submarine duties.

Yarmouth remained open until early 1920, and several of the seaplane station buildings lingered on until the 1990s. While no memorial is present at the seaplane station, the location of the RNAS HQ in Regent Street, Great Yarmouth, has a plaque on the outside recognising the efforts of South Denes and Hickling Broad during the anti-Zeppelin war. Another plaque is on the outside of Kimberley Terrace lodgings (now part of the Carlton Hotel), the residence of Major Cadbury (a member of the chocolate family dynasty), recognising his service at Yarmouth.

Yarmouth main units, 1918-19

War Flight RNAS Apr 1913; DB into RAF flights 1918

454(BS) Flt formed 25 May 1918;
absorbed into 229 Sqn, 20 Aug 1918 (Baby)

324(FB) Flt formed May 1918;
absorbed into 228 Sqn, 20 Aug 1918 (F.2A, H.12 and Baby)

325(FB) Flt formed May 1918;
absorbed into 228 Sqn, 20 Aug 1918 (F.2A, H.12 and Baby)

428(S) Flt formed May 1918;
DB Mar 1919 (Short 184 and Short 320)

429(S) Flt formed May 1918;
DB Mar 1919 (Short 184 and Short 320)

490(LB) Flt formed 25 May 1918;
absorbed into 212 Sqn, 20 Aug 1918 (DH.4 and DH.9A)

455(BS) Flt formed 15 Jun 1918;
absorbed into 229 Sqn, 20 Aug 1918 (Baby)

326(FB) Flt formed 15 Jul 1918;
absorbed into 228 Sqn, 20 Aug 1918 (F.2A, H.12 and Baby)

557(LB) Flt formed 26 Jun 1918;
absorbed into 212 Sqn, 20 Aug 1918 (DH.9A)

558(LB) Flt formed 26 Jun 1918;
absorbed into 212 Sqn, 20 Aug 1918 (DH.9A)

212 Sqn (ex-490, 557 and 558 Flts) 20 Aug 1918;
to Dover (Swingate Down), 7 Mar 1919 (DH.4, DH.9 and DH.9A)

228 Sqn (ex-324, 325 and 326 Flts) 20 Aug 1918;
to Killingholme, 5 Jun 1919 (Curtiss H.12 and F.2A)

229 Sqn (ex-428, 429, 454 and 455 Flts) 20 Aug 1918;
to Killingholme, 3 Mar 1919
(Short 184, 320, Fairey IIIB, IIIC and Baby)

273 Sqn cadre from Burgh, Jun 1919;
DB 5 Jul 1919

NORTHAMPTONSHIRE

Clipston (Market Harborough)

52°26'10"N/00°55'24"W, SP705823. 1.5 miles NE of Clipston, due S of Great Oxendon

THIS was the only ELG established in Northamptonshire during the war for the use of HD aircraft. Clipston was opened as an HD NLG2 in December 1916. From 30 June 1917 it was reclassified as a DLG until it was relinquished in late 1918.

Easton-on-the-Hill

52°36'33"N/00°30'18"W, TF013022. Off Cliffe Road from N and A47 from SW, within W boundary of RAF Wittering, 1 mile ESE of Collyweston

ESTABLISHED as a TDS from the start, construction began at Easton-on-the-Hill in the summer of 1917. On 15 September, with the site far from ready, 'A' Flight of 41 TS from Doncaster, 'B' Flight from 48 TS at Waddington, and 'C' Flight from 68 TS at Bramham Moor all arrived to provide the core of 5 TDS, formed here on the 24th. With construction of a permanent technical and domestic site progressing in the south-western corner of the aerodrome, seventeen Bessonneau hangars were erected for the TDS in the north-eastern corner along Cliffe Road.

RE.8 A4501 of 5 TDS at Easton-on-the-Hill would have provided many crews with a taste of operations before embarking to Northern France.

The aerodrome was large at 288 acres, and measured 1,100 by 1,100 yards. Once finished, it could boast seven 1918-pattern GS Sheds (170 by 100 feet) arranged in three coupled units, and a separate ARS Shed with a pair of aeroplane stores. 5 TDS's main role was to provide reconnaissance training, and at its peak seventy-two aircraft were on strength, the bulk of

The 'temporary' 5 TDS camp in the north-eastern corner of Easton-on-the-Hill, accessed from Cliffe Road and seen on 13 July 1918, remained in use until the aerodrome closed down. Note the standard accommodation tents at the bottom of the photograph.

them 504s and F.2Bs. Redesignated as 5 TS on 14 March 1919, then equipped with just the 504K, the unit was closed down in December. Returned to farmland in 1920, all trace of Easton-on-the-Hill was clinically removed. It was erased still further when the site became RAF Collyweston (initially known as Easton) in 1939, and when this airfield was swallowed up by RAF Wittering the site was covered by a nuclear weapons storage area and several V-bomber dispersals.

Easton-on-the-Hill main units, 1917-19

5 TDS formed 24 Sep 1917 ('A' Flt from Doncaster, 'B' Flt from Waddington and 'C' Flt from Bramham Moor (Tadcaster)); redesignated 5 TS, 14 Mar 1919
(DH.6, DH.9, BE.2, RE.8, 504, Camel and F.2B)

20th Aero Sqn, USAAS, detached from USA via Glasgow and Winchester, 7 Jan 1918;
to Delouze, 7 Aug 1918

127th Aero Sqn, USAAS, detached by 1918

20th Aero Sqn, USAAS, detached from Narborough, 1 May 1918;
to Delouze, 7 Aug 1918

138 Sqn nucleus flt formed (attached to 5 TDS), Sep 1918;
to Chingford, 30 Sep 1918

5 TS (ex-5 TDS) reformed 14 Mar 1919;
DB Dec 1919 (504)

Finedon

52°20'44"N/00°37'57"W, SP932728. 0.9 miles NE of Finedon off A510, 2.3 miles SE of Burton Latimer

FINEDON was an HD NLG2 allocated to 75(HD) Squadron, but was only active between January and 1 July 1917.

King's Cliffe (Peterborough)

52°34'13"N/00°29'21"W, TL025980. SE of RAF King's Cliffe memorial, S of Roman Road, 1.3 miles ENE of King's Cliffe village

ONLY used between December 1916 and July 1917 as an HD NLG2 for the use of 75(HD) Squadron, the same site was more exploited during the Second World War. RAF King's Cliffe (Station 367) became the home of 20th FG from 1943 to 1945 and remained open as an RAF station until 1959.

Litchborough

52°10'31"N/01°04'27"W, SP634533. SE of Tivy Farm, bisected by Knightley Way, 0.5 miles SSE of Litchborough, 4.5 miles NW of Towcester

THIS was another short-lived site that opened as an HD NLG2 in October 1916 and was closed down by March the following year. Only aircraft from 75(HD) Squadron are believed to have used the LG.

Moulton (Northampton)

52°17'07"N/00°50'49"W, SP787657. 0.3 miles SE of Moulton, 4.2 miles NE of Northampton town centre

AN HD NLG2 and DLG was open at Moulton for 75(HD) Squadron between December 1916 and 1918.

Stamford

52°37'00"N/00°27'08"W, TF046031. Current RAF Wittering, E end of station, W of Great North Road (A1), 2.4 miles SSE of Stamford

One of three aerodromes that would eventually be swallowed whole as RAF Wittering, Stamford first opened, close to the Great North Road, as an NLG for 'A' Flight of 38(HD) Squadron in October 1916. With excellent access, the site was soon viewed for a much larger purpose as the first of a number of new TDSs. The expansion work was carried out by P. & W. Anderson and included the construction of seven Aeroplane Sheds (180 by 100 feet). The aerodrome, now expanding to the west, took up 193 acres of land and measured 1,000 by 900 yards.

This excellent view of Stamford, nestling next to the Great North Road, shows the site at a time when it was expanding into a Training Depot Station. Just behind the aeroplane shed '38 HD STAMFORD' is marked out on the ground, and just to the north of the shed a large compass has also been painted or chalked on the ground.

The new unit, 1 TDS, was formed on 30 July 1917 after 4, 26 and 39 TS all donated a flight each to create it. Tasked with reconnaissance training, the TDS had a wide range of types on strength, but by 1918 these had been grouped down to 504s and F.2Bs.

In late 1918 Stamford also became a Flight Station for 'C' Flight of 90(HD) Squadron, equipped with eight 504K night fighters. Several USAAS units passed through Stamford in 1918, but with the disbandment of 1 TDS in March 1919 only 90(HD) Squadron remained until it departed for Buckminster. A Storage Depot moved in before the year was over, and by January 1920 Stamford was placed under Care & Maintenance.

The lack of activity was short-lived, because the aerodrome was brought back to life in 1924 as RAF Wittering, the home of the CFS. A complex and long history continued from that point, but since late 2010 the station is only shadow of its former self since the early retirement of the RAF's Harrier fleet.

Stamford/Wittering main units, 1916-18

38 Sqn 'A' Flt from Melton Mowbray, 1 Oct 1916;
to Buckminster, 31 May 1918 (BE.2C/E, BE.12 and FE.2B)

1 TDS 'A' Flt, 4 TS from Northolt, 30 Jul 1917;
DB 14 Mar 1919 (FK.3, DH.4, DH.6, DH.9, RE.8, BE.2D/E, FE.2B, F.2B, 504, Camel, JN.3 and JN.4)

1 TDS 'B' Flt, 26 TS from Turnhouse, 31 Jul 1917;
DB 14 Mar 1919

1 TDS 'C' Flt, 39 TS from Montrose, 31 Jul 1917;
DB 14 Mar 1919

1 TDS formed 31 Jul 1917;
DB 14 Mar 1919 (various aircraft)

11th Aero Sqn, USAAS, by 7 Jan 1918;
to Waddington, 24 Jun 1918

20th Aero Sqn, USAAS, by 7 Jan 1918;
to France, 7 Aug 1918

172nd Aero Sqn, USAAS, by 17 Jul 1918

120th Aero Sqn, USAAS, from New Romney, 10 Aug 1918;
to France, 27 Aug 1918

90 Sqn 'C' Flt formed Sep 1918;
to Buckminster May 1919 (504K(NF))

Welton

52°17'39"N/01°08'31"W, SP586665. N of Station Road, W of Crockwell Hill, NE of village, 2.3 miles NNE of Daventry

A TRAINING Squadron Station was recorded as being under construction on 1 April 1918, but appears not to be had been completed.

NORTHUMBERLAND

Acklington (Southfields)

55°18'00"N/01°38'22"W. Approximately 0.75 miles due S of Acklington village

ORIGINALLY the location of Southfields Farm, the landowner had 63 acres requisitioned for an NLG2 in 1916. By 31 October 1916 the small aerodrome, measuring 800 by 460 yards, was under RFC control, but was not ready for use until early 1917. The NLG was allocated to 36(HD) Squadron, whose main station was Newcastle with the BE.2E, FE.2B and FE.2D on strength. The LG was also the most southerly used by 77(HD) Squadron based at Edinburgh.

Southfields continued to be used until June 1919 when both HD units were disbanded, but flying would return in the late 1930s as the site would be at the centre of RAF Acklington.

Alnwick/Snipe House (Rennington)

55°22'21"N/01°44'55"W. Due N of Snipe House Farm, 2.3 miles W of Shillbottle

ALNWICK only saw brief service as an NLG2 for 36(HD) Squadron from October 1916. It is most likely that it was barely used, considering the autumn and winter period it was open. The site occupied 33 acres, measured 380 by 420 yards, and was closed down by March 1917.

Ashington

55°11'14"N/01°37'06"W, NZ243885. 2.3 miles WNW of Ashington centre, 1 mile NE of Pegswood

THIS extensively used HD Flight Station was opened north-west of Ashington in October 1916 for 36(HD) Squadron, which had just moved from Cramlington to Newcastle. The site occupied 105 acres, measured 730 by 700 yards, and was furnished with one Aeroplane Shed (56 by 140 feet) and at least one canvas hangar (60 by 90 feet), and also had the luxury of a 1912 R.A.F.-pattern canvas hangar for MT. Permanent staff during the period averaged 7 officers, 3 SNCOs, 2 JNCOs and 39 other ranks.

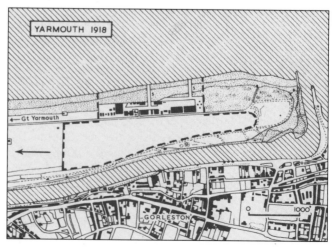

The first occupant was 'C' Flight of 36(HD) Squadron operating the BE.2C for aerial co-operation with coastal defence batteries. Redesignated as 'B' Flight on 12 August 1917, average aircraft strength by this time was four Pups, later complemented by four F.2Bs. 36(HD) Squadron continued to retain a presence here when the HQ moved to Hylton/Usworth in July 1918, the station then being reclassified as a Marine Operations (Aeroplane) Station.

On 28 June 1918 the DH.6s of 525(SD) Flight moved in from Prawle Point for anti-submarine patrol duties. To accommodate the small influx of extra personnel, several Armstrong huts and a small bomb stores were built, together with at least one extra Bessonneau. Under the charge of 254 Squadron, 525 Flight remained at Ashington until it was disbanded in June 1919. 36(HD) Squadron was disbanded at Hylton on 13 June 1919, and Ashington was closed down by the autumn.

Beacon Hill (Morpeth)

55°13'13N/01°46'15"W, NZ146918. N of Beaconhill Wood, 1.75 miles due S of Longhorsley

THIS short-lived NLG3 measured 500 by 300 yards and was for the use of 36(HD) Squadron between October 1916 and July 1917, until its duties were transferred to Longhorsley.

Benton

55°01'26"N/01°26'22"W, NZ270700. Due S of West Moor, N of Balliol Business Park

ONE of several LGs opened for 36(HD) Squadron, Benton was an NLG2, and opened in May 1917. Covered 42 acres and measuring 580 by 320 yards, Benton was relinquished on 29 May 1919.

Chathill

55°32'22"N/01°41'38"W, NU193273. 0.5 miles E of Chathill railway station, 1.2 miles NNW of Brunton airfield

THIS useful mooring-out station was opened on 22 July 1918 for non-rigid airships operating out of East Fortune. Located on Tileshed Plantation, Chathill was closed down in 1919.

Cramlington (I)

55°05'32"N/01°37'22"W, NZ240776. W of A1068, access road to Shotton Surface Mine passes through original site, 1.65 miles WNW of Cramlington

THE first RFC aerodrome to open in the North East of England, Cramlington was established as an HD Station from 1 December 1915 with an HD Flight equipped with the BE.2C. The flight formed the nucleus of 36(HD) Squadron, formed here on 1 February 1916, by which time Cramlington began to expand and from October was classified as an HD NLG2.

Occupying 155 acres and measuring 800 by 600 yards, three 1915-pattern Flight Sheds (210 by 65 feet) were erected on the eastern side of the aerodrome, while across the road, in the area now occupied by Bassington Industrial Estate, many technical and domestic building were built.

Despite the best efforts of 36(HD) Squadron, it could do little to stop a spate of airship raids on the North East during April 1916, which even resulted in a few bombs falling near the aerodrome. The squadron left Cramlington for Newcastle on 12 October 1916 having suffered several casualties in its efforts to deal with the Zeppelin threat with inadequate aircraft.

By early 1918 SD Flights were formed that would later be absorbed into 252 Squadron, equipped with the DH.6 for anti-submarine duties. Despite this role, Cramlington was not designated as a Marine Operations Station. The rare event of actually sighting an enemy submarine took place on 3 June 1918, when Capt F. W. Walker DSC spotted and attacked a U-boat 7 miles south-east of Creswell with no results observed.

The next stage of Cramlington's service was the formation of 52 TDS from 75 TS on 15 July 1918. A crowded aerodrome by this time, two Bessonneau hangars were erected together with a pair of 1918-pattern GS Sheds (170 by 100 feet), the latter being built on extra land requisitioned in the south-eastern corner of the aerodrome. Equipped with twenty-four Avro 504s and twenty-four DH.4s and/or DH.9s, Cramlington was a busy place right up to the Armistice, and 52 TDS continued in operation until disbanded in September 1919. An RAF presence remained until March 1920, and not long afterwards the site was taken over by Cramlington Aircraft Ltd, which operated several de Havilland Puss Moths and Gypsy Moths and two Simmonds Spartans. The Newcastle Aero Club arrived in 1925 and remained for ten years before moving to Woolsington.

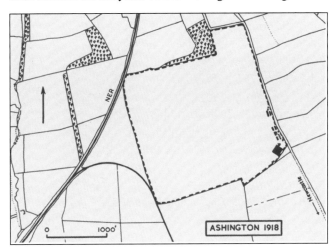

ASHINGTON 1918

One of only eight Armstrong Whitworth FK.10 quadruplanes built is seen at Cramlington while being trialled by 58 Squadron.

Cramlington (I) main units, 1915-19

HD Flt formed 1 Dec 1915;
redesignated 36(HD) Sqn, 1 Feb 1916 (BE.2C)

36 Sqn (ex-HD Flt) 1 Feb 1916;
to Newcastle, 12 Oct 1916 (BE.2C, BE.2E, BE.12 and Scout)

58 Sqn formed (nucleus from 36 Sqn) 8 Jun 1916;
to Dover (Swingate Down), 22 Dec 1916 (FE.2B)

76 Sqn formed (nucleus from 36 Sqn) 15 Sep 1916;
to Ripon, 10 Oct 1916 (BE.2C, BE.12 and DH.6)

63 Sqn from Stirling, 31 Oct 1916;
en route to ME, 23 Jun 1917 (DH.4, BE.12, BE.2E, 504 and FK.3)

47 TS formed (out of 58 Sqn) 2 Nov 1916;
to Waddington, 13 Nov 1916
(Shorthorn, RE.8, DH.9, DH.6, FK.3 and 504)

52 TS formed (out of 63 Sqn) 14 Jan 1917;
to Catterick, 18 Jan 1917 (BE.2C and DH.4)

61 TS formed 1 May 1917;
to South Carlton, 10 May 1917 (no aircraft)

69 TS from Catterick, 10 Oct 1917;
to Narborough, 9 Dec 1917 (DH.4 and DH.6)

75 TS from Waddington, 22 Dec 1917;
DB into 52 TDS, 15 Jul 1918
(DH.4, DH.6, DH.9, Elephant, RE.8 and BE.2E)

120 Sqn formed 1 Jan 1918;
to Bracebridge Heath, 3 Aug 1918 (various aircraft)

SD Flt: two SD Flts formed Mar 1918 for coastal patrol duty
over North East War Channels;
absorbed into 252 Sqn, 1 May 1918.

SD Flts formed Apr 1918;
redesignated 507 and 508 Flts, 24 May 1918 (DH.6)

507(SD) Flt, 252 Sqn (ex-SD Flt) 24 May 1918;
to Tynemouth, 8 Jun 1918 (DH.6)

508(SD) Flt, 252 Sqn (ex-SD Flt) 24 May 1918;
to Tynemouth, 8 Jun 1918 (DH.6)

509(SD) Flt, 252 Sqn formed 7 Jun 1918;
DB 25 Oct 1918 (DH.6)

52 TDS (ex-75 TS) formed 15 Jul 1918;
redesignated 52 TS, Sep 1919 (DH.6, DH.9, 504 and RE.8)

47th Aero Sqn, USAAS, by 17 Jul 1918

158th Aero Sqn, USAAS, by 17 Jul 1918

52 TS (ex-52 TDS) Sep 1919;
DB 2 Oct 1919 (504K)

Cramlington (Newcastle, aka Cramlington II)

55°05'35"N/01°36'03"W, NZ255777. Nelson village and South Nelson Industrial Park, N of Cramlington railway station, 1 mile NW of Cramlington centre

WORK began on this Class D Airship Station in early 1918 on an area of land on the opposite side of the railway line from the already established Cramlington aerodrome. The site occupied land from Cramlington railway station, nestling at the extreme southern boundary, with Crow Hill Lane as its eastern boundary, while the railway line was on its south-western boundary. The site occupied 238 acres and measured 870 by 680 yards. It was still under construction by the time the Armistice arrived, although a network of technical buildings had been erected to the west of Barry House. A single Airship Shed (300 by 100 by 70 feet) was also up, and by April 1919 the site was referred to in RAF listings as Newcastle Airship Station. Two flights of SS Twin airships were in residence by this time, and a variety of non-rigid patrol airships passed through Cramlington during the early 1920s.

The site was taken over by the Airship Development Company after the military departed. The company built an airship (the first private example in Britain), similar to an SS-Type, powered by a 75hp Rolls-Royce Hawk engine. Designated as the AD.1 and registered G-FAAX, the side of the airship could be hired for advertising and it was also used for aerial photography. Unfortunately it was wrecked in Belgium in 1930 and it appears that the company was wound up soon after. The giant airship shed remained as a local landmark until the late 1960s, when it was demolished as housing and industry took precedence.

The sole Armstrong Whitworth FK.12B, serialled 7838, pictured at Gosforth (Dukes Moor).

Currock Hill (Chopwell)

54°55'36"N/01°50'16"W, NZ104591. 0.3 miles SE of Currock Hill Farm, 1 mile NW of Chopwell

IN operation from April 1916 to March 1917, the HD NLG3 at Currock Hill served 36(HD) Squadron during that period. The LG was abandoned and replaced by Horsegate. Just half a mile to the north, aviation continues at Hedley-on-the-Hill, home of the Northumbria Gliding Club.

Gosforth (Newcastle/Duke's Moor)

54°59'45"N/01°37'32"W, NZ240668. Duke's Moor, N of Grandstand Road (A189), 0.9 miles SSW of Gosforth

AFTER receiving its first orders for new military aircraft in 1913, Armstrong Whitworth established a factory at the end of a narrow strip of land called Duke's Moor. Lined with trees and houses, this manufacturer's LG measured 600 by 150 yards. The factory itself was an old grandstand that had been used for the original Newcastle racecourse, dating back to the 1880s. On the outbreak of war orders increased rapidly, beginning with 250 BE.2Cs, forcing the factory to expand.

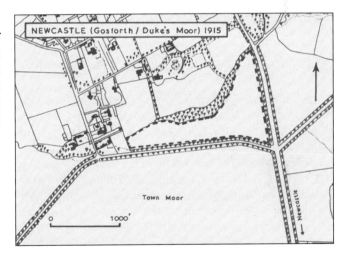

'C' Flight of 1 Sqn RNAS arrived with four TB.8s on 25 November 1914, which temporarily classified Gosforth as an RNAS HD Station. The unit was redesignated as the RNAS War Flight before moving out to Whitley Bay in March 1915.

While large sub-contract work continued to pour in, Armstrong Whitworth embarked on its own designs, the most successful of which was the FK.8 by Frederick Koolhoven. Gosforth remained in use until 1916, when it was declared too dangerous to use. Armstrong Whitworth established a new factory across the road at Town Moor, and Gosforth was closed down, to flying at least. Duke's Moor remains the same open strip of land, but the old grandstand and factory site at the western end are long gone.

Gosforth Park

55°01'51"N/01°36'50"W, NZ247707. High Gosforth Golf Club and Gosforth Park racecourse, 1.7 miles N of Gosforth town centre

ONE of many sites through which 2 Squadron staged on its journey from Farnborough to Montrose in February 1913, Gosforth Park was later used for airship moorings for the RNAS during 1917.

Holy Island

55°39'55"N/01°47'59"W, NU125413. In harbour, Holy Island (Isle of Lindisfarne)

LOCATED within The Harbour, overlooked by the 11th-century Benedictine Lindisfarne Priory, Holy Island was planned to open in May 1917 as a seaplane school to cut down the workload at Calshot, but this task was taken over by Lee-on-Solent instead. The site was then chosen to be the home of a flying-boat station in November 1917 rather than Seaton Carew II, but this plan also never came to fruition. The Harbour was used briefly in November and December 1918 as flying-boat moorings for the H.16s, F.2As and F.3s of 347 Flight out of Cattewater; part of 238 Squadron, the unit returned to Killingholme after only a few weeks.

Longhorsley

55°13'24"N/01°44'50"W, NZ161921. Due S of Longhorsley Common (Harelaw Common) off A697, 1.9 miles SSE of Longhorsley

A REPLACEMENT for Beacon Hill, Longhorsley was opened as an HD NLG2 and DLG3 for 36(HD) Squadron from January 1917. Occupying 58 acres and measuring 400 by 800 yards, the site remained open until June 1919.

Newcastle (Town Moor)

54°59'40"N/01°37'26"W, NX240666. Town Moor, S of Grandstand Road, W of Great North Road (B1318), N of A167, 1.5 miles N of Newcastle railway station

HAVING outgrown the Duke's Moor site to the immediate north, Armstrong Whitworth relocated its factory and flight-testing a few yards to the south, on the northern edge of the old racecourse at Town Moor. Opened in June 1916, the site was later shared with local aircraft manufacturer Angus Sanderson & Co Ltd, which built aircraft in St Thomas Street.

The 80-acre site, which measured 750 by 500 yards, was found to be suitable as an AAP and expansion work began in early 1917. In preparation for the new unit, an Aeronautical Inspection Department detachment was attached to Armstrong Whitworth, which was disbanded when 9 AAP opened on 8 August 1917. All buildings were lined along the southern edge of Grandstand Road, including one 1917-pattern timber GS Shed (170 by 80 feet), one 'French' shed (300 by 60 feet), and four Bessonneau hangars (80 by 60 feet).

The AAP accepted, erected and tested all of Armstrong Whitworth's aircraft, including its own FK.8s and F.2Bs, together with aircraft from Angus Sanderson, Blackburn and Pegler. The unit was redesignated 9 (Newcastle) AAP on 12 October 1917 and remained active at Town Moor until disbanded in July 1919. The RAF Aircraft Exhibition operated from here between 12 February and 1 April 1919 before moving to Leeds (Roundhay Park). Closed down by late 1919, the site was fully relinquished by early 1920 and remains open land today, without a trace of its First World War past.

New Haggerston (Berwick)

Site 1: 55°40'35"N/01°58'04"W, NU022425. 0.65 miles SW of New Haggerston Farm, N of Lickar Dean, 2.75 miles SW of Goswick
Site 2: 55°40'57"N/01°58'15"W, NU019432. Adjacent field due N, W of Barteyshill Plantation

THE first of two airfields to be named New Haggerston opened as an HD Flight Station for 77(HD) Squadron in October 1916. A few Bessonneau hangars were erected and 'B' Flight moved in from Edinburgh on the 16th. The flight moved to Whiteburn the following month and 'C' Flight took over until 10 August 1917, when it moved south to Penston. By this stage the field occupied 75 acres and measured 730 by 730 yards. Little activity took place for the remainder of 1917 until 77(HD) Squadron returned in January 1918, the site being classified as an HD NLG1, later downgraded to an NLG2.

In May 1918 New Haggerston was reclassified as a Marine Operations (Aeroplane) Station, and the heart of the airfield was moved a few hundred yards north to an adjacent field. On

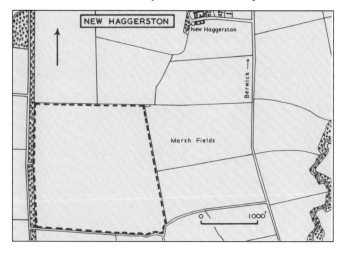

30 May 526(SD) Flight (possibly also known as 'B' Flight) was formed as part of 256 Squadron, flying six DH.6s. The flight's duties were to carry out anti-submarine patrols, which it performed until the Armistice. The aerodrome remained active until 526 Flight was disbanded on 30 June 1919. Relinquished in early 1920, the site today is exactly as it was during the First World War, right down to the narrow plantations along the roadside.

Old Heton (Cornhill)

55°40'01"N/02°09'39"W. 3.5 miles NE of Coldstream, due S of Castle Heaton

OPENED as an HD NLG3 in January 1917, this remote aerodrome was only used by 77(HD) Squadron until November 1917.

Ponteland (High West House)

55°02'50"N/01°46'19"W, NZ146725. S of Woodside Farm, 1.2 miles W of Ponteland village centre

THIS 56-acre site, which measured 600 by 600 yards, was opened in April 1916 as an HD NLG2. Only 36(HD) Squadron made occasional use of the site until it was relinquished on 13 August 1919.

Rennington (Stamford/Alnwick)

55°28'03"N/01°39'34"W, NU215915. 0.6 miles NNE of Rennington village, 4.3 miles NNE of Alnwick town centre

ORIGINALLY named Stamford/Alnwick when it was opened as an HD NLG2 in December 1916, this 72-acre site was renamed Rennington/Alnwick on 1 March 1917. The LG's classification was also changed on a number of occasions, beginning in July 1917 when it became an NLG3 and DLG3; it reverted to a DLG2 in September 1917, pending the arrival of 36(HD) Squadron.

It is not clear when 36(HD) Squadron gave up Rennington, but during June 1918 the newly formed 256 Squadron and its DH.6s briefly operated from here. During this period Rennington was designated as a Temporary Marine Operations (Aeroplane) Station. The LG, which measured 600 by 800 yards, was relinquished in June 1919.

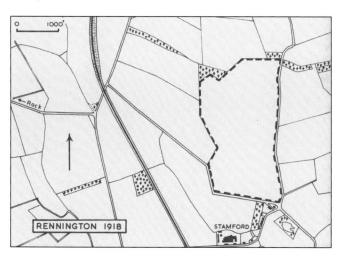

Seahouses (Elford)

55°34'48"N/01°42'04"W, NU189319. Due E of Reapers Hill, 0.6 miles N of Elford, 2 miles W of Seahouses

OPENED in October 1916 as one of 77(HD) Squadron's more southerly DLGs, Seahouses occupied 92 acres and measured 800 by 550 yards. By early 1918 the aerodrome's HD role had diminished, but rather than fade away the site was selected as a Marine Operations (Aeroplane) Station.

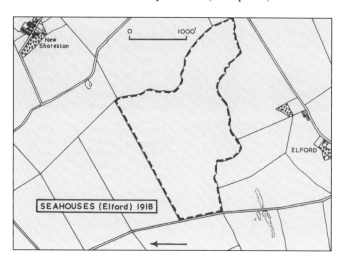

Several Bessonneau hangars were erected and a large number of the 130-plus personnel who served there were accommodated in Armstrong huts, although the majority of the twenty-seven officers were billeted in the local villages. The first units to serve in a marine capacity were 527 and 528(SD) Flights, which were formed at Seahouses with half a dozen DH.6s apiece on 6 June 1918. These two flights, together with 495, 525 and 526 Flights, made up 256 Squadron, which supported these units at New Haggerston, Rennington, Cairncross and Ashington. 256 Squadron briefly operated the Kangaroo from November 1918, but by January 1919 had been reduced to a cadre and moved south to Killingholme. The Bessonneau hangars were swiftly dismantled and the Armstrong huts sold off locally, leaving no trace of this once busy aerodrome's past.

South Shields

55°00'19"N/01°25'22"W, NZ370680. On Herd Sand, 0.6 miles NE of South Shields railway station

SOUTH SHIELDS opened as a seaplane station in April 1916 for an RNAS War Flight. Occupying 21 acres on the edge of Herd Sand, the station was furnished with five F-Type Seaplane Sheds (200 by 100 feet), and aircraft were launched into the calm waters of the River Tyne Entrance, protected by the North and South Piers. A seaplane depot opened in 1916, hence the size and number of Seaplane Sheds allocated to the station, and it remained as 2 (Northern) Marine Acceptance Depot until it was closed down in December 1919. The station itself was closed down in 1920.

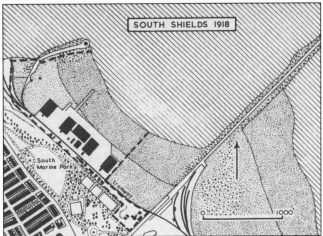

Two of the five F-Type Seaplane Sheds are visible in this north-easterly view from South Marine Park of South Shields Seaplane Station.

The location north of Stannington village is speculative, and to add to the mystery the former RAF Morpeth (Tranwell) was referred to as Stannington (55°07'43"N/01°44'08"W, NZ169816) during the King's Cup Air Races held in the late 1940s and early 1950s. Used as a turning point, Stannington was one of four points in the race, which set out from Newcastle Airport.

South Shields main units, 1916-19

War Flight RNAS formed Apr 1916;
DB 1918

Seaplane Depot RNAS/RAF formed 1916;
redesignated 2 (Northern) MAD, 22 Apr 1918

2 (Northern) MAD sub-station for Brough, 22 Apr 1918;
DB Dec 1919

18 Group Workshops formed 1918;
DB 1919

Storage Section formed 1919;
DB 1919

Tynemouth (Cullercoats)

55°01'45"N/01°26'04"W, NZ361706. In region of playing fields off A193 at Cullercoats, 1 mile NNW of Tynemouth

TYNEMOUTH was opened in December 1916 as an NLG2 for the use of Newcastle-based 36(HD) Squadron. Occupying 43 acres, the LG measured 680 by 320 yards, but its use as an HD LG was limited. By 1918 Tynemouth's status rose to that of a Marine Operations (Aeroplane) Station, and in response at least four Bessonneau hangars were erected. In May 252 Squadron was formed with DH.6s, comprising 495, 507, 508, 509 and 510 Flights. 507 and 508(SD) Flights, which had been formed at Cramlington, moved into Tynemouth on 8 June 1918 and, together with the main squadron, were disbanded on 30 June 1919.

Stannington

55°07'33"N/01°40'35"W, NZ210814. E of Dovecote Farm off Great North Road (A1), approximately 1.25 miles N of Stannington village

THIS small site served briefly as an LG for 52 TDS at Cramlington, between its formation in July 1918 and at least the end of the war. Whether the unit continued to use the LG afterwards as 52 TS is unknown; if it did, the site would have been active until October 1919.

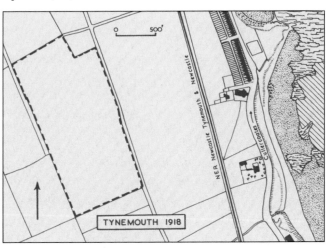

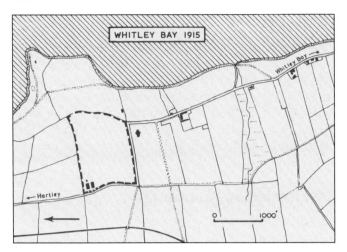

Whitley Bay

55°03'58"N/01°27'46"W, NZ346747. Due E of Whitley Bay Holiday Park off Blythe Road (A193), 1.7 miles NNW of Whitley Bay

ONE of several RNAS coastal LGs established during the early stages of the war, Whitley Bay was opened in late 1914 with hangarage provided by a pair of wooden aeroplane sheds. An RNAS HD War Flight was established here in January 1915 with four Bristol TB.8s, tasked with carrying out fleet reconnaissance, coastal patrols and defence from air raids. The flight was a detachment originating from Gosport, and before operating from Whitley Bay had served at Gosforth (Duke's Moor) as part of a forward operating base for 'C' Flight of 1 Squadron, RNAS. BE.2Cs became the main type used by the flight, although the Scout C, G.3 and 403C were also employed. Whitley Bay remained active until May 1916, when the War Flight was disbanded.

Woodbridge (Milfield)

55°35'28"N/02°04'43"W, NT952330. On opposite side of road from Borders Gliding Club at ex-RAF Milfield, 4 miles NW of Wooler

77(HD) Squadron first used the site in 1917 as an LG for its BE.2Es and RE.8s. Originally known as Woodbridge, the 90-acre field was the most southerly used by the squadron. The same area, next to the A697, south-east of Milfield, was surveyed again in late 1940, although this time the site would use 700 acres. The original intention was to build a typical A Class airfield for a bomber Operational Training Unit (OTU).

NORTH YORKSHIRE

Appleton Wiske

54°27'N/01°22'W, NZ402059. 1 mile NE of Appleton Wiske village

A 38-ACRE site opened in January 1917 for 76(HD) Squadron. Appleton Wiske then went through a not untypical period of reclassification, beginning on 31 March 1917 when it became an NLG3, then on 18 July it expanded its capability by becoming an NLG2 and DLG2. Remaining under 76(HD) Squadron's charge, Appleton Wiske was closed down on 13 August 1919.

Barlow (Selby)

53°45'26"N/00°59'59"W, SE658286. Due N of Drax power station, 3.7 miles SE of Selby

IN 1916 a large area of land east of the small village of Barlow was leased to Sir W. G. Armstrong Whitworth for the construction and testing of airships on a substantial site of 880 acres, measuring 3,760 by 2,260 yards. One Airship Shed (700 by 150 by 100 feet) was built, together with several technical buildings, and by 1917 the first airship to be built here, *R25*, was

By far the most successful British rigid airship of the war, the *R29*, built at Barlow, was the only example to actually see action. While operating from East Fortune, it sank the U-boat *UB-115* in September 1918.

launched. *R29* followed in 1918, and *R33*, although by then the war was over and the latter was scrapped without entering service. Armstrong Whitworth retained the site until 1920, and at one stage had planned to move all of its aircraft manufacturing to Barlow from Gosforth. Relinquished on 11 August 1921, the site remained in the hands of the Army until the 1970s, and the giant Airship Shed was not dismantled until 1982.

Binsoe (West Tanfield)

54°12′56″N/01°36′30″W. 0.5 miles NE of Binsoe, 1.5 miles NW of West Tanfield

OPENED in December 1916 for 76(HD) Squadron, Binsoe was designated as an HD NLG3 and remained so until its closure in June 1919. Sized at 35 acres, the LG measured 400 by 380 yards.

Carlton

53°42′10″N/01°02′13″W, SE636233. E of Coates and New Coates Farms off Hirst Road, 0.9 miles WSW of Carlton

A 39-ACRE NLG1 measuring 450 by 420 yards, Carlton was only open from March to November 1916 for 33(HD) Squadron, which was operating from Bramham Moor (Tadcaster) at the time.

Copmanthorpe

53°54′44″N/01°07′34″W, SE574466. Off Temple Lane (SW corner of old LG covered by housing), 0.65 miles E of Copmanthorpe, 3.3 miles SSW of York city centre

COPMANTHORPE was opened as a training squadron station, inaugurated by the formation of 57(HD) Squadron HQ and 'A' Flight on 8 June 1916, the nucleus of the unit being provided by 33(HD) Squadron. The main equipment was the BE.2C and the 504K, and four days after the HQ was formed the squadron was centralised with the arrival of 'B' and 'C' Flights of 57(HD) Squadron from Bramham Moor (Tadcaster).

The site occupied 98 acres and measured 700 by 600 yards, and facilities included a pair of HD-pattern Aeroplane Sheds (130 by 60 feet) and a single 1913-pattern Bessonneau, which was used for MT. Personnel strength averaged 2 officers, 7 SNCOs, 3 JNCOs and 39 other ranks.

On 20 August 1916 57(HD) Squadron moved out to Bramham Moor (Tadcaster), to be replaced by 'A' Flight of 76(HD) Squadron, which was detached from Ripon with various aircraft. Copmanthorpe was then classified as an HD Flight Station and remained so until 1919, when 76(HD) Squadron left for Bramham Moor (Tadcaster) on 5 May. The site was not fully relinquished until early 1920.

Dunkeswick

53°54′55″N/01°32′51″W, SE297467. 0.5 miles W of Dunkeswick, 1.6 miles NNW of Harewood House

OPENED for 33(HD) Squadron in April 1916 and classified as an HD NLG2, Dunkeswick was reclassified as an NLG3 and DLG2 on 18 July 1917. Covering 40 acres, the site measured 450 by 450 yards. 76(HD) Squadron also made use of the LG during the latter stages of the war. Dunkeswick was closed down in June 1919.

East Heslerton (Ganton)

54°10′55″N/00°34′06″W, SE934772. 0.5 miles NE of East Heslerton off A64, 3.5 miles WSW of Ganton

A GOOD-SIZED site at 82 acres and measuring 600 by 600 yards, East Heslerton was opened in April 1918 as an HD NLG2 for 76(HD) Squadron. The site was closed down in June 1919.

Filey (Filey Sands)

54°12′52″N/00°16′44″W, TA124813. 0.5 miles NE of Filey, 6.5 miles SE of Scarborough

THE sands at Filey, towards Filey Brigg, were first used for aviation by Robert Blackburn and B. C. Hucks from July 1910 through to early 1913. Work also commenced on a seaplane station for the RNAS from October 1912 through to early 1913, but appears not to have been occupied.

Gilling (New Malton)

54°09′25″N/01°04′08″W, SE608738. Due S of Ryebeck Farm, W of Black Gill Plantation, 1.9 miles SSW of Gilling East

ONE of the few options in the area for an NLG, Gilling was far from ideal, but still remained in military hands from December 1916 through to June 1919. Only occupying 28 acres, it measured 230 by 430 yards and was classified as an HD NLG3 and DLG2. Its first occupant was 33(HD) Squadron followed by 76(HD) Squadron. The site is still in its original form, but the surrounding plantations are much closer than they were nearly 100 years ago.

The ubiquitous bell-type military accommodation tent is demonstrated by a less than enthusiastic officer at Copmanthorpe.

Helperby (Brafferton)

54°07'40"N/01°21'17"W, SE422703. Between
Thornton Manor and Broomfield Farm, 1.2 miles W of
Helperby, 7 miles ENE of Ripon

HELPERBY began its association with aviation as a humble HD NLG1 for the use of the BE.2Cs of 'B' Flight, 33(HD) Squadron. By the late summer of 1916 Helperby had been singled out as an HD Flight Station, which warranted the construction of a pair of HD Aeroplane Sheds (90 by 60 feet) and several supporting wooden structures. Occupying 81 acres and measuring 1,000 by 800 yards, the first occupant of the new flight station was 'B' Flight of 76(HD) Squadron on 13 October 1916, three days after the HQ had moved from Cramlington to Ripon.

Equipped with various aircraft, 'B' Flight was joined by the main unit on 18 March 1919, by which time 76(HD) Squadron was equipped with the 504K(NF). Detachments to Copmanthorpe and Catterick were carried out before the squadron was reduced to a cadre and posted to Tadcaster. Helperby's relinquishment notice was issued on 6 November 1919, and confirmed on 22 January 1920.

Kettleness

54°31'38"N/00°42'36"W, NZ835155. E of Cliff House
Farm, 0.3 miles E of Kettleness, 4.6 miles NW of Whitby

THIS cliff-top site (328 feet amsl) was in use during 1915 and 1916 for RNAS aircraft transiting between Redcar and Scarborough.

Kirkleatham (Redcar)

54°35'23"N/01°05'15"W, NZ590220. Kirkleatham
Business Park off Kirkleatham Lane (A1042), 1.9 miles
SSW of Redcar Central railway station

ORIGINALLY called Redcar when it opened in May 1918, the name was changed to Kirkleatham on 27 August to avoid confusion with the Redcar racecourse site, which had been in operation since 1915. Kirkleatham served as a mooring-out station for non-rigid airships and a sub-station for Howden. The first airships to arrive were *SSZ54/55/62* followed by *SSZ31/33/56/64* from August through to October 1918. The station also served Cramlington from February to April 1919, but was closed down soon after.

Knavesmire (York Racecourse)

53°56'19"N/01°05'39"W, SE595495. York Racecourse,
1.65 miles SSW of York city centre

ROBERT Blackburn was the first person to introduce aviation to Knavesmire, when in 1912 he brought his Type E Monoplane here for flight-testing. The two-seater was tested by Norman Blackburn and R. W. Kenworthy, but refused to leave the ground. The site also witnessed the 'War of the Roses' Air Race, which took place between Lancashire's Avro 504 and Yorkshire's Blackburn Type I on 2 October 1913. One of the staging posts was at Bootham Stray (The Strays of York),

One of two Blackburn Type Es pictured at Knavesmire in 1912.

which was a large area that included Knavesmire. The race was ultimately won by the Yorkshire-built machine, flown by Harold Blackburn (no relation to the aircraft designer). Knavesmire was also used by the RFC when 2 Squadron staged through en route to Montrose on 21 March 1913, and again on 15 May 1914 when the squadron returned south.

The military returned to the racecourse in April 1916 when Knavesmire became an HD NLG for 'B' Flight, 33(HD) Squadron. The locals were not happy with the NLG being located so close to York, and their fears were realised on the night of 2 May 1916 when the glow of Knavemire's flare path drew the attention of a Zeppelin. At 1030hrs the airship dropped eighteen bombs, killing nine people and injuring forty. As a result, Knavesmire was closed down as an NLG forthwith, and 'B' Flight was moved to Copmanthorpe. The RFC remained, but the aerodrome was reclassified as a DLG only, still for the use of 33(HD) Squadron and briefly 57(HD) from Bramham Moor (Tadcaster). Various machines visited the aerodrome, until was relinquished in 1919.

The racecourse building also served as No 4 Area HQ, formed there on 1 April 1918. Redesignated as North-Eastern Area on 8 May, it controlled 16, 17 and 18 Groups, 19 (Equipment) Group and all HD units in 46 Wing until it was disbanded on 1 January 1919. 19 Group was also formed here on 1 April, but was disbanded by June.

Marske

54°35'41"N/01°01'58"W, NZ624225. Adjacent to
Ryehills Farm, N of Redcar Road, S of Coast Road
(A1085), 0.6 miles NW of Marske-by-the-Sea

It was Robert Blackburn who first brought aviation to Marske in 1910, when he tested one of his designs on the beach adjacent to the Coast Road. The land south of the road did not go unnoticed, and on 25 July 1910 a flying school was opened here.

The site was surveyed by the military during the early stages of the war but the land, measuring 1,000 by 900 yards, was not requisitioned until late 1917 for the use of a training school. On 1 November 1917 4 (Auxiliary) SoAG was formed here with a large array of aircraft types. The site was under construction from the day it opened almost to the day it closed, and at first hangarage was provided by seventeen Bessonneau hangars lined down the eastern side of Green Lane. These

would be eventually replaced by eight 1918-pattern GS Sheds (180 by 100 feet) with Esavian doors, together with a variety of supporting buildings, both north and south of Redcar Road, hemmed in by the railway line.

4 (A)SoAG was disbanded into 2 SoAF&G on 6 May 1918, which was redesignated to the much simplified 2 FS on 29 May, but still had no fewer than eighteen different types of aircraft on strength. The HQ for 2 FS was housed in Marske Hall, an impressive building north of the Redcar Road, between Dovedale and Hall Close. Following the Armistice life at 2 FS quickly calmed down and the school remained open until October 1919. The site was closed down in 1920.

Ryehill Farm and Marske Hall are still in place and a large portion of the flying field is extant. Housing now covers the main technical site area, but the road names have an aviation theme, ranging from de Havilland Drive to Beardmore Avenue.

Marske main units, 1917-20

4 (A)SoAG formed 1 Nov 1917;
DB into 2 SoAF&G, 6 May 1918 (various aircraft)

25th Aero Sqn, USAAS, from Ayr, 23 Apr 1918;
to France, 7 Aug 1918

2 SoAF&G formed 6 May 1918;
redesignated 2 FS, 29 May 1918 (Camel)

2 FS (ex-2 SoAF&G) 29 May 1918;
DB Oct 1919 (various aircraft)

17 (Training) Gp from 16 Windsor Crescent,
Newcastle-upon-Tyne, 1 Oct 1919;
absorbed into 20 Gp;
DB 18 Oct 1919

8th Wing HQ reformed 18 Oct 1919;
to Uxbridge, 1920

Above left: The first structures to be erected at Marske were seventeen Bessonneau hangars lined down the eastern side of Green Lane. *Via Stuart Leslie*

Left: The main technical and domestic site at Marske was in the south-eastern corner of the aerodrome, north of the railway line. Note in the upper centre of the frame the foundations of the eight GS Sheds and part-built sections. *Via Stuart Leslie*

The personnel of 2 Fighting School at Marske certainly enjoyed a high standard of comfort during their tour of duty. This room is described as the 'Men's Canteen', but it looks more like an officers' billiard room. *Via Stuart Leslie*

Menthorpe Gate (North Duffield)

53°48'40"N/00°56'50"W, SE697354. Near Longland Farm, 0.75 miles NNW of Menthorpe Gate, 1.7miles W of Breighton airfield

AN HD NLG3 and DLG2 for 76(HD) Squadron from January 1917, Menthorpe Gate occupied 67 acres and measured 730 by 700 yards. The site was officially relinquished on 29 May 1919.

Murton

53°58'01"N/01°00'10"W, SE642529. 0.5 miles E of Murton, 1 mile WNW of Dunnington

THIS small 23-acre LG, which measured 550 by 330 yards, was opened in October 1917 for 76(HD) Squadron until its closure in June 1919.

Redcar

54°36'12"N/01°04'21"W, NZ603237. W of Redcar racecourse, area now all housing in region called Westfield, 0.8 miles SSW of Redcar Central railway station

UNLIKE many other racecourse aerodromes across the country, Redcar did not take advantage of the three-quarters of a mile of flat grass already in place, but instead bordered up to its western boundary and extended to Low Farm.

Opened in July 1915 as an RNAS Flying School and RNAS HD Station, Redcar was a busy station from the outset. Facilities grew rapidly from three Bessonneau hangars to four Aeroplane Sheds (three at 180 by 60 feet and one at 200 by 100 feet). The site occupied 140 acres and measured 930 by 800 yards, virtually the same length as the neighbouring racecourse. The flying schools here taught pilots to become flying instructors and other specialist tasks, so the majority who passed through Redcar were already experienced flyers.

Redcar became a Temporary Marine Operations (Aeroplane) Station from September 1917 during a successful detachment by 7 Squadron RNAS, which brought its Handley Page O/100 bombers all the way from France. Gone by the following month,

A pair of RNAS Bristol Scout 'Cs' at Redcar in September 1915, serving as part of the resident RNAS HD War Flight.

A detachment from 7 Squadron, RNAS, under the command of Lt Cdr G. Sieveking, brought its Handley Page O/100 bombers to Redcar for a rest from operations in September/October 1917. The OC's aircraft, 3123, is pictured; it was called 'SPLIT PIN', which was Sieveking's nickname.

the aerodrome reverted to its original role until May 1918, when it once again became a Marine Operations Station with the formation 510(SD) Flight on 7 June, equipped with the DH.6 for anti-submarine duties. In November 1918 510(SD) Flight moved to West Ayton and Redcar took on its final role as a training squadron station from October with 63 TS as the main unit from Joyce Green. Together with the FIS, 63 TS was the last unit to serve here when it disbanded in September 1919. Today the entire site is covered in housing and is now known as Westfield.

Redcar main units, 1915-19

RNAS Preliminary Flying School formed 4 Jul 1915;
redesignated Instructors School, 1 Apr 1917

RNAS HD War Flight formed 4 Jul 1915;
DB Sep 1916

7 Sqn RNAS detached from Coudekerque, 5 Sep 1917;
to Manston, 2 Oct 1917 (O/100)

SoSF formed 1 Apr 1918 (
ex-Instructors School aka RNAS School Redcar);
redesignated 2 SoSF, 18 May 1918
(504A/J, DH6, Scout D, Pup and Camel)

2 SoSF (ex-SoSF) formed May 1918;
redesignated NE Area FIS, 1 Jul 1918
(504A/J/K, Scout D and Camel)

510 (SD) Flt formed 7 Jun 1918;
to West Ayton, Nov 1918 (DH.6)

NE Area FIS (ex-2 SoSF) 1 Jul 1918;
into NW Area FIS, 23 May 1919
(504, Camel, Pup, DH.9, SE.5A, Scout and Dolphin)

252 Sqn detached from Tynemouth, 1918;
to Tynemouth, 1918 (DH.6)

63 TS from Joyce Green, 5 Oct 1918;
DB Sep 1919 (504, DH.5, Pup and Camel)

NW Area FIS from Ayr, 15 Jan 1919;
DB 1919 (504 and F.2B)

Ripon (Racecourse)

54°07'15"N/01°29'50"W, SE330695. On current
racecourse, 1.5 miles SE of Ripon

RIPON went through several classifications during its existence between October 1916 and 1920. It was opened as an HD NLG3 for 76(HD) Squadron, which arrived from Cramlington on 10 October 1916 with BE.2Cs, BE.12s and DH.6s. On 18 July 1917 the LG was reclassified as an NLG2 and DLG2, and was upgraded to an HD Flight Station. Ripon occupied 81 acres of the racecourse and measured 720 by 500 yards.

189 NTS was formed on 20 December 1917 with a collection of machines including the BE.2C, Pup, RE.8 and Camel; the unit departed for Sutton's Farm on 1 April 1918. 76(HD) Squadron remained until 18 March 1919, when it moved to Helperby, and Ripon was closed down in early 1920.

Scalby Mills (Scarborough)

54°18'06"N/00°24'35"W, TA036906. On beach in
North Bay, 1.3 miles NNW of Scarborough

IN 1914 the newly formed Blackburn Aeroplane & Motor Company erected a hangar on the beach in North Bay for its Type L seaplane. Built for the *Daily Mail* Circuit of Britain air race, the war broke out before the event and the aircraft was requisitioned by the Admiralty. From August 1914 the Type L carried out reconnaissance patrols along the Yorkshire coast until early 1915, when it crashed into a cliff and was wrecked. No more flying ever took place from here, but Blackburn's shed remained until the late 1970s.

The Blackburn Type L seaplane was built for the *Daily Mail* Circuit of Britain air race in 1914.

Scarborough (Riggs Head Racecourse)

54°16'08"N/00°26'44"W, TA012870. NE of 'GCHQ' Wireless Station, 1.75 miles WSW of Scarborough railway station

THE old racecourse at Riggs Head attracted aircraft several years before the military was attracted to it. In May 1911 B. C. Hucks flew from Filey to Scarborough Racecourse, a distance of 8 miles, in a Blackburn Mercury. Henri Salmet also landed here during the 1912 Daily Mail air race before 2 Squadron briefly stopped here during its epic flight from Farnborough to Montrose in February 1913.

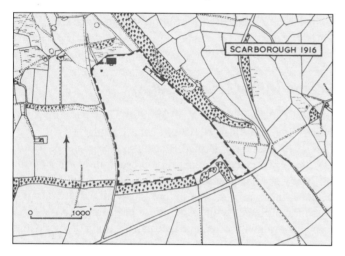

The racecourse was taken over on a more permanent basis in August 1915 when it became an HD Station for the RNAS. A single wooden hangar was erected and types operating here included the BE.2C and 504C on coastal patrol duties, until the site was closed down in February 1917.

Shipton

54°01'19"N/01°09'51"W, SE548587. Off Station Road between village and main railway line, 4 miles ESE of RAF Linton-on-Ouse

Shipton was brought into use for 76(HD) Squadron following the unit's move to Ripon in October 1916. Classified as an NLG2, it occupied just 36 acres, measured 550 by 400 yards, and was most likely relinquished by the Armistice.

The site became part of RAF Shipton during the Second World War and home to 60 MU, which was tasked with aircraft recovery and salvage across the region. Closed down in 1946, much of the later site remained until the 1980s.

South Otterington

54°16'51"N/01°24'13"W, SE389874. N of Leachfield Grange, 0.5 miles SW of Thornton-le-Moor, 1 mile ESE of South Otterington

THIS small LG, located closer to Thornton than South Otterington, was first used by the BE.2Cs of 76(HD) Squadron in late 1916. Occupying 28 acres and measuring 400 by 350 yards, the site was classified as a DLG2 and NLG2 and is believed to have remained open until the end.

Tadcaster (Bramham Moor)

53°51'56"N/01°19'22"W, SE445413. E of Spen Common Lane, S of Headley Hall, N of A64, 2.75 miles SW of Tadcaster

BUILT on Bramham Moor, by which name it was known until 1 April 1918, this aerodrome was opened as an HD NLG1 for 33(HD) Squadron, which arrived from Filton on 29 March 1916. Responsible for the defence of Leeds and Sheffield, 33(HD) Squadron was equipped for this daunting task with BE.2Cs and later BE.12s and Bristol Scouts, before relocating to Gainsborough in October 1916.

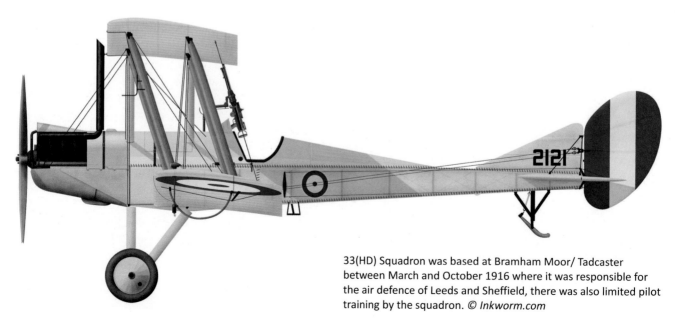

33(HD) Squadron was based at Bramham Moor/ Tadcaster between March and October 1916 where it was responsible for the air defence of Leeds and Sheffield, there was also limited pilot training by the squadron. © Inkworm.com

Units came and went until 46 and 68 TS arrived from Doncaster in December 1916 and Catterick in April 1917 respectively. These two units would be disbanded simultaneously on 15 July 1918 to form 38 TDS, tasked with carrying out single-seat fighter training. Now known as Tadcaster, the aerodrome occupied 198 acres and measured 1,450 by 800 yards. Six GS Sheds (170 by 80 feet) were constructed on the northern side of the aerodrome, together with enough accommodation for more than 800 personnel. The main equipment of the TDS was the 504 and SE.5A, and on average at least thirty-six examples of each were operating from here.

Three USAAS squadrons passed through in July 1918, and cadres of 76 and 94 Squadron were disbanded in June 1919. 38 TDS was redesignated 18 TS in August 1919, now equipped with the 504K, until it was disbanded in December 1919.

The site was quickly closed down and cleared by the early 1920s, although one GS Shed remains to this day, 250 yards south-east of Hedley Hall, visible from the A64 and Spen Common Lane. The latter road, a dual carriageway, encroaches onto the southern side of the flying field.

Tadcaster (Bramham Moor) main units, 1916-19

33 Sqn from Filton, 29 Mar 1916;
to Gainsborough, 3 Oct 1916 (BE.2C, BE.12 and Scout)

41 TS formed 5 Jul 1916;
to Doncaster, 16 Aug 1916 (Shorthorn, Longhorn and Caudron)

57 Sqn from Copmanthorpe, 20 Aug 1916;
to St André-aux-Bois, 16 Dec 1916 (BE.2C, 504K and FE.2D)

46 TS from Doncaster, 17 Dec 1916;
to Catterick, 23 Jul 1917 (various aircraft)

68 TS from Catterick, 14 Apr 1917;
DB into 38 TDS, 15 Jul 1918 (JN.4, Shorthorn, DH.6, FE.2D, DH.1, Camel and 504)

14 TS from Catterick, 23 Jul 1917;
DB into 38 TDS, 15 Jul 1918
(BE.2C, Shorthorn, Longhorn, 504 and Martinsyde)

74 TS from Castle Bromwich, 27 Jun 1918;
DB 15 Jul 1918 (Pup, 504 and Camel)

38 TDS formed (ex-14 and 68 TS) 15 Jul 1918;
redesignated 38 TS, Aug 1919 (SE.5, Pup and 504)

156th Aero Sqn, USAAS, by 17 Jul 1918

168th Aero Sqn, 'A' and 'B' Flt, USAAS, by 17 Jul 1918

176th Aero Sqn, 'D' Flt, USAAS, by 17 Jul 1918

94 Sqn cadre from Izel-le-Hameau, 3 Feb 1919;
DB 30 Jun 1919 (no aircraft)

76 Sqn cadre from Helperby, 30 May 1919;
DB 13 Jun 1919 (no aircraft)

38 TS (ex-38 TDS) Aug 1919;
DB Dec 1919 (504K)

24 (Northern) (Ops) Gp from Moor House, Leeds, 24 May 1919;
DB 13 Jun 1919.

16 (Training) Gp from Fossgate, York, 18 Oct 1919;
to Acomb Hall, York, late 1919

Thirsk (Racecourse)

54°13'54"N/01°21'29"W, SE420820. Current racecourse, off A61 (Station Road), 0.6 miles W of Thirsk town centre

NEEDING very little preparation to convert from a racecourse to an aerodrome, Thirsk was quickly brought into use for 76(HD) Squadron in 1916. With the HQ based at Ripon, the squadron would have operated a few BE.2Cs from here until no later than 1917.

Thornaby (Yarm)

54°32'19"N/01°17'49"W, NZ455161. In the region of Magister and Master Roads and Fullerton Way, 3.6 miles SW of Middlesbrough railway station

WHEN Matthew Young of Vale Farm was paid the princely sum of 100 gold sovereigns for the use of a field for an air show in the summer of 1912, the people of Thornaby-on-Tees were treated to an excellent display by the pioneering aviator Gustav Hamel. Apparently the very same field was used by the RFC from the beginning of the war as an ELG, and more officially from 1916, when it served 36(HD) Squadron. Classified as an NLG2, Thornaby occupied 34 acres and measured 360 by 450 yards.

The same site was the starting point for the much larger RAF Thornaby, which opened in 1930 and remained active until 1958. Both sites have long been swallowed up by housing, although remnants and thankfully memorials mark the location of this once busy RAF airfield.

West Ayton (Scarborough)

54°13'27"N/00°29'03"W, SE989820. Part of Wykeham Lakes, SW of Darrell's Low Farm, 5 miles SW of Scarborough

OFTEN confused with the HD LG on the old racecourse, West Ayton was a new site 3.5 miles to the south-west that saw brief service as a Marine Operations (Aeroplane) Station. The site occupied 100 acres and measured 840 by 650 yards with sparse facilities, including a few Bessonneau hangars. The 24 officers, 10 SNCOs and 60 other ranks that served here were all accommodated in local villages.

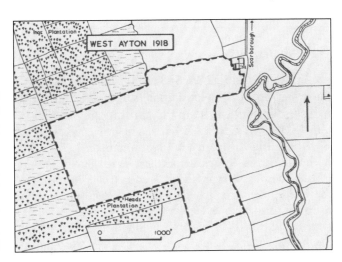

The first unit to arrive was 505(SD) Flight from Greenland Top with half a dozen DH.6s on 27 August 1918. Part of 251 Squadron, which retained its HQ at Hornsea, 505 Flight was joined by 510(SD) Flight from Redcar, also flying the DH.6, which was also referred to as 'C' Flight of 252 Squadron. West Ayton's units were tasked with carrying out anti-submarine and inshore reconnaissance patrols and general convoy duties off the Yorkshire coast.

Both flights were reduced to cadres by March 1919 and were moved to Killingholme to be disbanded on 30 June 1919. West Ayton was closed down not long after the two flights departed.

NOTTINGHAMSHIRE

East Retford

53°19'26"N/01°00'13"W, SK667812. Technical site now HM Prison Ranby off Straight Mile (A620), 2.1 miles E of Retford town centre

NESTLING between the Old London Road to the north-east and the Straight Mile to the south, East Retford was opened as an HD NLG1 for 33(HD) Squadron in April 1916. A large aerodrome, the site occupied 172 acres and measured 1,000 by 900 yards; it initially had Bessonneau hangars, until they were swept away in a gale in October 1917. By this time the site had been reclassified as an NLG3 in January 1917, only to be reinstated by September as an NLG1. In the meantime

several depot squadrons began to arrive and East Retford became a night training squadron station with an increasingly complex technical site that progressed north-westwards from the Old London Road and Straight Mile junction.

Four 1916-pattern GS Sheds (170 by 80 feet) replaced the Bessonneaus and, by the time construction was complete, buildings covered 30 acres of the aerodrome. All training operations centred on 187 and 186 NTS from April and May 1918 respectively, the former operating twenty-four 504s and DH.6s and the latter the same number of 504s, DH.6s, Elephants, Pups and Camels. Both units continued their trade until they were both disbanded on 1 May 1919. East Retford was closed down in March 1920, and today the area where the technical site once stood is completely covered by HMP Ranby, while the bulk of the extensive flying field has returned to agriculture.

East Retford main units, 1916-19

33(HD) Sqn 'A' Flt from Bramham Moor, Jun 1916 (BE.2C, BE.12 and Scout)	188 NTS formed 20 Dec 1917; to Throwley, 5 May 1918 (504, DH.6, Camel, Pup, BE.2E, FE.2B and FB.9)
99 Depot Sqn from Rochford, 12 Jun 1917; redesignated 199 Depot Sqn, 27 Jun 1917 (FE.2B, Farman, DH.1A and 1½ Strutter)	199 NTS (ex-199 Depot Sqn) 21 Dec 1917; to Harpswell, 26 Jun 1918 (various aircraft)
199 Depot Sqn (ex-99 Depot Sqn) 27 Jun 1917; redesignated 199 NTS, 21 Dec 1917	200 NTS (ex-200 Depot Sqn) 21 Dec 1917; to Harpswell, 10 Nov 1918 (various aircraft)
200 Depot Sqn formed Jul 1917; redesignated 200 NTS, 21 Dec 1917 (FE.2B, 504, Farman and DH.1)	187 NTS formed 1 Apr 1918; DB 1 May 1919 (504, DH.6, Pup, Camel, Elephant and BE.2C/E)
192 Depot Sqn from Gainsborough, 24 Sep 1917; to Narborough, 10 Oct 1917 (FE.2B/D and BE.2C/E)	186 NTS from Throwley, May 2918; DB 1 May 1919 (504 and DH.6)

Gainsborough

53°23'23"N/00°46'52"W, SK811888. On W bank of River Trent, S of The Flood Road (A631), 0.5 miles NW of Gainsborough Lea Road railway station

ALTHOUGH the town of Gainsborough, on the edge of the River Trent, is located in Lincolnshire, the LG to which it lends its name is located across the river in Nottinghamshire, on land known as 'Laynes Field'. It opened on 3 October 1916 for 33(HD) Squadron, which was engaged in anti-Zeppelin patrols. The squadron's HQ was established in the town at a large house called 'The Lawns' in Summerhill Road, North Sandfields, and it remained until 12 June 1918, when the role

of squadron was reduced to training and it moved to Kirton-in-Lindsey. In the meantime 192 Depot Squadron was formed on 5 September 1917, the unit's HQ also making use of 'The Lawns', before it moved out to East Retford on the 24th.

Occupying an area of 30 acres, Gainsborough was classified as an NLG2, later redesignated as an NLG3, and until 1918 had virtually no facilities that would have made it stand out as an aerodrome. It was not until late 1917 that a single shed was built by the Gainsborough engineering firm of Marshall & Co Ltd, which had won a contract to build 200 F.2B Fighters. It is presumed that 'Laynes Field' was used for flight-testing and subsequent delivery of the aircraft, which would have made Marshall the most active user of the site.

'The Lawns' also became the home of 48 Wing (ex-North Midland HD Wing), formed on 1 February 1918. The Wing controlled the operations of 33(HD) Squadron and 188, 189, 199 and 200 Depot Squadrons until it was disbanded on 18 April 1919. 'The Lawns' was de-requisitioned and handed back to its original owners, but has since been demolished and replaced by a more modern house with the original name.

Hucknall

53°01'06"N/01°13'16"W, SK526470. SE of Watnall Road (B6009), NE of Woodhall Farm, current Rolls-Royce plc (Hucknall), 1.3 miles SW of Hucknall

IT was in 1916 that a replacement site for Papplewick Moor was surveyed south-east of the Nottinghamshire town of Hucknall, and 135 acres of land belonging to the Duke of Portland was purchased. Blackpool-based builder Sir Lindsay Parkinson Ltd was commissioned to build a new TDS at a cost £700,000.

Completed by early 1918, the site featured the usual mass of buildings, with a domestic site on the north-west side of Watnall Road, and the flying site, which measured 850 by 800 yards, on the south-eastern side. The technical area included seven 1918-pattern GS Sheds (170 by 100 feet), three of them coupled and one on its own as an ARS.

Hucknall was quickly brought to life when 130 Squadron arrived from Wyton, and 135 Squadron and 15 TDS were formed here on 1 April 1918. The TDS was tasked with training aircrew to fly and fight in day bombers, and the main types on strength were the DH.6, DH.9 and 504. The TDS was redesignated 15 TS in March 1919 and disbanded in November. Only a cadre of 205 Squadron remained until January 1920, and a few weeks later the aerodrome was closed down.

The whole site was sold off but, rather than being completely dismantled, several of the hangars were occupied while the land was sold to local farmer George Elkington. However, the military had a change of heart and bought the land back from the farmer, and Hucknall became the home of the Nottingham Aero Club. The future RAF Hucknall was refurbished and was quickly re-established as a working airfield, which saw the significant arrival of Rolls-Royce in 1934, which took over two of the GS Sheds. The rest is history, as the bulk of the original site remains one of the domains of Rolls-Royce. All seven GS hangars survive, and many First World War-era buildings not only remain but are maintained in excellent condition by the many businesses that occupy them.

Hucknall main units, 1918-20

130 Sqn from Wyton, 1 Apr 1918;
DB 4 Jul 1918 (various aircraft)

135 Sqn formed 1 Apr 1918;
DB 4 Jul 1918 (various aircraft)

15 TDS formed 1 Apr 1918;
redesignated 15 TS, 14 Mar 1919 (DH.6, DH.9, 504, Pup and RE.8)

117 Sqn from Waddington, 3 Apr 1918;
to Norwich, 15 Jul 1918 (various aircraft)

23rd Aero Sqn, USAAS, detached from Thetford, 18 Aug 1918;
to Codford, 5 Nov 1918

218 Sqn cadre from Vert Galand, 7 Feb 1919;
DB 24 Jun 1919 (no aircraft)

15 TS reformed (ex-15 TDS) 14 Mar 1919;
DB 4 Nov 1919 (504K, DH.9 and F.2B)

205 Sqn cadre from La Louveterie, 18 Mar 1919;
DB 22 Jan 1920 (no aircraft)

DH.9 F1255 of 15 TDS stands in front of one of Hucknall's GS Sheds in late 1918. The aircraft was later presented to Canada as part of the nucleus that would become the RCAF.

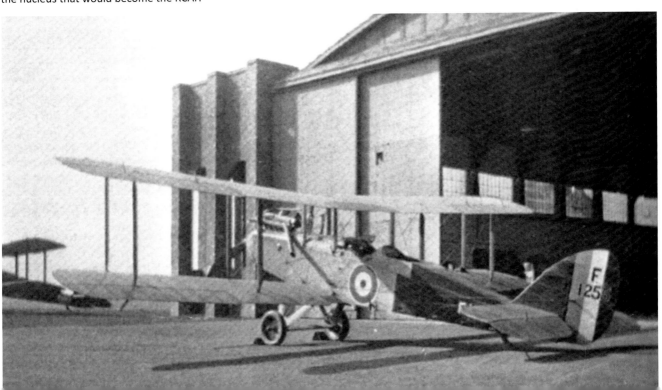

Hucknall in the 1960s was much as it was during the First World War, and even today, under Rolls-Royce ownership, the new buildings rub shoulders with the old without difficulty.

Papplewick Moor (Nottingham)

53°03'05"N/01°10'37"W, SK550510. E of Papplewick, 1.2 miles NE of Hucknall railway station

FOREVER in the shadow of its larger neighbour Hucknall, Papplewick Moor was declared open in April 1916, initially for 38(HD) Squadron and an HD detachment of 8th Wing. 54(HD) Squadron was also intended to use the LG in June 1916, but this plan was shelved, and 38(HD) Squadron, operating the BE.12, BE.2E and FE.2B, remained until May 1917. Prior to this, 'N' Flight was formed for service in Nigeria with a pair of Voisin LAS aircraft on 3 March 1917, only to be disbanded sixteen days later.

Papplewick was brought back into use in April 1918 as an RLG for 15 TDS at Hucknall until at least 1919, by which time the LG had been relinquished. Papplewick was used as an RLG again during the Second World War between 1941 and November 1945, and remains unaltered to this day.

Plungar

52°54'09"N/00°52'14"W, SK761345. 0.5 miles NW of Plungar village (Leicestershire), 1.5 miles NE of Langar airfield

38(HD) Squadron at Melton Mowbray and later Buckminster was the sole user of this 76-acre HD NLG1 from October 1916 to June 1919. Measuring 700 by 500 yards, Plungar was relinquished on 13 August 1919.

Radcliffe-on-Trent (Shelford)

52°58'40"N/01°01'04"W, SK660427. S of River Trent on land known as The Hams, 0.4 miles NW of Shelford, 1.4 miles W of ex-RAF Newton

AN HD NLG2 was located here between April and November 1916 for 38(HD) Squadron.

Ruddington

52°58'40"N/01°01'04"W, SK584320. E of Loughborough Road (A60), N of Mill lane, 1.2 miles SE of Ruddington

OPENED in October 1916 in place of Tollerton, Ruddington was an HD NLG2 used by 38(HD) Squadron. The acreage and size are unknown, but it is presumed to have been around 50 acres. The site, which remains open land, was abandoned by November 1917.

Thurgarton

53°02'28"N/00°59'25"W, SK678498. Between Far Barn and Foxhole Wood, 1.1 miles WNW of Thurgarton, 2 miles NE of Epperstone

CLASSIFIED as an NLG2, Thurgarton is credited with being used by 90(HD) Squadron during 1918, but only during the closing stages of the war. The aerodrome occupied 51 acres and measured 480 by 520 yards, and today is adjacent to a microlight strip.

Tollerton

52°55'09"N/01°04'45"W, SK617361. Current Nottingham City Airport, 3.9 miles SE of Nottingham city centre

THERE is believed to have been an LG at Tollerton, in the same position as the current airport, presumably for the use of HD squadrons.

Wigsley

52°12'N/01°43'W, SE06?35?. SW of Wigsley village

A 35-ACRE NLG2, measuring 500 by 400 yards, was established near Wigsley in October 1916 for 33(HD) Squadron. By November 1918 the site was closed down, but during the Second World War the more substantial RAF Wigsley was, presumably, built on the same site.

OXFORDSHIRE

Bicester

51°55'08"N/01°08'20"W, SP593248. Hangars and LG on current airfield site E of A4421, and domestic site S of Skimmingdish Lane, 1.2 miles NNE of Bicester railway station

THE first airfield to be located at Bicester was opened as a TSS and TDS in August 1918, and was typically furnished with seven 1917-pattern GS Sheds (170 by 100 feet).

Occupying 180 acres and measuring 1,150 by 1,000 yards, Bicester's first resident was 118 Squadron from Netheravon.

44 TS, formed from 35 and 71 TS, was the main unit from October 1918, until it was disbanded in December 1919. Many units were planned to reform at Bicester during 1918, but none came to fruition and the airfield was closed down in March 1920. However, by 1925 a more substantial Bicester emerged on the same site, destined to remain a busy airfield until its closure on 31 March 1976. The RAF did not actually leave Bicester until 2004, when the familiar site of the RAF Gliding & Soaring Association move to Halton. Sold off by the MoD in March 2013, the future of Bicester's architecturally important buildings seems secure.

Bicester main units, 1913-19

3 Sqn 'C' Flt from Netheravon, Sep 1913;
to Netheravon, Sep 1913 (BE.3, BE.4, F.20 and Type E)

118 Sqn from Netheravon, 7 Aug 1918;
DB 7 Sep 1918 (various aircraft)

44 TDS from Port Meadow, 1 Oct 1918;
redesignated 44 TS, Aug 1919 (504, F.2B and Pup)

2 Sqn (cadre) from Genech, 2 Feb 1919;
to Weston-on-the-Green, Sep 1919 (no aircraft)

44 TS (ex-44 TDS) Aug 1919;
DB Dec 1919 (504K)

Port Meadow

51°46'48"N/01°17'36"W, SP488093. Wolvercote Common, off Godstow Road, 2.4 miles NW of Oxford city centre

USING the full extent of Wolvercote Common, Port Meadow occupied 260 acres and measured 2,300 by 550 yards, making it one of the largest aerodromes in the country. Despite being susceptible to flooding, the site was used by several RE and RFC units before the First World War. Regardless of its size, and the fact that it opened as a training squadron station, the LG only had one 1915-pattern Flight Shed (140 by 65 feet) and seven Bessonneau hangars.

Only a few R.A.F. BE.2Es served with 35 TS and/or 71 TS at Port Meadow during 1917 and early 1918.

R.A.F. BE.2C 4377 of 17 TS at Port Meadow in 1917, with the aerodrome's single Flight Shed in the background.

Port Meadow main units, 1916-18

40 TS from Northolt, 21 Aug 1916;
to Croydon, 1 Jun 1917 (Scout D and 504)

17 TS from Croydon, 1 Jun 1917;
to Yatesbury, 8 Oct 1917 (504, BE.2C, RE.8 and BE.12)

1 TS from Narborough, 10 Oct 1917;
to Beaulieu, 15 Aug 1918 (Camel, Dolphin, 504 and Pup)

35 TS from Northolt, 16 Dec 1917;
DB into 44 TDS, 15 Aug 1918 (BE.2E, 504, F.2B and RE.7)

71 TS from Netheravon, 1 Apr 1918;
DB into 44 TDS, 15 Aug 1918 (BE.2E and Camel)

21st Wg Wireless Telephony Flt formed 1918;
redesignated No 2 School of Wireless Telephony (F.2B and BE.2)

186th Aero Sqn, 'A' Flt, USAAS, by 17 Jul 1918

44 TDS formed (ex-35 and 71 TS) 15 Aug 1918;
to Bicester, 1 Oct 1918 (504, F.2B and Pup)

2 SoWT formed (ex-Wireless Flt) by 24 Sep 1918;
DB Jun 1919 (F.2B and BE.2E)

93 Sqn reformed 14 Oct 1918;
DB 21 Nov 1918 (Dolphin)

The site was opened in April 1916, but it was not until 21 August that 40 TS arrived from Northolt, giving an early indication of Port Meadow's training role. 1 and 17 TS also passed through before the two units that would form a TDS arrived in October 1917 and April 1918 in the shape of 35 and 71 TS from Northolt and Netheravon respectively. The two squadrons formed 44 TDS on 15 August, but this much larger unit only remained at Port Meadow until 1 October, when it was moved to Bicester. This left 93 Squadron with Dolphins, which was disbanded on 21 November, having only been active for five weeks, and No 2 School of Wireless Telephony. It was the latter unit that closed the door on Port Meadow in June 1919.

Having the River Thames as its western boundary made Port Meadow susceptible to flooding, which resulting in the site being closed down promptly in mid-1919.

A line of 81 Squadron (aka 1 Squadron Canadian Air Force) Sopwith Dolphin fighters at Upper Heyford in late 1918.

Upper Heyford

51°56'13"N/01°15'09"W, SP515268. Ex-RAF Upper Heyford, 1 mile NE of Upper Heyford, 5 miles NW of Bicester

TO the majority of aviation enthusiasts the name of Upper Heyford conjures a vision of swept-wing F-111s, which thundered across Oxfordshire for almost a quarter of a century. On the very same site, which is still a complex mixture of runways, taxiways, dispersals and hardened shelters, sprang up the original LG, which was surveyed and opened in 1916.

Not a great deal happened here until late 1917, when Upper Heyford was selected as a TDS. Construction was very protracted, and by the time 157 Squadron was formed here in July 1918, and 158 Squadron in September, the TDS was still not ready. The site now occupied 257 acres and measured 1,200 by 950 yards, with six GS Sheds (170 by 100 feet) and one ARS Shed. The TDS was not completed by the time of the Armistice and Upper Heyford was only ever classified as a mobilisation station for three units, the third being 123 Squadron (2 Sqn CAF), which reformed here on 10 November 1918.

Upper Heyford's undistinguished First World War period came to an on 5 February 1920, when 2 Squadron CAF, equipped with the DH.9A, was disbanded and the aerodrome was closed down.

Reopened as a bomber station in 1927, Upper Heyford remained in RAF hands until 1950, when it was handed over to the USAF and later the USAFE until 1994. The substantial US expansion of the site has obliterated all trace of the original aerodrome, several times over!

Upper Heyford main units, 1918-20

157 Sqn formed (nucleus from CFS, 3, 43 and 56 TDSs) 14 Jul 1918;
DB 1 Feb 1919 (various aircraft)

158 Sqn formed (nucleus from CFS, 42, 50 and 53 TDSs) 4 Sep 1918;
DB 20 Nov 1918 (for Salamander)

123 Sqn (aka 2 Sqn CAF) reformed 10 Nov 1918;
to Shoreham, 31 Mar 1919 (DH.9A)

81 Sqn (aka 1 Sqn CAF) Wyton, 25 Nov 1918;
to <?>, 1 May 1919 (Dolphin)

2 Sqn CAF formed 28 Nov 1918;
DB 5 Feb 1920 (DH.9A)

Weston-on-the-Green

51°52'42"N/01°13'12"W, SP535205. Current RAF Weston-on-the-Green, off Northampton Road (B430), 3.3 miles SW of Bicester

REQUISITIONED in 1916, it was not until the following year that Weston-on-the-Green was selected as a TDS. Work appears not to have begun until early 1918 on a site that occupied 176 acres and measured 1,000 by 850 yards. Buildings were positioned on either side of Northampton Road – domestic on the western side and the technical area, with the flying field beyond, on the eastern side. Six GS Sheds of 180 by 100 feet and a seventh of 180 by 100 feet as an ARS Shed, complete with two aeroplane stores, were built.

On 17 July 1918 61 TS arrived from Cramlington and 70 TS from Beaulieu, neither with aircraft, to disband the same day to create 28 TDS, equipped with the Camel, Salamander and 504. Tasked with carrying out single-seat fighter training, the unit had up to seventy-two aircraft on strength, and could cater for 120 officer pupils and 60 NC pupils. 28 TDS was disbanded in March 1919, followed by only two squadron cadres, the last being 2 Squadron, which disbanded here on 20 January 1920.

Weston-on-the-Green was dormant from 1921, but appears to have remained in military hands, later serving as a satellite for Brize Norton and fully reactivated during the Second World War. Today, RAF Weston-on-the-Green is an increasingly rare survivor, serving as a drop zone for No 1 Parachute Training School at Brize Norton. The aerodrome is also the home of the very active Oxford Gliding Club.

Weston-on-the-Green main units, 1918-19

61 TS from Cramlington, 27 Jul 1918;
DB into 28 TDS, 27 Jul 1918 (no aircraft)

70 TS from Beaulieu, 27 Jul 1918;
DB into 28 TDS, 27 Jul 1918 (no aircraft)

28 TDS (ex-61 and 70 TS) 27 Jul 1918;
DB Mar 1919 (Camel, Salamander and 504)

2 Sqn cadre from Bicester, Sep 1919;
DB 20 Jan 1920 (no aircraft)

18 Sqn cadre from Merheim, 2 Sep 1919;
DB 31 Dec 1919 (DH.9)

Witney

51°47'24"N/01°31'15"W, SP332103. E and W of Downs Road, S of Burford Road (B4047), under Windrush Industrial Park, 1.5 miles E of Witney town centre

CONSTRUCTED as a training station from the outset, Witney came alive on 30 March 1918 when 24 TS brought its collection of aircraft from Netheravon. The aerodrome was a good size at 215 acres and measuring 1,100 by 900 yards, and had extensive facilities that included six Aeroplane Sheds (180 by 100 feet) and one ARS Shed (also 180 by 100 feet), and at least seven Bessonneau hangars. The arrival of 8 TS from Netheravon on 1 April 1918 with an even larger collection of aircraft made Witney a very busy place. Both TSs were disbanded into 33 TDS on 15 August 1918; by then the main types being operated were the 504, F.2B and the RE.8, with on average seventy-two aircraft on station. Redesignated as 33 TS on 6 September 1919, the unit was disbanded in October, and within weeks Witney fell silent and was closed down by the following year.

Civil flying took place during the 1930s, and at the beginning of the Second World War 2 SFTS used the field as an RLG. By 1940 de Havilland opened a CRO here, and by 1942 the first of 150 Dominies were built by Brush Electrical. The factory was closed down in 1946, and since then the site has slowly succumbed to industry. Many buildings from the two World Wars stand side by side with their modern counterparts.

Witney main units, 1918-19

24 TS from Netheravon, 30 Mar 1918;
absorbed into 24 TDS (Collinstown), 15 Aug 1918 (Shorthorn, Longhorn, F.2B, DH.6, FK.8, 504, Farman F.20 and BE.2E)

8 TS from Netheravon, 1 Apr 1918;
absorbed into 33 TDS, 15 Aug 1918 (Shorthorn, Longhorn, FK.3, JN.3, BE.2C/E, BE.8A, BE.12, 504, Farman F.20, F.2B, Camel, RE.5, RE.8, DH.6, Pup, FB.5, Voisin LA, DH.1 and Martinsyde)

7 TS from Netheravon, 30 Apr 1918;
absorbed into 33 TDS, 15 Aug 1918 (Shorthorn, Longhorn, FK.3, JN.3, BE.2C/E, BE.8A, BE.12, 504, Martinsyde, F.2B, FE.2B, Camel, RE.5. RE.8 and DH.6)

33 TDS (ex-7 and 8 TS) 15 Aug 1918;
redesignated 33 TS, 6 Sep 1919 (504, F.2B and RE.8)

33 TS 6 Sep 1919;
DB Oct 1919 (504K)

PEMBROKESHIRE

Fishguard

52°00'34"N/04°59'11"W, SM952393. Next to Fishguard railway station near ferry terminal, 1.25 miles NNW of Fishguard

SHELTERED by Fishguard Harbour's North Breakwater, this site occupied an area totalling only 2 acres, because its technical area was perched along the quayside. Regardless, there was still sufficient room for four Seaplane Sheds (one of 93 by 60 feet and three of 60 by 38 feet) and a single Bessonneau. Opened as a seaplane station for marine operations for the RNAS on 11 April 1917, the first occupant was the War Flight, formed with Short 184s. This unit was redesignated and divided into two flights, 426 and 427(S), on 20 May 1918, still equipped with the 184. These two flights formed the core of 245 Squadron, which was formed in August 1918 and remained at Fishguard until disbanded on 10 May 1919.

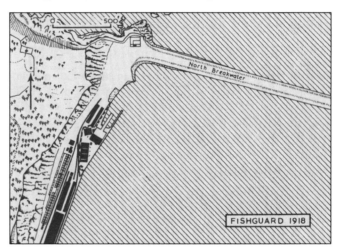

FISHGUARD 1918

Fishguard was redesignated as a Storage Station in 1919, but this was to be short-lived because the site was placed under Care & Maintenance on 20 May and closed down not long afterwards.

Milford Haven

51°42'28"N/05°01'11"W, SM914053. E of Castle Pill Swing Bridge, 1 mile ESE of Milford Haven railway station

ONLY occupying 6 acres, this site was opened as Kite Balloon Station Milford Haven in 1917. The station operated two balloons, which were housed in two canvas Balloon Hangars (100 by 36 feet). Redesignated as No 9 Balloon Base on 15 April 1918, this small unit was disbanded on 30 December 1918, and Milford Haven was closed early in 1919.

Pembroke

51°41′26″N/04°49′06″W, SN053027. Ex-RAF Carew Cheriton, 0.3 miles S of Sageston, 4.1 miles NE of Pembroke

ONE of only a few aerodromes in Britain that operated both airships and aeroplanes from the same location, Pembroke was a substantial site. Opened in January 1916 as a Class C Airship Station for non-rigid airships, it occupied 272 acres and measured 1,700 by 1,100 yards. Complete with its own sub-station at Wexford, Pembroke had one Airship Shed (302 by 50 by 70 feet) and one Portable Airship Shed (301 by 46 by 52 feet). At least fifteen airships were stationed at Pembroke up to early 1919.

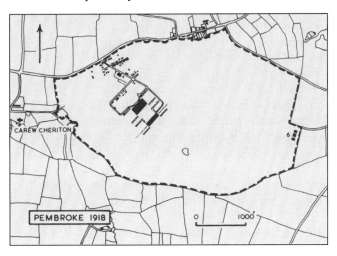

From May 1918 Pembroke also became a Marine Operations (Aeroplane) Station, although this part of the aerodrome was located on the extreme eastern boundary, well away from the airship sheds, and was furnished with three Bessonneau hangars. Several tents and Armstrong huts sprang up on this side, although the majority of the 130 personnel were billeted locally. 519 and 520 (SD) Flights, equipped with the DH.6, were formed on 6 June 1916 for anti-submarine duties over the Bristol Channel. Both Flights became part of 255 Squadron when this unit was formed at Pembroke on 25 July. The Flights carried out detachments at Llangefni and Luce Bay prior to the Armistice. 255 Squadron was disbanded on 14 January 1919 and airship operations ceased at a similar time, the site closing down in the spring of 1920.

The military returned in 1938 when the site became RAF Carew Cheriton, a Coastal and Flying Training Command station, which was closed down in 1945.

SHROPSHIRE

Newport (Chetwynd)

52°47′24″N/02°24′05″W, SJ730215. 0.5 miles W of Chetwynd Park, 2 miles NNW of Newport

FIRST surveyed as a potential LG on 13 July 1916, work reached a more than usually advanced stage because a size of 1,100 by 700 yards was recorded. However, no units ever made use of the LG.

Shawbury

52°47′46″N/02°40′21″W, SJ548223. Current RAF Shawbury, 6 miles NE of Shrewsbury

A TRAINING aerodrome from the start, Shawbury was established as a training squadron station in June 1917. 29th Wing ARS was the first unit to set up shop here on 1 June, and was destined to remain until April 1919. Shawbury occupied 259 acres and measured 1,400 by 1,100 yards. From the outset it was furnished with seven 1917-pattern GS Sheds (180 by 80 feet) made of timber and clad with iron sheeting.

The site was upgraded in early 1918, at a cost of £200,000, for 9 TDS, which was formed here in March 1918 to carry out day bombing training. The main equipment of the TDS was up to thirty-six Avro 504s and the same number of DH.4s and/or DH.9s. A storage detachment was established here in March 1919, just before the TDS was disbanded in April. By September Shawbury was also, albeit briefly, the home of an Airship Construction Section. A victim of the many post-war cuts, Shawbury was closed down in May 1920 and its buildings were either demolished or derelict within a short period of time. The airfield was reopened in 1935, swallowing up the First World War site, which was located on the western boundary of the current RAF Shawbury. Busy ever since, the airfield is another survivor and today is the home of the Defence Helicopter Flying School.

Shawbury main units, 1917-20

67 TS from Castle Bromwich, 11 Jun 1917;
to North Shotwick, 1 Apr 1917 (Camel, Pup, Nieuport and 504)

29 (Australian) TS formed 15 Jun 1917;
redesignated 5th TS AFC, 14 Jan 1918 (Shorthorn and Camel)

30 (Australian) TS formed 15 Jun 1917;
to Ternhill, 30 Jun 1917 (various aircraft)

10 TS from Ternhill, 30 Jun 1917;
to Lilbourne, 7 Apr 1918 (various aircraft)

90 Sqn formed (nucleus 10 TS) 8 Oct 1917;
to North Shotwick, 18 Oct 1917 (various aircraft)

5th TS AFC (ex-29 TS) 14 Jan 1918;
to Minchinhampton, 2 Apr 1918 (various aircraft)

131 Sqn formed 15 Mar 1918;
DB 17 Aug 1918 (various aircraft)

9 TDS formed 15 Mar 1918;
DB 25 Apr 1919 (DH.4, DH.6, DH.9, RE.8, 504 and BE.12)

137 Sqn formed 1 Apr 1918;
DB 4 Jul 1918 (DH.9)

Shrewsbury (Monkmoor)

52°43'02"N/02°43'10"W, SJ515135. E of Monkmoor
Road towards sewage works, 1.65 miles NE of
Shrewsbury town centre

LOCATED on the site of a pre-war aerodrome, work began
on an AAP in early 1918, but was destined never to be
completed. Despite still being under construction, 7 (North-
Western) ARD was formed here on 8 May 1918, comprising
an Engine Repair Section, MT section and salvage section, all
due to be open by October. However, despite a large array of
buildings at an advanced stage, the ARD was disbanded on 14
October 1918, while work continued on the AAP. Buildings
in situ by this stage were four GS Sheds (170 by 100 feet), a
pair of MT repair sheds (260 by 120 feet), a metal store (120
by 55 feet), a coach builders' shop (260 by 120 feet), and two
other sheds (200 by 140 feet and 120 by 120 feet).

The first aircraft to arrive belonged to the Observers School
of Reconnaissance & Aerial Photography, formed on 19 October
1918 with an establishment of twenty-four aircraft, including the
BE.2, RE.8, O/400 and DH.9. The school remained until 2 May
1919, when it was disbanded, and work on the unfinished AAP
ended in June 1919. Several of the buildings were taken over by
1 (Southern) ARD, which arrived from Farnborough on 28 June
1919 until disbanded on 30 April 1920.

The site was reactivated during the Second World War for
34 MU, a salvage unit that served from 1940 until 1945. Today
the site is covered in housing and light industry, but the four
GS Sheds remain in use and in good condition.

Ternhill (Stoke Heath)

52°52'29"N/02°32'04"W, SJ642308. Current RAF
Ternhill and Clive Barracks, off 'The Longford' (A41),
2.9 miles SW of Market Drayton

IN 1906 Major Atcherley landed a hot air balloon on an open
piece of land called Stoke Heath, south-east of rising ground
known as Grange Wood. Atcherley reported to the War Office
that the site could make a potential aerodrome, but it was not
until ten years later that his advice was taken up.

Ternhill opened in November 1916, the first residents
being 34 and 43 TS, both from Castle Bromwich, with a
variety of aircraft. A site with potential for much larger units,
Ternhill occupied 300 acres and measured 1,300 by 1,100
yards. Several TSs came and went, including two AFC units
that were resident from late 1916 through to April 1918.

In late 1917 work began on the construction of a TDS
designed for the training of Handley Page O/400 crews. The
site was rapidly expanded by building contractor Sir Lindsay
Parkinson Ltd at a cost of £500,000. Six GS Sheds (170 by 80
feet) were built, and on 1 March 1918 three units, 132, 133 and
134 Squadrons, were all formed to be equipped with the O/400.
On 1 April 13 TDS was opened with eighteen FE.2Bs, thirty
504s, ten O/400s and a few DH.6s on strength. Insufficient
O/400s arrived to justify the existence of the resident units, and
both 133 and 134 Squadrons were disbanded on 4 July; 132
Squadron was moved to Castle Bromwich.

13 TDS continued to operate at reduced capacity, later
being redesignated 13 TS on 14 March 1919 until March
1920. The site was sold off as a racehorse stables in 1922, but
was returned to the RAF as part of its expansion programme,
reopening in 1936. This picturesque site has remained in RAF
and Army hands ever since, serving the former as an RLG for
the Defence Helicopter School at Shawbury and the latter as
Clive Barracks.

An impressive group of R.A.F. SE.5As and Avro 504s of the 6th TS
(AFC) at Ternhill in February 1918.

Ternhill main units, 1916-20

34 TS from Castle Bromwich, 13 Nov 1916;
to Chattis Hill, 18 Mar 1918 (various aircraft)

43 TS from Castle Bromwich, 13 Nov 1916;
to Chattis Hill, 20 Mar 1918 (various aircraft)

33 (Australian) TS formed Dec 1916;
to Cirencester, May 1917 (BE.12)

63 TS formed 28 Mar 1917;
to Joyce Green, 1 Jun 1917 (504, DH.5 and Pup)

10 TS from Joyce Green, 1 Jun 1917;
to Shawbury, 30 Jun 1917 (various aircraft)

30 (Australian) TS from Shawbury, 30 Jun 1917;
redesignated 6th TS AFC, 14 Jan 1918 (various aircraft)

6th TS AFC (ex-30 (Australian) TS) 14 Jan 1918;
to Minchinhampton, 25 Apr 1918 (various aircraft)

No 1 ARS, AFC, formed 15 Jan 1918 in No 1 Training Wing, AFC;
to Minchinhampton, 11 Feb 1918

185th Aero Sqn, 'A' Flt, USAAS, from Hooton Park circa Mar 1918;
departed circa Apr 1918

132 Sqn formed 1 Mar 1918;
to Castle Bromwich, 19 Aug 1918 (various aircraft)

133 Sqn formed 1 Mar 1918;
DB 4 Jul 1918 (various aircraft)

134 Sqn formed 1 Mar 1918;
DB 4 Jul 1918 (various aircraft)

13 TDS formed 1 Apr 1918;
redesignated 13 TS, 14 Mar 1919 (O/400, FE.2B, 504 and DH.6)

87 Sqn cadre from Boussieres, 9 Feb 1919;
DB 24 Jun 1919 (no aircraft)

19 Sqn cadre from Genech, 17 Feb 1919;
DB 31 Dec 1919 (no aircraft)

13 TS (ex-13 TDS) 14 Mar 1919;
DB Mar 1920 (504K)

SOMERSET

Yeovil (Judwin)

50°56'19"N/02°39'06"W, ST540158. On current Agusta/ Westland Helicopters site, 1 mile W of Yeovil town centre

PETTERS Ltd of Yeovil, established in 1896, was an engineering company that specialised in the manufacturer of diesel and stationary petrol engines. At the beginning of the war the company answered the call to help support the war effort, expecting to be employed as a munitions factory. Extra land had already been purchased at Westland Farm, West Hendford, in 1913 for this purpose and, after offering its services to the War Office and the Admiralty, the latter responded, much to Petters' surprise, by contracting the company to build a dozen Short 184s. A further order for twenty Short 166s followed, all of these seaplanes being crated and delivered to Hamble and Rochester for flight-testing.

More land was purchased next to the factory and prepared as an LG because of more contracts for landplanes such as the 1½ Strutter, DH.4, DH.9 and later the Vimy bomber. The latter saw the factory expand again, including a larger erecting shop, which had an unsupported roof with a 140-foot span. As contracts were slashed at the end of the war, the Vimy contract was upheld, which helped to inspire the company to remain in aircraft manufacture. Indigenous Westland designs began to appear from 1917 and, after riding through the tough early 1920s, the company grew into one of the most successful in British aviation history.

Sopwith 1½ Strutter production in the Westland Factory at Yeovil would help steer the company into producing successful designs of its own in a tough post-war market.

SUFFOLK

Aldeburgh (Hazelwood)

52°10'34"N/01°34'10"W, TM442593. Off B1122 (Leiston Road), 2 miles due E of Thorpeness; original site extended S to A1094

ALDEBURGH can trace its aviation roots back to August 1915 when it was opened as an HD NLG for the RNAS; officially commissioned in October, it was under the command of Sub Lt A. Scarisbrick. It operated as a sub-station for Yarmouth until 1918, when the LG began a period of expansion, which included plans to turn the 105-acre site into a TDS. This never came to fruition, but Aldeburgh did gain four 1918-pattern GS Sheds with Esavian doors (170 by 100 feet), coupled as a pair of units, and another of 135 by 100 feet, complete with an aeroplane store for use as an ARS in 1918.

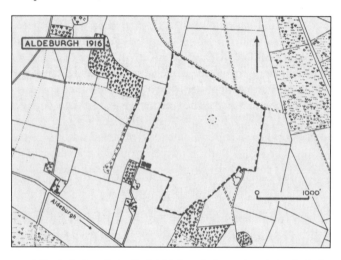

Aids to help pilots find Aldeburgh from the air included a chalk ring, 50 yards in diameter and 2 yards wide, although the nearby bunkers of the local golf course served as well. A 16-foot-long white wooden arrow also pointed out the direction of the wind.

In August 1918 the School for Anti-Submarine Inshore Patrol Observers (SASIPO) was formed to train aircrew for service with marine operations squadrons. Aircraft on strength included the BE.2C, DH.6, DH.9, Snipe and Kangaroo. Up to this point this important role was carried out by any rank that was prepared to fly! In October 1919 the SASIPO was redesignated as the School of Marine Observers, Aldeburgh, and on 1 January 1919 it was renamed again, to No 1 Marine Observers School. The latter was disbanded in September 1919, leaving Aldeburgh without a resident unit, and as such the airfield was closed down in 1920.

The remnants of a single hut can be seen from the A1094, while several timber buildings, bought by a local family and re-erected at Thorpeness, are still extant; one has been converted into three houses.

Bedfield

52°15'31"N/01°15'22"W, TM214668. 0.3 miles due E of Bedfield Long Green, 0.6 miles S of Worlingworth

THIS NLG2 was opened in April 1916 for 51(HD) and later 75(HD) Squadron until its closure in June 1919. Occupying 38 acres of land, Bedfield measured 500 by 300 yards.

Burgh Castle

52°35'02"N/01°39'52"W, TG483048. Off Butt Lane SE of Burgh Castle, 2.75 miles WSW of Great Yarmouth

ONLY occupying 50 acres of land, Burgh Castle proved to be a useful HD NLG and RNAS Flight Station in support of Great Yarmouth, located only a few miles to the east. Opened in November 1916 for the RNAS War Flight, the site was briefly upgraded to a Marine Operations (Aeroplane) Station. Facilities were improved by a trio of Aeroplane Sheds (66 by 42 feet), and the entire LG was operated by 6 officers and 20 other ranks. 273 Squadron, which established its HQ here in August 1918, was the last to leave in June 1919 to Great Yarmouth. It departed as a cadre, its aircraft having been relinquished in March. By July the site was farmland once more.

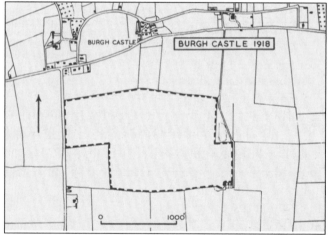

Burgh Castle main units, 1916-19

RNAS/RAF War Flt formed Nov 1916; DB Aug 1918

485(F) Flt formed, aka Temporary 'A' Flt, 7 Aug 1918; absorbed into 273 Sqn, 20 Aug 1919 (Camel)

486(F) Flt formed, aka Temporary 'C' Flt, 7 Aug 1918; absorbed into 273 Sqn, 20 Aug 1919 (Camel)

273 Sqn formed 20 Aug 1918; to Yarmouth (as cadre), Jun 1919 (DH.4, DH.9 and Camel)

219 Sqn detached from Westgate with DH.9 or Camel circa summer 1918.

470(F) Flt detached from Manston, 12 Nov 1918; to Manston, Jan 1919 (Camel)

534(LB) Flt from Covehithe by Nov 1918; to Covehithe, Mar 1919 (DH.4 and DH.9)

Bury St Edmunds

52°16'11"N/00°41'33"W, TL837669. Off Mildenhall Road (A1101), SE of Fornham All Saints, 1.4 miles NW of Bury St Edmunds railway station

THIS site is believed to have been used by RFC aircraft from Netheravon in October 1914, and later as an HD NLG for 51(HD) Squadron between April and October 1916.

Butley

52°06'09"N/01°25'17"W, TM343506. N and S of Woodbridge Road (B1084), Rendlesham Forest, E of Spratt's Street

SPLIT between two sites made up of an LG (550 by 450 yards) on the north side of Woodbridge Road and a technical and domestic site on the southern side, Butley still only covered 44 acres. Opened as an Acoustic Experimental Station in 1918, Butley was a sub-station for Orfordness Experimental Station. Some of the station's early work involved testing and silencing aero engines and aerial location of aircraft from the ground. Butley also briefly served as a Marine Operations (Aeroplane) Station when a Supernumerary Camel Flight was formed on 1 September 1918, although this unit was redesignated as 487(F) Flight three days later. As part of 230 Squadron, whose HQ was at Felixstowe, the Flight carried out escort duties from Butley. The Camels of 487 Flight were disbanded in January 1919 and the Acoustic Experimental unit was disbanded into AES Orfordness on 13 February 1919.

All structures were built on the south side of Woodbridge Road, and the clearing where they stood still remains, while the LG, which only had a pair of Bessonneau hangars, is now part of the new forest. The former RAF Woodbridge is 1 mile to the south, and the former RAF Bentwaters 1.5 miles to the north.

Cotton

52°15'30"N/01°01'18"W, TM063665. E of Ford's Green off B1113, 0.5 W of Cotton

A SHORT-LIVED LG was established at Cotton in October 1916 for 51(HD) Squadron. However, the site was abandoned two months later when its duties were transferred to Elmswell.

Covehithe

52°22'06"N/01°41'50"W, TM519809. On edge of Covehithe Broad, between Porter's Farm and Warren House, 3.1 miles N of Southwold

THIS 82-acre site located a mere 250 yards from the sea first saw service from March 1915 when it was the home of HD Flight RNAS, which was formed here under the control of RNAS Yarmouth. Twelve months later Covehithe was declared an HD Flight Station with a pair of wooden Aeroplane Sheds (60 by 42 feet), and measured approximately 600 by 400 yards.

The HD Flight, now serving the RAF, was redesignated as Temporary 'D' Flight on 30 May 1918, by which time plans were afoot to make Covehithe into a Marine Operations (Aeroplane) Station. By August 'D' Flight was redesignated as

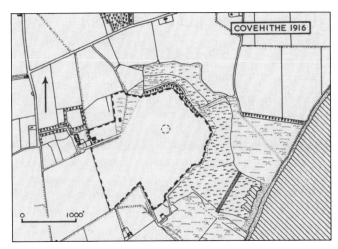

534(LB) Flight, under the charge of 273 Squadron, whose HQ was at Burgh Castle. Equipped with the DH.4 and DH.9, extra accommodation was built on the aerodrome for flight personnel. 534(LB) Flight moved to Burgh Castle in October 1918, but returned to Covehithe in March 1919, where it was disbanded. The site remained open until July 1919, but was fully relinquished by the end of the year.

Elmswell (Great Ashfield)

52°15'22"N/00°56'42"W, TM009660. 1.5 miles SE of Great Ashfield, in centre of WW2 site, 2 miles NE of Elmswell

OPENED in April 1916, it was not until December that 51(HD) Squadron began to make use of this large NLG1. On 14 September 1917 the LG was transferred to 75(HD) Squadron and, combined with a flurry of wooden buildings being erected, Elmswell was upgraded to an HD Flight Station and Squadron Station. During this time two HD-pattern Aeroplane Sheds (130 by 60 feet) were erected together with a single Bessonneau for MT. The site occupied 77 acres and measured 750 by 600 yards. The LG remained at this higher status until May 1919, despite 75(HD) Squadron's departure a year earlier.

Notification of Elmswell's closure came on 6 November 1919 and was confirmed on 1 January 1920. The site was swallowed up by RAF Great Ashfield during the Second World War, home of the 385th BG and its B-17 Flying Fortresses between 1943 and 1945.

Elmswell main units, 1916-18

51 Sqn from Hingham and Thetford, Dec 1916 to Aug 1917

75 Sqn HQ from Goldington, 8 Sep 1917;
to North Weald, 22 May 1918 (BE.2C/E and BE.12/B)

75 Sqn 'A' Flt from Harling Road, Feb 1918;
to Hadleigh, 18 Feb 1918

75 Sqn 'B' Flt from Yelling, 8 Sep 1917;
to Harling Road, Sep 1918

75 Sqn 'B' Flt from Harling Road, Sep 1918;
to North Weald, 22 May 1918

75 Sqn 'C' Flt from Hadleigh, Sep 1918;
to North Weald, 22 May 1918

Felixstowe (Landguard Common)

51°56'40"N/01°19'31"W, TM286325. Rear of Freightliner Terminal, 1.6 miles SE of Felixstowe town centre

THIS 42-acre site, situated directly behind Felixstowe Seaplane Station, was opened in September 1915 for the use of the RNAS. Designated as an HD Flight Station, the site, known as Landguard Common, was occupied by the HD War Flight RNAS until August 1916, when the unit was disbanded. The site was then classified as a DLG for the use of land-based communications aircraft serving the seaplane station. Under the Commander-in-Chief, The Nore RNAS, Landguard Common only remained in use until 1917.

Felixstowe Dock

51°56'41"N/01°19'10"W, TM282326. Freightliner and Container Terminal, 1.5 miles SW of Felixstowe town centre

THE long history of Felixstowe Dock (originally named Harwich) began in April 1913 at a sheltered location on the eastern edge of Harwich harbour. Positioned north of Landguard Fort, Felixstowe was opened as a seaplane and flying-boat station for the RNAS. The first unit was the RNAS Seaplane War Flight, formed on 5 August 1913, a year before it would be needed. The unit was joined by the RNAS Flying-Boat War Flights in 1915, and these two units were the main residents until the spring of 1918.

Only one slipway and a pair of Seaplane Sheds (90 by 70 feet) were here at first, but by 1917 the 38-acre site had been expanded dramatically. Three Flying-boat Sheds (330 by 160 feet), four Seaplane Sheds (one of 290 by 80 feet, one 200 by 80 feet, and two 180 by 60 feet) and a total of five slipways were built.

Felixstowe was a Marine Experimental Station from 1915 through to 1918, and a Seaplane Experimental Station from 1 April 1918 until 8 January 1919, tasked with experimental work of all kinds in connection with flying-boats and seaplanes. The RNAS Flying-Boat War Flights were redesignated as 327, 328, 329 and 330 Flights on 30 May 1918 when Felixstowe also became a Marine Operations (Seaplane) Station. Later, six seaplane squadrons would serve here until the end of the war, carrying out anti-submarine patrols, long-range reconnaissance and convoy escort duties.

Felixstowe's wartime experimental work certainly did it some good after the war, because it became the home of the MAEE from Grain in June 1924; apart from some Second World War service at Helensburgh/Rhu, the unit remained here until August 1954, when it was disbanded. RAF Felixstowe was closed down in August 1962 and, while remnants clung on for many years after, the site has been virtually eradicated by the requirements of the ever-growing container terminal.

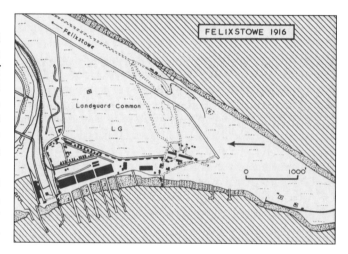

A general view of Felixstowe Dock, with its three 330-by-160-foot Flying-boat Sheds dominating the station. The LG at Landguard Common was on the extreme right of this photograph behind the row of houses. *Via Stuart Leslie*

Felixstowe F.2As are ready for operations from Felixstowe Dock in 1918. *Via Stuart Leslie*

Felixstowe Dock main units, 1913-22

RNAS Seaplane War Flights formed 5 Aug 1913;
DB 1918

RNAS Flying-Boat War Flights formed 1915;
redesignated 327-330 Flts 1918

Nore Defence Flight formed (within existing seaplane flights)
1916;
DB 10 Aug 1917

America School formed 1917;
DB into Small America Flight 1918

Small America Flight formed 1 Apr 1918 within America School;
DB 15 Jun 1918

327(FB) and 328(FB) Flt formed 30 May 1918;
absorbed into 230 Sqn, 20 Aug 1918 (F.2A)

329(FB) and 330(FB) Flt formed 30 May 1918;
absorbed into 231 Sqn, 20 Aug 1918 (F.2A)

333(FB) and 334(FB) Flt formed 31 May 1918;
absorbed into 232 Sqn, 20 Aug 1918 (F.2A)

335(FB) Flt formed 15 Jun 1918;
absorbed into 232 Sqn, 20 Aug 1918 (F.2A)

336(FB) Flt formed 31 Jul 1918;
absorbed into 247 Sqn, 20 Aug 1918 (F.2A)

C, D and E Boat Seaplane TF formed 8 Aug 1918;
DB 19 Mar 1919

230 Sqn formed (327, 328 and 487 Flts) 20 Aug 1918;
to Calshot, 7 May 1922

(F.2A, F.3, H.12, H.16, F.5 and Fairey IIIB/IIIC)

231 Sqn formed (329 and 330 Flts) 20 Aug 1918;
DB 7 Jul 1919 (F.2A, F.3 and F.5)

232 Sqn formed (333, 334 and 335 Flts) 20 Aug 1918;
redesignated as 4 (Comms) Sqn, 5 Jan 1919 (F.2A and F.3)

247 Sqn formed (336, 337 and 338 Flts) 20 Aug 1918;
DB 22 Jan 1919 (F.2A and F.3)

259 Sqn formed (342, 343 and 344 Flts) 20 Aug 1918;
DB 13 Sep 1919 (F.2A and F.3)

261 Sqn formed (339, 340 and 341 Flts) 20 Aug 1918;
DB 13 Sep 1919 (F.2A and F.3)

337(FB) Flt formed 15 Sep 1918;
DB 22 Jan 1919 (F.2A)

339(FB) Flt formed 20 Sep 1918;
DB Jan 1919 (F.2A)

341(FB) Flt formed 15 Oct 1918;
DB Jan 1919 (F.2A)

442(S) Flt formed 15 Oct 1918;
to Westgate, Nov 1918 (Fairey IIIB)

342(FB) Flt formed 31 Oct 1918;
DB Jan 1919 (F.2A)

4 (Comms) Sqn formed 6 Jan 1919;
DB 1919 (Short 184, F.5 and Fury)

Hadleigh

52°02′30″N/01°00′15″W, TM061424. Between Primrose Farm and Ramsey Wood, 2.2 miles E of Hadleigh

WHEN Hadleigh opened in April 1916 it was typical L-shaped LG, using the barest minimum of land to create a pair of landing strips. Classified as an HD NLG3 (an NLG1 from January 1917), Hadleigh was first occupied by 51(HD) Squadron but, with the arrival of 'C' Flight of 75(HD) Squadron from Therfield on 1 August 1917, the aerodrome began to expand. More land was acquired, making the site rectangular in shape, occupying 80 acres and measuring 700 by 550 yards.

Upgraded to an HD Flight Station from September 1917, when 'C' Flight was joined by 'A' Flight, 75(HD) Squadron, from Elmswell, Hadleigh gained a pair of HD-pattern Aeroplane Sheds (130 by 60 feet) and at least twenty other structures. These were concentrated in the south-west corner of the LG, now the location of Primrose Farm. By mid-1918 both Flights were equipped with eight 504K(NF) fighters, but their stay was to be short, 'C' Flight moving to Elmswell in September and 'A' Flight to North Weald Bassett on 7 November.

Hadleigh's short spell as an HD Flight Station was all over by the Armistice, but the site remained in military hands until it was closed in early 1920.

Levington

52°00′43″N/01°16′41″W, TM250398. NW of Walk Farm, bisected by A14, 1 mile ENE of Levington

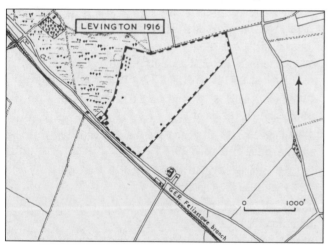

LEVINGTON briefly served as an NLG for the RNAS during 1916 and 1917 for the aircraft of ships that were anchored at Harwich.

Lowestoft

52°28′N/01°45′W, TM553933. Due N of Hamilton Dock, 0.5 mile NE of Lowestoft railway station

AN ideal location next to the sheltered Hamilton Dock, where kite balloons could be embarked in calm water, the site was opened as Kite Balloon Station Lowestoft in 1917. It was only 8 acres in size and only two balloons were stationed here at any one time, both having the luxury of their own 100-by-36-foot canvas hangar. Lowestoft was under RNAS control, under the command of Captain in Charge Naval Base Lowestoft RNAS until 1 April 1918, when the RAF took over, redesignating the unit as No 7 Balloon Station on 15 April. The unit disbanded on 14 October 1918 and the site was relinquished the following year.

Martlesham Heath

52°03′43″N/01°16′27″W, TM242454. Bisected by A12 with main technical site on either side of Gloster Road, 4.8 miles E of Ipswich

FOREVER associated with trials and evaluation of service aircraft, which would evolve into the A&AEE, formed here in March 1924, Martlesham Heath was first opened as a humble HD NLG3 in April 1916. The aerodrome, which was reclassified as an NLG2 on 5 January 1917 and again to an NLG1 on 31 March, was first used by 51(HD) Squadron, then 37(HD) Squadron and finally 75(HD) Squadron until 1919.

From January 1917 Martlesham became an Experimental Station for the Testing Squadron from Upavon and 'A' Flight of the Armament Experimental Squadron from Orfordness. The latter disbanded into the former on its arrival, then was redesignated as the Aeroplane Experimental Station from 16 October 1917. The unit settled in to a period of experimental and testing work that included carrying out performance trials of every type of aircraft and their engines entering service. The many enemy aircraft captured during the war were also evaluated here.

By late 1917 the aerodrome occupied 900 acres and measured 1,850 by 1,700 yards. By 1918 it was furnished with three 1918-pattern timber GS Sheds (170 by 80 feet), one 1918-pattern GS Shed (170 by 80 feet) with sliding doors, and a single 1918 GS Shed (228 by 100 feet) with a pitched roof.

After the war Martlesham overcame the swingeing cuts and was destined to remain the centre for flight testing when the Armament Experimental Station was redesignated as the Aeroplane Experimental Establishment on 16 March 1920, then the A&AEE on 24 March 1924, remaining until September 1939, when it moved to Boscombe Down. Martlesham remained an active RAF station until 25 April 1963 and today all remnants are from the Second World War onwards. These include the preserved tower, which is the home of the excellent Martlesham Heath Aviation Society & Control Tower Museum.

Just a glimpse of one of Martlesham's Aeroplane Sheds can be seen on the right, while O/100 3138 is the photographer's main quarry in this image, taken in September 1917.

Newmarket

52°14'14"N/00°22'28"W, TL622625. Close to Millennium Grandstand, Newmarket Racecourse, 1.5 miles SW of Newmarket

WITH little preparation or ceremony, Newmarket was transformed from one of the country's oldest racecourses to an HD NLG1 for the use of 51(HD) and 75(HD) Squadrons. A generous 100 acres of the course was used for aviation, measuring 1,000 by 600 yards, with twelve Bessonneau hangars. Opened in April 1916, the site was reclassified as an NLG2 by September 1917, and shortly afterwards had its role changed to that of a night training squadron station in November.

192 Depot Station moved in from Marham on 14 November equipped with the FE.2B/D and BE.2C/D and E. The unit was redesignated 192 NTS and was destined to remain at Newmarket until it was disbanded on 31 May 1919. It was joined by 190 NTS from Rochford on 14 March 1918 flying the DH.6, BE.2C/E, 504J/K and Pup. That unit moved to Bury (Upwood) on 5 October 1918 and, despite 192 NTS's demise in May, Newmarket remained an RAF station until early 1920. Less than twenty years later the RAF would return.

Orfordness

52°05'10N/01°33'27"W, TM437490. Between River Ore and Stoney Ditch, 0.9 miles SE of Orford, 4.4 miles SSW of Aldeburgh

A DESOLATE, lonely and very secret location, Orfordness was nevertheless one of the most important aerodromes of the First World War and would continue to remain important through the Second and on into the Cold War. A large site occupying 2,527 acres and measuring 1,500 by 1,400 yards, Orfordness opened as an HD NLG for 37(HD) Squadron and an Experimental Armament Establishment in April 1916. All of the buildings ran along the southern boundary close to Stoney Ditch. These included two 1915-pattern Flight Sheds

(210 by 65 feet), one 1916-pattern GS Shed (170 by 80 feet), one 1917-pattern GS Shed (180 by 100 feet), three Aeroplane Sheds (two of 105 by 40 feet and one of 106 by 33 feet), and two Balloon Sheds (100 by 36 feet and 50 by 30 feet).

37 Squadron formed the core of the first unit, the Experimental Flight, on 20 May 1916, and the site was classified as an Experimental Station the same day. A wide variety of testing was carried out, well away from prying eyes, including work with machine guns and cannon, gun sights, bombs and bomb sights, and well as general testing of aircraft that had been suffering unexplained failures in service.

The site continued its important work until June 1921, when the AES moved out to Grain and the site was placed under Care & Maintenance. Remaining in military hands, the aerodrome site remained untouched and at least two hangars were still standing after the Second World War; the majority of their bases can still be seen today. A few smaller First World War-era buildings also remain, thanks to the long military occupation.

Bottom: Dazzle-type camouflage is evaluated on the fuselage of a redundant Sopwith Camel at Orfordness.

Below: One of many camouflage schemes experimented with during the war is tested by O/100 3126 at Orfordness.

Orfordness main units, 1916-21

37 Sqn from Norwich (Mousehold Heath), 4 Apr 1916;
DB into Experimental Station 20 May 1916

Experimental Flt from Upavon, May 1916;
DB into Experimental Station 20 May 1916

Experimental Station 20 May 1916;
redesignated Armament Experimental Station, 13 Oct 1917

Experimental Station 'A' Flt formed from parent unit Jan 1917;
to Martlesham Heath, Jan 1917

Armament Experimental Station 13 Oct 1917;
redesignated AES detachment, 16 Mar 1920

AES detachment 16 Mar 1920;
to Grain, Jun 1921

Shotley (Harwich)

51°57'31"N/01°16'15"W, TM248339. Located within ex-HMS *Ganges* at Shotley Gate, 1 mile SE of Shotley

The operation of balloons above HMS *Ganges* on the edge of Harwich Harbour was first witnessed in 1912, and within two years a more permanent kite balloon station was established. Taking up just 5 acres, Shotley had four Balloon Sheds (100 by 36 feet) and several technical and domestic buildings. The station was run by 9 officers, 4 SNCOs, 7 corporals and 90 other ranks.

Shotley's main role was that of convoy and offensive patrol duties in support of the Royal Navy's Harwich Force. Only two balloons were ever operational and all tasking was controlled by the Senior Naval Officer, Harwich.

On 15 April 1918 No 12 Balloon Base was formed in place of Shotley's original title of Royal Navy Kite Balloon Station. The unit was closed down on 30 June 1919, while HMS *Ganges* remained open until 1976.

Stutton

51°58'21"N/01°08'03"W, TM156351. N of Holbrook Road (B1080), W of entrance to Alton Reservoir car park, 1.3 miles SW of Holbrook

Established as an NLG2 initially for 37(HD) Squadron from early 1917, Stutton occupied 52 acres and measured 580 by 410 yards. 75(HD) Squadron is also recorded as serving here until at least November 1918, when the LG was returned to the land.

Trimley

52°00'07"N/01°17'54"W, TM265389. 0.9 miles NNW of Trimley St Martin, N of A14, 3.5 miles NW of Felixstowe

A SMALL LG was established here in December 1916 in support of Martlesham Heath, located just over 4 miles to the north, and Felixstowe, which was 3 miles to the south. At least one Aeroplane Shed was built for the purpose of erecting aircraft allocated for flight-testing and/or trials. One

of the first was Sopwith Pup 9911, which arrived via Felixstowe on 10 January 1917. After a test flight back to Felixstowe, the fighter remained until 2 February, when it departed for Levington. Pup 9910 also arrived via Felixstowe for erection on 10 January. The aircraft was fitted with a set of Le Prieur rockets on the struts, and left for Levington on the same day as 9911. It is most likely that many more aircraft passed through Trimley; one of the last was DH.4 A7671 from RAE Farnborough on 8 May 1918. Unfortunately the aircraft broke up over the LG, killing the pilot, Lt L. F. D. Lutyens, and his passenger, Mr D. H. Pincent.

Today nothing remains of the original LG and the military buildings that can be seen off the A14 belong to the GCI Station that was built here during the Second World War.

SOUTH YORKSHIRE

Brampton

53°22'47"N/01°15'17"W, SE490877A. 1 mile SE of Brampton-en-le-Morthen and 1 mile due W of Laughton Common

ALLOCATED to 33(HD) Squadron in April 1916, Brampton was not used a great deal once the parent unit moved to Gainsborough in October 1916. Classified as an NLG3, this small LG was abandoned on 24 March 1917.

Brancroft (Finningley)

53°27'51"N/01°00'10"W. S of Robin Hood Airport between A614 and end of runway 02

Opened as an HD NLG3 for 33(HD) Squadron at Gainsborough in December 1916, Brancroft was made up of two fields located alongside the Hatfield to Bawtry road. Named after the local farm, Brancroft was reclassified as an HD NLG2 on 31 March 1917, and by June 1919 the airfield was closed.

Broomhill (Wombwell)

53°31'19"N/01°22'53"W, SE415032. 0.5 miles W of Broomhill, 0.75 miles W of Wombwell, on N side of Waterside Park

AN HD NLG3 for 33(HD) Squadron, Broomhill was opened in June 1916, reclassified as an HD NLG2 on 31 March 1917, and remained open until late 1918.

Doncaster

53°31'28"N/01°06'18"W, SE596036. Intake, NE of Town Moor Avenue, due N of Doncaster Racecourse, 1.5 miles E of Doncaster railway station

EVEN though the neighbouring Doncaster Racecourse had hosted a large aviation meeting before the war, the site was not selected as a military aerodrome, but land due north across Leger Way (the A18) was. The site occupied 248 acres of land

Major E. L. Foot MC is at the controls of Camel F6491 of 47 TDS at Doncaster in 1918.

belonging to Intake Farm, which, surprisingly, remained in situ on the site, which measured 1,100 by 1,100 yards.

Opened as a training squadron station in January 1916, the first occupant was 15 TS from Thetford equipped with the 504, RE.8 and FK.3. By March 1916 the site also served as an NLG1 HD Flight Station for a detachment of 47(HD) Squadron, which was redesignated as 33(HD) Squadron after a few months before departing or Bramham Moor. Training units were the main occupants, 41 TS from Tadcaster in August 1916 sowing the seeds for the LG's final and major role as a TDS. Before this role the site slowly developed with three 1915-pattern Flight Sheds (210 by 65 feet) and one 1916-pattern GS Shed, erected in the south-western corner.

47 TDS was formed here from 41 and 49 TS in July 1918, its main role being to carry out single-seat fighter training. Personnel strength at Doncaster by this time had expanded to an average of 34 officers, 80 officer pupils, 40 NCO pupils, 31 SNCOs, 22 JNCOs, 214 other ranks and 152 women. The TDS flew a variety of aircraft, but generally had at least twenty-four 504s and the same number of SE.5s on strength at any one time. The TDS was the last major unit to serve here until it was disbanded on 13 February 1919. By the end of that year the relinquishment notices came through and the site was close down in the spring of 1920.

A sub-depot for No 7 Stores Depot was also located at Doncaster from May 1918; the main section of the unit moved to the aerodrome from Mexborough on 2 February 1919 until it was disbanded in January 1920.

Doncaster main units, 1915-19

15 TS from Thetford, 1 Jan 1916;
to Spittlegate, 15 Sep 1917 1 Jun 1917 (504, RE.8 and FK.3)

HD detachment (three BE.2Cs attached to 15 TS) from Feb 1916; dispersed to HD Sqns, 25 Jun 1916

47 (HD) Sqn detached from Beverley, Mar 1916; redesignated 33(HD) Sqn detachment, Jun 1916 (BE.2C, BE.12 and FK.3)

33(HD) Sqn detachment (ex-47(HD) Sqn detachment) Jun 1916; to Bramham Moor, 1916 (BE.2C/D)

41 TS from Tadcaster, 16 Aug 1916;
DB into 47 TDS, 15 Jul 1918 (Shorthorn, Longhorn and G.3)

46 TS formed 23 Oct 1916;
to Tadcaster, 17 Dec 1916 (various aircraft)

82 Sqn formed (nucleus from 15 RS) 7 Jan 1917;
to Beverley, 6 Feb 1917 (various aircraft)

80 (Canadian) TS formed (nucleus from 15 RS) Jan 1917;
to Canada, 27 Feb 1917

90 (Canadian) TS formed (nucleus from 36 RS) 15 Mar 1917;
to Beverley, 18 Apr 1917 (no aircraft)

49 TS from Spittlegate, 15 Sep 1917;
DB into 47 TDS, 15 Jul 1918
(Shorthorn, Longhorn, 504, FK.3, RE.8, BE.2E and DH.4)

47 TDS (ex-41 and 49 TS) formed 15 Jul 1918;
DB 20 Feb 1919 (Shorthorn, SE.5A, 504J/K, Camel and Pup)

168th Aero Sqn, 'C' and 'D' Flts, USAAS, by 17 Jul 1918

Ecclesfield

53°26'22"N/01°27'16"W, SK363937. Potentially on St Michaels Sports Ground, 0.5 miles ESE of Ecclesfield centre, 3.8 miles WNW of Rotherham

ONLY open from April until the autumn of 1916, Ecclesfield was classified as an HD NLG. Allocated to 33(HD) Squadron, the site closed down when its duties were taken over by Broomhill.

Redmires (Sheffield)

53°21'45"N/01°35'17"W, SK274851A. At Fulwood Booth, 0.4 miles E of Redmires Reservoir, 5 miles WSW of Sheffield city centre

THIS HD NLG3 was allocated to 33(HD) Squadron from April 1916 until September 1917.

Thorne

53°35'30"N/00°53'45"W, SE732111. NE of Thornebrook Primary School, 3.5 miles NE of Hatfield & Stainforth railway station

THIS 94-acre NLG1 was used briefly by 'A' Flight, 33(HD) Squadron, from October 1916. Measuring 750 by 650 yards, it would have remained in military hands until at least November 1918.

STAFFORDSHIRE

Chasetown (Lichfield)

52°40'12"N/01°55'40"W, SK050080. Due W of Ridgeway Primary School, Chasetown, 0.75 miles from Burntwood centre

AN HD NLG3 when it opened for 38(HD) Squadron in October 1916, Chasetown was reclassified as a DLG3 by September 1917. However, by that date notification of the site's impending closure was issued and there was little activity beyond October 1917.

Great Barr (Walsall)

52°32'41"N/01°54'18"W, SP065940. Opposite Great Barr School across Aldridge Road in Queslett Park, 1.4 miles NE of Hamstead (Birmingham) railway station

A SHORT-LIVED HD NLG2, it was used by 38(HD) Squadron from April to December 1916.

Kingswinford (Dudley, aka Wall Heath)

52°30'07"N/02°11'59"W, SO863892. Between Staffordshire & Worcestershire Canal and Mile Flat Road, 1.35 miles WNW of Kingswinford

NESTLING next to the Worcestershire border, Kingswinford was opened as an HD NLG2 for 38(HD) Squadron in April 1916. One of the unit's most westerly LGs, the site was closed down in June 1917. The fields are still as clear as they would have been during the First World War, although the farm on Mile Flat was much smaller.

Perton (Fern Fields/Wolverhampton)

52°35'25"N/01°13'09"W, SO853993. 0.5 miles NW of Perton village, site now partly covered by Perton Park Golf Club

THE first of three airfields named Perton was opened in April 1916 for 38(HD) Squadron, which did not arrive until the unit moved to Melton Mowbray in October. Covering 66 acres, Perton was an NLG3/2 and a DLG right through to its closure in August 1918.

SURREY

Addlestone

51°22'28"N/00°28'56"W. E end of Station Road, Addlestone, now Aviator Park

A LARGE Blériot aircraft factory was built here in 1917, and the several hundred aeroplanes produced there were taken by road to Brooklands for final assembly and test-flying. The factory was taken over by Weymann to build bus and coach bodies (the company built the prototype Routemaster) before closing down in mid-1960s.

Brooklands

51°20'48"N/00°28'21"W, TQ065620. 'Brooklands Airfield (disused)', 1.7 miles SSW of Weybridge, 1.8 miles NNE of Wisley

THE very early romantic days of aviation and motor racing in Britain can be linked back to 1906, when Hugh Locke King started building his circuit, and the following year, when Lord Brabazon tried to fly an aircraft of his own design. While the racing circuit went on to be a successful venture, Brabazon's early attempts to fly failed, but in 1908 a young A. V. Roe was successful. Roe was not popular with the motor racing fraternity and, after crashing a Triplane in the middle of the circuit during an event, he was 'invited to leave'. However, together with the Short Brothers and Martin & Handasyde (later Martinsyde), Roe was invited back to Brooklands in 1910, making the site the most significant aviation centre in the country.

Vickers established a flying school here in 1911, and just before the outbreak of war the first military unit arrived in the shape of 1 Squadron, which was reactivated on 1 August 1914.

Some of the pre-war civilian flight sheds at Brooklands, which backed onto the racing circuit.

Hubert Latham managed to park his Antoinette VII, without injury, on the roof of the Martin & Handasyde shed at Brooklands in June 1911.

The aerodrome, which occupied 290 acres and measured 2,150 by 1,000 yards within the confines of the racing circuit, was until 1919 classified as an HD NLG and DLG for various detachments, including 141(HD) Squadron from 1918.

The main technical site of the aerodrome was concentrated in the south-western corner and was quickly expanded to not only cope with normal operations, but also to cater for companies such as Sopwith and Vickers, which were destined to build aircraft by the thousand. As well as the original pre-war Flight Sheds erected along the edge of the circuit, seven 1918-pattern GS Sheds (170 by 100 feet) and a single 1915-pattern HD Shed (190 by 70 feet) were built. By the end of the First World War Brooklands-based aircraft manufacturers had produced more than 4,600 aircraft. To help cope with the outflow, 10 AAP was established here in October 1917 to handle SE.5s built by Blériot, Martinsyde and Vickers, the latter alone producing 1,650 aircraft.

At Brooklands in the 1930s the original pre-war sheds can be seen in the lower left corner within the racing circuit, and the First World War expansion in front.

After the war the airfield grew from strength to strength, and even motor racing returned, making Brooklands a very exciting place to be. It continued to be a centre for Hawker and Vickers, which later purchased the site outright as Vickers-Armstrong in 1948. Vikings, Viscounts, One-Elevens and VC10s were all built here, the latter being the last to be designed and built completely at Brooklands. The last VC10 flew out in February 1970, heralding the closure of the airfield, which still retained a large number of original First World War buildings. Today the site has been consumed by modern businesses, but large sections of the racing circuit still remain and the outstanding Brooklands Museum will forever keep aviation alive at this historic site.

Brooklands main units, 1914-20

1 Sqn re-established as cadre 1 May 1914, and reactivated 14 Aug 1914;
to Netheravon, 13 Nov 1914 (Longhorn, Boxkite and S.1)

2 RS formed 12 Nov 1914;
to Northolt, 31 Jan 1917 (various aircraft)

8 Sqn formed 1 Jan 1915;
to Gosport (Fort Grange), 6 Jan 1915 (BE.2C)

10 Sqn from Farnborough, 8 Jan 1915;
to Hounslow, 1 Apr 1915
(Longhorn, Shorthorn, Blériot XI, S.1 and BE.2C)

9 Sqn reformed 1 Apr 1915;
to Dover (Swingate Down), 23 Jul 1915 (BE.2, Blériot XI and Longhorn)

Wireless Exp Flt formed Dec 1915;
redesignated Wireless School, 24 Aug 1916

46 Sqn formed (nucleus from 2 RS) 19 Apr 1916;
to Wyton, 20 Apr 1916 (BE.2C and BE.2E)

23 RS formed;
attached to 2 RS, Jun 1916;
to Egypt, Aug 1916

Wireless School (ex-Wireless Exp Flt) 24 Aug 1916;
redesignated Wireless & Observers School, 24 Oct 1916
(RE.7, BE.2C and BE.2E)

Wireless & Observers School (ex-Wireless School) 24 Oct 1916;
to Hursley Park, 2 Oct 1917 (RE.7, BE.2C and BE.2E)

Wireless Testing Park formed Oct 1916;
to Joyce Green, 21 Oct 1916

AAP formed 1 Aug 1917;
redesignated 10 AAP, 12 Oct 1917 (accepted SE.5A and Snipe)

10 AAP (ex-AAP) 12 Oct 1917;
closed Apr 1920 (accepted SE.5A and Snipe)

Despite predominantly serving in France, 208 Squadron briefly returned to the UK in 1918 when it was likely to have received the Snipe, E8176 was photographed whilst at Brooklands Acceptance Park, 9th October 1918 with squadron identification bars on the fuselage. Due to a German offensive the squadron soon returned to France. © Inkworm.com

Chessington,
London Borough of Kingston-upon-Thames

51°21'23"N/00°18'52"W, TQ174633. Nigel Fisher Way, Chessington, 0.3 miles W of Chessington railway station

ESTABLISHED for the use of 39(HD) Squadron from October 1916, Chessington was initially classified as an HD NLG2. Reclassified as a DLG2 from 14 September 1917, the site was abandoned the following month.

Croydon (Beddington)

51°21'16"N/00°07'46"W, TQ306635. Off Mollison Drive (ex-Plough Lane), South Beddington, 2 miles SW of Croydon

ONE of many early HD Stations established around London to counter the Zeppelin threat, the first aerodrome to be named Croydon was located on 81 acres of land belonging to New Barn Farm, Beddington. Initially classified as an HD NLG2, Croydon first hosted a small detachment (possibly only two BE.2Cs) of 17 TS, which formed here on 15 December 1915. The unit was destined to remain and grow substantially in size, just like the aerodrome around it. Overall, Croydon was classified as a training squadron station, and as such three 1918-pattern GS Sheds (two of 170 by 70 feet and one 130 by 80 feet) were built on the western side of Plough Lane, while a complex technical and domestic site rose up on the eastern side. The construction work was carried out by Holland, Hannen & Cubitt, and on average the aerodrome contained up to thirty aircraft, by which time the main resident unit was 40 TS, tasked with single-seat fighter training with several Camels on strength. This unit was replaced by 29 TS from Stag Lane on 14 December 1918, which remained until June 1919.

Croydon remained a busy place throughout 1919, with several squadrons passing through, although all were cadres. The RAF remained in residence until February 1920, when the Air Council Inspection Squadron was disbanded. Civilian flying crept into Croydon, but the nearby Waddon aerodrome was causing conflict and it was decided to move the centre of the Beddington site eastwards towards Purley Way and amalgamate it with Waddon. The site slowly dissolved into the western side of Croydon Airport. The area today is covered in housing, but the developers have recognised the area's history and virtually every road is named after an aircraft or aviator.

Croydon main units, 1915-19

17 TS HD detachment formed 15 Dec 1915;
to Port Meadow, 1 Jun 1917 (504, JN.2, BE.2C and RE.8)

19 TS HD detachment from Hounslow, 1 Feb 1916;
to Hounslow, 15 Apr 1916 (DH.1 and FE.2B)

22 TS formed (attached to 17 TS) 22 May 1916;
to Aboukir, 24 Aug 1916 (504)

65 TS formed 1 May 1917;
to Sedgeford, 10 May 1917 (FK.3 and FK.8)

40 TS from Port Meadow, 1 Jun 1917;
to Tangmere, 14 Dec 1918
(Scout, 1½ Strutter, DH.5, Pup, Camel and 504)

93 Sqn formed (nucleus from 40 TS) 23 Sep 1917;
to Chattis Hill, 3 Oct 1917 (various aircraft)

24th Aero Sqn detachment, USAAS, from Wye, 31 Jan 1918;
to Wye, 7 Mar 1918 (DH.4)

29 TS from Stag Lane, 14 Dec 1918;
to Netheravon, 30 Jun 1919
(DH.6, DH.9, F.2B, 504, Camel and Snipe)

Air Council Inspection Sqn formed 25 Jun 1919;
redesignated 24 Sqn, 1 Feb 1920 (504, DH.9, F.2B, BE.2C and F.4)

32 Sqn cadre from Tangmere, 8 Oct 1919;
DB 29 Dec 1919 (no aircraft)

41 Sqn cadre from Tangmere, 8 Oct 1919;
DB 31 Dec 1919 (no aircraft)

84 Sqn cadre from Tangmere, 8 Oct 1919;
to Kenley, Jan 1920 (no aircraft)

207 Sqn cadre from Tangmere, 8 Oct 1919;
to Uxbridge, 16 Jan 1920 (no aircraft)

3 Sqn cadre from Dover (Swingate Down), 15 Oct 1919;
to Uxbridge, 27 Oct 1919 (no aircraft)

10 Sqn cadre from Ford Junction, 15 Oct 1919;
DB 31 Dec 1919 (no aircraft)

83 Sqn cadre from Lympne, 15 Oct 1919;
DB 31 Dec 1919 (no aircraft)

22 Sqn cadre from Ford Junction, 20 Nov 1919;
DB 31 Dec 1919 (no aircraft)

Frensham Great Pond

51°09'17"N/00°47'30"W, SU845402. 1 mile due S of Frensham, 4 miles S of Farnham

THE large 'pond' at Frensham was used for hydro-aeroplane experiments by the Royal Aircraft Factory at Farnborough during 1913.

Hurst Park,
London Borough of Kingston-upon-Thames

51°24'31"N/00°21'38"W, TQ140692. Due S of Garrick's Eyot, on edge of River Thames, 1 mile NW of Hampton Court railway station

HURST PARK was opened as a racecourse in 1890, which made it an ideal location from which to operate aircraft. The course was occupied by the military in 1916, when it was requisitioned as an Examination Ground and Aircraft Park for the RFC on 27 May. From its opening, the park took delivery of BE.2Es built by British & Colonial and Ruston Proctor, and DH.5s built by Darracq.

Under the command of Southern Aircraft Depot on 1 January 1917, Aircraft Park, Hurst Park, came under the Central Aircraft Depot ten days later, only to be closed down completely on 27 January, with all duties transferred to the Aircraft Erection Park at Lympne. On 22 December 1917 the site was closed to flying, and by January 1918 Hurst Park was under the control of Southern Group Command, later transferred to SE Area in November.

No 7 (MT) Stores Depot was then formed at Hurst Park on 7 February 1918, but was redesignated No 1 (MT) Depot on 7 March 1918. An MT School of Instruction was also formed here in 1918, as was 11th Brigade (Independent Force) on 29 September. The Brigade was supposed to leave for France on 31 October, but instead was disbanded at Hurst Park on 15 November.

The RAF departed from Hurst Park in 1919 and the site continued to operate as a racecourse until its final meeting in 1962.

Kenley Common,
London Borough of Croydon

51°18'09"N/00°05'42"W, TQ329576. Current Kenley Airfield, 0.75 miles SW of Upper Warlingham railway station, 1.5 miles SSE of Kenley

THE vital role Kenley played during the Battle of Britain, possibly only overshadowed by Biggin Hill, has thankfully been recognised by English Heritage and the Croydon and Tandridge councils, who both designated this site a conservation area in 2006.

Kenley's long and continuous career began in early 1917 when 174 acres of land on Kenley Common was requisitioned as an AAP. The common was cleared of trees and scrub by the Canadian Forestry Corps and in June 1917 the AAP was opened on the aerodrome, which measured 1,350 by 850 yards. Construction was still under way when the AAP opened, and as a temporary measure eighteen Bessonneau hangars were erected on the western side of Hayes Lane (since moved further west for the later airfield). Fourteen 1918-pattern GS Sheds (170 by 100 feet) were eventually constructed for the AAP, which was renamed 7 (Kenley) AAP on 12 October 1917. Kenley was also classified as an Experimental Station from June 1917, with a specialist photographic unit in residence, although the Photographic Experimental Section was not formed until May 1918.

The AAP was a hive of activity and aircraft were accepted from Croydon Assembly (Handley Page), Short Brothers (DH. 9), Holland, Hannen & Cubitt (DH.9), Sopwith Aviation (Dolphin and Salamander), Darracq Motor & Engineering (Dolphin), Hooper (Camel), Vickers, Crayford (SE.5), D. Napier (RE.8), and Whitehead (DH.9). The AAP not only carried out acceptance of new aircraft but also delivery work, erection, general testing and the installation of specialist instruments and guns.

A wide variety of units continued to pass through Kenley during the late war and post-war period and the airfield was

Pranged Bristol F.2B Fighter H1400 has already been part salvaged at Kenley, with its mainplanes removed.

one of the chosen few retained by the RAF. The site was expanded, but the majority of the First World War buildings remained until 1940, when the Luftwaffe destroyed several of the original GS Sheds. At least one was extant until the late 1970s, when vandals saw fit to destroy one of the last pieces of the airfield's First World War history.

Kenley Common main units, 1917-20

AAP formed Jun 1917;
redesignated 9 (Kenley) AAP, 12 Oct 1917

7 (Kenley) AAP formed (from existing AAP) 12 Oct 1917;
DB 1919
(DH.9, Dolphin, Camel, RE.8, SE.5A, O/400 and Salamander)

88 Sqn from Harling Road, 2 Apr 1918;
to Capelle, 16 Apr 1918 (F.2B)

Photographic Flt from Chingford, 21 May 1918;
redesignated Photographic Experimental Section, 21 May 1918

Photography Experimental Section 21 May 1918;
DB 20 Aug 1919

108 Sqn from Lake Down, 14 Jun 1918;
to Capelle, 22 Jul 1918 (DH.9)

110 Sqn from Sedgeford, 15 Jun 1918;
to Bettoncourt, 1 Sep 1918 (DH.9)

116 Sqn from Netheravon, 27 Jul 1918;
to Feltham, 28 Sep 1918 (O/400)

91 Sqn from Tangmere, 27 Aug 1918;
to Lopcombe Corner, 7 Mar 1919 (Dolphin)

95 Sqn reformed 1 Oct 1918;
DB 20 Nov 1918 (no aircraft)

1 (Comms) Sqn from Hendon, 13 Apr 1919;
redesignated 24 Sqn, 1 Apr 1920 (DH.4, DH.9, 1½ Strutter, O/400, BE.2C, Scout, F.2B and 504)

Storage Park, Kenley, formed (ex-7AAP) 13 Sep 1919;
DB 1920

Lingfield

51°10'03"N/00°00'32"W, TQ392428. Lingfield Park Racecourse, 0.65 miles SSE of Lingfield

NEEDING virtually no preparation to change this site into an aerodrome, the racecourse was active as an HD NLG from the spring of 1916 through to October. It is most likely that Newchapel (East Grinstead) was favoured instead.

Newchapel (East Grinstead)

51°10'21"N/00°02'32"W, TQ369435. 0.75 miles NE of New Chapel, 1.5 miles W of Lingfield Park Racecourse

MOST likely a replacement for nearby Lingfield, Newchapel was opened in October 1916 as an HD NLG2 for 39(HD) Squadron. Both 50(HD) and 78(HD) Squadrons also made use of the LG. Newchapel was temporarily closed between 24 May and July 1919, and was completely relinquished on 13 August 1919.

Roehampton, London Borough of Wandsworth

51°27'26"N/00°14'49"W, TQ218746. NW of Roehampton University on edge of Roehampton Golf Club

COVERING an area of 130 acres, Roehampton Kite Balloon Training Station & School opened in 1915 to train Royal Navy and RNAS personal. RFC personnel were also trained here until the nearby Richmond Park opened in late 1915.

No 2 Balloon Section, RNAS, was formed in 1915 until it was redesignated No 1 Balloon Training Wing Depot when the RAF took over in April 1918. The unit's HQ was also formed at the same time, both units remaining at Roehampton until they were disbanded in 1919.

The Kite Balloon Experimental Park was formed in December 1918, but this was later amalgamated with the Balloon Testing Section at Richmond Park, and was then moved out to Fulham. The final unit to serve here was No 1 Free Balloon School, which arrived from Hurlingham on 31 January 1919 but was disbanded by September. Presumably Roehampton was then closed down.

Waddon (Croydon), London Borough of Sutton

51°21'35"N/00°07'03"W, TQ311639. Spitfire Business Park, off Purley Way (A23), 0.25 miles N of Croydon Tower, 0.5 miles S of Waddon railway station

WORK began on this 198-acre site, due north of Croydon (Beddington) aerodrome off Purley Way, in September 1917, but progress was slower than expected thanks to poor weather and a lack of steel. Despite this, the site was opened as National Aircraft Factory No 1 in October under the management of Holland, Hannen & Cubitt. On 18 January 1918 the impressive frontage of the factory for the use of the offices was opened, and manufacturing began in March 1918, but the factory was not fully completed until 13 July. The first of 241 DH.9s built here was rolled out on 9 March 1918, and 3,000 CC-type interrupter gears were also made here before the war's end.

Looking north across the ADC factory at Waddon, with Purley Way and Stafford Road junction in the distance.

The Aircraft Disposal Company (ADC) took over several National Aircraft Factories after the war, including Waddon. These ex-military DH.9s are being refurbished for the civilian market.

NAF No 1 was redesignated as No 3 National Aircraft (Salvage) Depot from 9 January 1919, handling the familiar DH.9 and several O/400s. The depot was closed down by late 1919. Today the entire office section of the factory, a building 240 feet long, is extant along the edge of Purley Way, and a 60,500 sq ft section of the building survives to the rear off Queensway and Hawker Road.

Wimbledon Common

51°26'08N/00°15'00"W, TQ220720. Close to Great War memorial, SW of Kingston University, 2 miles WSW of Southfields underground station

OPENED in 1914, this site in the north-west corner of Wimbledon Common occupied 40 acres and measured 600 by 350 yards. The LG was available to all aircraft, but it was not until 1918 that it was classified as an NLG3 and allocated to 141(HD) Squadron, whose HQ was at Biggin Hill. It was most likely closed down by the Armistice, and definitely by March 1919, because 141 Squadron left for Tallaght.

SUSSEX

Arlington (Hailsham)

50°51'N/00°11'W, TQ542066. 3 miles W of Hailsham, 3 miles NW of Polegate railway station

OPENED in December 1916, Arlington was initially allocated to 78(HD) Squadron based at Hove. An NLG3 at first, the airfield was reclassified as an NLG1 on 31 January 1917 and again as a DLG1 on 14 April. Following 76(HD) Squadron's move to Sutton's Farm, Arlington was transferred to 39(HD) Squadron on 14 September 1917. The LG was no longer used and was closed in 1919.

Blackboys (Uckfield)

50°57'34"N/00°09'04"W, TQ512203. 1 mile WSW of Blackboys, 2.4 miles E of Uckfield town centre

78(HD) Squadron's most inland LG was located near the Sussex village of Blackboys. Designated as an HD NLG2, Blackboys was only open from December 1916 until August 1917.

Chichester (Shopwhyke)

50°51'37"N/00°45'26"W, SU875075.
Chichester/Goodwood Aerodrome and Motor Racing
Circuit, 1.75 miles NE of Chichester city centre

DESTINED to become one of the most famous Battle of
Britain stations during the Second World War, Chichester
first saw aviation in January 1917. Classified as an HD NLG1,
the only occupant was 78(HD) Squadron and its BE.2Cs from
Hove. 39(HD) Squadron also briefly used Chichester until it
was closed down in later 1917.

Cobnor

Aerodrome: 50°48'53"N/00°52'36"W, SU792023. 0.2
miles due N of Cobnor Point, 2 miles E of Thorney
Island airfield (Baker Barracks)
Seaplane School: 50°48'53"N/00°52'36"W, SU792019.
Cobnor Point

THIS was the location of a private aerodrome and Seaplane
School for the use of Wells Aviation Company Limited
during 1918.

Crawley

51°06'11"N/00°13'28"W, TQ241351. NE of Bewbush
Manor (now redeveloped as housing), 1.7 miles WSW
of Crawley

THIS HD NLG1 was only in existence for a few weeks
during January and February 1917 for 78(HD) Squadron.
It is possible that the site suffered from flooding problems
owing to two streams that were fed from Bewbush Pond (now
Ifield Mill Pond) to the north-west.

Earnley

50°45'38"N/00°50'39"W, SZ815963. 0.5 miles E of
Bracklesham, 3 miles NW of Selsey

EARNLEY did not open as a DLG2 until 1918 under the
control of SACCDB at Gosport and for 78(HD)
Squadron. A 45-acre site measuring 600 by 400 yards, Earnley
was closed down in August 1919.

Eastbourne (The Crumbles)

Slipways: 50°46'52"N/00°18'52"W, TQ632005. Behind
Sovereign Centre off Royal Parade, Eastbourne
Factory: 50°47'38"N/00°19'10"W, TQ635019.
St Anthony's Hill, 1.75 miles SW of Pevensey Bay

THE Eastbourne Aviation Co Ltd built seaplane slipways
at The Crumbles in February 1913, which remained in use
until early 1920.

Eastbourne (St Anthony's Hill)

50°44'26"N/00°18'18"W, TQ625016. NE of Lottbridge
Drove (A2290) and NW of Seaside/St Anthony's
Avenue (A259), 1.75 miles NE of Eastbourne

NOT the most ideal of locations for an early aerodrome,
owing to a myriad of drains in an area known as Willingdon
Level, Eastbourne was opened in December 1911 for the use of
the Eastbourne Aviation Co Ltd, owned by Major Frederick
Bernard Fowler, which remained until August 1914. The
company also established a flying school from January 1912, as
did the Fowler Flying School, again until the outbreak of war.

The RNAS took over the site in August 1914, and in April
1915 formed the Preliminary Flying School with a variety of
aircraft. On the formation of the RAF on 1 April 1918 the school
was redesignated as 206 TDS, and by this time the site occupied

An Eastbourne Aviation Company-built Biplane at Eastbourne in 1914.

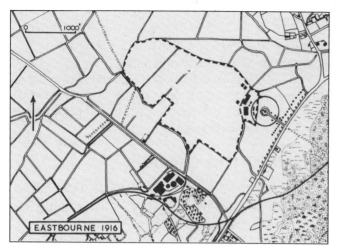

EASTBOURNE 1916

242 acres and measured 2,000 by 1,000 yards. Two Aeroplane Sheds (179 by 59 feet and 69 by 69 feet) had been built, together with six Bessonneaus running in a line off St Anthony's Avenue, and three more on the edge of Lottbridge Drove. The TDS operated up to seventy-two aircraft, mainly 504s and Camels, and was tasked with single-seat fighter training, with up to 120 officer and 60 NCO pupils at any one time. The TDS grew even larger when, together with 54 TS from Castle Bromwich, it was absorbed into 50 TDS in July 1918.

After the Armistice 50 TDS was steadily wound down until it was disbanded in October 1919, and handed back to Major Fowler in 1920, including all of the buildings placed there by the military. A licence was issued for civilian flying to return, but this only lasted until December, and Eastbourne was closed down in 1921 and returned to agriculture. Aerodrome-related buildings slowly disappeared from the site, and today, thanks to it being inhabited, the original First World War guard room is the only remnant, located in Leeds Avenue (50°47'26"N/00°18'28"W).

Eastbourne main units, 1914-19

RNAS Preliminary Flying School formed Apr 1915; redesignated 206 TDS, 11 Apr 1918 (various aircraft)

206 TDS (ex-RNAS FS) 1 Apr 1918; absorbed into 50 TDS, 15 Jul 1918 (DH.6, Camel, Pup and 504)

154th Aero Sqn, USAAC, from Chattis Hill, Apr 1918; to Flower Down, 30 Aug 1918

54 TS from Castle Bromwich, 6 Jul 1918; absorbed into 50 TDS, 15 Jul 1918 (DH.6, Camel, Pup and 504)

50 TDS (ex-54 TS) formed 15 Jul 1918; to Manston by Oct 1919 (DH.6, F.2B, Camel and 504J/K)

158 Sqn nucleus flight formed (attached to 50 TDS) Sep 1918; to Upper Heyford, 4 Sep 1918

Ford (Ford Junction/Yapton)

50°49'02"N/00°35'54"W, SU988029. Off B2233, 0.75 miles E of Yapton, on W side of later Ford airfield

THE first of two airfields by the name of Ford was opened in March 1918 as a training squadron station. While under the charge of the RAF, only two units, 148 and 149 Squadrons, both with FE.2Bs, ever passed through the unit in wartime. The latter unit had departed for France by June 1918, but this did not stop the airfield expanding into a complex well-facilitated site with a generous number of hangars, including seven 1918-pattern GS Sheds (170 by 100 feet) and two aeroplane stores, one as an ARS. The site occupied 145 acres and measured 950 by 850 yards.

In September 1918 the unit was passed to the USAAC and the same month the 92nd Aero Squadron (equipped with Farman F.20s), the 140th Aero Squadron (with equally antiquated BE.2Cs) and the 326th Aero Squadron (with DH.4s) made Ford their home until November 1918. Plans were already in place for the erection and operation of American-built Handley Page O/400s by the USAAC, including specially built sheds, but the war was over before work commenced. However, at least ten sets of O/400 components where sent from National Aircraft Factory No 1 at Waddon.

Throughout late 1918 several RAF units returning from France, Belgium and Greece passed through Ford to be disbanded, until the airfield was closed down in 1920. It was reactivated in 1930 when Dudley Watt Aviation renovated a pair of the original hangars. While this venture came to nothing, aviation never left and the military returned in 1936. By the Second World War the airfield had expanded to incorporate the vast majority of the First World War infrastructure. However, the Luftwaffe flattened several of the early hangars during a devastating attack on 18 August 1940, although the remainder survived until at least the late 1960s, and the First World War area of the airfield was still easy to see during the 1980s. Today this area of Ford is now housing, while it is only a matter of time before the later site is swallowed up as well.

This is Ford aerodrome during the early 1930s, when it was being leased by the Ford Motor Company in an effort to increase sales of its Trimotor airliner. Virtually all of the First World War infrastructure remains intact.

Ford main units, 1918-19

148 Sqn from Andover, 1 Mar 18;
to St Omer, 20 Mar 1918 (FE.2B/D)

149 Sqn formed 3 Mar 1918;
to Marquise, 2 Jun 1918 (FE.2B/D)

92nd Aero Sqn, USAAS, from USA, Sep 1918;
to Tangmere, 15 Nov 1918 (Farman F.20)

140th Aero Sqn, USAAS, formed Sep 1918;
to Tangmere, 15 Nov 1918 (BE.2C)

326th Aero Sqn, USAAS, formed Sep 1918;
to Tangmere, 15 Nov 1918 (DH.4)

Night Bombardment Training School (USAAC) formed Sep 1918;
DB 15 Nov 1918

144 Sqn (cadre) from Mudros, 15 Dec 1918;
DB 4 Feb 1919

215 Sqn from Alquines, 2 Feb 1919;
DB 18 Oct 1919 (O/400)

97 Sqn from St Inglevert, 4 Mar 1919;
en route to India, 19 Jul 1919 (O/400 and DH.10)

115 Sqn (cadre) from St Inglevert, 4 Mar 1919;
DB 18 Oct 1919

50 TS formed Jul 1919;
DB 6 Dec 1919 (504K)

22 Sqn from Spich, 1 Sep 1919;
DB 31 Dec 1919 (F.2B)

Goring-by-Sea

50°49'16"N/00°25'02"W, TQ115035. Centre of aerodrome would have been close to current Field Place First School and The Orchards Community Middle School, 0.4 miles NW of Durrington-on-Sea railway station

CONSTRUCTION work began on a new TDS for the USAAS in August 1918, but with the arrival of the Armistice in November, and the site far from complete, all work was halted. With a typical range of Aeroplane Sheds, a Handley Page Shed and an ARS all planned, the site occupied 168 acres and would have measured 910 by 900 yards.

Hooe (Bexhill)

50°50'54"N/00°23'27"W, TQ684081. SE of New Lodge Farm, dissected by A259, 0.9 miles SSW of Hooe

HOOE had a short career as an LG, beginning in December 1917 when it served 39(HD) Squadron as an HD NLG2. Reclassified as an NLG3 and DLG3 on 31 March 1917, 39(HD) Squadron's tenure was taken over by 78(HD) Squadron until the site was closed down in mid-1918.

Lower Beeding (Horsham)

51°02'05"N/00°14'56"W, TQ228276. Approximately 3.5 miles from Horsham railway station

THIS 69-acre HD NLG2 and DLG1 was opened in January 1917 for the use of 78(HD) Squadron based at Hove with the BE.2C and BE.12. 39(HD) Squadron also made use of the LG, which measured 880 by 530 yards and closed down on 13 August 1919.

Middleton-on-Sea (Sands)

Manufacturer's aerodrome: 50°47'25"N/00°36'19"W, SU982001. On beach due S of Elmer, 0.6 miles from Middleton-on-Sea centre, 3.2 miles WSW of Littlehampton
Seaplane slipways: SZ982997

THIS stretch of sand was regularly used by White & Thompson Ltd and later Norman Thompson for test-flying their seaplanes and flying-boats. It is quite possible that the site was used from 1912, but it is officially credited as in use from 1915 to 1919, when the company was liquidated and taken over by Handley Page.

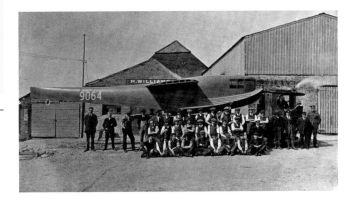

Staff of the Norman Thompson Flight in front of NT.4 No 9064 at the Middleton factory. Following a sudden change in RNAS requirements, which resulted in the cancellation of twenty N.T.4As, combined with continuous problems with the N.T.2B's engines, the company went into receivership on 19 April 1918. Liquidated in July 1919, the company's remaining assets were bought by Handley Page Limited. *Via Stuart Leslie*

Newhaven (Tide Mills)

50°47'00"N/00°03'49"W, TQ455002. Tidemills, between Mill Creek and Seaford Bay, 0.6 miles SE of Newhaven Harbour railway station

NEWHAVEN was overlooked by the military until February 1917, when enemy U-boat activity became unrestricted. Following a survey along the South Coast, a 5-acre section of shingle foreshore was selected despite the top of the beach being 15 feet above the normal high-tide level. Two concrete bases were laid for one Type-G Seaplane Shed (180 by 60 feet) and one Seaplane Shed (120 by 50 feet). The men's living quarters were Army huts on piles behind the hangars, while officers were accommodated at Bishopstone, and the Tidemill was used as a mess. The usual collection of huts made up the main station's technical buildings, although three old railway carriages also served as offices and a crewroom. Because of the high tide fall, the station's two slipways were 150 yards long so that they could reach the water's edge at low tide.

RNAS Newhaven opened as a seaplane station and a kite balloon station in May 1917, the first main unit being the War Flight equipped with four Short 184s, increased to six by the end of the year. By early 1918 the site was expanded by a further 6 acres to the north-east, to an area known as the drill ground, which was large enough to be employed as an LG. In May 1918 the War Flight became 408(S) Flight, and in July gained a few Campanias. A typical patrol for a Short 184 could be anything up to 5 hours, and these where flown between Dungeness and the Isle of Wight, paying particular attention to any Allied convoys.

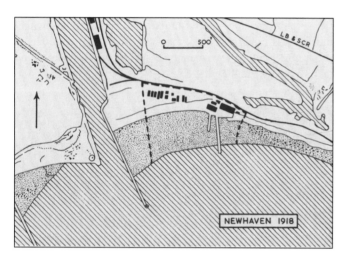

NEWHAVEN 1918

Sightings of U-boats were rare, but on 7 July Lt E. M. Ackery and his observer Lt Dangerfield could not believe their eyes when one surfaced below them, after failing to hit the lead ship of a convoy with its torpedo. Lt Ackery turned to attack, by which time the German crew began to scramble back into the conning tower, only moments before Lt Dangerfield dropped a 112lb bomb within 5 feet of the hull. Despite a huge explosion and oil left on the surface, the U-boat managed to escape.

409(S) Flight was formed on 15 August 1918, also equipped with the 184. At the same time 242 Squadron, which now controlled 408 and 409 Flights, was also formed at Newhaven, also being responsible for 513(SD) Flight operating the DH.6, which had formed at Chickerell on 7 June. Anti-submarine patrols continued right up to the Armistice, but 409 Flight was the first to be disbanded in late November. 242 Squadron and 408 Flight soldiered on until they were also disbanded on 15 May 1919. Newhaven was closed down in the autumn and all buildings were sold by auction in 1920.

Today a large area of concrete still remains, once the bases to the two large Seaplane Sheds. The beginnings of the two long slipways can also be seen, now extending just a few feet towards the sea.

Pett (Hastings)

50°54'14"N/00°40'28"W, TQ881150. Between Pannel Farm and Factory Wood, 5.5 miles NE of Hastings town centre

THIS small LG was active from December 1916 through to August 1918, the only recorded user being 50(HD) Squadron. Designated as an HD NLG3, a 53rd Wing survey in 1918 recorded the LG as being 300 yards wide.

Polegate (Wilmington/Eastbourne)

50°48'38"N/00°14'30"W, TQ581035. Sheds were due SE of Willingdon Community School, 1 mile S of Polegate

THIS Class C Airship Station was opened on 6 July 1915 for the use of non-rigid airships operated by the RNAS and later the RAF. Accommodation was provided for 14 officers and 137 enlisted men, and at first at least three SS-Type non-rigid airships were stationed here. The site was dominated by two large sheds (323 by 70 by 60 feet and 317 by 69 by 50 feet) on a technical site that was accessed from Wannock from the west, and Lower Willingdon from the east. The entire site took up 142 acres and measured 970 by 830 yards. Polegate also had two sub-stations at Slindon and Poole (Upton).

The Airship Wing was formed at Polegate in December 1918 and remained until at least 1 May 1919. It is presumed that the site was closed down not long afterwards.

Ringmer

50°53'58"N/00°04'03"W, TQ455131. 0.3 miles E of Broyle Side village, 0.75 miles NE of Ringmer village

RINGMER served as a temporary LG for the use of aircraft from RNAS Eastbourne during late 1915 and possibly early 1916. During this period 'B' Flight of the Preliminary Aeroplane School carried out manoeuvres with the SW Mounted Brigade, and it is most likely that this was the most activity the site experienced. A survey was carried out in March 1916 for potential use as an NLG for the RFC, but this plan was not carried through.

Rustington

50°48'29"N/00°29'58"W, TQ058020. Centre of aerodrome would have been close to Priory Hospital, 0.7 miles SW of Angmering railway station

IT is now very hard to imagine an aerodrome being located here today, but in mid-1917 159 acres of land was requisitioned between the then villages of Rustington and East Preston. Measuring 717 by 1,033 yards, this DLG was only used by aircraft from Gosport that were engaged for local gunnery practice.

Re-surveyed in 1918, Rustington was chosen as one of several sites for a three-unit TDS for the USAAC operating O/400s. Thirty-two acres of the site were covered in the usual technical and domestic buildings, including six Handley Page single and twin Aeroplane Sheds (225 by 75 feet), a Handley

Page erection and repair shed (408 by 75 feet), and a single ARS Shed (180 by 100 feet). However, before this extensive site was completed the Armistice arrived and all work was halted. The part-built site then languished until October 1919, when the buildings were sold off and the aerodrome returned to fields.

Rye

50°57'05"N/00°45'04"W, TQ936194. Off Camber Road, N of Northpoint Beach, 1 mile E of Rye railway station

CLASSIFIED as an NLG3, Rye measured 150 by 580 yards and was open from March until at least November 1918.

Shoreham (Brighton/Hove/Worthing)

50°50'04"N/00°17'33"W, TQ202055. Current Shoreham (Brighton City) Airport, 0.75 miles W of Shoreham-by-Sea railway station

THE aviator Harold Piffard first drew attention to a flat area of land west of the River Adur and north of the Shoreham to Lancing railway line in 1910. On 20 June 1911 a large aerodrome of 191 acres, measuring 1,100 by 650 yards, was opened, and on 25 May 1912 the Sussex Aero Club Ltd was formed here under agreement with the site's owners, Brighton/Shoreham Aerodrome Ltd. Prior to the official opening Shoreham had already been placed on the aviation map when it was used in the Brooklands to Brighton air race, won by Gustav Hamel in May 1911. Several flying schools, including Shoreham's own, the Chanter Flying School and the Avro Flying School, were using this large aerodrome from 1912. A dozen Aeroplane Sheds (three 130 by 80 feet, three 50 by 45 feet, and six 45 by 45 feet) were built along the southern boundary alongside the railway line.

The RFC took over Shoreham in August 1914, but it was not until January 1915 that 3 TS moved in from Netheravon, and was destined to remain until July 1918. Training was the main occupation here for the bulk of the war, pilots being churned out with only a few hours under their belts before being dispatched to France. The SE Area FIS was formed here in July 1918 to train flying instructors of varying abilities using the Avro 504. The FIS was closed down in March 1919, but Shoreham remained in military hands, becoming the home to a large number of Canadians from Upper Heyford in the shape of 1 Squadron CAF equipped with SE.5As. This unit was disbanded in February 1920, leaving just a Packing Section, which was closed down in December 1921.

Shoreham was not quiet for long, as civilian aviation returned in 1923. Following another period of military occupation during the Second World War, this picturesque airfield has grown from strength to strength.

Shoreham main units, 1915-20

3 TS from Netheravon, 21 Jan 1915;
DB 15 Jul 1918 (various aircraft)

14 Sqn formed 3 Feb 1915;
to Hounslow, 11 May 1915 (Longhorn)

21 TS formed 22 May 1916;
to Abbassia, Jun 1916 (Maurice Farman)

86th Aero Sqn, USAAS, arrived 25 Mar 1918;
to France, 11 Aug 1918 (no aircraft)

SE Area FIS formed 1 Jul 1918;
DB 31 Mar 1919 (504, SE.5A, Pup, Camel and M.1C)

82 Sqn cadre from Bertangles, 15 Feb 1919;
to Tangmere, May 1919 (FK.8)

123 Sqn from Upper Heyford, 31 Mar 1919;
DB 5 Feb 1920 (DH.9A)

81 Sqn/1 Sqn CAF from Upper Heyford, Mar 1919;
DB 1 Feb 1920 (SE.5A)

A Maurice Farman S.11 Shorthorn at Shoreham in 1915. Several early units operated this type here.

Slindon

50°53'07"N/00°38'48"W, SU952104. Near Nore Wood, 1 mile NE of Eartham, 4.5 miles NW of Arundel

SERVING as a sub-station for Polegate, Slindon was brought into use in 1918 under the command of Capt E. L. D. Batley. With moorings for a three SS-Type airships, long anti-submarine patrols over the Channel were carried out from here, including one in *SSZ28* that lasted for 26hr 30min. Nore Folly to the south of the wood was used as a wireless station and, like the clearing where the airships were moored, still remains today.

Southbourne (Emsworth)

50°51'10"N/00°54'58"W, SU763065. Between A27 to N and Chichester to Southampton railway line, due W of Bourne Community College, 0.75 miles NW of Southbourne

CONSTRUCTION of a new TDS to train three American squadrons with the Handley Page 0/400 began in early 1918. The generous site north-west of Southbourne occupied 247 acres and measured 1,300 by 966 yards. All essential services were in place by August, when work began on the construction of seven Handley Page Sheds (222 by 75 feet), a single ARS Shed (172 by 100 feet) and a pair of aeroplane stores.

The site was planned to be completed by 1 November, but as the Armistice passed it was clear that Southbourne would not be ready. Whether it was fully completed is not clear, but it certainly was never occupied, and the entire infrastructure was auctioned off in 1919. The flying ground has remained free from development ever since and only the college on the eastern boundary has encroached on the original site.

Stonegate (Ticehurst)

51°01'57"N/00°22'55"W, TQ671286. 0.3 miles E of Stonegate, N of Cottenden Road

THIS HD NGL3 served 78(HD) Squadron from November 1916 to March 1917.

Tangmere

50°50'53"N/00°42'32"W, SU911060. Site of ex-RAF Tangmere, 3 miles ENE of Chichester

ON 25 September 1917 200 acres of land was requisitioned south of the village of East Hampnett for the construction of a new aerodrome. By the beginning of 1918, with the site nearing completion, it was decided to allocate it, now named Tangmere, to the USAAS for use as a TDS.

The site measured 1,000 by 950 yards, and by mid-1918 seven GS Sheds (170 by 80 feet) and a single Handley Page Shed (330 by 90 feet) were reaching an advanced stage of construction. Both 91 and 92 Squadrons passed through Tangmere before the first USAAS unit arrived in July 1918. More USAAS units followed, but by the time 61 TDS had established itself the war was already over. Many units returned from France as cadres during early 1919, the majority of them to disband here.

Closed down in 1920, the Air Ministry retained the site and by 1926 RAF Tangmere was reactivated and would remain a busy airfield until it was finally closed down in 1970. The site's rich Second World War history has overshadowed its early incarnation, but thanks to the resident Tangmere Military Aviation Museum the spirit lives on.

Tangmere main units, 1918-19

91 Sqn from Chattis Hill, 15 Mar 1918;
to Kenley, 27 Aug 1918 (various aircraft)

92 Sqn from Chattis Hill, 17 Mar 1918;
to Bray Dunes, 2 Jul 1918 (Pup and SE.5A)

163rd Aero Sqn, 'D' Flt, USAAS, by 17 Jul 1918

92nd Aero Sqn, USAAS, from Ford, 15 Nov 1918;
departed 22 Nov 1918

140th Aero Sqn, USAAS, from Ford, Nov 1918

326th Aero Sqn, USAAS, from Ford, Nov 1918

40 TS from Croydon, 14 Dec 1918;
redesignated 61 TDS, 15 Dec 1918 (504 and Camel)

61 TDS (ex-40 TS) 15 Dec 1918;
redesignated 61 TS, 20 Jun 1919 (504, Camel and F.2B)

14 Sqn cadre from Salonika, 1 Jan 1919;
DB 4 Feb 1919 (no aircraft)

41 Sqn cadre from Halluin, 7 Feb 1919;
to Croydon, 8 Oct 1919 (no aircraft)

40 Sqn cadre from Orcq, 13 Feb 1919;
DB 4 Jul 1919 (no aircraft)

148 Sqn cadre from Serny, 17 Feb 1919;
DB 4 Jul 1919 (no aircraft)

32 Sqn cadre from Serny, 4 Mar 1919;
to Croydon, 8 Oct 1919 (no aircraft)

82 Sqn cadre from Shoreham, May 1919;
DB 30 Jun 1919 (no aircraft)

61 TS (ex-61 TDS) 20 Jun 1919;
DB Dec 1919 (504K)

84 Sqn cadre from Eil, 12 Aug 1919;
to Croydon, 8 Oct 1919 (no aircraft)

207 Sqn from Hangelar, 22 Aug 1919;
to Croydon, 8 Oct 1919 (no aircraft)

Telscombe Cliffs (Newhaven)

50°47'51N/00°00'17"W, TQ407016. E of Ambleside Avenue, NW of Peacehaven Community School, 2.4 miles W of Newhaven

ESTABLISHED in response to increasingly deeper Zeppelin raids across the South East of England, Telscombe Cliffs opened as an HD NLG in late 1916. Occupying 50 acres and measuring 550 by 500 yards, the LG's first occupant was a detachment of BE.2Cs and BE.12s from 78(HD) Squadron in November 1916, although a detachment 50(HD) Squadron is also credited with being here at a similar time. Bessonneau hangars protected the aircraft, while airmen either slept under canvas or a few lucky ones were accommodated in the local

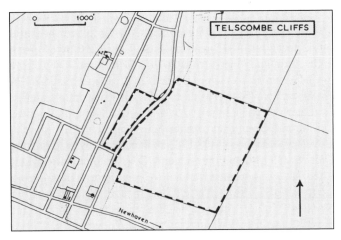

village. Not one Zeppelin ventured close to Telscombe during 78(HD) Squadron's tenure and the unit left for Sutton's Farm in September 1917. In the meantime some expansion took place when 13 AAP was formed on 7 June 1918; later redesignated 13 (Telscombe) AAP, the unit was closed down by 10 March 1918.

A change of role came in the spring of 1918 when the aerodrome, which had been downgraded to an ELG since 78(HD) Squadron's departure, was upgraded to a Marine Operations (Aeroplane) Station when 514(SD) Flight was formed with six DH.6s on 7 June 1918. Two Aeroplane Sheds (120 by 60 feet) were erected in place of the Bessonneaus, a new access road was built, a guard hut near the entrance was expanded into a mess, and several Armstrong huts were erected. Unit strength rose to 12 officers, 5 SNCOs and 30 other ranks, who faithfully maintained the DH.6s for their anti-submarine duties along the South Coast. 514(SD) Flight became part of 242 Squadron – whose HQ was down the road at Newhaven from August 1918 – with little effect on the routine that the flight was already performing. The Flight was disbanded on 20 January 1919 and Telscombe Cliffs was closed down soon afterwards. The site has seen been erased from the map and is now under the town of Peacehaven.

Telscombe Cliffs main units, 1916-19

50 Sqn detached from Dover (Swingate Down), 1 Oct 1916; to Harrietsham, 1916 (BE.2C, BE.12 and ES.1)

78 Sqn detached from Newhaven and later Hove, 1916; to Sutton's Farm, Sep 1917 (BE.2C/E and BE.12)

13 AAP formed 27 Aug 1917; redesignated 13 (Telscombe)AAP, DB 10 Mar 1918

514 (SD) Flt formed 7 Jun 1918; absorbed into 242 Sqn, 15 Aug 1918 (DH.6)

242 Sqn (ex 408, 409 and 514 Flts) formed Aug 1918; DB 15 May 1919 (DH.6)

Thakeham (Billingshurst)

50°58'07"N/00°24'16"W, TQ120199. E of Ingram's Furze, E of Sincox Lane, 2.4 miles NNW of Ashington

THIS small HD NLG1 and DLG was established for the use of 39(HD) and 78(HD) Squadrons between March 1917 and February 1918.

WARWICKSHIRE/ WEST MIDLANDS

Birmingham (Adderley Park)

52°28'52"N/01°51'36"W. In region of Birmingham Wheels Raceway, S of railway line

HOME of Wolseley Motors Ltd, a subsidiary of Vickers Ltd, approximately 240 BE-type aircraft and 450 SE.5As were built at Adderley Park during the war. The site covered 23 acres and it is presumed that the factory's own LG was located to the south of the railway line.

Castle Bromwich

52°31'00"N/01°47'23"W, SP144911. Area now known as Castle Vale, bounded by railway lines to S and E, 4 miles NE of Birmingham city centre

FAMOUS for its colossal aircraft production during the Second World War, which included nearly 12,000 Spitfires, there is barely a trace of its existence today, other than a few aeronautically names roads.

Originally open playing fields, Alfred Maxfield flew his own aeroplane from here in November 1909, followed by B. C. Hucks, who demonstrated a Blériot on the same fields in 1911. Castle Bromwich was also used as a turning and stopping point for many air races before the war, including the *Daily Mail* London to Manchester event in June 1914. The site was requisitioned by the War Office in August 1914, and by May 1915 a reserve and training squadron station was established here; the first unit, 5 RAS (later RS & TS) was formed on the 5th.

From May to October 1916 Castle Bromwich was classified as an HD Flight Station, then as an HD NLG1 and DLG for the use of 38(HD) Squadron, and later 90(HD) Squadron until mid-1919. By 1917 the site occupied 262 acres and measured 1,700 by 900 yards and was being prepared as an AAP. Expansion included six 1915-pattern Flight Sheds (210 by 65 feet)and one 1916-pattern GS Shed (170 by 80 feet) to serve the new AAP, a pair of Handley Page Sheds (280 by 150 feet) and twenty-one storage sheds (200 by 60 feet). 14 (Castle Bromwich) AAP did not open until 1 July 1918, tasked with the erecting, testing and delivering of Handley Page O/400s, supplied by the Metropolitan Wagon Co Ltd and the Birmingham Carriage Co Ltd. SE.5s built by the Austin Motor Co Ltd were also handled by the AAP, which remained at Castle Bromwich until it was wound down to a cadre and moved to Shrewsbury (Monkmoor) in April 1920. By March the site had been virtually de-requisitioned by the RAF, but the future of Castle Bromwich was bright, the aerodrome remaining active until 1954; the site closed down for good on 1 April 1958.

Castle Bromwich main units, 1915-19

5 TS formed 11 May 1915;
to Wyton, 12 Dec 1917
(Shorthorn, Longhorn, BE.2C/E, BE.12 and DH.8)

19 Sqn formed 1 Sep 1915;
to Netheravon, 31 Jan 1916 (various aircraft)

34 Sqn formed 12 Jan 1916;
to Lilbourne, 15 Jun 1916 (G.3, BE.2C/E)

54 Sqn formed 15 May 1916;
to London Colney, 22 Dec 1916 (BE.2C, BE.12 and 504)

28 TS formed 1 Jun 1916;
DB into 42 TDS, 15 Jul 1918 (504, Scout and 1½ Strutter)

55 Sqn formed 8 Jun 1916;
to Lilbourne, 10 Jun 1916 (BE.2C)

38 Sqn reformed 14 Jul 1916;
to Melton Mowbray, 1 Oct 1916 (BE.12)

34 TS formed 1 Nov 1916;
to Ternhill, 13 Nov 1916 (various aircraft)

43 TS formed 2 Nov 1916;
to Ternhill, 13 Nov 1916 (various aircraft)

71 Sqn formed 27 Mar 1917;
to St Omer, 18 Dec 1917 (Camel)

67 TS formed 3 Jun 1917;
to Shawbury, 11 Jun 1917 (various aircraft)

7 TDS 'C' Flt formed 15 Oct 1917;
to Feltwell, 1 Nov 1917

74 TS from Netheravon, 1 Dec 1917;
to Tadcaster, 27 Jun 1918 (Pup, 504 and Camel)

54 TS from Harlaxton, 12 Dec 1917;
to Eastbourne, 6 Jul 1918 (various aircraft)

55 TS reformed 15 Jan 1918;
to Lilbourne, 1 Feb 1918 (Camel, SE.5A and 504)

49th Aero Sqn, USAAC, from USA, 1 Feb 1918;
to France, 24 Jun 1918 (no aircraft)

14 (Castle Bromwich) AAP formed 1 Jul 1918;
to Shrewsbury (Monkmoor) as cadre, Apr 1920

115 Sqn from Netheravon, 17 Jul 1918;
to Roville-sur-Chênes, 29 Aug 1918 (various aircraft)

132 Sqn from Ternhill, 19 Aug 1918;
DB 23 Dec 1918 (various aircraft)

9 Sqn cadre from Ludendorf, 30 Jul 1919;
DB 31 Dec 1919 (no aircraft)

Coventry (Radford)

52°25'35"N/01°30'39"W, SP333810. King Automotive Systems Ltd now occupies part of area of original factory, rest now under houses E of Cheveral Avenue, Radford

THIS large manufacturer's aerodrome for the Daimler Motor Co Ltd occupied 208 acres and measured 1,050 by 1,000 yards. The site opened as an Examination Ground in 1916 and was steadily expanded into an AAP by early 1917. The site was extensive with two wooden Aeroplane Sheds (60 by 42 feet), one 1915-pattern Flight Shed (210 by 65 feet), eight Aeroplane Sheds (four 200 by 53 feet and four 170 by 84 feet), and sixteen storage sheds that were GS Sheds (170 by 80 feet) configured as three trebles and two coupled units.

Later designated as 1 (Coventry) AAP, the unit accepted new aircraft from local manufacturers such the RE.8 from the Coventry Ordnance Works Ltd, the Standard Motor Co Ltd, the Daimler Co Ltd, and the Siddeley-Deasy Motor Car Co Ltd. The DH.9 was accepted from the Vulcan Motor & Engineering Co Ltd, the SE.5 from Wolseley Motors Ltd, and the Pup from Standard Motors. The AAP handled thousands of aircraft for the RFC and later RAF until it was closed down in 1919.

Coventry (Radford) main units, 1916-20

Aeronautical Inspection, Coventry, formed by Apr 1916;
became 1 AAP, 22 Mar 1917 (BE.2C/D, BE.12, RE.7 and Pup)

1 AAP formed 22 Mar 1917;
redesignated 1 (Coventry) AAP, 12 Oct 1917

1 (Coventry) AAP (ex-1 AAP) 12 Oct 1917;
DB 1919

Packing Case Section formed 4 Oct 1918;
DB 1919

Storage Park formed 1919;
DB after June 1920

King's Heath (Billesley)

52°25'25"N/01°52'08"W, SP090806. E of Yardley Wood Road, due S of Billesley Primary School, 1.2 miles SE of King's Heath

THE aerodrome has its roots in the Birmingham Aero Club, which moved its HQ from 62 Albion Street to Billesley Farm, Yardley Wood Road, King's Heath, in 1911. Also the home of the Midland School of Flying, the military requisitioned the site in April 1916 as an HD NLG 2 for the use of 38(HD) Squadron until mid-1918.

Knowle (Widney Manor)

52°23'20"N/01°45'43"W, SP163768. Bordered by Browns Lane, Smiths Lane and Widney Manor Road, 0.7 miles SE of Widney Manor railway station

THIS was an HD NLG that served 38(HD) and 54(HD) Squadrons (both formed at Castle Bromwich) from April through to the autumn of 1916, by which time both units had moved out of the area.

A few years before Lilbourne became an aerodrome, the same area was used for aerial manoeuvres in 1913, during which 3 Squadron, among others, brought its sole BE.3, No 203.

Lilbourne

52°22'28"N/01°11'16"W, SP554753 (aerodrome) and SP553763 (domestic site). W of Roman Road (A5), S of 'The Meadows', 1 mile SW of Lilbourne, 2.75 miles E of Rugby railway station

THE village of Lilbourne from which this aerodrome took its name is located in Northamptonshire, but the main aerodrome site lay to the west of the old Roman Road and as such resides in Warwickshire. Opened in June 1915, the 115-acre site, which measured 800 by 600 yards, was first occupied by a detachment from 54 Squadron on the 5th, from Castle Bromwich. The aerodrome was classified as a TSS and Flying School from March 1916, and an HD NLG1 for the use of 38(HD) Squadron, also from Castle Bromwich. By this time three 1915-pattern Flight Sheds (210 by 65 feet) had been built on the aerodrome site, and a large domestic site off the Roman Road between Rugby Road and Hillmorton Lane was becoming established, not to mention a small site north of the Rugby Road.

By late 1917 Lilbourne began to feel more like a training station as 59 and 71 TS arrived from Netheravon in December, and 55 TS moved in from Castle Bromwich, all flying a wide variety of aircraft. All of the TS units had moved out by June 1918, allowing Lilbourne to take its final and most important role since opening. On 17 June the Midland Area SoSF was formed here to train pupil instructors in a wide range of skills. The school was twice the size of similar units, with eighteen instructors on strength training up to fifty-four pupils in an intensive course that lasted for two weeks. Pupil instructors were taught the art of telephone communications between pupil and instructor, all rules, and manoeuvres in which a potential instructor might find himself once in the hands of an inexperienced pupil pilot, not normally taught at a TDS. Potential instructors were either creamed off from the TDS or were more experienced pilots returning from overseas postings.

Up to thirty-eight Avro 504Js were used by the school, which was later redesignated as the Midland Area Flying Instructors School from 1 July 1918. As the year progressed

the school also gained a number of other aircraft, including the Snipe, DH.4/9 and F.2B, before it was transferred to Feltwell on 22 April 1919, and Lilbourne was returned to agriculture by late 1920.

The aerodrome today is much as it was, while the large domestic site on the eastern side of the Roman Road is completely covered by a Nightowl Truckstop.

Lilbourne main units, 1916-19

54 Sqn detached from Castle Bromwich by 5 Jun 1916 (BE.2C and BE.12)

55 Sqn from Castle Bromwich, 10 Jun 1916;
to Fienvillers, 6 Mar 1917 (BE.2C, FK.3, 504K and DH.4)

34 Sqn from Beverley, 15 Jun 1916;
to Allonville, 10 Jul 1916 (BE.2C/E)

44 RS formed 2 Nov 1916;
to Harlaxton, 13 Nov 1916 (504, RE.7 and DH.4)

84 Sqn from Beaulieu, 22 Mar 1917;
to Liettres, 23 Sep 1917
(Nieuport 12, JN.4, 504, 1½ Strutter and SE.5A)

73 Sqn from Upavon, 10 Jul 1917;
to St Omer, 9 Jan 1918 (Camel)

71 TS from Netheravon, 10 Dec 1917;
to Netheravon, Feb 1918 (BE.2C and Camel)

59 TS from Netheravon, 16 Dec 1917;
to Rendcomb, 1 Feb 1918 (various aircraft)

55 TS from Castle Bromwich, 1 Feb 1918;
to North Shotwick, Jul 1918 (Camel, SE.5 and 504)

10 TS Shawbury 7 Apr 1918;
to Gosport, 25 Jun 1918 (various aircraft)

Midland Area SoSF formed 17 Jun 1918;
redesignated Midland Area FIS, 1 Jul 1918 (504J)

Midland Area FIS (ex-Midland SoSF) formed 1 Jul 1918;
to Feltwell, 22 Apr 1919 (504J/K, Snipe, DH.4, DH.9 and F.2B)

Meriden

52°26'05"N/01°38'10"W, SP237819. SW of village next to disused quarry pits, 4 miles ESE of Birmingham Airport

THIS small HD NLG2 and DLG was used by 38(HD) Squadron based at Melton Mowbray and later Buckminster between April 1916 and August 1918.

Smethwick

52°30'23"N/01°58'00"W, SP022901. W of Halford Lane opposite West Bromwich Albion football ground, 3.7 miles NW of Birmingham New Street railway station

A MANUFACTURER'S LG for the Birmingham & Midland Carriage Co, located 400 yards to the east in Middlemore Lane, Handsworth, Smethwick was an area of open land west of Halford Lane. The company was awarded a contract for 100 de Havilland DH.10s (only sixty of which were actually built) and 140 Handley Page O/400s. The site is now covered by sports facilities and industry.

Stretton-under-Fosse (Rugby)

52°26'11"N/01°20'46"W, SP445822. Between Fosse Way (B4455) and Main Street (B4027), W of Stretton-under-Fosse

A SHORT-LIVED NLG for the use of 38(HD) Squadron between October 1916 and June 1917, Stretton-under-Fosse occupied approximately 50 acres and measured 500 by 300 yards.

Whitley Abbey (Coventry)

52°22'56"N/01°29'23"W, SP347761. Jaguar Land Rover Ltd, Engineering Centre, Abbey Road, 0.75 miles NW of Midland Air Museum

CONSTRUCTION of an AAP began on land south-west of Whitley, north of the River Sowe, in the spring of 1918. The site, which occupied 177 acres and measured 800 by 600 yards, was still under construction when it opened in July as a storage AAP. Hangars were four GS Sheds coupled, and a pair of GS Sheds (170 by 80 feet) also coupled, together with several Bessonneaus. The site was never fully completed, but at its peak 428 aircraft were stored here before construction work on the site was halted in December 1918.

The site was bought by Sir John Siddeley in late 1923, and during the late 1920s through to the 1930s large numbers of Armstrong Whitworth aircraft, including the Whitley bomber, were built here. Armstrong Whitworth concentrated its activities at Baginton and Bitteswell from the 1940s, but Whitley Abbey continued to be used for missile development work until the 1950s. Today the site has been erased by the substantial Jaguar Land Rover factory, although one early test shed (140 by 130 feet) is still extant on the eastern side of the factory site.

Whitley Abbey is seen not long after Armstrong Whitworth purchased the site in the early 1920s. The large shed, set an angle to the furthest set of GS Sheds, survives today.

A Farman biplane being put through its paces at the Dunstall Park meeting in 1910.

Wolverhampton (Dunstall Park Racecourse)

52°36'15"N/02°08'36"W, SJ903007. Current Dunstall Park Racecourse, 1.25 miles from Wolverhampton city centre

AFTER months of build-up, the first all-British flying meeting was organised at Dunstall Park, Wolverhampton, between 27 June and 2 July 1910. The event was arranged by the Midland Aero Club, whose headquarters was located at the Grand Hotel, Birmingham, and the club president was the Earl of Dartmouth. The week's events included a bomb-throwing competition with a first prize of £100, and a special prize for the aviator flying for the longest duration, another £100 being available to the winner. The Lord Plymouth Prize was for the competitor who completed three laps of a special circuit laid out within Dunstall Park in the fastest time, and the Earl of Plymouth would present the trophy to the winner. Another challenge was the Sir John Holder Prize, awarded to the competitor who achieved the highest flight.

Competitors began arriving from 6 June, and six wooden hangars had been erected by the Midlands Aviation Syndicate (the company running the meeting). The event attracted great names of the day including Charles Rolls, one partner of the

fledgling Rolls Royce, and Claude Grahame-White, one of the great British aviation pioneers. Ten budding aviators were listed to take part in a variety of aircraft including Blériot, Humber and Lane, together with locally built Star and Hartill monoplanes. Other types included Farman, Short-Wright and Roger Sommer Biplanes, as well as a Macfie Empress, Short S.27 and Howard Wright Avis.

WEST YORKSHIRE

Catterick

54°22'00"N/01°37'14"W, SE248969. Current Marne Barracks, off A1, 0.5 miles S of Catterick, 5.3 miles SE of Richmond

UNDOUBTEDLY influenced by the location of the huge Catterick Garrison (aka Richmond and Catterick Camp), located 4 miles to the west, work began on the aerodrome, south of the town of Catterick, in late 1914. Constructed as a training squadron station, the first resident was 14 TS, which was formed on 12 January 1915. The aerodrome, which covered 240 acres and measured 1,600 by 770 yards, took on a dual role when it also became an HD NLG for 33(HD) Squadron.

Avro 504K D2059 of 49 TDS is seen after crashing onto a hut at Catterick in 1918.

The core purpose of the aerodrome was to train pilots, and to achieve this Catterick was designed to accommodate a pair of TSs. Each had three 1915-pattern Flight Sheds (210 by 65 feet), which were later joined by one 1916-pattern GS Shed (170 by 80 feet) and one 1918-pattern GS Shed (170 by 100 feet). On the northern side of the site the MT section operated from a pair of Bessonneau hangars.

By late 1916 Catterick became an HD Flight Station for 'C' Flight, 76(HD) Squadron, and its eight Avro 504s, which took over one of the 1915-pattern sheds from October. Throughout 1917 more TSs were formed, with the resident 14 TS usually providing the nucleus for the new units. 14 TS made way for 46 and 52 TS, which in turn were disbanded

into 49 TDS in July 1918. This unit was tasked with carrying out day bombing training and was equipped with thirty-six Avro 504s and the same number of DH.4s and/or DH.9s. 49 TDS remained until it was disbanded on 10 March 1919, then, unlike many other aerodromes after the war, Catterick was retained by the RAF more for its location and facilities, as flying did not fully return until 1927.

The site remained RAF Catterick until 1994, when it was handed over to the Army and renamed Marne Barracks. Three and half of the original 1915-pattern sheds still survive on the site.

115 squadron was formed on 1st December 1917 at Catterick, during the following year it operated the HP Type O/400, moving to France in late August 1918. © Inkworm.com

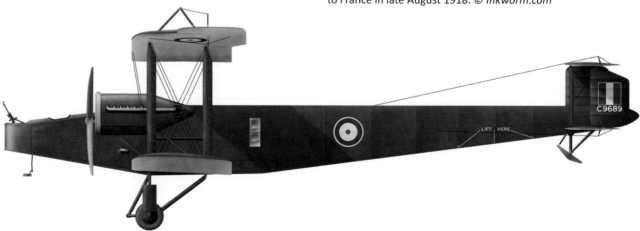

Catterick main units, 1915-19

14 TS formed 12 Jan 1915; to Bramham Moor (Tadcaster),
23 Jul 1917 (Shorthorn, Longhorn, Martinsyde, 504 and BE.2C)

6 TS from Montrose, 27 Nov 1915;
to Montrose, 24 Nov 1917 (various aircraft)

44 Sqn formed (nucleus from 6 TS) 15 Apr 1916;
to Turnhouse, 18 Apr 1916 (various aircraft)

53 Sqn formed (nucleus from 14 TS) 15 May 1916;
to Farnborough, 11 Dec 1916 (FK.3, 504 and BE.12)

37 TS formed 2 Nov 1916;
to Brattleby, 13 Nov 1916 (various aircraft)

52 TS from Cramlington, 18 Jan 1917;
to Stirling, 18 Mar 1917
(BE.2B/C/E, DH.4, 504, RE.8 and Elephant)

83 (Canadian) TS formed (nucleus from 14 TS) 9 Feb 1917;
to Beverley, 9 Mar 1917 (no aircraft)

52 TS from Cramlington, 18 Jan 1917;
to Stirling, 18 Mar 1917 (various aircraft)

88 (Canadian) TS formed (nucleus from 14 TS) 15 Mar 1917;
to Canada, 16 Apr 1917 (no aircraft)

68 TS formed (nucleus from 14 TS) 7 Apr 1917;
to Bramham Moor (Tadcaster), 14 Apr 1917 (various aircraft)

46 TS from Tadcaster, 23 Jul 1917;
DB into 49 TDS, 15 Jul 1918 (DH.1, FE.2B/D)

89 Sqn formed (nucleus from 6 TS) 24 Jul 1917;
to Harling Road, 1 Aug 1917 (various aircraft)

76 Sqn 'C' Flt formed 10 Oct 1916;
to Tadcaster as cadre, 10 May 1919 (BE.2C/E and BE.12/B)

69 TS formed (nucleus from 14 TS) 1 Oct 1917;
to Cramlington, 10 Oct 1917 (various aircraft)

107 Sqn formed (nucleus from 46 TS) 8 Oct 1917;
to Stonehenge, 18 Oct 1917 (various aircraft)

52 TS from Montrose, 24 Nov 1917;
DB into 49 TDS, 15 Jul 1918
(BE.2B/C/E, DH.4, 504, RE.8 and Elephant)

115 Sqn formed 1 Dec 1917;
to Netheravon, 15 Apr 1918 (various aircraft)

118 Sqn formed 1 Jan 1918;
to Netheravon, 15 Apr 1918 (various aircraft)

127 Sqn formed 1 Jan 1918;
DB into 49 TDS, 4 Jul 1918 (various aircraft)

166th Aero Sqn, USAAS, from USA, 25 Mar 1918;
to Delouze, 7 Aug 1918 (DH.4)

49 TDS (ex-46 and 52 TS) formed 15 Jul 1918;
DB 10 Mar 1919 (DH.4, DH.6, DH.9, 504, RE.8 and FK.8)

Coal Aston (Greenhill) (formerly Derbyshire)

53°19'26"N/01°28'02"W, SK355808. S/SE of Meadowhead School and Norton College in region now known as Batemoor and Jordanthorpe

IN late 1915 work began to prepare an LG south of Norton Lane and west of Jordanthorpe House for the use of 33(HD) Squadron. By February 1915 the site was opened as an HD Station and RFC NLG, occupying 203 acres and measuring 1,800 by 600 yards. 'A' Flight of 33(HD) Squadron was the first to make use of the LG, joined by a detachment of 47(HD) Squadron in March and a further detachment of 33(HD) Squadron in April. The latter moved out to Brattleby (Scampton) on 2 October 1916 as Coal Aston was being prepared for a new role.

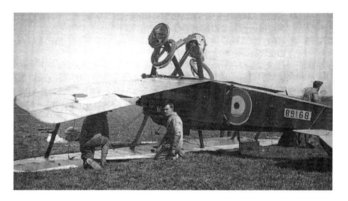

It is not certain whether the incident in which Camel B9168 ended up on its back took place at Coal Aston, but the aircraft was certainly repaired by 2 (Northern) ARD, as were many others.

From December 1916 the site quickly expanded to become the home of the Northern ARD Depot. Hangars began to appear in the shape of two 1915-pattern Flight Sheds (210 by 65 feet), four Aeroplane Sheds (160 by 75 feet), one salvage shed (150 by 150 feet), and one general shed (130 by 30 feet). The site by early 1917 had spread itself across six separate camps, including the LG itself. The ARD, which handled the RE.8, all FKs, BE.12, FE.2B, 1½ Strutter, a variety of Fleet machines and Scouts, occupied the northern part of the LG south-west of Jordanthorpe House, extending to north of Dychelane Farm. Further to the south-west was the Engine Repair Section, which handled R.A.F. 4A and BHP-type aero engines, and to the north, across Norton Lane, was a substantial Stores Depot. Large MT Sections and a Salvage Section capable of handling all aircraft salvage from the North of England were also present. Three domestic camps, to the south and south-west of Little Norton, were made up of two male camps and one female to accommodate the nearly 2,000 other ranks and close to 800 women who were working at this vibrant station.

The ARD was redesignated as 2 (Northern) ARD on 12 October 1917 until it was disbanded on 31 October 1919. Personnel from the ARD retained a presence until August 1920 and the site was not fully closed down until late 1921.

Coal Aston main units, 1916-19

33 Sqn 'A' Flt from Filton, Feb 1916;
to Tadcaster, 29 Mar 1916 Tadcaster (BE.2C and BE.12)

47 Sqn detached from Beverley, Mar 1916;
DB Apr 1916 (various aircraft)

33 Sqn detached from Tadcaster, Apr 1916;
to Brattleby, 2 Oct 1916 (BE.2C and BE.12)

Northern ARD Depot formed Dec 1916;
absorbed into Northern ARD, 28 Apr 1917

Northern ARD HQ from Bradford, 28 Apr 1917;
redesignated 2 (Northern) ARD, 12 Oct 1917

2 (Northern) ARD (ex-NARD) 12 Oct 1917;
DB 31 Oct 1919

The multiple sets of Bessonneau hangars at Roundhay Park appear to comprise two outer rows with four hangars apiece and the centre row with six. *www.loedis.net*

Farsley

53°48'40"N/01°40'54"W, SE210350. In region of Fairfield School, next to A6120, 1.5 miles NW of Pudsey

ONLY in service from April 1916 until 31 March 1917, Farsley was an NLG3 allocated to 33(HD) and 76(HD) Squadrons.

Leeds (Roundhay Park)

53°50'17"N/01°29'45"W, SE329375. Military Field/Sports Grounds, E of Princes Avenue, 3.1 miles NE of Leeds railway station

THE Blackburn Aeroplane & Motor Co Ltd was formed in June 1914 with a working capital of £20,000 and three premises. These were workshops at Benson Street, off North Street, Leeds, disused stables at 18 Spencer Place, Balm Road, and the Olympia Works in a disused skating rink in Roundhay

One of fifty DH.9As built by Mann Egerton at Norwich, J570 is pictured within one of the multiple Bessonneau hangars during the RAF Aircraft Exhibition at Roundhay Park in May 1919. Sopwith Camel D9564, in the background, previously served with 34 TDS at Scampton. *www.loedis.net*

Park. The latter, which used the neighbouring park as an LG, produced 111 BE.2Cs, 186 Sopwith Babys and a pair of AD Scouts under contract during the war. Blackburn also built several of its own designs, including nine Twin Blackburns, one Triplane, two GP Floatplanes and twenty Kangaroo anti-submarine patrol bombers. The Olympia Works remained open until 1930, when Blackburn transferred to Brough.

In May 1919 the RAF Aircraft Exhibition descended upon Roundhay Park from Newcastle (Town Moor). Three multiple sets of Bessonneau hangars were erected in the north-eastern corner of the park for the exhibition, which closed in July and all exhibits were moved to Tadcaster.

Manywells Height (Cullingworth)

53°48'57"N/01°54'07"W, SE066355. Due E of Hewenden Reservoir, 5 miles from Bradford railway station

AN HD NLG3 and DLG were opened at Manywells Heights (named, incorrectly, Manywell Heights in original RFC and RAF documents) in April 1916, for the use of 'B' Flight of 33(HD) Squadron, whose main operating base was Tadcaster. When the unit moved to Gainsborough, the LG, covering 40 acres and measuring 550 by 420 yards, was taken over by 76(HD) Squadron from Ripon with a variety of BEs and RE.8s. The site was relinquished on 26 June 1919.

Middleton

53°44'52"N/01°31'59"W, SE308280. On sports ground near council offices, 0.6 miles E of Middleton centre, 2.75 miles E of Morley town centre

OPENED in April 1916 for the use of 33(HD) Squadron based at Gainsborough, Middleton was an HD NLG 3, but was later reclassified as an HD NLG2 on 31 March 1917. 76(HD) Squadron took over from Ripon and occasionally used the LG until the summer of 1918.

Phoenix Aerodrome

53°47'26"N/01°43'43"W, SE186340. Hubert Street, Leeds Road, Bradford, 1.3 miles ESE of Bradford city centre

THIS manufacturer's aerodrome was located next to the Phoenix Dynamo Company works in Bradford from January 1916 to 1919.

Pontefract Racecourse

53°42'04"N/01°19'57"W, SE441229. Current racecourse, 1.2 miles NW of Pontefract town centre

MAKING full use of the area within Pontefract Racecourse, this site could boast 174 acres with a usable landing area measuring 1,300 by 800 yards. First opened in April 1916 as an HD NLG2 for 33(HD) Squadron, the site was reclassified as an NLG3 from January 1917. The racecourse was later used by 76(HD) Squadron and was relinquished in June 1919.

Seacroft (Winn Moor)

53°49'27"N/01°27'42"W, SE355365. Due N of Seacroft Shopping Centre, 1.5 miles ESE of Roundhay

SEACROFT was one of three LGs placed around the city of Leeds, although it was the most basic example of an NLG. It was established for the use of 'B' Flight, 33(HD) Squadron, during the unit's tour of duty at Tadcaster, which lasted from March to October 1916.

A pair of Felixstowe F.3s are about to embark on the 60-mile journey to Brough, where they will assembled and flight-tested.

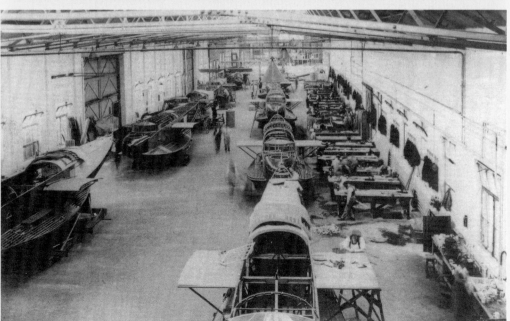

Felixstowe F.3s are under construction by the Phoenix Dynamo Company in Hubert Street, Bradford.

Sherburn in Elmet

53°47'11"N/01°13'35"W, SE512326. Current Sherburn in Elmet airfield, WWI technical area now covered by trading estate, 0.9 miles NE of South Milford

THE first of two airfields constructed at Sherburn in Elmet was opened in 1917 for the use of 76(HD) Squadron operating out of Ripon, but its use appears to have been infrequent at best. By early 1918 the site began to come alive as it had been chosen as an AAP and Storage Section. The aerodrome was expanded to 177 acres, measured 1,100 by 700 yards, and was furnished with eight 1918-pattern GS Sheds with Esavian doors (170 by 100 feet) together with twenty-one storage sheds (200 by 60 feet). The site also became a manufacturer's aerodrome for Blackburn, which built 162 Sopwith Cuckoos here, the first of which, N6950, made its maiden flight in May 1918. The AAP was active from that year, as was 2 (Northern) MAD Stores Section, which was formed in 1918. A storage detachment was formed in 1919, by which time this large and expensive aerodrome was relinquished, then closed down in 1920.

The buildings did not go to waste, however, nor did the flying field, which was taken over by the Yorkshire Aero Club in 1926, later moving to Yeadon in 1931. Blackburn also built aircraft during the Second World War, including 1,700 Swordfish. Aviation continues at this historic site in the shape of the Sherburn Flying Club, which operates from three grass strips, one of which runs adjacent to the Second World War concrete runway.

WILTSHIRE

Boscombe Down (Red House Farm)

51°09'47"N/01°44'46"W, SU178404. Current MoD Boscombe Down, 1.6 miles SE of Amesbury

KNOWN as Red House Farm until 6 October 1917, Boscombe Down was opened as a TDS the previous August. A large unit from the outset, the main resident was 6 TDS, which was created from three flights donated by 82 Squadron at Waddington, 83 Squadron at Spittlegate and 59 TS at Yatesbury. Occupying 333 acres and measuring 1,250 by 1,000 yards, facilities at first revolved around eleven Bessonneau hangars on the western edge of the aerodrome. These were later complemented and eventually replaced by seven 1918-pattern GS Sheds (170 by 100 feet); these were also used by 11 and 14 TDS, which arrived in November 1918. On average there were now up to seventy-two aircraft on the aerodrome, made up of Avros, DH.4s and DH.9s. Personnel strength was 52 officers, 90 officer pupils, 90 NCO pupils, 49 SNCOs, 26 JNCOs, 336 other ranks, and 215 women. 6 TDS was the last flying unit to serve here when it disbanded on 15 May 1919. A Storage Section was formed in 1919, and this was the final resident when the site was closed down in March 1920.

The site was left to languish until the military returned in 1927, taking over the First World War hangars and buildings that remained. Later home to many RAF units, Boscombe

Photographed by a 98 Squadron DH.9 from Old Sarum on 24 February 1918, this view of Boscombe Down shows eight Bessonneau hangars and at least eleven aircraft of 6 TDS. *Via Stuart Leslie*

Down is best known for being the home of the A&AEE and the ETPS, and today is run by QinetiQ. Two GS Sheds, coupled together, survive today, surrounded by an array of modern buildings.

Boscombe Down main units, 1917-19

6 TDS formed from nucleus flights from Waddington ('A' Flt), Spittlegate ('B' Flt) and Yatesbury ('C' Flt) 12 Oct 1917; DB 15 May 1919
(BE.2, BE.12, 504, DH.4, DH.6, DH.9, FK.8 and Pup)

161st Aero Sqn, USAAS, by 17 Jul 1918

188th Aero Sqn, USAAS, by 17 Jul 1918

11 TDS from Old Sarum, Nov 1918;
to Beaulieu, Apr 1919
(DH.4, DH.6, DH.9, BE.2, 504, Pup and Dolphin)

14 TDS from Lake Down, Nov 1918;
DB Mar 1919 (DH.6, DH.9 and 504)

Brigmerston Down

51°13'23"N/01°42'49"W, SU210476. 2.5 miles SW of Tidworth

OPENED as an LG for the CFS at Upavon, this remote LG was later used as a bombing range. Under the control of the Bombing Ground Section, 4th Wing, 7(Training) Group, which was established at Brigmerston on 11 October 1918, the area remained a range until April 1919.

Druid's Lodge, then HQ 33 Wing, is in the foreground, and there is a glimpse of the southern side of Lake Down aerodrome across the road, including all twelve Bessonneau hangars.

Codford

51°10'08"N/02°03'09"W*, ST971411*. Possibly due N of Codford St Peter, W of Green Road

THIS was another LG that was used for a just a few weeks during the closing stages of the war, and appears not to have warranted any details about its exact location and size. The 43rd Aero Squadron, USAAS, arrived here from South Carlton on 14 October 1918, but took its DH.4s to France one week later. Another American unit, the 23rd Aero Squadron, USAAS, also equipped with DH.4s, arrived from Duxford on 5 November 1918 and left for France six days later. The only infrastructure at this temporary LG would have been tented accommodation.

* Both positions approximate

Earl's Farm Down

51°10'28"N/01°44'17"W, SU184415. 0.75 miles NNE of Boscombe Down airfield, 1.75 miles E of Amesbury

BELIEVED to have been the location of a DLG, there is some doubt as to its true identity, which could have been the original name for Boscombe Down. It is also possible that it served as an LG for nearby Netheravon or Upavon.

Lake Down

51°08'58"N/01°51'15"W, SU105389. E and W of A360, with aerodrome over road from Druid's Lodge, 6 miles NNW of Salisbury

BUILT as a TDS and TSS from the outset, Lake Down was established in 1917 with the formation of 2 TDS of 15 August. Like most TDSs, the unit was formed from three other units, namely 'A' Flight, 35 TS from Northolt, 'B' Flight, 19 TS

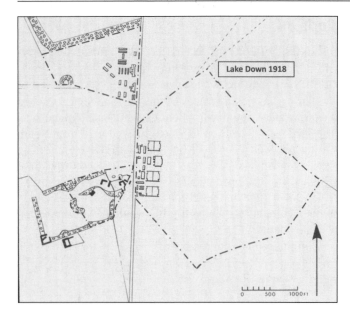

Lake Down 1918

from Hounslow, and 'C' Flight, 9 TS from Norwich. Equipped with the DH.4, BE.2E, RE.8 and FK.8, this busy training unit quickly brought Lake Down to life, occupying land on both sides of the Devizes to Salisbury road, from Druid's Lodge to the southern tree line of The Park on the western side, and a flying field that extended eastwards towards Westfield Farm.

The site occupied 160 acres and measured 950 by 880 yards, and among the many smaller technical and domestic buildings constructed there were seven 1917-pattern GS Sheds (170 by 100 feet) that would have dominated the skyline. 2 TDS made the short move to Stonehenge on 2 December 1917 to be replaced at Lake Down by 107, 108 and 109 Squadrons, which moved out of Stonehenge with DH.9s. Only 107 Squadron left Lake Down to fight in Northern France in June 1918, while 108 Squadron left for Kenley the same month, and 109 Squadron was disbanded here in August.

In the meantime, 14 TDS was formed on 6 June 1918, tasked with carrying out day bomber training, the dominant type once again being the DH.9. To cope with the number of aircraft now on station, which averaged no fewer than seventy-two, at least a dozen Bessonneau hangars were erected along the southern boundary. In June 1919 14 TDS was redesignated 14 TS, by which time the main equipment was the 504K. In September 1919 the unit was disbanded, and the aerodrome

closed down in 1920. Lake Down had been under the control of the 33rd Wing from 30 August 1917, whose HQ was formed at 2a Winchester Street, Salisbury, on 30 August 1917. The HQ moved to Druid's Lodge on 5 January 1919 and remained until it was disbanded on 15 May.

Today the flying field to the east of the A360 is undisturbed, although there is little sign of military occupation. However, the water tower on the edge of the A360 was part of the Larkhill military light railway, built in 1914, which would have served Lake Down during its existence.

Lake Down main units, 1917-19

2 TDS formed 15 Aug 1917;
to Stonehenge, 2 Dec 1917 (DH.4, BE.2E, RE.8 and FK.8)

107 Sqn from Stonehenge 2 Dec 1917;
to Le Quesnoy, 5 Jun 1918 (DH.9)

108 Sqn from Stonehenge, 2 Dec 1917;
to Kenley, 14 Jun 1918 (DH.9)

109 Sqn from Stonehenge, 2 Dec 1917;
DB 19 Aug 1918 (DH.9)

136 Sqn formed 1 Apr 1918;
DB 4 Jul 1918 (various aircraft)

14 TDS formed 6 Jun 1918;
redesignated 14 TS, Jun 1919 (DH.6, DH.9, 504, BE.2E and BE.12)

201 Sqn from Bethencourt as cadre, 17 Feb 1919;
to Eastleigh, 2 Sep 1919 (no aircraft)

14 TS (ex-14 TDS) formed Jun 1919;
DB Sep 1919 (504K)

Larkhill

51°11'28"N/01°47'47"W, SU141438. 0.9 miles ESE of Larkhill, 1.6 miles NW of Amesbury

ONE of the oldest aerodrome sites in Britain, Larkhill was first used by Horatio Barber in 1909 and C. B. Cockburn for aeronautical experiments. The site was then purchased by the British & Colonial Aeroplane Co Ltd in June 1910, giving the company good access for potential military aircraft sales. It was used as a control point during the *Daily Mail* Round

This pre-war view shows Larkhill with the Bristol Aeroplane Company sheds and several examples of its early machines in the foreground. The five sheds closest the camera survive today and thanks to a Grade II listing in 2005 should remain for the foreseeable future.

Britain Air Race in July 1911, and the Military Aeroplane Competition was held here in August 1912.

The military first arrived on 1 April 1911 when 2 (Aeroplane) Company Air Battalion, Royal Engineers, was formed. Coupled and treble Aeroplane Sheds had already been erected, but with the arrival of the military a total of twelve Aeroplane Sheds were built at Larkhill, as well as several ancillary buildings.

3 Squadron was also formed from a detachment of 2 (Aeroplane) Company on 13 May 1912. It had a typically eclectic mix of machines including the Henry Farman III, Avro Type E, Bristol Boxkite, Deperdussin Monoplane, Nieuport Monoplane, Bristol-Prier Monoplane and BE.3. 3 Squadron moved to Netheravon on 16 June 1913, and in 1914 the aerodrome was closed down to make way for garrison buildings. The only military unit to serve here during the war was the 154th Aero Squadron, USAAS, whose personnel stayed from 9 to 19 March 1918, before leaving for Lopcombe Corner.

Today five of Bristol's original sheds still survive on Woods Road, which follows the same line where all twelve were originally placed. Believed to be the oldest surviving military aerodrome buildings in the country, these excellent structures were Grade II listed in 2005.

Market Lavington

51°16′46″N/01°57′39″W, SU028535. On Gibbet Knoll, 1.2 miles E of Market Lavington, 5 miles SSE of Devizes. NB: Located in active 'Danger Area'

AN RAF LG opened here in 1918 and was only used by local artillery co-operation squadrons until its closure in June 1919.

Netheravon

51°14′30″N/01°45′57″W, SU165493. Current Airfield Camp, Netheravon, 4.5 miles N of Amesbury

IN 1912 the recently formed Air Battalion of the Army (soon to be renamed the RFC) occupied several unused cavalry school buildings east of Netheravon. Work began on the construction of fifteen 1912-pattern Aeroplane Sheds (70 by 65 feet), and the gallops to the east made a reasonably good LG. 4 Squadron from Farnborough was the first resident on 14 June 1913, followed two days later by 3 Squadron from Larkhill. Twelve months later the entire Military Wing of the RFC descended upon Netheravon to evaluate the use of aeroplanes in the event of war, which began not long after.

From 1915 Netheravon became a training squadron station, which later helped to form a large number of RFC squadrons. Hangarage increased from 1915 with a pair of Flight Sheds (210 by 65 feet) and a single Handley Page Shed (200 by 106 feet), and a twin Aeroplane Shed (two 100-by-53-foot units) was added. By then the site occupied 283 acres and measured 2,270 by 520 yards. The aerodrome also served as an annex for the CFS, a major training school and the home of 8 and 12 TDS, formed here on 1 April 1918. Both of these units were intended for Handley Page O/400 training but, as well as an establishment of twenty O/400s apiece, both TDSs operated up to sixty Avros and thirty-six FE-types. 12 TDS was completely disbanded on 15 May 1919, while 8 TDS was redesignated 8 TS, which in turn

Maurice Farmans, Blériots and BE-types at Netheravon during a pre-war concentration camp of the entire Military Wing of the RFC just before the conflict began.

Netheravon main units, 1913-19

4 Sqn from Farnborough, 14 Jun 1913;
to Eastchurch, 24 Jul 1914 (various aircraft)

3 Sqn from Larkhill, 16 Jun 1913;
to Dover (Swingate Down), 13 Aug 1914 (various aircraft)

5 Sqn from Farnborough, 28 May 1914;
to Gosport (Fort Grange), 6 Jul 1914
(Sopwith Three-Seater, RE.1 and Tabloid)

6 Sqn from South Farnborough, 21 Sep 1914;
to Farnborough, 4 Oct 1914 (BE.8, BE.2A and F.20)

7 Sqn detached from Farnborough, Sep 1914;
to Farnborough, Oct 1914 (various aircraft)

7 Sqn from Farnborough, 24 Oct 1914;
to St Omer, 8 Apr 1915 (Avro Type E and FB 'Gun Carrier')

1 Sqn from Brooklands, 13 Nov 1914;
to St Omer, 7 Mar 1915 (504, BE.8 and G.3)

3 RS formed 21 Jan 1915;
to Shoreham, 21 Jan 1915 (no aircraft)

11 Sqn formed (from 7 Sqn) 14 Feb 1915;
to St Omer, 25 Jul 1915 (FB.5)

12 Sqn formed (nucleus from 1 Sqn) 14 Feb 1915;
to St Omer, 6 Sep 1915 (504 and BE.2C)

10 Sqn from Hounslow, 7 Apr 1915;
to St Omer, 25 Jul 1915 (BE.2C)

21 Sqn formed (nucleus from 8 RAS) 23 Jul 1915;
to Boisdinghem, 23 Jan 1916 (RE.7)

7 TS formed 28 Jul 1915;
absorbed into 33 TDS, 15 Aug 1918 (various aircraft)

8 TS formed 28 Jul 1915;
to Witney, 1 Apr 1918 (various aircraft)

20 Sqn formed (nucleus from 7 RAS) 1 Sep 1915;
to Filton, 15 Dec 1915 (JN.3, BE.2C and S.1)

26 Sqn formed (from South African Flying Unit) 8 Oct 1915;
to East Africa, 23 Dec 1915

32 Sqn formed (nucleus from 21 Sqn) 12 Jan 1916;
to St Omer, 28 May 1916 (ES.1 and DH.2)

19 Sqn from Castle Bromwich, 31 Jan 1916;
to Filton, 4 Apr 1916 (various aircraft0)

42 Sqn formed (nucleus from 19 Sqn) 26 Feb 1916;
to Filton, 1 Apr 1916 (BE.2D/E)

48 Sqn formed (nucleus from 7 RS) 15 Apr 1916;
to Rendcomb, 8 Jun 1916 (various aircraft)

24 RS formed 25 May 1916;
redesignated 24 TS, 1 Jun 1917 (Maurice Farman)

66 Sqn from Filton, 2 Jul 1916;
to Filton, 30 Jul 1916 (BE.2B/C/D, BE12 and 504K)

43 Sqn from Stirling, 30 Aug 1916;
to Northolt, 8 Dec 1916 (Scout, BE.2C and 1½ Strutter)

Artillery Co-operation Sqn, 'A' Flight, formed 13 Jan 1917

92 Canadian RS formed (out of 27 RS) 15 Mar 1917;
to Canada, 16 Apr 1917

24 TS (ex-24 RS) 1 Jun 1917;
to Witney, 30 Mar 1918

72 Sqn from Upavon, 8 Jul 1917;
to Sedgeford, 1 Nov 1917 (504 and Pup)

74 TS formed 21 Oct 1917;
to Castle Bromwich, 1 Dec 1917 (Pup, SE.5A, 504 and Camel)

59 TS from Beaulieu, 20 Nov 1917;
to Lilbourne, 6 Dec 1917 (various aircraft)

71 TS formed (out of 7 TS) 28 Nov 1917;
to Lilbourne, 10 Dec 1917 (BE.2E and Camel)

70 TS formed (out of 24 TS) 20 Dec 1917;
to Gosport, 20 Dec 1917 (no aircraft)

71 TS from Lilbourne, Feb 1918;
to Port Meadow, 1 Apr 1918 (BE.2E and Camel)

104th Aero Sqn, USAAS, from Upavon, 24 Mar 1918;
to Salisbury, 6 Jun 1918 (no aircraft)

97 Sqn from Stonehenge, 31 Mar 1918;
to Xaffévillers, 9 Aug 1918 (O/400)

8 TDS formed 1 Apr 1918;
redesignated 8 TS, 15 May 1919
(O/400, FE.2B, 504, Camel, DH.6 and Shorthorn)

12 TDS formed 1 Apr 1918;
DB 15 May 1919 (O/400, FE.2B, 504, DH.6 and RE.8)

115 Sqn from Catterick, 15 Apr 1918;
to Castle Bromwich, 17 Jul 1918 (O/400)

207 Sqn from Coudekerke, 22 Apr 1918;
to Andover, 13 May 1918 (O/100 and O/400)

215 Sqn from Coudekerke, 23 Apr 1918;
to Andover, 15 May 1918 (O/100 and O/400)

187th Aero Sqn, USAAS, by 17 Jul 1918

42 Sqn cadre from Abscon, 18 Feb 1919;
DB 26 Jun 1919

52 Sqn cadre from Aulnoye, 18 Feb 1919;
to Lopcombe Corner, 28 Jun 1919 (RE.8)

35 Sqn cadre from Ste-Marie-Cappel, 3 Mar 1919;
DB 26 Jun 1919

8 TS (ex-8 TDS) reformed 15 May 1919;
redesignated Netheravon Flying School, 29 Jul 1919 (504K)

Netheravon Flying School (ex-8 TS) 29 Jul 1919;
redesignated 1 FTS 23 Dec 1919 (504)

208 Sqn from Eil, 9 Sep 1919;
DB 7 Nov 1919 (Snipe)

1 FTS (ex-Netheravon FS) 23 Dec 1919;
DB 1 Feb 1931 (504, DH.9 and F.2B)

This aerial view of Netheravon, looking north-west, shows eight of the fifteen 1912-pattern Aeroplane Sheds. Six were coupled and one was a treble (extreme right).

became the Netheravon Flying School from 29 July. This unit was one of the post-war survivors and one of the main reasons why Netheravon remained in military hands when it became 1 FTS on 23 December.

Netheravon remained an active airfield, serving under Army Co-Operation Command during the Second World War and the Army Air Corps from the early 1960s. The airfield only closed down in 2012, all resident units moving to Upavon. A single 1915-pattern Flight Shed still remains close to a pair of Second World War survivors.

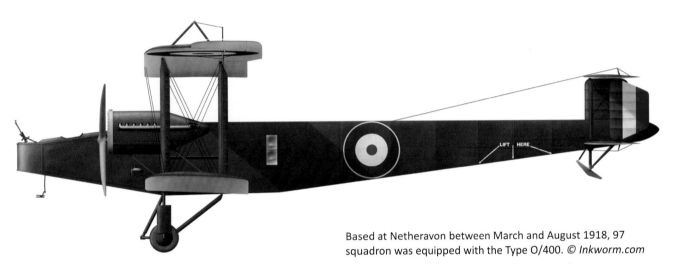

Based at Netheravon between March and August 1918, 97 squadron was equipped with the Type O/400. © Inkworm.com

Old Sarum (Ford Farm)

51°06'00"N/01°47'04"W, SU152331. Current Old Sarum Airfield/Castle Gate Business Park, off Portway, 0.3 miles NW of Ford, 2 miles NNE of Salisbury

182 ACRES of land was purchased from Ford Farm by the War Department in early 1917, the site opening as a training squadron station in August 1917. The first occupants were 98 and 99 Squadrons, which arrived from Harlaxton and Yatesbury respectively on 30 August 1917. Measuring 1,000 by 900 yards, Ford Farm aerodrome, as it was known locally, was contained south of Portway and the old Roman road. Facilities included seven 1917-pattern GS Sheds (170 by 80 feet), one of which was a single ARS Shed.

Old Sarum became the home of 11 TDS, formed on 1 April 1918 and tasked with training day bomber crews. The main equipment by this time was on average thirty-six 504s and the same number of DH.6s or DH.9s. The TDS moved to Boscombe Down in November 1918, but returned in the shape of 11 TS, which was reformed in July 1919. Old Sarum survived post-war cuts and would become the home of RAF Army Co-operation, its location close to Salisbury Plain making it ideal for this role.

Old Sarum looking north-east from an 11 TDS machine on 28 September 1918. All but the two GS Sheds in the foreground, which were destroyed by fire in 1987, survive to this day.

Old Sarum remained in RAF hands until 1971 and served on with Army until 1979. All seven GS Sheds survived until 1987, when two were claimed by fire; the remainder, together with a few First World-era buildings, are extant.

Old Sarum main units, 1917-19

98 Sqn from Harlaxton, 30 Aug 1917;
to Lympne, 1 Mar 1918 (various aircraft including DH.9)

99 Sqn from Yatesbury, 30 Aug 1917;
to St Omer, 25 Apr 1918 (BE.2E, DH.6 and DH.9)

103 Sqn from Beaulieu, 8 Sep 1917;
to Serny, 12 May 1918 (DH.9)

104th Aero Sqn, USAAS, from Upavon, Dec 1917;
to Winchester, 10 Jul 1918

124, 125 and 126 Sqn formed 1 Feb 1918;
to Fowlmere, 1 Mar 1918 (various aircraft)

11 TDS formed 1 Apr 1918;
to Boscombe Down, Nov 1918
(BE.2C, DH.4, DH.6, DH.9, Pup and 504)

104th Aero Sqn, USAAS, from Andover, Netheravon and Yatesbury, 6 Jun 1918;
to Winchester, 10 Jul 1918

School of Instruction, Southern TB, from Beaulieu, 1918;
to Andover, 10 Jun 1918 (DH.9, RE.8 and BE.2E)

23rd Aero Sqn, USAAS, from Thetford, Jul 1918;
to Codford, 5 Nov 1918

337th Aero Sqn, USAAS, from Stonehenge, 24 Jul 1917;
to Codford, 5 Nov 1918

841st Aero Sqn, USAAS, from Yatesbury, 16 Aug 1918

Artillery Co-operation Sqn from Tilshead, Nov 1918;
to Stonehenge, Aug 1919

53 Sqn cadre from Laneffe, 17 Mar 1919;
DB 25 Oct 1919

34 Sqn cadre from Caldiero, 3 May 1919;
DB 25 Sep 1919

11 TS reformed Jul 1919;
DB Mar 1920 (504K)

7 Sqn from Heumar, 21 Sep 1919;
reduced to cadre and to Eastleigh, 27 Oct 1919 (RE.8)

Rollestone Camp (Larkhill)

51°12′15″N/01°51′55″W, SU095450. Rollestone Camp, N of The Packway (B3086), 1.75 miles NE of Shrewton

STILL in military hands, Rollestone Camp opened in July 1916 for the use of 1 Balloon School of Instruction. The 180-acre site, opposite Rollestone Bake Farm, had a single Balloon Shed (100 by 36 feet) and three sheltered areas carved out of Rollestone Clump, a copse located within the camp boundary. The school trained officers as balloon observers, and subjects including artillery co-operation and map-reading. The course lasted one month and the average pupil capacity of the school was twenty-four.

The 154th Aero Squadron, USAAS, passed through Rollestone in March 1918, and in July 1919 No 2 Balloon Training Depot arrived from Richmond (Beverley Brook), only to be disbanded into 1 Balloon School. Not long afterwards the school was redesignated as 1 Balloon Training Centre, and on 16 March 1920 it became the School of Balloon Training. In 1931 the unit's name changed again to the RAF Balloon Centre. which retained a presence at Rollestone until 1939, when the whole operation was moved to Cardington.

Stonehenge

51°10′36″N/01°50′18″W, SU113420. W of Stonehenge stone circle, hemmed in by B3086 to N, A344 to W, and A303 to S, 2.65 miles W of Amesbury

WITH the famous ring of stones on the eastern boundary, from which this aerodrome took its name, work began on Stonehenge in early 1917. A near triangular-shaped site, thanks to the roads by which it was bounded, Stonehenge occupied 230 acres and measured 1,450 by 850 yards. The main technical area was located in the south-eastern corner of the aerodrome, straddling the A303. A dozen Bessonneau hangars provided cover for the aircraft at first, followed by construction of four GS Aeroplane Sheds (180 by 100 feet) and eight 'semi-permanent' Handley Page Sheds.

The first units to arrive were 107, 108 and 109 Squadrons in October and November 1917, which travelled the short distance to Lake Down on 2 December to make way for 2 TDS from Lake Down. By 5 January 1918 2 TDS was redesignated as No 1 SoN&BD, which was divided into two squadrons, one tasked with teaching crews to fly day bombers and the other night bombers. Subjects taught for the day crews including aerial navigation, flying on instruments, and formation flying, while the night course included map and compass flying by day and night, and working with vertical searchlights. Pupil throughput saw thirty pilots and forty-eight observers pass through Stonehenge every week on their respective day and night courses.

A low pass by an aeroplane of 14 TDS from Lake Down on 29 September 1918 reveals a busy flightline at Stonehenge. Considering how complex this site was, not even the smallest scar on the landscape is left today.

A Handley Page O/100 (possibly 3118 or 3133) at Stonehenge in 1918.

No 1 SoN&BD was absorbed by the SoAP at Andover in September 1919, while Stonehenge became the home of the Artillery Co-operation Squadron flying the 504K. This unit became the SoAC and specialised in supporting large troop exercises on Salisbury Plain with its F.2Bs. In January 1921 the school left and Stonehenge was closed down, with some of the buildings being quickly auctioned off. The Handley Page Sheds clung on until the 1930s, sections of them being re-erected at High Post, Woodley and Old Warden; the latter location represents the only surviving remnants of this big, busy aerodrome, which is now completely erased.

Stonehenge main units, 1917-20

107 Sqn from Catterick, 18 Oct 1917;
to Lake Down, 2 Dec 1917 (various aircraft)

108 Sqn from Montrose, 12 Nov 1917;
to Lake Down, 2 Dec 1917 (various aircraft)

109 Sqn from South Carlton, 12 Nov 1917;
to Lake Down, 2 Dec 1917 (various aircraft)

2 TDS from Lake Down, 2 Dec 1917;
redesignated 1 SoN&BD, 5 Jan 1918 (DH.4, BE.2E, RE.8 and FK.8)

1 SoN&BD (ex-2 TDS) formed 5 Jan 1918;
DB into SoAP at Andover, 23 Sep 1919 (various aircraft)

97 Sqn from Waddington, 21 Jan 1918;
to Netheravon, 31 Mar 1918 (various aircraft)

140th Aero Sqn, USAAS, by 17 Jul 1918;
to Ford, 1918

377th Aero Sqn, USAAS, by 17 Jul 1918

Artillery Co-Operation Sqn from Old Sarum
(detachment to Worthy Down) Jul 1919;
redesignated SoAC, 8 Mar 1920 (504K)

School of Army Co-Operation reformed 8 Mar 1920;
to Old Sarum, Jan 1921 (F.2B)

4 Sqn 'C' Flt formed 8 Mar 1920;
to Old Sarum, 1920 (F.2B)

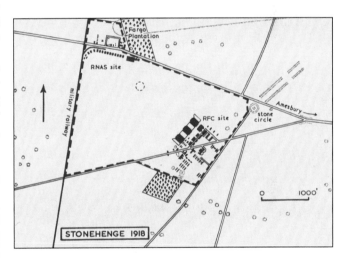

Tilshead

51°13'49"N/01°58'09"W, SU021478. Horse Down, W of A360, 1.2 miles W of Tilshead Camp

LITTLE more than a rolling area of grass, Tilshead was located in the south-eastern corner of West Lavington Down. There would have been little ceremony to its opening, the first recorded unit being the aircraft of the Artillery Co-operation School, which arrived from Netheravon in June 1918. Supporting local artillery units training on Salisbury Plain, the unit used a collection of aircraft, such as the Pup, RE.8 and 504K. The school left for Old Sarum on 1 September 1918 and, other than a few weeks of use by 'A' Flight of the Army Co-operation Squadron in October, the site was no longer recognised as an LG from November 1918.

The Central Flying School at Upavon employed a wide range of aircraft for training, including FK.8 'A411' which was at Upavon in June 1916. © Inkworm.com

Upavon's main domestic site, looking north-east with York Road in the lower centre of the photo, which today leads to married quarters.

Upavon

51°17'12"N/01°47'00"W, SU152542. Current Trenchard Lines, bisected by Andover Road (A342), 1.3 miles ESE of Upavon

REFERRED to as 'the birthplace of the Royal Air Force', Upavon was certainly where the RFC began to become an organised entity, thanks to the formation of the CFS on 13 May 1912. The CFS was under the command of Capt G. M. Paine RN, with Major H. Trenchard (the future 'Father of the RAF') as his assistant. The site was originally Army training gallops and, considering the number of potential locations across Salisbury Plain, Upavon was far from the best – the site was split by Andover Road, with its flying area to the south and domestic area to the north.

The flying site was large and was facilitated by seventeen Aeroplane Sheds (fourteen at 70 by 65 feet and three at 140 by 70 feet). The CFS was divided up into four training squadrons, 'A' to 'D', the main task being to train pilots as flying instructors on a variety of types, which were later dominated by the 504, SE.5 and Camel. The CFS was joined by the Testing Flight, later Squadron, in November 1914, a significant unit that moved to Martlesham Heath in 1917 to become the A&AEE.

Four squadrons were formed here in 1917, all from a nucleus provided by a CFS Flight. In 1919 after a major reorganisation of the RAF, the FOIS was formed, and in December this unit and the CFS were absorbed into the FIS. After much confusion, the FIS was reinstated as the CFS in 1920, which after several moves continues to serve at RAF Cranwell today. Upavon enjoyed a long and rich RAF history until 1993, when it was passed to the Army, which appropriately renamed the site Trenchard Lines. The airfield remains all grass and is mainly used for gliding by Wyvern Gliding Club, the Army Gliding Association and 662 VGS.

Upavon main units, 1912-20

CFS formed 13 May 1912;
absorbed into FIS, 23 Dec 1919 (various aircraft)

Testing Flt/Sqn formed Nov 1914;
to Martlesham Heath, 16 Jan 1917 (various aircraft)

Experimental Flt formed May 1916;
to Orfordness, May 1916

73 Sqn formed (nucleus from 'B' Flt, CFS) 1 Jul 1917;
to Lilbourne, 10 Jul 1917 (various aircraft)

72 Sqn formed (nucleus from 'A' Flt, CFS) 2 Jul 1917;
to Netheravon, 8 Jul 1917 (various aircraft)

85 Sqn formed (nucleus from 'C' Flt, CFS) 1 Aug 1917;
to Norwich, 10 Aug 1917 (various aircraft)

87 Sqn formed (nucleus from 'D' Flt, CFS) 1 Sep 1917;
to Sedgeford, 15 Sep 1917 (various aircraft)

104th Aero Sqn, USAAS, from Winchester, 24 Dec 1917;
to Netheravon, 24 Mar 1918 (DH.4)

FOIS formed 14 Aug 1919;
absorbed into FIS, 23 Dec 1919 (various aircraft)

FIS (ex-FOIS) formed 23 Dec 1919;
absorbed into CFS, 26 Apr 1920 (F.2B)

Yatesbury (Calne/Cherhill/Compton Bassett)

Western aerodrome: 51°26'20"N/01°55'33"W, SU052712. Off Jugglers Lane, W of The Avenue, 0.9 miles WSW of Yatesbury village, 1 mile SE of Compton Bassett
Eastern aerodrome: 51°26'10"N/01°54'45"W, SU062717. E of The Avenue, N of A4, 0.5 miles S of Yatesbury village

YATESBURY was a large site that was made up of two aerodromes and three different camps. Opened in 1916 for 55 TS, which moved in from Filton on 22 November, Yatesbury was a training station from the outset and would remain so until its closure in early 1920. By late 1917 the two aerodromes, which were split by a minor road leading to the village, were occupied by 16 and 17 TS on the western aerodrome (aka No 1 Aerodrome), while 13 and 66 TS were resident on the eastern site (aka No 2 Aerodrome).

Camp No 1 West at Yatesbury, with Avro 504s and Sopwith Pup A6193 of 16 and/or 17 TS in July 1917.

The western aerodrome occupied 260 acres, measured 1,100 by 1,050 yards, and supported two camps (Camp No 1 West and No 2 East) on its northern boundary, south of Jugglers Lane. Between the two camps four Aeroplane Sheds (170 by 80 feet) and one ARS Shed (170 by 80 feet) were erected. Camp No 1 was the most complex, with a large number of workshops and accommodation huts behind the flightline. The eastern aerodrome, which occupied 278 acres and measured 1,400 by 1,200 yards, had its technical and domestic site positioned in the south-western corner, close to the A4. Fronted by four Aeroplane Sheds (170 by 80 feet), an equally complex array of buildings made up what was known as Camp No 2.

On 15 July 1918 Yatesbury was reorganised when 13 and 66 TS became 36 TDS, and 17 TS was disbanded into 37 TDS, both new units remaining within their original camps. Both were tasked with carrying out corps reconnaissance training and on average had nearly 100 Avro 504s and RE.8s apiece on strength. Both TDSs were disbanded into 36 TS on 15 May 1919, until this much smaller unit was closed down on 29 October 1919.

By early 1920 both aerodromes were closed, but the site was reactivated in 1936 when it became an RAF reserve training school. Yatesbury became one of the busiest training schools in the country, and a huge camp sprang up on the old eastern aerodrome. The station was not closed down until 1969 and, while the eastern aerodrome has been clinically returned to its original pre-war state, much of Camp No 1 West is extant today. Aircraft still fly from the old eastern site from a strip called Yatesbury Field.

A Sopwith Pup and pilot pose in front of one the nine Aeroplane Sheds at Yatesbury in 1918.

Yatesbury main units, 1916-19

55 TS from Filton, 22 Nov 1916;
to Gosport, 23 Jul 1917 (504 and DH.5)

59 TS from Gosport, 30 Apr 1917;
to Beaulieu, 30 Oct 1917 (various aircraft)

62 TS from Gosport, 10 May 1917;
to Dover (Swingate Down), 1 Jun 1917 (various aircraft)

66 TS from Wye, 20 May 1917;
absorbed into 36 TDS, 15 Jul 1918 (BE.2C/E, BE.12, RE.8 and Pup)

13 TS from Dover (Swingate Down), 1 Jun 1917;
absorbed into 36 TDS, 15 Jul 1918 (various aircraft)

28 Sqn from Gosport (Fort Grange), 23 Jul 1917;
to St Omer, 8 Oct 1917 (Pup, DH.5, 504, Scout and Camel)

99 Sqn formed (from 13 TS) 15 Aug 1917;
to Ford Farm (Old Sarum), 30 Aug 1917 (various aircraft)

17 TS from Port Meadow, 8 Oct 1917;
absorbed into 37 TDS, 15 Jul 1918 (various aircraft)

32 TS (AFC) formed Oct 1917;
redesignated 7 TS (AFC), 14 Jan 1918
(BE.12A, 504, RE.8, Pup and 1½ Strutter)

16 TS from Beaulieu, 30 Oct 1917;
absorbed into 37 TDS, 15 Jul 1918 (various aircraft)

104th Aero Sqn (USAAS) detached from Upavon, 24 Dec 1917;
departed, DB Jul 1918 (DH.4)

7 TS (AFC) (ex-32 TS) 14 Jan 1918;
to Leighterton, 23 Feb 1918 (various aircraft)

36 TDS (ex-13 and 66 TS) 15 Jul 1918;
DB into 36 TS, 15 May 1919
(RE.8, 504, F.2B, BE.2E, BE.12, SE.5A and DH.6)

37 TDS (ex-16 and 17 TS) 15 Jul 1918;
DB into 36 TS, 15 May 1919
(BE.12A, DH.6, RE.8, BE.2C/E, F.2B, 504 and Pup)

199th Aero Sqn (USAAS) arrived Jul 1918

73 Sqn cadre from Baizieux, 10 Feb 1919;
DB 2 Jul 1919 (no aircraft)

65 Sqn cadre from Bisseghem, 12 Feb 1919;
DB 25 Oct 1919 (no aircraft)

54 Sqn cadre from Merchin, 17 Feb 1919;
DB 25 Oct 1919 (no aircraft)

66 Sqn cadre from San Pietro-in-Gu, 10 Mar 1919;
to Leighterton, 29 Mar 1919 (no aircraft)

36 TS reformed 15 May 1919;
DB 29 Oct 1919 (504K)

WORCESTERSHIRE

Broom (Hagley)

52°24'23"N/02°07'57"W, SO910787. S of Broome Lane, 0.8 miles W of Holy Cross

ONLY in operation for six months between April and October 1916, Broom was an HD NLG2 allocated to 38(HD) Squadron.

Channel Islands

St Peter Port (Guernsey)

49°27'09"N/02°31'51"W. Castle Pier, 0.3 miles SE of St Peter Port

THE AERONAVALE operated CAM flying-boats from here between July 1917 and December 1918.

Isle of Man

Ramsey

54°20'14"N/04°26'10"W, SC417962. 1.1 miles SW of Regaby, 2.5 miles NW of Ramsey

MOORINGS were established here for non-rigid airships operated by the RAF during 1918.

Isle of Wight

Bembridge Harbour (Bembridge Point)

50°41'40"N/01°05'34"W, SZ641887. On N edge of Bembridge Harbour at Bembridge Point, 0.3 miles NW of Bembridge village centre

BEMBRIDGE was no stranger to aviation before the military descended upon it in 1915. The sight of a Maurice Farman S.11 Shorthorn or two was fairly common from 1914 onwards. In 1915 the RNAS established a small seaplane sub-station, covering an area of only 5 acres, in support of aircraft operating from Calshot.

In November 1916 Bembridge became a seaplane station in its own right, and what limited expansion that followed included the erection of two Seaplane Sheds (one 96 by 60 feet and the other 71 by 71 feet). The first unit to operate from here was the RNAS Seaplane War Flight with Short 184s, a unit that was redesignated as 412(S) Flight on 20 May 1918. The flight still operated the Short 184, but by then had gained a few Campanias and Hamble Babys.

On 7 June 1918 Bembridge played host to the formation of 253 Squadron, which was created from 412, 511, 512 and

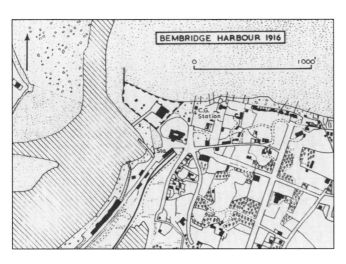

BEMBRIDGE HARBOUR 1916

513 Flights with 184s, Campanias and Hamble Babys, while several land-based DH.6s were detached to Foreland, Brading and Chickerell (511 and 512(SD) Flights). 413(S) Flight was also formed here on 15 September 1918 with 184s, but was disbanded in November when the war came to an end. This left 253 Squadron, which by this time had a dozen aircraft on strength until its disbandment on 31 May 1919.

Bembridge was closed down in 1920, and as with most ex-RAF establishments the buildings were sold off in a public auction. One of the two hangars served as a theatre in Shanklin, then as part of the Summerland Amusement Arcade located on the Esplanade (50°37'45"N/01°10'18"W), where it remains to this day.

Brading

50°42'14"N/01°08'02"W, SZ614894. 0.8 miles WSW of Nettlestone, 1 mile NW of St Helens

OPENED as a DLG for the RFC in December 1917, Brading was only a 26-acre site measuring 400 by 330 yards. Some cover was provided by Bessonneau hangars for the DH.6s of 511(SD) Flight and 512(SD) Flight, both formed here under the control of 253 Squadron on 7 June 1918. Both flights left for New Bembridge on 8 August 1918, while Brading lasted until January 1919.

Cliff End

50°41'52"N/01°31'14"W, SZ339888. 0.4 miles SW of Norton, 1 mile SW of Yarmouth

CLASSIFIED as a DLG, Cliff End only took up 18 acres and measured 350 by 200 yards. The small LG was only used by aircraft of 78(HD) Squadron and the School of Aerial Co-Operation with Coastal Defence Batteries (SACCDB) at Gosport. Cliff End was only used from early to late 1918.

Norman Thompson NT.2Bs under construction at the S. E. Saunders factory at East Cowes.

Cowes East and West

East: 50°45'35"N/01°17'24"W, SZ501958. Next to Classic Boat Museum, Columbine Road, 0.3 miles W of East Cowes

West: 50°45'36"N/01°17'37"W, SZ499958. Off Medina Road, 0.3 miles from Cowes centre

BOTH OF these slipways were used by J. Samuel White & Co Ltd for Short 184 flight-testing, while the Cowes East site was also shared with S. E. Saunders & Co Ltd. The eastern site was developed into SARO's main factory and the home of the ill-fated Princess flying-boat.

Foreland (New Bembridge)

50°41'03"N/01°04'40"W, SZ654877. SE area of Bembridge, mainly under housing with exception of Forelands Fields, 1.4 miles E of current Bembridge airfield

THIS SMALL Marine Operations (Aeroplane) Station, measuring 600 by 500 yards on the eastern tip of the Isle of Wight, was ready for occupation by late May 1918. In June 253 Squadron had been formed at Bembridge from several flights, two of which, 511 and 512(SD), were formed at Brading with DH.6s. Both flights were detached to Foreland from 8 August and are believed to have remained until they were disbanded together with the main unit on 31 May 1919.

Golden Hill

50°41'20"N/01°31'90"W, SZ338878. Golden Hill Fort, 0.7 miles N of Freshwater

GOLDEN HILL was briefly the home of a kite balloon station during 1919, presumably operating outside the fort's walls, which were considerably more open than they are today. The Coastal Defence Artillery School based at Gosport carried out experiments and target practice here.

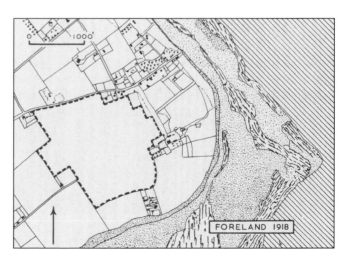

Wight (Cowes/Somerton)

50°44'47"N/01°18'31"W, SZ487942. W of Newport Road (A3020), current BAE Systems (Cowes) factory, 1.25 miles SW of Cowes

DURING the early stages of the war J. Samuel White & Co purchased a field near Three Gates Road to test landplanes built in its factory at Cowes. White expanded the airfield in 1916 and built a new factory there. Rather than requisitioning it, the RAF shared the airfield from September 1918, when the School of Aerial Co-Operation arrived from Gosport. Equipped with the BE.2C, BE.12 and DH.9, the unit was tasked with working with local coastal defence batteries. On 15 September 1919 the unit was disbanded into the Coastal Battery Co-Operation School and moved to Gosport. The previous July White had also ended aircraft production. The site was used by light aircraft during the 1920s until 1929, when SARO moved in for its own flight-testing. The company shared the site with Spartan Aircraft from 1931, and the Isle of Wight Gliding Club. Somerton Airways operated from here from August 1946 to April 1951, and the airfield closed down soon after.

Isles of Scilly

Porth Mellon, Isles of Scilly

49°55'03"N/06°18'28"W, SV908108. N end of Porth Mellon beach near Harry's Walls Battery on St Marys

A SINGLE Seaplane Shed (145 by 45 feet) was built here for the use of seaplanes from Tresco during 1917, just east of the lifeboat station. The shed was later dismantled and re-erected at Tresco.

Tresco (Abbey Wood), Isles of Scilly

49°56'56"N/06°19'49"W, SV895145. N of Abbey Road, S of Great Pool, Tresco

NOTHING more than a clearing in Abbey Wood, moorings for airships operating from Mullion were active here during 1918.

Tresco (New Grimsby), Isles of Scilly

49°57'01"N/06°20'15"W, SV890149. Off Farm Beach near Abbey Farm, S of New Grimsby, Tresco

BEING located on the edge of the sheltered New Grimsby harbour, with calm water 1½ miles long and half a mile wide, made this site ideal for the vital flying-boat operations urgently needed to help protect the shipping passing the Isles of Scilly. There was enough space to moor six large flying-boats, while the facilities on shore were basic with only Bessonneau hangars, a rudimentary slipway and a few tents for the personnel, who in 1917 were ferried daily to and from Tresco from St Mary's. By the summer of 1917 a permanent flying-boat station was given the go-ahead and work began on a single steel-framed Seaplane Shed of 200 by 100 feet, and another of 105 by 45 feet. A few tents would remain until the end, but by 1918 approximately twenty-five buildings occupied the main technical area of 20 acres, together with six smaller sites that raised the total by another 10 acres. The slipway was upgraded to one with a 2-ton capacity, complete with a track-mounted trolley to make it much easier to manoeuvre the larger flying-boats, such as the Felixstowe F.3 and Curtiss H.12.

Four flying-boat flights, 350 to 353, were formed here between May and September 1918, all under the charge of 234 Squadron, which was also formed at Tresco on 20 August 1918. The Tresco flying-boats were some of the hardest working in the country and as result recorded thirteen attacks on enemy submarines as well as carrying out untold convoy escorts and numerous rescue operations, some successful, many fruitless. 234 Squadron was disbanded in May 1919, but the site remained useful for RAF flying-boats until the early 1920s, and again for Sunderlands between 1941 and 1944. Today the only real clue to the site's past is the decaying slipway and half a dozen concrete bases to the south-west of the site.

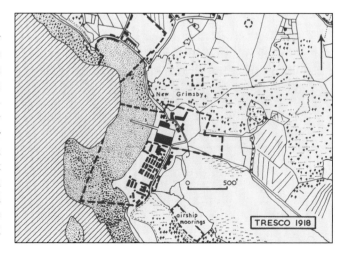

This excellent view of Tresco in the summer of 1918 shows a Felixstowe F.3 on the beach and a second Felixstowe-type flying-boat being assembled. Note the 200-by-100-foot Seaplane Shed under construction in the centre of the photo, and the trolley tracks on the main slipway. *Via Stuart Leslie*

Tresco main units, 1918-19

350(FB) Flt formed 31 May 1918;
absorbed into 234 Sqn, 20 Aug 1918 (F.3 and Short 184)

351(FB) Flt formed 30 Jun 1918;
absorbed into 234 Sqn, 20 Aug 1918 (F.3 and Short 184)

352(FB) Flt formed 15 Sep 1918;
DB 15 May 1919 (F.3 and Short 184)

353(FB) Flt formed 30 Sep 1918;
DB 15 May 1919 (F.3 and Short 184)

234 Sqn (350, 351, 352 and 353 Flts) formed 20 Aug 1918;
DB 15 May 1919 (F.2A and F.3)

Northern Ireland

ANTRIM

Ballycastle

55°12'15"N/6°15'30"W, 05/D11100 41000. SW of
Ballycastle

THIS mysterious LG was believed to have been established
south-west of Ballycastle in 1918. It was still under
construction for 25 Group, RAF, at the end of the war, and
was most likely abandoned soon after.

Bentra (Whitehead, aka Larne)

Airship station: 54°45'89"N/05°43'64"W, 15/J46249
93143. 1 mile NW of Whitehead railway station
Landing ground: 54°45'84"N/05°43'35"W, 15/J46569
93072

IN 1917 a military airship station and LG was opened at Bentra
near Whitehead. It was conveniently positioned so that its SS
Class airships and fixed-wing aircraft could patrol the Irish Sea
on the hunt for U-boats. It was officially designated as an Airship
Station Class A and operated as a sub-station for Luce Bay for
the operation of non-rigid RNAS and later RAF airships. Patrols
were also regularly flown from Luce Bay to help protect the
Larne-Stranraer ferry, *Princess Maud*, whose service continued
throughout the war. On 5 June 1917 the first airship, *SS20*,
arrived at Bentra, having flown its operation across the Irish Sea,
returning safely to Luce Bay that evening.

Although it was only classed as a mooring-out station, it
had at least one 'portable' hangar (150 by 45 by 50 feet), and
the fixed-wing types operated from an LG approximately 400
by 400 yards. Flying ceased in 1919, and on 20 February
1920, the site was relinquished by the military.

Broughshane

54°53'00"N/06°13'00"W. SE edge of village, 3 miles
from Ballymena railway station

THIS small DLG was briefly used by 105 Squadron's
RE.8s during its tenure at Omagh, circa late 1918.

DOWN

Aldergrove

54°39'12"N/06°13'77"W, J145795. 2 miles N of
Crumlin, 4 miles S of Antrim via A26 and A50

ORIGINALLY surveyed back in 1917 by Sholto Douglas,
Aldergrove was one of eight training stations that were
selected for use by the RFC. Starting out at 360 acres, and
measuring 1,400 by 1,200 yards, today Aldergrove is by far
the biggest and busiest airfield in Northern Ireland.

Above: A glimpse of Aldergrove, with Lough Neagh in the
background, a few years before the site was changed forever
into a thriving RAF station and later as Belfast International
Airport.

By the time the aerodrome opened, the RFC had passed into history and it was only thanks to aircraft production continuing at Harland & Wolff that a role for Aldergrove was found. On 15 October 1918 16 (Aldergrove) AAP was formed, primarily to accept the Harland & Wolff-built Handley Page V/1500, but only a handful ever arrived. Hangars and several substantial technical and domestic buildings were built for the new AAP, including one Aeroplane Shed (585 by 85 feet) and one erecting shed (510 by 147 feet). 16 AAP was closed on 4 December 1919, but the RAF wisely retained the airfield, initially for annual exercises.

Ballywalter

54°33'18"N/05°29'40"W. N of Dunover Road, 0.75 miles NNW of Ballywalter

THE first of two flying sites located near Ballywalter on the Ards Peninsula was active between 1918 and 1922. Its exact use is unclear, other than it was used by the RAF probably as an ELG.

Bangor

54°39'07"N/05°39'95"W, 15/J50631 80630. SW of Bangor

TWO sites on the outskirts of Bangor were used for military aviation during the 20th century. The first was a small LG used by land-based aircraft from the USN serving in Ireland during 1918. As usual it would have been little more than a flat, reasonably unobstructed field, and no specific units can be connected to it.

Bryansford (Newcastle)

54°13'73"N/05°55'86"W, 29/J34902 33108. 1.5 miles NW of Newcastle

THIS small LG, which is believed to date back to 1913, was briefly in civilian hands before the outbreak of war. It is not clear when, but it obviously has to be before April 1918, when the 'field strip' was used by the RFC. It probably ceased to be used before the end of the war.

Slidderyford Bridge

54°14'31"N/05°51'60"W, 29/J395343. 1.9 miles NE of Newcastle bus station

ORIGINALLY described as a 'field strip', it was in civilian hands from September 1913, and at some point was taken over by the RFC. Unfortunately no further details are available to expand on this.

Scotland

BORDERS

Cairncross (Reston)

55°51'55"N/02°10'04"W, NT892630. 1.5 miles SSW of Coldringham, 3 miles W of Eyemouth

CAIRNCROSS was the most southerly of 77(HD) Squadron's LGs, situated just 5 miles from the English border. The small aerodrome measured 1,000 by 750 yards and took up 115 acres east of the hamlet of Cairncross. Classified as an NLG2, Cairncross opened in October 1916.

77(HD) Squadron, which alone was operating six different types of aircraft in 1917, first made use of the LG from October of that year. Also during that year a detachment of 528 Flight, a unit operating within 256 Squadron, brought its DH.6s from Seahouses on 6 June 1918. 528 Flight returned to Seahouses on 15 August, but despite no resident units the airfield remained open until 13 August 1919.

Eccles Tofts

55°41'58"N/02°22'58"W, NT759452. 3 miles ESE of Greenlaw off A697 at Eccles Tofts

A TYPICAL basic NLG1, Eccles Tofts had a brief existence. One of many LGs used by 77(HD) Squadron between late January 1917 and early 1918, there is little evidence that it was used a great deal. The 110-acre LG measuring 850 by 600 yards and was closed down in June 1919. To the north-east, RAF Charterhall enjoyed a much busier history during the Second World War.

Horndean

55°52'07"N/02°22'37"W, NT892503. N of Winfield Cottage off B6461, on W edge of ex-RAF Winfield, 6.75 miles WSW of Berwick-upon-Tweed

OPENED for just twelve months between December 1916 and December 1917, Horndean was used by 77(HD) Squadron. The eastern side of this HD NLG2 was swallowed up by RAF Winfield, a satellite of RAF Charterhall, during the Second World War.

Whiteburn (Grantshouse)

55°52'07"N/02°22'37"W, NT 765639. 1 mile N of Abbey St Bathans, 15 miles NW of Berwick

POSITIONED on 120 acres of open moorland and measuring 850 by 800 yards, Whiteburn was on the fringe of the Lammermuir Hills. One of the highest aerodromes of the war at 750 feet amsl, it became the home of 'C' Flight, 77(HD) Squadron, which arrived from New Haggerston in November 1916.

More established than most aerodromes of this type, Whiteburn had a single Aeroplane Shed (125 by 60 feet), at least one workshop, a technical store, several offices, and accommodation for up to sixty personnel, including an officers' mess. Further facilities included a compass platform, machine-gun range, ammunition dump and a small bomb dump.

Above: One of several early aviation events at Alloa (overleaf), on 17 August 1910, is viewed from the grandstand.

In August 1917 'B' Flight, 77(HD) Squadron, arrived, followed in early 1918 by 'A' Flight, making the unit complete for the first in its short history. Despite the aerodrome being so well equipped, the sortie rate was not high, and meteorological observations carried out during 1917 and 1918 revealed that flying was only possible for 25% of the daylight hours.

In May 1918 the entire squadron left for Penston, returning for just a few weeks for a detachment back at Whiteburn. Not long after the end of the war the site was abandoned.

CENTRAL

Alloa (Forthbank/Caudron)

56°6'50"N/03°46'02"W, NS889914. 1.1 miles due E of Alloa on A907/A910 Clackmannan Road, due S of A907/B909 junction on N bank of Firth of Forth

ALTHOUGH more associated with flying at Hendon during the pre-war period, the W. H. Ewen Aviation Co Ltd had already opened a flying school in 1911 at the Lanark Racecourse. The company was officially registered at 28 Bath Street, Glasgow, from 1913, but the outbreak of the war would see the company expand rapidly.

Contracts for the supply of aircraft to the RFC and RNAS were already being undertaken at the Hendon factory, so Ewen Aviation looked for an additional plant further north. The company's second site, described as the 'Scottish factory and aerodrome', was established at Alloa in 1914. The same year the company was renamed The British Caudron Co Ltd, indicating its alliance to the French aircraft manufacturer founded back in 1909.

Production focused on Caudron types, namely a single G.2 and the more prolific G.3 at first, sixty-one of the latter being built at Alloa. As pressure for more aircraft increased, the factory became a sub-contractor for other companies for the remainder of the war. Fifty BE.2Cs and Es were built, as well as twenty-two Avro 504Bs and 100 Sopwith Camels.

The Armistice brought an end to the factory, but it was licensed for a short period during the 1920s for recreational flying. Today, unusually, the site has not been over-developed and the flying field is much the same as it was. However, no physical evidence of a factory or airfield remains.

Stirling (Kincairn/Gargunnock)

56°08'18"N/04°04'29"W, NS710960. W of Kirk Lane (B8075), 0.4 miles NW of The Offers Farm, 1 mile NNE of Gargunnock

THIS small HD NLG3 was laid out for 36(HD) Squadron, but was instead transferred to 77(HD) Squadron, which used the site from August 1916 until March 1917. Not in the best of locations, at the foot of the unforgiving Gargunnock and Touch hills, this, combined with its westerly location for Zeppelin defence, probably brought about its premature closure.

Stirling (Raploch/Falleninch Farm)

56°07'23"N/03°57'50"W, NS785945. 1 mile NNW of town centre

LITTLE more than an open field, this small aerodrome was located west of Castle Hill, Stirling, and north of the Dumbarton road. A handful of temporary wooden hangars provided protection for aircraft undergoing maintenance, while all personnel were accommodated under canvas.

43 Squadron from Montrose was the first resident, bringing its FK.3s to Raploch on 19 April 1916. By June the squadron began to receive the BE.2C and 504 before it moved by road to Netheravon on 30 August 1916.

Raploch lay silent until 18 March 1917 when 52 TS brought in its large collection of aircraft from Catterick. Equipped with at least ten different types, this training squadron departed for Montrose on 1 September 1917, becoming the last unit to operate from Raploch.

77(HD) Squadron also based aircraft at Raploch during 1916 and 1917 but, as with Kincairn, its use for Zeppelin defence patrols was limited.

DUMFRIES & GALLOWAY

Castle Kennedy

54°54'00"N/04°56'03"W, NX119598. 3 miles ESE of Stranraer off A75

THE area now known as Castle Kennedy Airfield forms part of Cults Farm, about 5 miles east of Stranraer. It was here that fixed-wing aircraft recorded the first landings in Galloway, in August 1913. The aircraft involved were a contingent of one Maurice Farman MF.7 Longhorn and five BE 2s belonging to 2 Squadron from Montrose, and they were on their way to Ireland to take part in military manoeuvres. While at Castle Kennedy they were fitted with flotation bags to assist them in the event of ditching in the Irish Sea. At the conclusion of the exercise only three of the original six aircraft were able to complete the journey from Castle Kennedy to Montrose, the remainder having suffered mechanical or navigational problems. The arrival of the aircraft predictably created much local interest; schools were closed and special trains organised to Castle Kennedy station to view the new machines.

During the First World War, and in the intervening period, the airfield was used intermittently for the transport of mail and small goods across the water to Ireland, but generally the area returned to agriculture.

Luce Bay's 300-foot-long Airship Shed dominates the centre of station while an SS Class airship is prepared for operations on the right.

Luce Bay

54°51′17″N/04°55′46″W, NX120550. E of East Galdenoch off B7077, now covered by N edge of West Freugh Airfield

CONSTRUCTION of a substantial airship station and aerodrome began in early 1915 on low-lying ground, close to the long sand dunes at the head of Luce Bay. The site occupied 444 acres, although only 6 acres were actually covered in buildings, the largest being a single Airship Shed (300 by 70 by 50 feet).

Luce Bay was opened as a Class B Airship Station for non-rigid RNAS airships on 15 July 1915. Sub-stations were located at Ballyliffan, Larne, Machrihanish and Ramsey during its existence, and its SS Class airships saw a great deal of action while patrolling off the north-western Scottish coast.

By June 1918 the station was under RAF control for marine operations, and on 5 June 523 and 524(SD) Flights were formed within 255 Squadron, operating from an LG that measured 2,270 by 1,530 yards. 255 Squadron was already detached here with its DH.6s and remained until the end of the year. Also referred to as 'A' and 'B' Flights, the two SD units became part of 258 Squadron when it formed on 25 July. The squadron re-equipped with Fairey IIIAs until it was disbanded in March 1919.

25 (Operations) Group was formed on 12 August 1918 to control the North Western Area, 258 and 278 Squadrons, Luce Bay and Larne. Three days later 529(SD) Flight was formed within 258 Squadron with DH.6s, but was disbanded by March 1919. 244 Squadron was detached from Bangor with its DH.6s during late 1918, leaving 25 Group to be the last RAF unit to operate from here, finally disbanding on 12 June 1919.

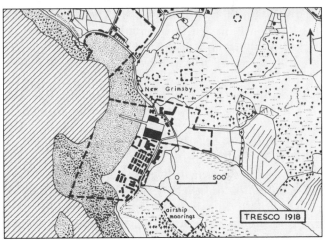

The site has now been completely swept away as the area was developed into West Freugh Airfield during the Second World War. The general location of the Airship Shed is now the bomb dump, although the taxiways and access roads that surround it seem to follow the same alignment as the First World War access roads.

Tinwald Down Farm

55°05′49″N/03°34′29″W, NX996792

THERE is evidence of a First World War LG here, but its purpose is unknown. The site was covered by the main technical site of RAF Dumfries during the Second World War.

FIFE

Crail

56°16'18"N/02°36'40"W, N625085. 1 mile NNE of Crail, 8 miles SE of St Andrews

THE remote but beautiful fishing village of Crail, located at Fife's most easterly point, lent its name to two airfields during the 20th century. The first briefly opened during the latter stages of the First World War, only to be reopened during the early months of the Second. Supporting at least thirty-six Fleet Air Arm squadrons alone during the Second World War, Crail became the premier and most important airfield for training aircrews in the art of attacking the enemy using a torpedo.

Opened in 1918, Crail's first airfield was a well-equipped complex with no fewer than seven 1918-pattern GS Sheds (170 by 100 feet) together with a host of technical and domestic buildings. The flying field took up approximately 170 acres, making it sufficient in size to cater for all of the aircraft of the day. The build was originally commissioned for use by the RFC and RNAS, but by the time it opened the RAF had been formed and thus took control of the new airfield. The first unit to arrive was 58 TS from Spittlegate on 15 July 1918, followed by 64 TS from Harlaxton. Both squadrons brought a variety of aircraft with them, including the FK.3, Nieuport 17, F.2B, Shorthorn, Avro 504 and many more. Both of these units were destined to be disbanded into 27 TDS, which was formed at Crail on 15 August 1918. The 20th Group, whose headquarters were at 14 Randolph Crescent, Edinburgh, controlled 27 TDS. Its name changed to the North Western Area in May 1918, controlling all of Scotland's TDSs.

27 TDS had a short life and, with the end of the First World War, the RAF was wound down dramatically. 27 TDS was disbanded on 31 March 1919, leaving Crail with only a Delivery Station (Storage), which was formed on 1 March, and a single squadron. 104 Squadron arrived at Crail on 3 March as a cadre, having disposed of its DH.9s and 10s. The personnel remained at Crail until the squadron was disbanded on 30 June 1919. This was the end for Crail and, despite such a lot of money, time and effort being put into building the significant aerodrome, it was closed in the spring of 1920.

Crail main units, 1918-19

50 TS from Spittlegate, 8 Aug 1918;
DB into 27 TDS, 15 Aug 1918

64 TS from Harlaxton, 8 Aug 1918;
DB into 27 TDS, 15 Aug 1918

120th Aero Sqn, USAAS, detached from New Romney, 9 Mar 1918;
to Stamford (Wittering), 10 Aug 1918

27 TDS formed 15 Aug 1918;
DB 31 Mar 1919

Donibristle

56°02'29"N/03°20'59"W, NT155834. 2 miles E of Rosyth off A92

AFFECTIONATELY known as 'Donibee' by the many thousands of military and civilian workers who passed through it, Donibristle had a diverse history that could be dated back to 1917 and continued almost uninterrupted for a further 42 years. Industry and housing have virtually removed it from the aviation map, but its memory will live on as one of Scotland's earliest airfields.

The explanation for an airfield being built on the northern edge of the Firth of Forth, on rising ground above Dalgety Bay, could be traced back to 1903. It was then that the decision was made to build a new naval dockyard at Rosyth, upstream from the Forth railway bridge. Work began in 1909, but it was not fully completed and ready for operation until March 1916. The Admiralty initially saw aircraft as nothing more than a novelty but, as the conflict developed, their importance, especially in support of warships, grew rapidly.

In late 1916 various sites surrounding Rosyth were inspected and surveyed for the location of a landing ground and eventual storage area for large numbers of aircraft belonging to the RNAS. In early 1917, as part of the aerial defence of the Firth of Forth and Edinburgh, 77(HD) Squadron RFC established a small emergency landing ground on land belonging to the Earl of Moray at Donibristle House. The Earl was none too happy about aircraft using his land, but the commanding officer of 77

F.2B Fighters and a 504K belonging to 27 TDS are seen at Crail in early 1919. Note the substantial hangar behind, which was razed to the ground only months later.

Squadron was a good friend and coaxed him round to the idea. Several trees had to be removed to clear a runway, then a single guard hut and a few ancillary buildings were constructed.

Not a single aircraft used the small LG before the arrival of the RNAS in August 1917. Allocated to the Admiralty on 17 September, work began on building a large ARD. The site was expanded with four Type-F Sheds (200 by 100 feet), one erecting shed (200 by 100 feet) and two storage sheds (200 by 100 feet and 120 by 35 feet). This task brought about the formation of the Fleet Aircraft Acceptance Depot in October 1918, which was changed to the Fleet Aircraft Repair Depot not long after.

Highlighting the importance of the airfield's first major role, Donibristle was kept open after the Armistice and continued to overhaul carrier-based aircraft until it was reduced to Care & Maintenance in 1921.

Donibristle main units, 1918-22

F Sqn from East Fortune, Mar 1918;
to HMS *Furious*, Mar 1918

Fleet ARD formed 1918;
redesignated Coastal ARD 1922

Fleet AAP formed 1918;
redesignated Coastal Area Aircraft Depot 15 Sep 1919

Fleet Stores Distributing Park formed 1918;
DB 1919

Coastal AAD 15 Sep 1919;
DB Mar 1922

Hawkcraig Point

56°03'01"N/03°17'20"W, NT201849. Hawkcraig Point, 0.5 miles ESE of Aberdour

POSITIONED at the bottom of the cliffs on the western side of Hawkcraig Point, no specific unit was ever allocated to this small seaplane station.

Operations began as early as 1913, initially with the Sopwith Baby and later with the Short 184. A single Bessonneau was constructed on the shoreline with its own simple slipway, together with a few technical buildings behind the hangar. One 184, N1650, served at Hawkcraig from 1918 and was still there by January the following year, by which time the site was soon closed down.

Inverkeithing Bay

56°01'33"N/03°23'25"W, NT133822. General area occupied by Stone Marine Services, 0.4 miles SE of Inverkeithing, 1.65 miles SW of Dalgety Business Park (former Donibristle technical site)

INVERKEITHING BAY was a convenient location for distributing new and repaired aircraft back into fleet service. Joined to the parent unit at Donibristle by a railway line, a Fleet ARD sub-station was established at Inverkeithing Bay in 1918. Complete with two large storage sheds (240 by 138 feet), the ARD only remained open until 1919.

Kilconquhar

56°12'28"N/02°50'23"W, NO478020. Due S of Kilconquhar Loch

KILCONQUHAR was an HD NLG2 for the use of 77(HD) Squadron during its anti-Zeppelin campaign towards the end of the First World War. Facilities would have been sparse on this level piece of land located south-east of Broomlees Farm; it occupied 45 acres and measured 650 by 500 yards. 77(HD) Squadron was allocated this landing ground from May 1918 to May 1919.

Leuchars (Leuchars Junction)

56°22'23"N/02°52'06"W. 5 miles NW of St Andrews off A919

LAND clearance began for a new aerodrome at Reres Farm, south-east of Leuchars village on the edge of the River Eden estuary, in 1916. A large site occupying 220 acres and measuring 1,250 by 900 yards, Leuchars was furnished with seven 1918-pattern GS Sheds (170 by 100 feet).

By 1918 the site was ready for occupation and was placed under the control of 78 Wing based in Dundee; it was classified as a School and Ships Aeroplane Base from July. Its first unit was 1 Torpedo Training Squadron, formed from 208 TDS, which only remained a few weeks before departing for East Fortune. The TTS was followed on 10 November 1918 by the (Grand) Fleet School of Aerial Fighting & Gunnery. Leuchars was intended to be a temporary mobilisation station with the task of training aircrew from basic flying through to fleet co-operation work.

This is RAF Leuchar's original neat, technical site complete with seven 1918-pattern GS Sheds. *Via Stuart Leslie*

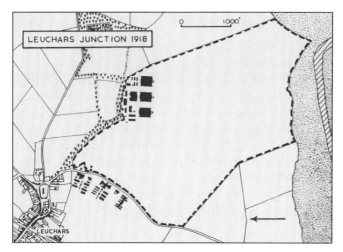

Today much of the original First World War site has been retained, including seven of the original hangars. From its official opening, Leuchars has been in virtually uninterrupted use until recent years, when it was announced that this historic airfield will be closing and handed over to the Army by 2015.

Leven

56°11'32"N/02°59'43"W, NO382003. On beach near Leven on edge of Largo Bay

A TEMPORARY seaplane base made the beach near Leven its home during the summer of 1913. Several aircraft used it, including a Borel monoplane on floats, which took part in a large naval exercise. The site was meant to have been cleared away, but instead provided a stepping stone while more suitable seaplane stations were being built, and as a result was closed down in 1914.

Methil

56°10'59"N/03°00'34"W, NO377995. Located on edge of current No 2 Dock, 0.3 miles from Methil centre

O PENED as Kite Balloon Station Methil in 1917, the unit was to be the home of 11 Balloon Base, which was planned to be formed on 15 April 1918, but this never took place. During the Second World War 13 ASRMCU operated from the harbour.

North Queensferry

56°00'41"N/03°24'16"W, NT125807. 0.5 miles North Queensferry railway station

O PENED in the summer of 1917, North Queensferry was a small Royal Navy kite balloon station approximately 5 acres in size. It was equipped with eight kite balloons, complete with six canvas Balloon Hangars (100 by 36 feet). Personnel were accommodated in wooden huts on the site, while the officers enjoyed the Ferry Gate House. Designated as 18 Balloon Base from 15 April 1918, the unit was disbanded on 1 December 1919.

Port Laing (Carlingnose)

56°01'00"N/03°23'27"W, NT133814. Near beach at Port Laing, 0.5 miles N of North Queensferry

E STABLISHED in 1912, this small seaplane base was not particularly busy until just before the beginning of the First World War. At least Maurice Farman Longhorn seaplane No 71 and Borel monoplane No 86 were operating from here until early 1914. However, on 28 February of that year the entire station had to be moved and dispersed thanks to the expiry of the lease. The station's three Seaplane Sheds were later moved to Stannergate.

The location, which is most likely to have been near the beach at Port Laing, is now occupied by 'executive'-type houses.

Rosyth

56°01'18"N/03°25'45"W, NT111818. E of Rosyth Europarc, 1 mile SW of Inverkeithing

A SMALL hydro-aeroplane station was established at Rosyth by late 1912. However, by early 1914 what little had been built here was moved to Dundee. Not to be confused with Port Laing, the Rosyth seaplane station was later developed and located within the naval base. It consisted of a pair of Seaplane Sheds (200 by 100 feet), one of which was used as a store, and a single slipway.

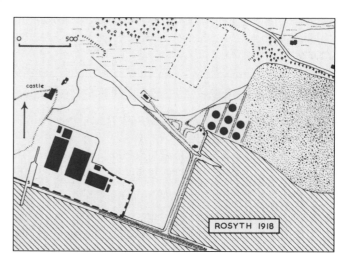

Rosyth was also the home of No 9 (Edinburgh) Stores Distributing Park, which supplied technical stores of Fleet aircraft units until October 1918. The station's main role was the servicing of naval aircraft, a task that it carried out until its closure in late 1918, following transfer of the work to Donibristle.

St Andrews Sands

56°21'44"N/02°48'37"W, NO501195. West Sands, SE of Out End, E of St Andrews golf course, 1.7 miles NNW of St Andrews

W ITH uninterrupted approaches from any direction, the obstacle-free open sands north of St Andrews were used by 2 Squadron from Montrose for training during 1913 and 1914.

South Kilduff (Kinross)

56°12'02"N/03°28'43"W, NO083017. SW of Killoch
Bridge, 1.1 miles SW of ex-RAF Balado Bridge

THE useful landmark of the nearby Loch Leven may have
helped the pilots of 77(HD) Squadron find this small LG.
It operated between 1916 and 1918, was classified as an
NLG3, occupied 27 acres, and measured 480 by 270 yards.

GRAMPIAN

Auldbar (Albar/Montrose)

56°41'38"N/02°42'10"W, NO578554. 3.5 miles SW of
Brechin, 3.75 miles from Auldbar Road railway station

IT was common for airship stations to have mooring-out sites,
where airships could be diverted in bad weather if unable to
return to their home bases safely. Lenabo had a mooring-out base
at Auldbar in Angus, about 70 miles south of the home station.
This was the only known mooring-out site in Scotland and
consisted of four airship bases cut out of the forest and known
as the 'Nest'. A cleared area for landing and take-off and a few
huts completed the base. The idea was for the airship to be
guided into one of the berths until its cable could be fastened to
a mooring mast. Each berth also had a rectangular pit large
enough to house the control car and skids for maintenance.
Auldbar was used as a forward operating base in 1918, with
airships *SSZ57*, *SSZ58*, *SSZ65* and *SSZ66* shuttling to and fro
from Lenabo for overhaul and maintenance between patrols.

Over the years the base at Auldbar has largely disappeared
apart from the mooring pits, but efforts are now being made
to reclaim the area.

Longside (Lenabo/Peterhead)

57°28'21"N/01°57'08"W, NK030421. 0.5 miles E of
Easterton at Lenabo Farm, 1 mile ENE of Newton

RNAS Longside, also
known as Lenabo, was
first established in March 1916
as a Class G Airship Station for
non-rigid airships complete
with a sub-station at Auldbar.
The site was typically large at
950 acres, and measured 2,730
by 2,330 yards. It was furnished
with three sheds, one rigid (711
by 150 by 105 feet) and two
non-rigid (323 by 113 by 80
feet).

An artist's impression of Longside
airship station, showing a single
large shed protected by a pair of
smaller SS-Type sheds, to help
reduce crosswinds.

Longside briefly became a marine operations station from
November to December 1918 for 492 Flight of 254 Squadron.
The station remained open until 1921, when the site was sold.
Now covered by forest, all three airship shed bases are still
easy to find and the original access remains intact.

Peterhead Bay

57°29'31"N/01°47'18"W, NK130447. 1 mile from
Peterhead railway station

A seaplane station and seaplane repair depot for the RNAS
and later the RAF was opened here in 1918, with
Strathbeg serving as a sub-station. A 90-acre site located on
the south side of the bay, Peterhead had a single Seaplane Shed
(200 by 100 feet).

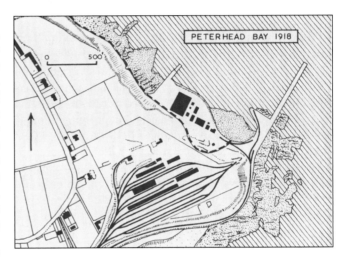

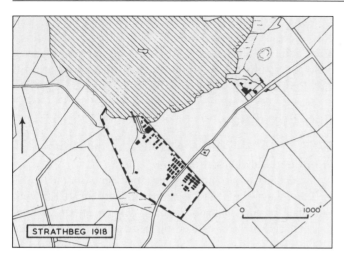

STRATHBEG 1918

HIGHLAND

Cromarty

57°41'01"N/04°02'09"W, NH795671. Near old lighthouse and coastguard station in Cromarty

THE Cromarty Firth is a superb natural deep harbour that provided the Royal Navy with safe anchorage for many years. On 7 May 1913 one of the officers on board HMS *Hermes*, Lt Cdr A. Longmore, was appointed as commander of Cromarty Air Station. At this time no such place existed, but it was up to Longmore to establish it to support those ships operating from the firth.

Not the easiest of tasks, Longmore eventually plumped for a site near the lighthouse and coastguard station. It was an area of land used by local fishermen to dry their nets, but it was sufficiently large to accommodate at least one hangar and close enough to the foreshore to launch seaplanes. It was not clear who actually owned the land, but the Admiralty had already allocated up to £10,000 to spend on the new station, which would have easily covered the purchase of land and any construction needed.

A single Bessonneau hangar arrived on 4 July 1913 after a long journey on a lighter from Sheerness. Recruitment at the time was fascinating, with only half of the twenty ratings taken on for the new station having actually seen an aircraft before. Fitter and rigger training was carried out in-house, with most rectification faults cured by trial and error!

Strathbeg

57°36'33"N/01°51'45"W, NK082577. SE end of loch of Strathbeg, near Old Rattray, 2.2 miles ENE of Crimond

THE loch at Strathbeg was used as a sub-station for Dundee, which was a very busy seaplane station. It is possible that the small base was opened as early as 1916, but there is little evidence of a permanent unit or flying from the loch. The first unit to arrive in August 1918 was 401(S) Flight operating the Short 184. They were joined by 249 Squadron from September 1918, also flying the 184, and by the end of the war both units returned to Dundee. The station could accommodate six seaplanes, and had a single Seaplane Shed (70 by 70 feet) and one slipway.

Sopwith seaplane No 59 was the second aircraft to arrive at Cromarty in 1913.

Aircraft began arriving by rail and boat in dribs and drabs, the first being Maurice Farman seaplane No 117, followed by Sopwith biplane No 59 and Borel monoplane No 85. Longmore wasted no time in using these aircraft in Fleet exercises, proving that air-sea cooperation was more than feasible when he spotted a periscope off Nairn on 26 July 1913. Using an Aldis lamp, Longmore signalled his find to a nearby ship, much to the enthusiasm of senior officers taking part in the exercise.

Despite quickly establishing Cromarty as a useable seaplane station, the Army barracks at Fort George was found to be more than adequate, and from October 1913 Cromarty was literally moved piece by piece by boat across to Fort George.

Delny House

57°43'08"N/04°08'04"W, NH730720. Off A9 W of Delny, 2.5 miles NE of Invergordon

VERY little is known about this small landing ground other than it was in use from 1918. It was used by aircraft flying off warships anchored in the Cromarty Firth, and was still in limited use by June 1920. At this time a single DH.9A took part in wireless and range-finding experiments with HMS *Barham* and HMS *Warspite* as moving targets.

Delny was inspected in 1921 with potential expansion plans in mind, but nothing ever came of it and Novar (Evanton) was chosen instead. Nothing remains today.

Fort George

57°34'58"N/04°03'52"W, NH767566. Near East Gate entrance close to sports field, 1.5 miles NW of Ardersier

ON the outbreak of war there were only two active RNAS stations in Scotland, both operating seaplanes and neither with facilities for land-based aircraft. These were Dundee and Fort George, which had been in operation since 1913.

Fort George came about following the ending of seaplane operations from Cromarty in late 1913. At least one Bessonneau hangar was dismantled at Cromarty and transported by tug to Fort George in October 1913. On the 27th the tug *Resource* was used to deliver the advance party and stores, and it took the remainder of the year to move all the equipment to Fort George, aggravated by poor weather conditions. Now under the command of Lt Cdr A. Longmore, potential landing grounds at Ardersier and Carse of Delnies were inspected but not considered to be suitable. Longmore was later posted to Calshot, handing over command to Lt Oliver on 26 January 1914.

No specific unit was ever based at Fort George, but the main and most common type to be seen there was the Wright Navy seaplane. These flimsy looking biplane pusher seaplanes continued to fly from the Moray Firth until 1916, with only one ever being recorded as lost during this existence: Wright No 155 was wrecked during a gale on 8 April 1915, becoming Fort George's only recorded casualty.

At least one shed (70 by 70 feet) was constructed at Fort George during the war, and was removed to Smoogroo on 25 June 1918.

Nigg

57°41'33"N/04°01'12"W, NH797687. Nigg ferry at end of B9175, 1.75 miles SSW of Nigg

A SMALL seaplane station was established here in 1913, but does not seem to have been used a great deal and was not developed. During the Second World War a torpedo boat was established on the same site near the Nigg ferry.

Thurso

58°35'55"N/03°30'48"W, ND121689. W of River Thurso entrance, 0.5 miles NE of town centre

THURSO briefly existed as a 'knee-jerk' response to the potential U-boat threat at the beginning of the war, when it and Scapa Flow were chosen as sites for seaplane stations to help protect the Fleet on 13 August 1914. Not long afterwards a single S.38 biplane was delivered by rail, but had already left by the end of the month. Before the end of 1914 all plans to establish a station at Thurso had been abandoned, and all equipment and personnel were merged with Scapa Flow.

LOTHIAN

Belhaven Sands, East Lothian

56°00'14"N/02°33'02"W, NT652792. 1.5 miles W of Dunbar, 0.7 miles due N of West Barns

BELHAVEN SANDS was a temporary landing ground laid out on a broad beach for the use of Sopwith Cuckoos that were carrying out torpedo-dropping trials in the Firth of Forth from June to November 1918. Work began in April 1918 and, as well as preparing the beach, several huts were erected as workshops. A pair of Bessonneau hangars were also provided, but accommodation remained at East Fortune.

A Sopwith Cuckoo drops its torpedo in a scene representative of what took place off Belhaven Sands nearly 100 years ago.

The aircraft of 208 TDS are dwarfed by the *R.29* at East Fortune in 1918. *H. A. Vasse via A. P. Ferguson*

Colinton (Edinburgh), Mid-Lothian (Edinburgh)

55°53'55"N/03°15'53"W, NT222692. Adjacent to Redford Barracks, 3.75 miles SW of Edinburgh city centre

ONE of three small LGs located close to Scotland's capital, Colinton was established in April 1916. Little more than a reasonably level square field, Colinton was used by 77(HD) Squadron until the autumn of 1916 in response to the increasing Zeppelin threat.

East Fortune, East Lothian

56°00'02"N/02°44'03"W, NT555786. 3 miles NE of Haddington

FROM the beginning of 1915, the first Zeppelin attacks began on Great Britain and a 'knee-jerk' reaction at the time was to build a plethora of HD LGs to deal with this new threat. One of these sites was located 3.5 miles south of North Berwick and 3 miles north-east of Haddington near the small village of East Fortune, all within East Lothian. Positioned south of the village, with the East Coast railway line curving its way to the north, the small LG first saw aircraft in September 1915. The Director of Naval Air Services, which came under control of the Admiralty that same month, commissioned the site and the intention was to operate airships from here.

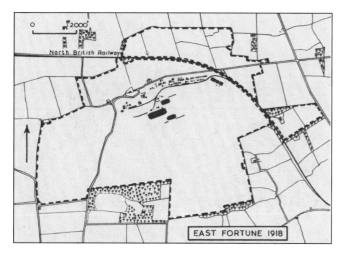

EAST FORTUNE 1918

Before the arrival of airships, the first aircraft types arrived from Montrose. They consisted of a single Maurice Farman and a pair of Sopwith Scouts, followed later by Avro 504s and BE.2Cs. These aircraft were initially housed in a hired marquee, but this proved to be completely inadequate in providing protection against the Scottish elements. Coastal-type airships began to arrive in mid-1916, and construction of a pair of North Sea Airship Sheds (320 by 100 by 80 feet) began not long after. Rapid construction of both technical and domestic buildings quickly changed the small airfield from an LG to a fully functional airfield and airship station covering 1,330 acres, measuring 4,000 by 2,700 yards.

During the only Zeppelin attack on Edinburgh during the night of 2/3 April 1916, a single aircraft was dispatched from East Fortune to intercept. The 504C, piloted by Sub-Lt Cox, attempted to attack Zeppelin *L14*, which had been spotted near St Abbs Head, 28 miles east of the airfield. An overcast sky protected the enemy raider and Cox was unable to find it. On returning to the airfield, the 504 crashed on landing and Cox was seriously injured.

RNAS East Fortune was officially commissioned on 23 August 1916, and development of the airfield continued into 1917. A third, much larger, Rigid Airship Shed (700 by 180 by 100 feet) was built during 1917. By July of that year the large hangar was accommodating the new North Sea Class non-rigid airships, which served until the Armistice and beyond. The first rigid airship, HMA No 24, arrived in late 1917, followed by the successful *R29* a few months later.

208 TDS was formed at East Fortune in June 1918 with a host of aircraft including the Sopwith Camel, 1½ Strutter and Pup. This unit was disbanded a few weeks later to form the Fleet Aerial Gunnery School and No 1 TTS. The latter was created to train crews on the new Sopwith Cuckoo torpedo plane, the first example of its type to be able to operate from an aircraft carrier. 1 TTS only existed for a few weeks and the result was the formation of 185 Squadron, which would go on to operate from HMS *Argus*.

By mid-1920 the airfield was reduced to Care & Maintenance, and by 1922 the giant Airship Sheds had been dismantled. More than 350 acres of the land was sold to the South Eastern Counties of Scotland Joint Sanatorium Board and a tuberculosis hospital was established in the vast majority of the former airfield buildings.

East Fortune main units, 1915-20

RNAS Home Defence detached from Dundee, Sep 1915;
to Dundee, Aug 1916

RNAS War Flt formed Aug 1916;
DB 1916

Observers School Flt formed Mar 1917

'F' Sqn RNAS formed 20 Dec 1917;
to HMS *Furious*

Naval Flying School formed 1917;
DB Jun 1918

208 TDS formed Jun 1918;
DB 19 Jul 1918 (M.1C, Camel, 504, Pup and 1½ Strutter)

Torpedo Aeroplane School formed 3 Jul 1918;
absorbed into 201 TDS, 14 Aug 1918
(Cuckoo, Short 310 and Shirl)

Fleet AGS (ex-208 TDS) 19 Jul 1918;
DB 10 Nov 1918

1 TTS (ex-208 TDS) 19 Jul 1918;
absorbed into 201 TDS, 14 Aug 1918 (F.2B, Cuckoo and Shirl)

201 TDS reformed 14 Aug 1918;
redesignated TTS, 30 Apr 1919 (various aircraft)

HQ Unit/Flt HMS *Argus* formed 17 Aug 1918;
embarked at Rosyth, 7 Oct 1918

185 Sqn formed 19 Oct 1918;
DB 14 Apr 1919 (Cuckoo)

TTS (ex-201 TDS) 30 Apr 1919;
DB 1920 (Cuckoo)

Gifford (Townhead/Haddington), East Lothian

55°55'03"N/02°43'54"W, NT545695. 0.3 miles E of Chippendale International School of Furniture, 1.2 miles NE of Gifford, 3.2 miles SE of Haddington

ESTABLISHED specifically for the use of 77(HD) Squadron in January 1917, this small LG did not see a great deal of aerial activity. Covering approximately 35 acres and measuring 700 by 400 yards, it was classified as an NLG3. The LG remained in military hands until mid-1919.

Gilmerton (Edinburgh), Edinburgh

55°53'57"N/03°07'18"W, NT297678. S of Gilmerton Station Road (A772), A720 passes through W edge of site, 0.7 miles SE of Gilmerton

THIS was another LG for the use of 77(HD) Squadron, opened to help it defend Edinburgh. It was brought into use in December 1916 and used by the squadron until 1918. It covered 59 acres, was classified as an NLG2, and measured 600 by 470 yards.

Granton, Edinburgh

55°58'58"N/03°13'23"W, NT240775. In region of Royal Forth Yacht Club, 2.5 miles NNW of Edinburgh city centre

A PERMANENT detachment of seaplanes had been operating from Granton Harbour since November 1914, the site being designated as a sub-station for Dundee. This continued into 1915, but comings and goings began to tail off by the end of the year. The occasional Beardmore-built seaplane also used Granton Harbour, but in 1916 the site was probably closed.

Gullane (West Fenton), East Lothian

56°01'09"N/02°48'01"W, NT505810. 2 miles S of Dirleton off B1345

FIRST opened in early 1917, West Fenton was one of many landing grounds for 77 (HD) Squadron. This small aerodrome, classified as an HD NLG1, had only the most basic of facilities at first. It was later surveyed for further development and renamed Gullane, becoming the home of 2 TDS, which was formed here on 15 April 1918.

Seven 1918-pattern GS Sheds (170 by 100 feet) were built as well as an array of timber technical and domestic buildings. By now the airfield was also known as Gullane, after the village located 3 miles north-west; it occupied 186 acres and measured 1,100 by 900 yards. The only operational unit to serve at Gullane during this time was the 41st Aero Squadron, equipped with the Camel and SPAD. The 41st operated from Gullane from April to August 1918 before it departed for Northern France.

With the massive run-down of the newly formed RAF at the end of the war, 2 TDS, like so many others, was also run down. It was officially closed on 21 November 1919 and was abandoned, but would rise as one of Scotland's most famous fighter stations, RAF Drem.

Gullane main units, 1918-19

77(HD) Sqn from Turnhouse, Jan 1917;
DB 13 Jun 1919 (various aircraft)

2 TDS formed 15 Apr 1918;
DB 21 Nov 1919 (Scout, Pup, Camel, SE.5A and 504)

41st Aero Sqn, USAAC, from Montrose, Apr 1918;
to France, 14 Aug 1918

151 Sqn cadre from Liettres, 21 Feb 1919;
DB 10 Sep 1919 (Camel)

152 Sqn cadre from Liettres, 21 Feb 1919;
DB 30 Jun 1919 (Camel)

Sopwith F.1 Camel E1450 served with 2 TDS at Gullane from July 1918. *Via Ray Sturtivant*

Hoprig Mains, East Lothian

55°57'08"N/02°53'20"W, NT446736. SE of Hoprig
Mains, W of go-kart racetrack off B6363, 1.1 miles NE
of Macmerry

THIS small HD NLG2 was allocated to 36(HD) Squadron, but transferred to 77(HD) Squadron when it opened in August 1916. The site was closed down in favour of Penston in July 1917.

Myreside (Edinburgh), Edinburgh

55°55'43"N/03°14'03"W, NT2297726. In region of
Borough Muir Rugby Club, W of Union Canal, 2.5 miles
SW of Edinburgh city centre

ANOTHER LG located around the outskirts of Edinburgh, Myreside is not credited as being used by 77(HD) Squadron, but this is the only unit that was most likely to have used it.

Penston I, East Lothian

55°55'59"N/02°53'19"W, NT445715. W of B6363, 0.5
miles due S of Penston Farm, 1 mile SE of Macmerry

THIS replacement for Hoprig Mains was opened as an HD NLG1 in December 1916 for 77(HD) Squadron. Occupying 94 acres, the LG's service was short because on the opposite side of the B6363 yet another aerodrome was set to supersede it. The first of two sites named Penston was closed down in August 1917.

Penston II, East Lothian

55°55'58"N/02°52'43"W, NT451715. E side of B6363,
NW of Hodges and W of Butterdean Wood, 1.3 miles
SE of Macmerry

AS the original Penston site across the road closed, the new aerodrome opened in August 1917 as an HD Flight Station for the use of 77(HD) Squadron. The largest of three sites located close to Macmerry, Penston II occupied 106 acres and measured 900 by 700 yards. It was also the best equipped, with a pair of HD-pattern Aeroplane Sheds (130 by 60 feet) and several technical and domestic buildings all huddled around Hodges Farm.

'A' Flight, 77(HD) Squadron, was the first to move in from Turnhouse, followed by 'B' Flight from New Haggerston and the main squadron HQ from Edinburgh by January 1918. All three of the squadron's Flights were in residence by April 1918, carrying out aerial cooperation duties with local coastal batteries. The main equipment was the 504K(NF) from April 1918, with on average sixteen aircraft on strength. 'A' and 'B' Flights were detached to Whiteburn, but on 13 June 1919 the squadron centralised for one final time, only to be disbanded the same day. The station was wound down by late 1919 and closed by February 1920.

Skateraw (Innerwick), East Lothian

55°58'05"N/02°24'59"W, NT740751. Above Skateraw
harbour, possibly located W of Torness Nuclear Power
Station

DESCRIBED as 'on cliffs of sea coast', that was literally where Skateraw was. Also known as Innerwick, this small HD NLG3 extended across 53 acres and measured 650 by 400 yards. It served as a landing ground for 77(HD) Squadron during 1917 and 1918 in its defence of Edinburgh and the Firth of Forth.

South Belton (Dunbar), East Lothian

55°59'11"N/02°33'22"W, NT654775. E of Thirstly
Cross, N of A1, 1.75 miles WSW of Dunbar

COVERING just 44 acres and measuring 480 by 450 yards, South Belton was another of 77(HD) Squadron's landing grounds, and was open from 1916 to late 1918 and classified as a DLG2 and NLG3.

Turnhouse (Edinburgh), Mid-Lothian

55°57'09"N/03°21'46"W, NT60735. Current Edinburgh
Airport, 5 miles W of Edinburgh city centre

LOCATED to the west of Scotland's capital, this once busy fighter station is still bustling as Edinburgh Airport after nearly 100 years of almost continuous activity. Steady development over the years has significantly changed the airfield, and it is now a serious international airport that can cater for the largest modern airliners.

The site for a new aerodrome was quickly requisitioned by the Ministry of Munitions in 1914. The land originally belonged to the Dalmeny Estate, owned by the Earl of Rosebery since 1665. This also included land at Turnhouse Farm and Craigihall, all of which was owned by the Earl.

The airfield's first unit can be traced back to 1915 when the Aeroplane Barrage Line constructed a flight station for the RFC. 44 Squadron arrived without aircraft on 18 April 1916, after forming at Catterick in Yorkshire. Before any flying machines arrived, the unit was disbanded into 26 TS on 22 May 1916. The new unit took charge of eighteen Maurice Farman Short and Longhorn trainers, which had arrived on 1 May, under the control of No 19 (Training) Wing.

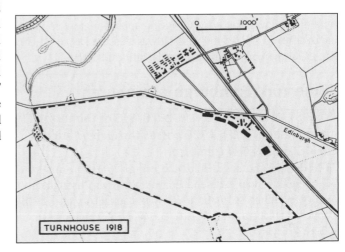

TURNHOUSE 1918

This is Turnhouse not long after it opened in 1916, with aircraft of 26 RS (later 26 TS). *Via Stuart Leslie*

By 1916 German Zeppelin raids were on the increase, but they remained few and far between over Scottish soil. A Zeppelin raid on Edinburgh during the night of 2/3 April 1916 resulted in a permanent detachment of 77 Squadron being based there.

Under the control of 19 Wing, an ARD was formed at Turnhouse and more permanent facilities were established. Now covering 149 acres and measuring 1,550 by 450 yards, hangarage included five Aeroplane Sheds (two at 200 by 70 feet, one 130 by 120 feet, one 170 by 80 feet, and one 150 by 70 feet).

77 Squadron's responsibilities began to shrink by 1918 and it moved as a whole to Penston. After re-equipping with the 504K, a better aircraft but still unsuitable for tackling Zeppelins, the squadron disbanded on 13 June 1919.

A period of inactivity followed before the airfield was taken over by the Admiralty and the Firth of Forth Group on 1 November 1918. The Group was formed under the control of the Commander-in-Chief of the Grand Fleet and controlled the RAF bases at Turnhouse, Rosyth and Donibristle. Turnhouse remained in this role until December 1919, when the Group was disbanded. The airfield was briefly the home of 103 Squadron, which arrived from Maisoncelle in France on 1 February 1919. By 3 March it had taken its DH.9s and DH.10s to Crail, and Turnhouse fell silent.

An early Submarine Scout airship about to embark on a patrol from Caldale in 1917.

Tynehead, Mid-Lothian

55°48'58"N/02°59'24"W, NT380585. N of A7, NW of Middleton Mains, 1 mile SW of Tynehead

PROBABLY little more than field with a few tents in the corner, this small LG was used by 77(HD) Squadron during 1917 and 1918. One of many used by the squadron in its efforts to defend Edinburgh from the Zeppelin, Tynehead occupied 114 acres and measured 850 by 650 yards.

ORKNEY

Caldale

58°58'22"N/03°01'09"W, HY415099. W of Bloomfield Road off Old Finstown Road, 2.2 miles WSW of Kirkwall

CALDALE was located in a low-lying area sheltered to the west by Keelylang Hill and Wideford Hill to the north, both of which rose to more than 700 feet. Its main role was to provide anti-submarine patrols and convoy escort in the waters surrounding the islands using the SSPs (Sea/Submarine Scout Pushers). To accommodate these airships a pair of large sheds, one Coastal Type (220 by 70 feet) and one Submarine Type (150 by 45 feet), were built. The sheds were staggered, and six giant windbreaks were also constructed to help when manoeuvring the airships in and out of them. A technical area was also constructed as well as accommodation for at least 200 personnel, which was located next to the minor road at the site entrance.

The 146-acre site was officially opened in July 1916, although the large Coastal Shed was not completed until September 1917. This was aggravated by the remote location and the difficulty in obtaining stores. Designated as a Class B Airship Station, the first airships to arrive were a pair of Submarine Scouts, *SS41* and *SS43*.

On 22 January 1918 an order was received from the Admiralty to close the airship station. It would now change roles and become a kite balloon base using 19th-century balloon technology to simply lift observers into the air. This seemingly backward step was very effective on a clear day, with a potential height of between 2,000 and 3,000 feet being achieved. With the formation of the RAF, Caldale had another

Caldale's 150-foot-long Submarine Type Airship Shed survived until the 1930s.

name change, this time becoming 20 Balloon Base on 15 April 1918. The name was later modified again to Balloon Training Base at the end of the war. The unit was disbanded on 15 September 1919 and Caldale was abandoned not long afterwards, although several of the buildings, including the giant sheds, survived into the 1930s, and virtually all of their concrete bases remain today.

Houton Bay

58°55'01"N/03°11'03"W. E and W of Houton Bay, 10 miles SW of Kirkwall off A964

HOUTON Bay was the largest seaplane and kite balloon station constructed on the Orkney mainland during the war. It spread itself across 188 acres from Quoy of Houton in the west, through the Houths to Midland Ness in the east, all of which surrounded the Bay of Houton. This natural harbour was perfect for seaplane operations, combined with the added protection of the Holm of Houton, which extends around the southern half of the bay.

Construction began in 1916 and buildings included two F-Type Sheds (200 by 100 feet), one Seaplane Shed (180 by 60 feet), ten canvas Balloon Hangars (100 by 36 feet) and three slipways. It also had an engineers' workshop, which included a carpenter, tinsmith and blacksmith. It even had its own meteorological section, an engine store and a test house, as well as its own butcher and tailor for the 350-plus personnel that were posted here.

Felixstowe F.3 N4403 of 306 Flight at Houton Bay in late 1918.

One of many Felixstowe F.2As that served at Houton Bay was N4517, pictured in late 1918.

By late 1917 various aircraft, including the H.16 'Large America', F.2 and F.3 flying-boats, were stationed here on the hunt for enemy U-boats. A huge submarine net had been strung across the English Channel, forcing the enemy boats to travel around Scotland to and from Germany. During early 1918 the Kite Balloon Section was formed here, remaining in service until it was closed down on 23 April 1919. The section was complemented by the formation of 19 Balloon Base on 15 April 1918. The former Royal Navy Kite Balloon Station unit was disbanded on 15 April 1919. The first of several seaplane and flying boat flights was formed at Houton on 30 May 1918. The first was 430(S) Flight, which was created from the station's 'War Flight', flying the Short 184. 306(FB) Flight followed on 31 July 1918 with a variety of aircraft including the H.16, F.3, Short 184 and Baby.

Even after the war new units continued to be formed, including Orkney Wing, which only lasted from June to 27 October 1919. The previous month both 306 and 430 Flights had also been disbanded, leaving Houton in a temporary state of flux. This lasted until 16 March 1920 when the station was retitled RAF Practice Base (Houton Bay) using aircraft that had been on Houton's establishment. By 1921 this once busy seaplane station had no further purpose or role to play in peacetime, and was closed by September.

Houton Bay main units, 1917-21

Seaplane War Flight formed 1917;
redesignated 430 (Independent) Flt, 30 May 1918

Kite Balloon Station Houton Bay formed 1917;
redesignated 19 BB, 1 Apr 1918

19 BB formed 1 Apr 1918;
DB 23 Apr 1919

Flying-Boat War Flt formed 1918;
redesignated 306 (Independent) Flt, 31 Jul 1918

430 (Independent) Flt formed (ex-Seaplane War Flight)
30 May 1918;
DB 19 Sep 1918

306 (Independent) Flt formed (ex-FB War Flt);
DB Mar 1919

F Boat Seaplane Training Flt formed 15 Aug 1918;
DB 25 Nov 1918

Wireless Station formed 1919;
DB 1921

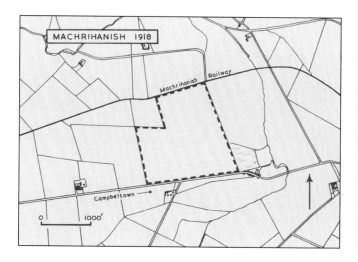

Houton (Orphir)

58°55'05"N/03°09'53"W, HY330040. Head of Banks, S
of Gyre Road, 0.5 miles SW of Orphir

ONE of the balloon units quoted as being stationed at
Houton Bay was most probably stationed at Orphir, just
a few hundred yards up the road.

Kirkwall Bay

58°59'17"N/02°58'16"W, HY442115. Close to
Granshore Road, SE edge of later RNAS Hatston site

AN RNAS seaplane station is believed have been located
on the edge of the bay during 1913, but was not expanded
or used to any great extent.

Pierowall (Westray)

59°21'03"N/02°57'00"W, HY440482. Bay of Pierowall,
Westray

A SMALL seaplane station was established here by early
1917 in a strategically good position, 30 miles north of
Scapa Flow. Sopwith Babys were the first to make use of the
site during the summer of 1917. Not extensively used, a
detachment of two F.3s of 306(FB) Flight from Houton Bay
stayed here from 10 August 1918. One of the aircraft, N4411,
flown by Capt P. Bend, attacked a U-boat on 29 August, but
beyond that very little is known about Pierowall, and it is
surprising that it was not used more.

Scapa

58°57'42"N/02°58'12"W, HY441090. 1 mile due S of
Kirkwall, at Nether Scapa on shore of Scapa Bay

SOME of the earliest seaplane patrols of the war were flown
by Scapa's seaplane station. Opened around August 1914,

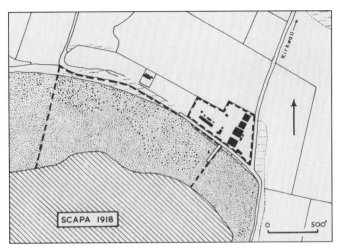

SCAPA 1918

Henry Farman Pusher-type seaplanes were recorded as
patrolling from here in September. Initially, very ramshackle
temporary structures were erected to protect the two seaplanes
serving here from the unforgiving weather. By the end of
September these were replaced by the slightly more
substantial Bessonneau and a pair of Piggot tents. It was not
long before the weather got the better of the hangars, and on
21 November 1914 one collapsed in a gale. A Sopwith Boat
Pusher Amphibian, one of only two serving with the RNAS
at the time, was destroyed.

A solid pair of hangars (69 by 69 feet) were later added to
the canvas Bessonneaus, and additional technical buildings
such as an engineering workshop and a variety of tradesmen's
huts were also built. Two accommodation huts and a separate
officers' quarters were also built. Expansion steadily continued
as the war progressed, and by 1918 a Fleet Aircraft Repair
Base and Stores Depot was established here.

This is one of just two Felixstowe F.3s of 306 Flight that saw
service at Pierowall during the last few months of the war.

Smoogroo

58°55'09"N/03°07'49"W, HY350052. E of The Breck at Toy Ness, 1 mile ESE of Orphir

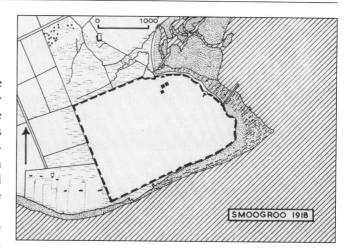

SMOOGROO 1918

IN mid-1917 an uneven but open piece of land on the northern edge of Scapa Flow found itself becoming the only airfield available to the Grand Fleet while berthed in the Orkney Islands. Smoogroo was used as a safe haven for pilots who were taking part in the first experiments of flying land-based aircraft from ships. After launching there was no return to the ship other than a risky ditching and, however rough and ready Smoogroo was, it would have been a welcome place under the wheels of any man's aircraft.

It was from Smoogroo that RNAS history was made when Sqn Cdr E. H. Dunning took off in his Sopwith Camel and successfully landed on the moving deck of HMS *Furious* on 2 August 1917. This was the first time an aircraft had landed on a moving ship, and from that moment the aircraft carrier was born.

Designated as a fleet practice station, facilities were few and far between, with shelter provided by just three Bessonneau hangars (66 by 66 feet) located in the north-east corner of the field, which occupied a total of 66 acres. Any repairs were carried out at Houton Bay or Scapa Flow

seaplane stations, and aircraft were transferred by ship via a lengthy jetty on the eastern shore of the site. On 16 March 1920 RAF Practice Base (Smoogroo) was formed out of the old Smoogroo station establishment, the majority of which had been based at Houton Bay. By 1921 this small but useful little site had been abandoned, leaving little to indicate any aviation history. Today the site is still as open as it was nearly 100 years ago and only the jetty remains, still providing a useful berth for small vessels.

It was from Smoogroo that history was made when Sqn Cdr E. H. Dunning took off in his Camel and successfully landed on the moving deck of HMS *Furious* on 2 August 1917.

Stenness (Stenness Loch)

58°59'18"N/03°13'04"W, HY300117. W of Standing Stones Hotel, off A965, 10 miles W of Kirkwall

ONLY 5 miles north of Houton Bay, another, much smaller seaplane station was established on the edge of Stenness Loch, the largest brackish lagoon in Great Britain. More than 200 personnel were stationed here; the majority, and the lucky ones (23 officers), were accommodated in the Standing Stones Hotel, and the unlucky ones in eleven wooden huts.

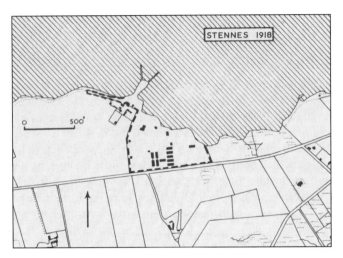

Three new flights, namely 309, 310 and 311(FB) Flights, were formed in May and July 1918. All three operated the F.3, tasked with flying anti-submarine patrols and operations for the Grand Fleet. However, the loch was found to be shallow and exposed for flying-boat operations, and all flying took place from Houton Bay, although all three Flights are credited with being disbanded at Stenness by September 1918. The Standing Stones Hotel continued to play an important role in the region, becoming the home of 28 Group (Orkney & Shetland) on 13 July 1918. It remained in this role under the control of the C-in-C Grand Fleet until it was disbanded into 29 Group on 15 April 1919.

SHETLAND

Balta Sound (Unst)

60°45'37"N/00°50'18"W, HP639105. S of Springfield Road, Baltasound jetty, 0.7 miles ENE of Baltasound

AN advanced mooring station was established here during the war for the use of Catfirth-based flying-boats. There was very little activity beyond 1919, but a seaplane slipway was built by an auxiliary battalion of the Royal Marines along the edge of Balta Sound in April 1940.

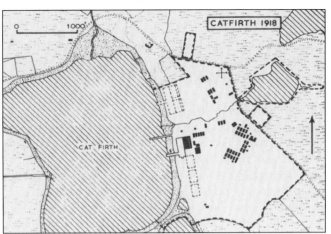

Catfirth

60°15'51"N/01°11'28"W, HU448552. 0.5mile NW of Freester, 0.8 miles SE of Catfirth

THE Shetland Islands' first seaplane station arrived too late in the war to play a significant role. Work began in early 1918 on the well-equipped station, with facilities including a large slipway and a hangar (200 by 100 feet) capable of accommodating the RNAS's largest flying-boats of the day.

With the formation of the RAF, plans to accommodate a larger flying-boat unit were reduced to just a single flight. This took the form of 300(FB) Flight, which was formed at Catfirth within 28 Group on 14 June 1918. The flight was equipped with the Felixstowe F.3 and the Porte FB.2, both capable medium-range flying-boats of sturdy design. Their task during the final months of the war would have been to patrol for enemy ships and submarines, although encounters in this region by late 1918 would have been rare, if made at all.

Five further flights, 301 to 305(FB) Flights, also operating the F.3, were also scheduled to arrive at Catfirth. However, the end of the war was in sight and none of them were formed. 300(FB) Flight continued to operate alone from Catfirth until the end of March 1919, then the site was clinically closed on 15 April.

Surprisingly, considering the short time it was in service, a great deal of Catfirth remains today. The slipway and hangar base are easy to find, and several accommodation huts still stand as you approach the shoreline. Its condition during the Second World War attracted the attentions of Luftwaffe aerial reconnaissance – Catfirth was obviously giving the impression that it was still in use!

Lerwick (Grimista/Gremista)

60°09'32"N/01°08'56"W, HU465433. 2 miles N of Lerwick

OCCUPYING just 15 acres of land, construction of a kite balloon station at Lerwick began in late 1917; it was located on the shore of Bressay Sound, the strait between Bressay Island and the Shetland mainland.

Facilities included twelve sheds (100 by 36 feet) designed to accommodate kite balloons. A hydrogen production plant was also built, as well as five piers positioned along the shoreline heading north-east, at which Royal Navy ships berthed to collect the kite balloons.

By the end of the war the site was still occupied, but beyond that its use was probably very limited and it was probably closed by 1919. Today the landscape has completed changed, with modern roads straddling the site and a large marina now occupying the original shoreline.

STRATHCLYDE

Ayr (Racecourse)

55°27'54"N/4°36'91"W, NS350220. NE area of Ayr

THIS airfield was established, as the name suggests, on Ayr Racecourse, which had opened in 1907. It is quite possible that an aircraft or two visited the flat expanse of grass before the arrival of the RFC on 17 September 1917. Occupying 138 acres and measuring 1,250 by 670 yards, the aerodrome later supported sixteen Bessonneau hangars and a single GS Shed, which survived until the 1990s.

The first occupant that would continue to re-manifest itself at Ayr in several different forms was No 1 SoAF. On 10 May 1918 it became No 1 SoAF&G, only to be redesignated again on the 29th to become No 1 FS. The diverse range of aircraft now operating from Ayr increased again, including the DH.9, Pup, Snipe, Dolphin and even the large Handley Page O/400 bomber.

The North Western Area FIS was the next and final unit to be formed during the airfield's short history. Both of Ayr's resident units survived long enough to become part of the new RAF, but the instructors school was disbanded on 15 January 1919 and 1 FS closed on 1 April.

Little if any evidence of continued aviation activity has been recorded, although it can be safely said that the original flying field is still fairly well preserved today in the shape of Ayr Racecourse.

Ayr main units, 1917-19

1 SoAF formed 17 Sep 1917;
to Turnberry and DB into 1 SAF&G, 10 May 1918
(Camel, DH.2, 504J and SE.5A)

25th Aero Sqn, USAAS, from USA, 23 Jan 1918;
to Marske, 23 Apr 1918

105 Sqn from Andover, 10 May 1918;
to Omagh, 19 May 1918 (RE.8)

106 Sqn from Andover, 21 May 1918;
to Fermoy (RE.8)

NW Area FIS formed 1 Jul 1918;
to Redcar, 15 Jan 1919 (504J/K)

Bogton (Dalmellington)

55°19'24"N/04°24'35"W, NS472057. SW of Dalmellington, on edge of Loch Bogton

AFTER the failure of trying to build an aerodrome near Loch Doon, an alternative with an unpromising name was found near Dalmellington. Named after Loch Bogton, the site was still a marshy one and was prone to flooding, but it was hoped with time and drainage that the new aerodrome would improve.

First surveyed in March 1917, work was carried out swiftly and by early April a pair of 1916-pattern GS Sheds (180 by 80 feet) had been erected and two aircraft, a BE.2C and a de Havilland Scout, had arrived. By the summer the aerodrome had continued to develop with workshops, stores, vehicle sheds and eighteen brick-built accommodation buildings, each designed for thirty men. Even the two hangars were centrally heated, which, combined with the comfortable accommodation, made this a very pleasant posting.

'Y' Squadron formed here as part of the SoAG School in April 1917, but the failure and eventual cancellation of the Loch Doon aerial gunnery range in December 1917 resulted in Bogton seeing very little use.

Carmunnock (Cathcart/Glasgow)

55°47'34"N/04°14'30"W, NS595578. S of Carmunnock Road, 0.25 miles NW of Carmunnock

HUNDREDS of brand-new aircraft first took to the air from this small grass aerodrome during the war, all of them built by G. & J. Weir. Weir combined with several other companies to become the Scottish Group of Manufacturers, all engaged in the mass-production of military aircraft. Contracts came in thick and fast, beginning with an order for 450 FE.2Bs and 600 DH.9s, although 200 of these were later cancelled. As part of the Scottish Group, Weir also worked with Alexander Stephen, North British Locomotive Company and Barclay, Curle & Company. Within this partnership Weir helped to build 300 BE.2s and had at least a hand in building up to another 300 FE.2Bs. By 1918 all Weir-built aircraft were test-flown from Renfrew, and Carmunnock's brief but very busy existence came to an end.

Dalmuir (Robertson's Field)

55°54'39"N/04°26'39"W, NS475712. W of Duntocher Burn, S of Forth & Clyde Canal on edge of River Clyde (bonded warehouse site)

TO meet the huge number of orders for aircraft that had fallen upon W. M. Beardmore & Co Ltd, the company constructed a massive building on the north bank of the River Clyde in 1915. It was called the 'Seaplane Sheds', and by the time it was finished the company had more than 63,000 sq ft of floor space. At a similar time a small airfield was established at Dalmuir, next to the shipyard, known as Robertson's Field after the local farmer, Peter Robertson. By 1916 a pair of hangars were built and the first batch of sixty BE.2Cs were the first aircraft to be reassembled here, test-flown, then transferred to Inchinnan. Beardmore went on to

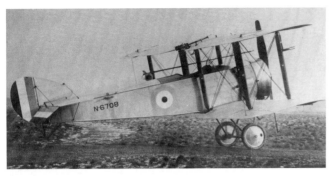

Beardmore WB.3 N6708 at Dalmuir; this aircraft was based on the Sopwith Pup, but lacked its performance.

produce the Camel in great numbers as well as its own WB.2, and a few V/1500s were also flown from here.

Beardmore also produced hundreds of seaplanes during the war, and these were also built in the 'Seaplane Sheds' and launched onto the Clyde for their first flights via a slipway at Dumbarton.

Helensburgh

55°00'47"N/04°46'21"W, NS272834. Rhu Marina, 1.65 miles WNW of Helensburgh Central railway station

W. M. Beardmore & Co Ltd build at least one seaplane slipway at Rhu in 1915, and the same site was taken over by the MAEE during the Second World War.

Inchinnan

55°53'01"N/04°26'22"W, NS476684

IN late 1915 Beardmore won a contract to build a very large naval airship, and to carry out this work a new giant Airship Shed (720 by 230 by 122 feet) was constructed a mile south of the Dalmuir shipyard at Inchinnan. Work began on the building

in January 1916 and was completed by September, the site by then occupying 413 acres and measuring 1,830 by 1,400 yards. The first airship built was the *R24*, followed by the *R27*, and the more famous *R34* was also constructed at Inchinnan.

In 1917 No 6 AAP was established, having been formed as the Glasgow AAP for the acceptance of locally built aircraft. These included Cuckoos built by Fairfield, and G. & J. Weir-built DH.9s and FE.2Bs. Beardmore-built aircraft were also received here, but test-flown at the company's own small aerodrome across the Clyde at Dalmuir. On 12 October 1917 the unit was restyled, rather than redesignated, as No 6 (Glasgow) AAP, and continued to operate from Inchinnan until it moved to Renfrew on 10 March 1918.

With the AAP gone and no more orders for new airships, the site was closed down just after the end of the war. The giant shed lingered on for a few years, but in 1923 it was sold and reduced to scrap.

Loch Doon I, II and III

Site I: 55°15'11"N/04°23'10"W, NX483980. 0.4 miles W of Craigencolon
Site II: 55°15'29"N/04°22'36"W, NX490983. 0.4 miles N of Craigencolon, W edge of Loch Doon
Site III: 55°13'09"N/04°22'30"W, NX490943. Portmark, E edge of Loch Doon

LOCATED in one of the most beautiful parts of Scotland, Loch Doon was little more than a very expensive attempt to establish an aerial gunnery and seaplane school. The concept was the brainchild of Brig Sefton Brancker who, having recently returned from France, saw the importance of thorough training in the art of aerial fighting.

Despite being offered alternative sites all over the British Isles, work began here in mid-1916. An elaborate moving target range was also constructed at the north-eastern corner of the

The 643-foot-long *R34* emerges from the giant 720-foot-long Airship Shed (the largest built in Scotland at the time) at Inchinnan for the first time in March 1919.

loch. The aerodrome was located on a flat piece of land south of Garpel, and by the spring of 1917 more than 3,000 men were working on the site. The SoAG was formed here in January 1917, and on the very edge of Loch Doon a seaplane school was also formed. By January 1918 both aerodrome and seaplane sites had been abandoned, and a third site on the eastern of the loch was also attempted as a seaplane station, only to suffer the same fate. Despite thousands of yards of pipe being laid, the marshy soil could not be drained adequately, and the site was abandoned in favour of Dalmellington a few miles north.

Machrihanish (Strabane)

55°25'13"N/05°39'50"W, NR682201. 1 mile W of Stewarton, N of B843, 2 miles SE of West Darlochnan/Campbeltown Airport

THE first airfield to bear the name Machrihanish was established in 1917 as sub-station for Luce Bay. The site was a combined aerodrome and airship sub-station, which provided nothing more than a place to land when the weather prevented a return to Luce Bay. No more than 600 yards by 550 yards in size, spread across 65 acres, the site was located north of Strath Farm and hemmed in by the Campbeltown & Machrihanish Light Railway to the north.

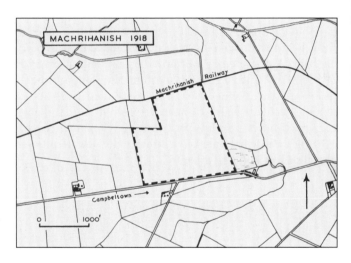

272 Squadron was formed here on 25 July 1918 from 531, 532 and 533 Flights, flying the DH.6 on 'scarecrow' anti-submarine patrols. From November 1918 the more purposeful Fairey IIIA was introduced before the squadron disbanded on 5 March 1919. The airfield was closed down not long afterwards, but enjoyed a second existence as Campbeltown from the 1930s, before being overshadowed by its much larger neighbour.

A visiting North Sea Aerial Navigation Blackburn Kangaroo generates a lot of interest at Moorpark.

Renfrew (Moorpark)

55°52'00"N/04°23'26"W. M8 motorway follows line of runway

IT was local manufacturer G. & J. Weir that first flew its aircraft from Renfrew in late 1915. Contracts for the mass-production of the BE.2C/E and FE.2B saw the establishment of Aeronautical Inspection, Glasgow, at Renfrew from April 1916. The AI was formed in the 19th Wing, Scottish Command, specifically for the acceptance of all the Weir-built aircraft. On 10 March 1918 6 AAP moved in from Inchinnan and the resident AI was dissolved into it. By 2 May the unit was redesignated as 6 (Renfrew) AAP before closing down on 31 May 1919. In the meantime, 55 Squadron, albeit as a cadre, moved in from St Andre-aux-Bois and 6 (Scottish) ARD was formed here on 31 May 1919. The ARD only lasted until 29 September, and 55 Squadron was moved to Shotwick on 1 January 1920, bringing this first phase of Renfrew's history to an abrupt end.

A brightly coloured BE.2C has its prop swung at Turnberry in late 1917.

Turnberry

55°19'32"N/04°49'27"W. S of Maidens, N of
Turnberry, A719 passes through airfield site

IT is very unusual to record an airfield that has a history covering almost a century, has been used in four different guises, and is still used in a limited capacity today.

For those who are subservient to the world of golf, it would seem sacrosanct to plant an airfield in the middle of one of the most historic courses in Scotland. Established formally on 6 July 1901, Turnberry Golf Course was quickly acknowledged as a potentially great one, but the outbreak of the First World War focussed a great deal of attention away from the sport.

The course and level ground south of Maidens right up to the coastline near Turnberry Castle and lighthouse was not overlooked by the RFC, and in January 1917 2 (Auxiliary) SoAG was formed here. By 17 September 1 SoAF was also formed here under the Training Division.

Both the SoAG and SoAF were disbanded and joined to form 1 SoAF&G, which was jointly operated by Turnberry and Ayr. Aircraft types had now been streamlined to the DH.9, SE.5A and FE.2B but, despite some improvements in maintenance, pilots were still losing their lives before getting anywhere near a front-line squadron. A final change of name came on 29 May 1918 when the SoAF&G became 1 FS before disbanding on 1 April 1919, the aerodrome closing down not long after.

Bristol M.1C C5017 of No 1 School of Aerial Fighting at Turnberry in 1918.

Turnberry main units, 1917-19

2(Aux) SoAG formed Jan 1917;
DB into 1 SoAF&G, 10 May 1918
(Camel, FB.9, DH.2, FK.3, Shorthorn, BE.2C/E and FE.2B)

1 SoAF&G formed (ex-1 SoAF) 10 May 1918;
redesignated 1 FS, 29 May 1918 (DH.9, SE.5A and F.2B)

1 FS formed (ex-1 SoAF&G) 29 May 1918;
DB 25 Jan 1919 (various aircraft)

TAYSIDE

Balhall

56°45'42"N/02°47'02"W, NO521635. E of Mains of
Balhall, 5 miles NW of Brechin

AN LG and possible DLG for Montrose, Balhall was only
a temporary site that opened in 1915.

Porte Baby No 9810 is pictured at Dundee (Stannergate) while en
route to Houton Bay on 18 May 1918. *Via Stuart Leslie*

Barry

56°29'34"N/02°45'16"W, NO532334. 0.3 miles W of
Barry Links railway station, 1.2 miles NNE of Buddon

CREATED during the early stages of the war for use by
RNAS landplanes, this temporary LG was opened in May
1915, but for how long is not known.

Broughty Ferry

56°27'50"N/02°52'16"W, NO464305. Slipway off
Beach Crescent, 0.25 miles SSE of Broughty Ferry
railway station

ALTHOUGH all coordinates draw this site to the harbour,
Broughty Ferry is consistently described as an LG. It is
doubtful that there was enough room north of the castle (Castle
Green) for land-based machines, but it is more likely that the
slipway was used by RNAS machines between 1915 and 1918.

Dundee (Stannergate)

56°28'N/02°56'W, NO433307. 2 miles E of Dundee off
A930

STANNERGATE can trace its roots back to 1914 when a
small seaplane station was first established for the RNAS
as a base for reconnaissance and anti-submarine operations.
Very little evidence exists with regard to units or activity

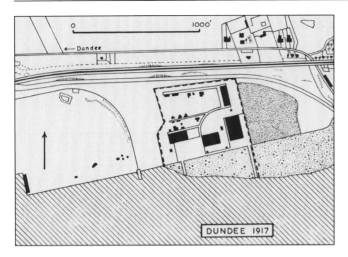

DUNDEE 1917

during the majority of the war, but from May 1918 a whole host of movements took place.

The first of these occurred on 30 May 1918 when what was by then a well-equipped seaplane base saw the formation of 318 and 319(FB) Flights, 400 and 401(S) Flights and 450(B) Seaplane Flight.

Now occupying more than 24 acres, the station's original two Seaplane Sheds (170 by 90 feet and 180 by 60 feet), which may have been moved from Port Laing on the River Forth, were joined by a third F-Type Shed (200 by 100 feet) in April 1918, and a pair slipways were constructed leading from a large concrete apron.

Stannergate's rapid transition from a sleepy backwater to an important seaplane station continued when 78 (Operations) Wing was formed in 22 Group on 8 August 1918. 2 (Northern) Marine Acceptance Depot set up camp at Stannergate from August to October 1918 while its new station at Brough was being completed. Another small unit, 419(S) Flight, brought a handful of Short 184s over from Strathbeg, making the Short torpedo bomber the most prolific aircraft type at Stannergate. Even more flying-boats descended upon the station when 306(FB) Flight brought its H.16s and F.3s from Houton Bay for a short detachment in November and December 1918. Finally, with 1918 drawing to a close, another half-dozen Short 184s made Stannergate their home when RAF unit HMS *Pegasus* was formed in December.

With the end of the war, it was only a matter of time before the fate that was befalling nearly all of the nation's seaplane stations was shared by Stannergate. 78 Wing had already been prematurely disbanded back in September 1918, reducing dramatically the operations that the resident 249 and 257 Squadrons had been flying. 249 Squadron was the first to go as a cadre to Killingholme on 3 March 1919. 257 Squadron was also reduced to a cadre in April 1918, but was not officially disbanded until 30 June 1919, together with 419(S) Flight, which was disbanded the same month. Going against the grain, yet another unit was formed here under the guise of Delivery Station (Storage), and was destined to remain until September 1919.

This just left the HMS *Pegasus* force of Short 184s, which was due to sail for the Mediterranean on 15 December 1919. However, this did not occur until 6 March 1920, at which time Stannergate fell silent and was closed soon afterwards.

Dundee (Stannergate) main units, 1914-20

318(FB) Flt formed 30 May 1918;
absorbed into 257 Sqn, 18 Aug 1918 (F.2A and H.16)

319(FB) Flt formed 30 May 1918;
absorbed into 257 Sqn, 18 Aug 1918 (F.2A and H.16)

400(S) Flt formed 30 May 1918;
absorbed into 249 Sqn, 18 Aug 1918 (Short 184)

401(S) Flt formed 30 May 1918;
absorbed into 249 Sqn, 18 Aug 1918 (Short 184)

450(BS) Flt formed 30 May 1918;
absorbed into 249 Sqn, 18 Aug 1918 (Baby and Hamble Baby)

'G' Boat Seaplane Training Flt formed 15 Aug 1918;
DB 25 Nov 1918

249 Sqn (formed from 400, 401, 419 and 540 Flts) 18 Aug 1918;
to Killingholme, 3 Mar 1919 (Short 184, Baby, H.12, F.2A and F.3)

257 Sqn (formed from 318 and 319 Flts) 18 Aug 1918;
DB 30 Jun 1919 (F.2A, Campania and Baby)

Edzell

56°49'38"N/02°36'49"W, NO626708. Inch of Arnall, 1 mile NNE of WWII technical site, 2.2 miles NE of Edzell village

THE first of three airfields at Edzell was opened as a TDS in July 1918, a generous site that occupied 211 acres and measured 1,200 by 900 yards. Facilities were equally generous, the hangars comprising seven 1917-pattern GS Sheds (170 by 100 feet), six of which were coupled and the extra was employed as an ARS.

On 15 July 1918 26 TDS was established following the dissolving of 36 and 74 TS. Fighter training was its main task, using the Camel, Pup and SE.5A as its main aircraft types, with many more in support. The nucleus of 155 Squadron was also formed here in early September 1918 but, after being attached to 26 TDS for a few days, the unit moved south to Chingford on 14 September, where it equipped with the DH.9A.

After an initial flurry of activity, the end of the war saw a steady decline of the TDS, which did well to last as long as 25 April 1919, when the site was placed under Care & Maintenance and closed in early 1920.

Edzell main units, 1918

36 TS from Montrose, 15 Jul 1918;
DB into 26 TDS, 15 Jul 1918

74 TS from Tadcaster, 15 Jul 1918;
DB into 26 TDS, 15 Jul 1918

26 TDS formed 15 Jul 1918;
to Chingford, 14 Sep 1918

155 Sqn nucleus flight formed Sep 1918;
to Chingford, 14 Sep 1918

A Sopwith Camel of 26 TDS at Edzell in late 1918.

Montrose (Broomfield)

56°43'50"N/02°27'03"W, NO725598. 1 mile N of Montrose, off A92

THE history of Montrose spans both of the 20th century's World Wars, and its establishment in early 1914 makes it one of the oldest military airfields in Scotland.

The second of Montrose's aerodromes came about when the CO of 2 Squadron, Major J. Burke, began a local search for an alternative to Upper Dysart Farm, which was only deemed as temporary. Burke discovered the Broomfield site in the summer of 1913, and later that year kit-form wooden hangars, intended for Dysart, were diverted to Broomfield instead. Before Broomfield was completed, 2 Squadron moved its operations to the second oldest military airfield in Scotland on 1 January 1914. The new airfield not only provided a better airfield from which to fly, but was also more comfortable from an accommodation point of view. 2 Squadron was only to enjoy its new surroundings for a few months before taking its ten BE.2Cs south to Netheravon on 11 May 1914.

A pair of Blériot XIs formed the CPF here in August 1914, but had disbanded by the end of the year. A period of quiet then followed, and it was probably during this time that the airfield began to expand. Several sheds were built, including three 1915-pattern Flight Sheds (210 by 65 feet) and three 1916-pattern GS Sheds (170 by 80 feet), together with an extensive wooden technical and domestic area, in preparation for Montrose becoming a training station.

1916 at Montrose saw the formation of 18 TS, which, like its predecessor, provided the nucleus for another famous fighter squadron on 15 April, but 43 Squadron did not stay here for long, moving to Stirling four days later. 39 TS was formed on 29 August 1916, and by the end of the year the unit had at least eighteen Maurice Farmans on strength.

The formation of the RAF brought many changes to the old RFC training structure, and by 15 July 1918 Montrose's TSs were dissolved into a single unit, 32 TDS. This introduced several new fighters to the airfield, including the Nieuport 17, SE.5A, Camel and Pup, as well as the now traditional collection of Avro 504s. On 30 May 1919 32 TDS was disbanded, and not long afterwards Montrose was left to its fate.

Sopwith Camel C6753 '3' of 32 TS at Montrose in early 1918.

A 2 Squadron BE.2C at Montrose in May 1914, only days before the unit left for Netheravon.

Montrose main units, 1913-18

2 Sqn from Farnborough, 26 Feb 1913;
to Farnborough, 5 Aug 1914 (various aircraft)

6 TS formed 17 Jul 1915;
became nucleus for 25 Sqn, 25 Sep 1915 (various aircraft)

25 Sqn formed 25 Sep 1915;
to Thetford, 31 Dec 1915
(Shorthorn, G.3, JN.4, S.1, 504 and BE.2C)

6 TS reformed/revived 20 Oct 1915;
to Catterick, 27 Nov 1915 (various aircraft)

18 TS formed 1 Jan 1916;
DB into 32 TDS, 15 Jul 1918 (various aircraft)

43 Sqn formed (nucleus from 18 TS) 15 Apr 1916;
to Stirling, 19 Apr 1916

39 TS formed 26 Aug 1916;
DB into 46 TDS, 27 Jul 1918 (various aircraft)

83 Sqn formed (nucleus from 18 TS) 7 Jan 1917;
to Spittlegate, 15 Jan 1917 (various aircraft)

82 (Canada) Res Sqn formed Jan 1917;
to Beverley, 20 Feb 1917 (JN.4)

85 (Canada) Res Sqn formed Jan 1917;
to Canada, Mar 1917 (JN.4)

11 (Reserve) Sqn reformed 7 Apr 1917;
to Spittlegate, 14 Apr 1917 (various aircraft)

1 TDS 'C' Flt formed (nucleus of 39 TS) 20 Jul 1917;
to Stamford, 31 Jul 1917 (various aircraft)

80 Sqn from Thetford, 10 Aug 1917;
to Beverley, 1 Nov 1917 (Camel)

52 TS from Stirling, 1 Sep 1917;
to Catterick, 24 Nov 1917
(BE.2B/C/E, DH.4, 504, RE.8 and Elephant)

108 Sqn formed (nucleus from 52 TS) 1 Nov 1917;
to Stonehenge, 12 Nov 1917 (various aircraft)

6 TS (Advanced Training Sqn) from Catterick, 24 Nov 1917;
DB into 32 TDS, 15 Jul 1918 (various aircraft)

36 TS from Beverley, 27 Nov 1917;
DB into 26 TDS, 15 Jul 1918 (JN.4, BE.12, FK.3, BE.2C, Camel, Pup, 504, RE.8 and 1½ Strutter)

41st Aero Sqn, USAAS, from USA, 10 Mar 1918;
to Gullane, Apr 1918 (no aircraft)

32 TDS formed 15 Jul 1918;
DB 30 May 1919 (SE.5A, Camel, 504 and Pup)

138th Aero Sqn, USAAS, by 17 Jul 1918

176th Aero Sqn, 'C' Flt, USAAS, by 17 Jul 1918

21 Gp formed 1 Apr 1918 in No 5 Area;
DB into 20 Gp, 1 Jul 1918

BE.2C '5384' served with 18 TS at Montrose circa January 1916.
© Inkworm.com

Montrose (Upper Dysart)

56°40'13"N/02°31'05"W, NO685545. 3 miles S of Montrose

SCOTLAND'S oldest military airfield was created on 26 February 1913 with the arrival of 2 Squadron after an epic 360-mile flight from Farnborough with its BE.2As. The first aircraft missed the small aerodrome and landed at Sunnyside Royal Hospital before continuing to Upper Dysart Farm. An advance party had already travelled to the site in January to erect several 1912-pattern RAF and RE canvas hangars to protect the aircraft, while the vast majority of the 130 personnel serving in the squadron were accommodated in an Army barracks in the town.

From the start 2 Squadron was not happy with its new location but, thanks to several detachments, they did not operate from here for very long. Six aircraft departed for a detachment to Limerick in March 1913, and in November Capt C. A. H. Longcroft flew 650 miles non-stop from Montrose, via Portsmouth, landing at Farnborough.

A temporary camp was also set up on St Andrews beach during 2 Squadron's stay, to practise take-offs and landings. Tents were erected on Bruce Embankment, and the flying drew quite a crowd. ELGs were also made available to the unit at Muirhouses, Kirriemuir and Edzell; the latter was more often than not covered in sheep. Various aircraft types passed through the squadron during its tour at Upper Dysart before it moved to Broomfield on 1 January 1914. Upper Dysart is credited with remaining under military control until April, and it is possible that the site was used further as a landing ground by 2 Squadron during its tour of duty at Broomfield.

Wales

Gwynedd

Anglesey (Llangfni or Llangefni), Anglesey

53°15'10"N/04°20'56"W, SH432750. 0.6 miles NW of Rhostrehwfa, 1.5 miles W of Llangefni

Anglesey was opened on 26 September 1915 as a Class B Airship Station complete with a sub-station at Malahide. This substantial site occupied 242 acres and measured 1,600 by 1,200 yards, making it large enough to support land-based aeroplane operations as well. Six acres of the site was covered in buildings, a large part of this figure being accounted for by a single Airship Shed (302 by 69 by 50 feet), with annexes on both sides. Personnel strength at its peak was 18 officers, 12 SNCOs, 27 JNCOs, 146 other ranks, 18 women and 16 'household' women.

On 6 June 1918 521 and 522(SD) Flights were formed here within 255 Squadron, whose home station was Pembroke. Equipped with DH.6s, Anglesey was redesignated as a Temporary Marine Operation Station under the control of 14 (Operations) Group until the two Flights were disbanded on 15 August 1918. Anglesey remained an active airship station until 1919, when the site was abandoned and returned to farmland.

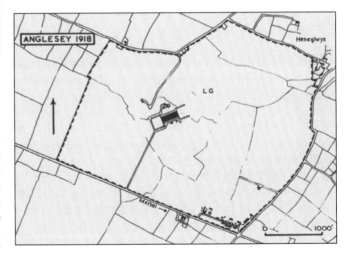

Anglesey had a single 302-foot-long Airship Shed complete with large screens at both ends. *Via Stuart Leslie*

Bangor, Caernarvonshire

53°13'47"N/04°03'56"W, SH623723. Due E of Glan-y-môr-isaf, 2.6 miles E of Bangor

IN July 1918 Bangor was one of the few LGs specifically opened as a marine operations station. The first occupant was 244 Squadron, formed here on 25 July 1918 with DH.6s, followed by 530(SD) Flight, which was also referred to as 'C' Flight. The squadron was joined by 521(SD) and 522(SD) Flights from Anglesey on 15 August 1918 with six DH.6s apiece. Originally formed within 255 Squadron at Pembroke, on moving to Bangor the Flights transferred to 244 Squadron.

Bangor occupied 35 acres and measured 600 by 500 yards; facilities were limited, although at least two, possibly three, Bessonneau hangars were erected, affording some protection to the eighteen or more DH.6s on the aerodrome. Personnel strength during 1918 averaged 39 officers, 21 SNCOs and 119 other ranks, the majority of whom were accommodated in Armstrong huts around the site.

The only unit movement from Bangor was when 530 Flight went to Tallaght on 18 October 1918, but it was back on 26 November. 244 Squadron's Flights were also detached to Llangefni and Luce Bay before the unit was disbanded on 22 January 1919. A relinquishment notification was issued on 15 May, and it was not long before Bangor was returned to its original owners.

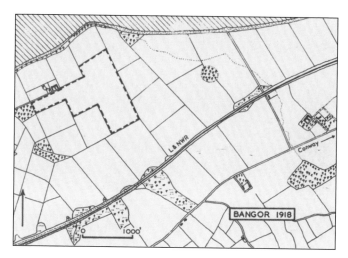

BANGOR 1918

Bibliography

Ashworth, C. *Action Stations 5* (PSL)

Action Stations 9 (PSL)

Blake, R., Hodgson, M. & Taylor, B. *Airfields of Lincolnshire* (Midland Counties)

Bowyer, M. J. F. *Action Stations 6* (PSL)

Chorlton, M. *Plane to Plane* (Old Forge Publishing)

Doyle, P. A. *Fields of the First* (Forward Airfield Research)

Fife, M. *Scottish Aerodromes of WW1* (Tempus)

Francis, P. *British Military Airfield Architecture* (PSL)

Goodall, M. H. *The Norman Thompson File* (Air Britain)

Green, P. & Hodgson, M. *Cranwell* (Midland Publishing)

Halpenny, B. Barrymore *Action Stations 8* (PSL)

Harding, E. D. & Chapman, P. *A History of 16 Squadron, RNAS*

Jefford, C. G. *RAF Squadrons* (Airlife)

McMahon, L. & Partridge, M. *Eastbourne Aviation Company* (Eastbourne Local History)

Morris, A. *First of Many* (Jarrold)

Morris, J. *German Air Raids on Britain 1914-18* (The Naval & Military Press)

Robertson, B. *British Military Aircraft Serials* (Ian Allan)

Sopwith – The man and his aircraft (Air Review)

Simmons, G. *East Riding Airfields 1915-20* (Flight Recorders)

Smith, R. *British Built Aircraft Vol 5* (Tempus)

Sturtivant, R. & Hamlin, J. *RAF Flying Training & Support* (Air Britain)

Sturtivant, R. & Page G. *RN Aircraft Serials & Units* (Air Britain)

The Camel File (Air Britain)

The D.H.4/9 File (Air Britain)

Treadwell, T. C. & Wood, A. C. *Airships of WW1* (Tempus)

Various archive material from the National Archives

Index